Can We Still Believe the Bible?

Can We Still Believe the Bible?

An Evangelical Engagement with Contemporary Questions

Craig L. Blomberg

BrazosPress
a division of Baker Publishing Group
Grand Rapids, Michigan

Published by Brazos Press
a division of Baker Publishing Group
P.O. Box 6287, Grand Rapids, MI 49516–6287
www.brazospress.com

Printed in the United States of America

Library of Congress Cataloging-in-Publication Data
Blomberg, Craig.
Can we still believe the Bible? : an evangelical engagement with contemporary questions / Craig L. Blomberg.
pages cm
Includes bibliographical references and index.
ISBN 978-1-58743-321-4 (pbk.)
1. Bible—Evidences, authority, etc. I. Title.
BS480.B548 2014
220.1—dc23 2013036161

16 17 18 19 20 7 6 5 4

To the faculty, administration, and trustees
of Denver Seminary,
who from 1986 to the present
have created as congenial a research environment
as a professor could hope for,
upholding the inerrancy of Scripture
without any of the watchdog mentality
that plagues so many evangelical institutions

Contents

Preface

I wrote this book sooner than I had planned. I typically have multiple writing projects to which I have committed—lined up like airplanes on a runway, waiting to take off. I arrange them chronologically, according to their due dates. When one is finished, I proceed to the next. Of course, there is inevitably some overlap in projects here and there, but I really dislike being late on anything.

Finishing this book at this time, however, has meant pushing some other things back that I thought I would be working on by now. Publishers have been gracious enough to allow me to extend some deadlines. Like the prophet Jeremiah, with fire in his bones preventing him from being silent (Jer. 20:9), I had to speak. The reliability of Scripture is the topic that first catapulted me into biblical scholarship; I would not be surprised if it turns out to be the last thing I am studying academically whenever the Lord decides I am writing my last work. It is the topic on which I am most often invited to speak, and the need is decidedly urgent. In the nonrefereed world of the internet, so much gibberish masquerades as truth, confusing or misleading web-surfers daily. In the refereed world of academic publishing, too frequently publishers are more interested in cents than in sensibility, so that they intentionally publish books with dramatically conflicting viewpoints on the same issue, knowing that each work will have a separate market and generate more income than either work would by itself. Unfortunately, Christian publishers are not exempt from this temptation.

Readers, therefore, need help in weaving their way through the maze of competing claims.

Few academic disciplines yield a greater diversity of perspectives than biblical studies. In some ways this is a backhanded compliment to the Christian Scriptures. If correctly understanding them and evaluating their claims were not of monumental importance for each person on the planet, there would be far fewer scholars either attacking and trying to debunk them or supporting and trying to defend them. There would also be fewer subdivisions within each of these two categories of scholarship, where writers debate the correct way to critique and dismiss the Bible or to interpret and apply it in our contemporary world.

This book does not pretend to have discovered some new breakthrough that will make the media swarm to examine its novel claims. It does represent perspectives that are widely held in mainstream evangelical circles, even though evangelicalism itself is fragmented into numerous subgroups, so we dare not claim more consensus than exists. This book does not follow the trend in certain circles of lobbying for the acceptance of more of the methods and conclusions of the critical establishment, represented by many in organizations such as the Society of Biblical Literature and the American Academy of Religion. But it also refuses to try to turn back the clock and retreat to the mythical "good old days" by disregarding genuine advances in biblical studies and censuring those who accept them.

I wish to thank my research assistants over the past two academic years, Luke Hoselton and Emily Gill, for their superb work in helping me with this project. I owe a debt of gratitude to all of the people and organizations who over the years have invited me to speak on the topics addressed in this book at conferences, churches, campus outreach events, retreats, and the like. All these people have considerably improved my awareness of the questions our culture is most asking and the most common misconceptions they have about the answers to those questions—in terms of both what we do know and what we do not yet know. As I complete my twenty-eighth year of teaching at Denver Seminary, I am profoundly grateful for the numerous colleagues, staff, students, trustees, and other members of our constituency who have encouraged me in my work and enabled it to flourish. Years ago our late chancellor,

Dr. Vernon Grounds, penned the statement that is now inscribed in our student center named after him and his wife, Ann: "Here is no unanchored liberalism—freedom to think without commitment. Here is no encrusted dogmatism—commitment without freedom to think. Here is a vibrant evangelicalism—commitment with freedom to think within the limits laid down in Scripture." Having discussed my perspectives on several of the issues treated in this book with Vernon over the years, I think that he would be pleased with this offering as in keeping with the spirit that he so deeply engraved on Denver Seminary during the fifty-nine years (1951–2010) he was a part of it. In any event, I dedicate this book to all of the wonderful people I have been associated with here at the seminary since my arrival in 1986.

Abbreviations

Bibliographic and General

AB	Anchor Bible
AD	*anno Domini*, in the year of the Lord
ad loc.	*ad locum*, at the place discussed
Alex.	Plutarch, *Alexander*
Anab.	Arrian, *Anabasis*
Ant.	Josephus, *Jewish Antiquities*
AOTC	Apollos Old Testament Commentary
ASV	American Standard Version
b.	Babylonian Talmud
B	Codex Vaticanus
BC	before Christ
BCOTWP	Baker Commentary on the Old Testament Wisdom and Psalms
BECNT	Baker Exegetical Commentary on the New Testament
BSC	Bible Student's Commentary
CBMW	Council on Biblical Manhood and Womanhood
CBT	Committee on Bible Translation
CC	Continental Commentaries
CEB	Common English Bible
CEV	Contemporary English Version
cf.	*confer*, compare
chap./chaps.	chapter/s
CJB	Complete Jewish Bible
ConcC	Concordia Commentary
CSG	Colorado Springs Guidelines
DSS	Dead Sea Scrolls

ed./eds.	editor/s, edited by, edition
e.g.	*exempli gratia*, for example
EGGNT	Exegetical Guide to the Greek New Testament
esp.	especially
ESV	English Standard Version
et al.	*et alia*, and others
ETS	Evangelical Theological Society
Gen. Rab.	*Genesis Rabbah*
GNB	Good News Bible
Gos. Thom.	*Gospel of Thomas*
GWN	God's Word to the Nations
HCSB	Holman Christian Standard Bible
ICC	International Critical Commentary
i.e.	*id est*, that is
Ign. *Trall.*	Ignatius, *To the Trallians*
JB	Jerusalem Bible
JST	Joseph Smith Translation
KJV	King James Version
LBP	Living Bible Paraphrased
lit.	literally
LXX	Septuagint (Greek OT)
mg.	marginal note or footnote
MT	Masoretic Text (Hebrew OT)
NAB	New American Bible
NAC	New American Commentary
NASB	New American Standard Bible
NCB	New Century Bible Commentary
NCBC	New Cambridge Bible Commentary
NCCS	New Covenant Commentary Series
NEB	New English Bible
NET	New English Translation
NHL	*Nag Hammadi Library in English*. Edited by J. M. Robinson. 4th rev. ed. Leiden: Brill, 1996
NIBC	New International Biblical Commentary
NICNT	New International Commentary on the New Testament
NICOT	New International Commentary on the Old Testament
NIGTC	New International Greek Testament Commentary
NIrV	New International Readers' Version
NIV	New International Version
NIVAC	NIV Application Commentary
NIVI	New International Version, Inclusive-Language Edition
NJB	New Jerusalem Bible

NKJV	New King James Version
NLT	New Living Translation
NRSV	New Revised Standard Version
NT	New Testament
NTL	New Testament Library
NWT	New World Translation
OT	Old Testament
par./pars.	and parallel/s
pl.	plural
PNTC	Pillar New Testament Commentary
Q	*Quelle*, hypothetical source of Jesus's sayings shared by only Matthew and Luke
REB	Revised English Bible
repr.	reprinted
RSV	Revised Standard Version
SBC	Southern Baptist Convention
TNIV	Today's New International Version
TNTC	Tyndale New Testament Commentaries
TOTC	Tyndale Old Testament Commentaries
UBC	Understanding the Bible Commentary
v./vv.	verse/s
WBC	Word Biblical Commentary
y.	Jerusalem Talmud
ZCCS	Zondervan Classic Commentary Series
ZECNT	Zondervan Exegetical Commentary on the New Testament

Old Testament

Gen.	Genesis	Neh.	Nehemiah
Exod.	Exodus	Esther	Esther
Lev.	Leviticus	Job	Job
Num.	Numbers	Ps(s).	Psalm(s)
Deut.	Deuteronomy	Prov.	Proverbs
Josh.	Joshua	Eccles.	Ecclesiastes
Judg.	Judges	Song	Song of Songs
Ruth	Ruth	Isa.	Isaiah
1–2 Sam.	1–2 Samuel	Jer.	Jeremiah
1–2 Kings	1–2 Kings	Lam.	Lamentations
1–2 Chron.	1–2 Chronicles	Ezek.	Ezekiel
Ezra	Ezra	Dan.	Daniel

Hosea	Hosea	Nah.	Nahum
Joel	Joel	Hab.	Habakkuk
Amos	Amos	Zeph.	Zephaniah
Obad.	Obadiah	Hag.	Haggai
Jon.	Jonah	Zech.	Zechariah
Mic.	Micah	Mal.	Malachi

New Testament

Matt.	Matthew	1–2 Thess.	1–2 Thessalonians
Mark	Mark	1–2 Tim.	1–2 Timothy
Luke	Luke	Titus	Titus
John	John	Philem.	Philemon
Acts	Acts	Heb.	Hebrews
Rom.	Romans	James	James
1–2 Cor.	1–2 Corinthians	1–2 Pet.	1–2 Peter
Gal.	Galatians	1–3 John	1–3 John
Eph.	Ephesians	Jude	Jude
Phil.	Philippians	Rev.	Revelation
Col.	Colossians		

Introduction

Questions about the Bible have flourished since its inception. People have always wrestled with the problem of evil and why there is so much suffering in the world. Bible readers have regularly assessed the adequacy of the Jewish and Christian responses to that question found in the Scriptures, which focus on God's desire for a freely offered love relationship with humanity that likewise allows the freedom to rebel against God, with all of the resulting consequences.[1] Other religions and ideologies regularly suggest discrete answers as well. Many religions have likewise debated the fate of those who never had a reasonable chance to respond to their message. Will God or the gods treat them in the same way as those who have rejected the message outright? The Bible only hints at answers to this question, yet Christians have made numerous suggestions that merit evaluation and are by no means limited to the notion that all such people are lost.[2] Closely related are issues of pluralism versus exclusivism. What is the destiny of those who consciously reject a given religion? Do they all fall into one homogeneous group, or are there subdivisions of some kinds? Again, Christian responses have often been far more nuanced than many people realize.[3]

In a different vein, any anthology of sacred literature written in diverse literary genres over many centuries, and to a wide variety of audiences for many different purposes, will inevitably exhibit apparent contradictions and theological diversity along with some measure of continuity and unity. With respect to the Bible, from at least the second century onward Christians have been well aware of the similarities and differences among the four Gospels and have offered a variety of explanations for both minute apparent discrepancies and broad, varying emphases.[4] The same is true for the seeming dissonance *within* a wide variety of passages in both Testaments, either with each other or with information from outside of Scripture. Not a single supposed contradiction has gone without someone proposing a reasonably plausible resolution.[5]

A third important area of conversation involves biblical ethics. Many people with only superficial or secondhand familiarity with the Bible's contents wrongly believe, for example, that the Bible promotes slavery. It is true that some Christians in later centuries supported their defense of slavery from Scripture, but the Bible has been twisted and distorted to support countless bizarre beliefs throughout history. The most important matter is what it actually says, and there is not a single text anywhere in the Bible that commands slavery. God allowed it in Old Testament times, as it was universal among the people groups of the ancient Near East. He enacted legislation, however, to make it more humane than in any other ancient context, often more akin to what might better be called indentured servanthood. In Israel it was primarily an institution for enabling individuals to work themselves out of debt and return to free status. In the New Testament even more countercultural teaching appears, with numerous seeds that would eventually germinate into its abolition altogether—abolition that was disproportionately spearheaded by Christians.[6]

Many people, even many evangelical Christians, have never engaged in a detailed study of what the Bible permits women to do either. On this issue there *are* legitimate debates over the interpretation of key texts and over which passages were meant to be timeless in application and which were more situation-specific.[7] But it is a simple fact that women are described with approval in the Old Testament as judges, prophets, and queens and in the New Testament as deacons, as coworkers with Jesus and the Twelve, and as having and exercising the spiritual gifts of pastor, teacher, apostle, evangelist, and the like. Whether it is significant for today's world that they could not be priests in the Old Testament, were not chosen as Jesus's closest followers, and do not appear as presbyters or elders in the New Testament—all this is a matter of ongoing, lively discussion and research. The vast majority of all interdenominational evangelical Christian institutions nevertheless recognize that diversity of opinion here is not a reason to keep anyone from becoming a believer and fellowshiping and working together with other believers across theological boundaries. The evangelical egalitarian position has become an established and credible part of the scholarly and ecclesiastical worlds alike, even if a handful of Protestant denominations have yet to recognize this.[8]

A quite different ethical topic involves the so-called attempted genocide in the Old Testament. Unfortunately, this very label misleads. The only offensive war ancient Israel ever fights is against the Canaanites when they enter the promised land; all the others are defensive (even if individual battles within larger wars are sometimes initiated by the Israelites), as they are attacked by Philistines, Assyrians, Babylonians, Persians, and so on. Even then, archaeological research has increasingly shown that of the few cities Joshua describes the Israelites as actually attacking, several were probably little more than armed encampments, much like modern-day military bases, where the only civilians present are the family members of soldiers and a few basic service personnel. Moreover, all of them had heard of the Israelites and their God, as proved by Rahab's testimony and action in Joshua 2. This account illustrates how anyone could have peacefully chosen to serve Israel's God without repercussions. To make a sweeping generalization, the Canaanites also were among the most debased of human cultures ever, and God had waited patiently for over four hundred years until their behavior had reached its lowest point (Gen. 15:16; cf. Deut. 9:5).[9] Finally, the ancestors of the Canaanites had freely entered into treaties with Abraham and the other patriarchs, on which their descendants were now reneging (Gen. 21:27; 26:28). Unlike so often in today's overpopulated world, there was plenty of good land for all of the people, if the inhabitants of the country had been willing to allow Israel to settle there as well, and the laws of Moses repeatedly required the Israelites to treat the foreigners in the land with the same justice that they were to administer among themselves (Exod. 20:10; 22:21; 23:9–12; Lev. 16:29; 17:8–15; 19:33–34; etc.).

At the same time, there are a variety of Old Testament ethical issues that understandably trouble interpreters even after the most careful historical-critical research is undertaken. These are not always identical to those mentioned by some of the most outspoken atheists of recent years, such as Richard Dawkins, Christopher Hitchens, or Sam Harris;[10] no one should read the works of these individuals without constantly checking the Bible itself, because many of their descriptions of events are significant distortions of the actual accounts.[11] In any event, given the amount of clarification that a study of comparative literature and culture has shed on these items even just in recent decades,[12] it is likely that scholars will continue to learn still more about ancient culture, thus enabling us to view ancient customs and languages in a more accurate historical light and removing even more of the objections. But for the Christian, it is also always important to stress that central to Jesus's ministry was the abolition of some of the potentially most offensive practices in ancient Israel. It seems impossible to avoid the conclusion that God has worked with humanity gradually over time, progressively revealing more and more of himself and his will as humans have been able to receive it, which also suggests that there are trajectories of moral enlightenment established on the pages of Scripture that we should continue to push even further today.[13]

However, this book is about none of these topics. All of them are worthy of continued study, but excellent resources abound for those who are interested. These topics have been addressed in detail many times in recent years, as well as throughout history. Frequently, the more aggressive atheists—as Dawkins, Hitchens, Harris, and like-minded individuals are often called—write as if the historical, theological, and ethical problems of Scripture that they believe merit the rejection of Christianity are somehow new discoveries of recent times and are problems that earlier generations and centuries of believers weren't aware of or just didn't understand.[14] This is utter nonsense. After careful study, one may decide that the best defenses of the faith prove inadequate, but let no one pretend that such defenses do not exist or have not existed throughout church history. Sadly, the most virulent anti-Christian voices of our day seem woefully ignorant of this body of literature.[15] Moreover, what one deems plausible depends much on whether one adopts a "hermeneutic of consent" or a "hermeneutic of suspicion" when approaching the biblical text.[16] Literary critics routinely explain that the only way to truly understand another author's communicative processes, before ever beginning to assess and evaluate them, is to enter empathetically into the worldview presupposed in that communication.[17] As a culture we excel in doing this with science fiction, with romance novels, with political docudramas, and the like, but we seem to shelve all those skills when it comes to the Bible. In any case, one looks in vain for signs of such empathy in the writings of Dawkins, Hitchens, Harris, and their ideological kin, and even in much liberal biblical scholarship.

Also remaining unchanged over the centuries are some of the classic reasons *for* believing the Bible to be a trustworthy depository of Jewish and Christian history, divinely given theology and ethics, and a collection of masterpieces of religious literature. The astonishing amount of archaeological corroboration of the kinds of details in the Bible that can be tested grows steadily with each generation.[18] The theological unity of Scripture, even amid all of its diversity, enables readers of all sixty-six books to discern a coherent narrative plot, profound wisdom, and a metanarrative that explains human nature from its origins to its final destiny. No other anthology of literature in the history of the world even attempts to undertake all three of these tasks simultaneously.[19] The lives transformed for the better by the Bible's witness and the contributions to civilization that those people have made throughout history are disproportionately larger than in any other religion or ideology.[20] None of this is to deny some very horrible things that a few Christians (and a few others masquerading as Christians) have perpetrated over the years,[21] but the complaints from some of Christianity's harshest critics have often grossly exaggerated these actions and failed to acknowledge the worse and more widespread atrocities committed under the banners of other religions and especially atheism.[22]

Yet this book is about none of these topics either. *What this book does address is why I still believe the Bible as I write these words in 2013.* Because my reasons for belief are not idiosyncratic but generalizable, I have titled the book *Can We Still Believe the Bible?*

I came to faith in my sophomore year of high school, in the spring of 1971. In college, from 1973 to 1977, I majored in religion at a private liberal arts college that in many respects was running from its Christian heritage as fast as it could.[23] Between actively engaging anyone in my public high school who would talk with me about Christian faith and delving into the whole gamut of a liberal arts curriculum in college, I think I encountered virtually every major historic challenge to traditional, orthodox Christianity during those seven years of schooling. Rarely were the classic or contemporary Christian responses to those challenges ever presented or acknowledged in my classrooms. Fortunately, my college had an excellent library, and in both my high school and college years, a good percentage of the Christian bookstores nearby were still stocked with serious academic works. Local pastors and parachurch leaders pointed me to still other texts that I needed to know about in order to gain a balanced education and to decide for myself where I fell on the spectrum of responses to the key issues of faith versus unbelief.[24]

Study at an evangelical Christian seminary in the United States for my masters in New Testament studies (Trinity Evangelical Divinity School) and at a public university in the United Kingdom for my doctorate in that same field (University of Aberdeen) rounded out my formal education. Both institutions provided far more balance in presenting all sides to key issues, before the professors would indicate their own preferences, than my undergraduate education had done, which overly stressed the latest avant-garde approach to most of the subdisciplines of religious studies.

Our liberal American love affair with the newest and the novel seems to condemn each new generation to rehearse the same debates as in the past, making some of the same mistakes all over again, even if minor variations and changes of nomenclature intrude. One key branch of today's postmodernism is little more than the existentialism of the 1960s.[25] A generation ago, the Graf-Wellhausen theory of sources in the Pentateuch was well entrenched in Old Testament scholarship, parceling up the writings traditionally attributed to Moses in the fifteenth century BC and assigning them to anonymous tenth-through-fifth-century *J*ahwist (Yahwist), *E*lohist, *P*riestly, and *D*euteronomistic writers (conventionally labeled J, E, P, D).[26] Today in some circles, the so-called Old Testament minimalists have replaced them. Sometimes stressing the literary unity of books more than their predecessors, these scholars nevertheless date the final form of various Old Testament books well into the Persian and Hellenistic ages of the fifth through second centuries BC, largely apart from any substantial new discoveries that would actually make their theories plausible.[27] The study of the historical Jesus has now embarked on its third main phase (often called a "quest"), and some scholars are now calling for a fourth quest.[28] There are important differences among the various phases or quests, but the same debate remains: Can historical argumentation bolster faith? Does it hinder faith? Or is it altogether unrelated to faith?[29]

New methodologies in biblical studies come and go: the academy is extremely faddish. Liberationist exegesis has mutated into postcolonialism.[30] Form criticism and structuralism have seen their heyday, but a close analysis of texts as literary artifacts continues unabated with narrative and genre criticisms.[31] Rudolf Bultmann's great mid-twentieth-century program of demythologizing the Bible—looking for the core theological truths that can still be believed in a scientific age, truths wrapped in the husks of the mythical miracles—had just about died out, only to be given new life by the Jesus Seminar in the 1990s and 2000s.[32] Examples could be multiplied. What goes around comes around. Most of my reasons for believing the Bible thus remain unchanged from thirty and forty years ago.

There are some areas, nevertheless, where a curious phenomenon has occurred over the past generation. *I am thinking of areas of scholarship where new findings, or at least much more intense study of slightly older discoveries, have actually strengthened the case for the reliability or trustworthiness of the Scriptures, even while the most publicized opinions in each area have claimed that there are now reasons for greater skepticism!* Six in particular have captured my attention enough for me to devote some specialized study to them. They involve textual criticism, the canon of Scripture, the proliferation of English (and other) translations of the Bible, the doctrine of biblical inerrancy, the diversity of literary genres among books or sections of books that appear to many as historical narrative, and the manifestations and meanings of the miraculous. So I have subtitled this book *An Evangelical Engagement with Contemporary Questions.*

Sadly, there has also been a backlash in each of these six arenas. A handful of very conservative Christian leaders who have not understood the issues adequately have reacted by unnecessarily rejecting the new developments. To the extent that they, too, have often received much more publicity than their small numbers would warrant, they have hindered genuine scholarship among evangelicals and needlessly scared unbelievers away from Christian faith. As my Christian eighth-grade public school history teacher, Dorothy Dunn, used to love to intone with considerable passion, after having lived through our country's battles against both Nazism and Communism: "The far left and the far right—avoid them both, like the plague!"[33] A brief overview of the six areas of study will set the stage for our more detailed examination of them in the chapters ahead.

Textual criticism has come of age in the last generation. Due partly to discoveries of new manuscripts, partly to scholars' completing the translation of copies of Old Testament books discovered among the Dead Sea Scrolls in the 1940s and 50s, and partly to the tireless efforts of centers for textual research in Germany and the United States in compiling and collating facsimiles of the thousands of biblical manuscripts still in existence from antiquity, we are now in a better position than ever to reconstruct with confidence the most likely wording of the original writings of the biblical authors.[34] The vast majority of textual critics of all theological or ideological stripes recognize this, but somehow a few dissenters have captured the attention of the popular media and the blogosphere: far too many people think that the situation is just the opposite, that the proliferation of manuscripts has made us less certain than ever about what the biblical authors first wrote. This is simply false, but we need to go into more detail to demonstrate it. At the other end of the spectrum, a tenacious and vocal, even if tiny, minority of Christians continues to maintain, against virtually all the evidence, that God actually *preserved* every biblical book perfectly in some ancient manuscripts somewhere. Usually this belief is joined to the one alleging that the King James Version of 1611 is by far the closest English approximation to that inerrantly preserved text. This too is completely misguided.

A second issue involves the biblical canon, the collection of books that the Christian church deems authoritative and inspired. Some discussion continues concerning the Old Testament Apocrypha, that is, the books that Roman Catholics treat as canonical but Protestants do not. But here about the only widespread trend noticeable over the past generation has been a move in at least some Catholic circles to treat these books as "deuterocanonical"—authoritative, yes, but not as centrally important as the sixty-six books that all branches of Christianity have historically agreed on as Scripture. What *has* become a virtual cottage industry of new study are the post–New Testament apocryphal works, especially the so-called gnostic gospels. From time to time, even calls for reconsidering the New Testament canon have been sounded.[35] The popular press and the average layperson, including the unchurched, have probably heard more about the noncanonical *Gospel of Thomas* than the canonical Gospel of Mark, and much of what they have heard has been at least misleading if not downright inaccurate. The real state of affairs is that every noncanonical document from ancient Christianity known to us has been given far more scrutiny than ever in the history of the church during the last generation, and the reasons for *not* treating them on a par with the New Testament documents are clearer than ever.[36] At the same time, especially among grassroots evangelicals, the notion that the canon of Scripture is not only uniquely adequate to address spiritual matters but also sufficient for addressing numerous other topics of human inquiry has led to some bizarre approaches to the Bible, which need to be avoided.

A third phenomenon is the rampant proliferation of English translations of Scripture. Other modern languages have also seen a flurry of new versions, but nowhere nearly so prolifically as in English. Many of these are justifiable once one understands the translation theory utilized and the target audience in mind. Yet some seem to replicate previous efforts unnecessarily. A few try to establish themselves by touting their merits at the expense of the alternatives, thus giving the public the impression that we really aren't sure how to translate significant parts of the Bible at all. And if we can't even be sure what it *means* in our own language, how can we ever hope to have it function as a reliable and adequate authority for Christian living more generally? But in fact, our understanding of the nature of language, recognition of the strengths and weaknesses of various approaches to translating from one language to another, and the sophistication of the discipline of linguistics more generally have never been greater. Significant strides have been taken in just the last generation.[37] Nevertheless, huge misunderstandings remain about the strengths and weaknesses of so-called literal translations. Indeed, the term *literal* itself is used in a variety of inconsistent and sometimes incompatible ways. Add in some of the unfounded claims that have been made about the dangers of using inclusive language when referring to humanity, and it appears to many that the various Bible translations are much less reliable than they actually are.

Fourth, we consider the question of the "inerrancy" of the Bible. The term itself has not always been used throughout church history, but the concept that dominated Christianity until modern times was that, of all the writings in human history, the biblical books are uniquely accurate and reliable, historically and theologically. The late eighteenth century's Scientific Enlightenment, as it is often called, spawned for the first time a substantially liberal branch of Christianity, which continued to grow until about a generation ago. But it is only in the last generation that expressions such as "I swear on the Bible . . ." or "It's the gospel truth" have largely fallen out of use, because they do not carry the force they once did. Ironically, as liberal Protestants and Catholics have steadily decreased in number both at home and abroad over the last half century and as conservative or "evangelical" Christians have exploded in number, now for the first time in history significant numbers of those evangelicals have begun to question belief in inerrancy, at least as it has usually been framed.[38] At the same time, historians today have an unprecedented understanding of what would or would not have been considered reliable history in the biblical cultures,[39] so that inerrantists have the ability to define and nuance their understanding of the doctrine better than ever before. Sadly, some extremely conservative Christians continue to insist on following their modern understandings of what should or should not constitute errors in the Bible and censure fellow inerrantists whose views are less anachronistic.

Closely related to this discussion is a fifth area of research: biblical genres. With unprecedented access to most ancient documents relevant for understanding biblical history and literature, with a large percentage of them available in English (and often German, French, and/or Spanish as well), and with the ease of consulting them in a digital world, we are aware more than ever before of the diversity of literary forms contained within biblical documents and the array of literary genres that entire biblical books comprise.[40] Most important, simply because a work appears in narrative form does not automatically make it historical or biographical in genre. History and biography themselves appear in many different forms, and fiction can appear identical to history in form. Other contextual and extratextual indicators must be consulted as well, including comparisons with noncanonical literature of similar form, in order to determine the kinds of narrative we are reading. Occasionally, what has seemed to many throughout the centuries to reflect straightforward history can now be seen to represent a different genre. In most cases, what has usually been viewed as historical is rightly understood as such, but the way in which the ancients wrote history is clearer now than ever before. Once again the result is that we know much better what we should be meaning when we say we "believe the Bible," and therefore such belief is more defensible than ever. Yet once again, unfortunately, a handful of ultraconservatives criticize all such scholarship, thinking they are doing a service to the gospel instead of the disservice they actually render.

Finally, there is the question of the miraculous. Thanks to twenty-first-century communication technology, we have unprecedented numbers of carefully documented accounts (sometimes recorded in audio or video) of physical healings, exorcisms, and even more dramatic supernatural (or at least paranormal) events, often in quick response to public and explicitly Christian prayer, for which science and medicine have no explanation.[41] A variety of classic objections to the concept of miracles, which have been put forward over the centuries, have been successfully rebutted.[42] More important, no convincing explanations have emerged for the innumerable miraculous events attested just in the last generation alone. The biblical miracles dovetail remarkably with these recent miracles in nature and purpose. Also, the biblical miracles prove far less random or fanciful than those in other literature from the ancient world. In most instances, the way the biblical accounts differ from the classic Greco-Roman and ancient Near Eastern myths proves particularly striking, despite the occasional superficial similarity. Where such parallels with the Old Testament are closer, the biblical authors are usually rebutting pagan claims and showing how God and not some other deity is in charge of some part of the world. Where the parallelism between the New Testament and the surrounding world proves to be close, the pagan accounts almost always turn out to be post–New Testament, too late to have influenced the Bible's composition.[43] Once again, however, we would scarcely suspect this if we relied solely on some recent works that have received widespread attention. And a small rearguard of hyperconservative believers, usually reacting to certain excesses in the charismatic movement, attribute all or virtually all contemporary "miracles" to human manufacture or diabolical counterfeit, when they should instead be rejoicing at the powerful workings of God's Spirit for good in our world.

I have read and heard numerous accounts of people who are "deconverting" from Christianity, to use the fashionable and euphemistic term for reneging on one's faith commitments or baptismal pledges.[44] There is almost a definable literary genre of autobiographical writings explaining why a person who once believed no longer does.[45] Unfortunately, most people who once believed *and still do*, or believe even more strongly than in the past, never think to publicize their faith journeys. Perhaps they assume few would be interested. Perhaps they are right; if so, it is a shame. But I suspect that biblical scholars who, like me, have found their faith fortified by the evidence the longer they have studied it may have an increasing obligation in our pluralistic world to give an account of the hope that is in them (1 Pet. 3:15).[46]

The six areas of scholarship that this book presents explain why I still believe the Bible *in the twenty-first century*, and why I believe that *we* can *still* believe the Bible. These topics may not produce the most important reasons for belief. But they do debunk widespread misconceptions about what belief entails, and they present exciting recent developments in scholarly arenas that are not nearly as well known or understood as they should be. Let us begin, then, with what for many readers may be the most opaque of the six fields of study to be investigated here, textual criticism.

1

Aren't the Copies of the Bible Hopelessly Corrupt?

Some scholars estimate that there are four hundred thousand textual variants among the ancient New Testament manuscripts.[1] From this observation alone, certain skeptics conclude that it is ridiculous to imagine ever reconstructing the original text of Scripture, much less being able to affirm its trustworthiness. How should Christians reply? What do Christian scholars do with this statistic? If we really can have no confidence that we know what the original authors of the Bible wrote, then it is pointless to ask about their *accuracy* in what they wrote. What we have might not correspond at all to the original documents. In this case, all we could look at would be hopelessly corrupt copies!

It is depressing to see how many people, believers and unbelievers alike, discover a statistic like this number of variants and ask no further questions. The skeptics sit back with smug satisfaction, while believers are aghast and wonder if they should give up their faith. Is the level of education and analytic thinking in our world today genuinely this low? Anyone learning about four hundred thousand variants should immediately want to ask a variety of questions: Is this statistic accurate? If so, what *kinds* of variations appear among the manuscripts? Are they minor or major? Do they affect the meanings of texts and, if so, to what degree? Across how many manuscripts are these four hundred thousand variants spread? Do they fall into identifiable patterns? If so, what is the significance of those patterns? How did these variations come into existence? And all of this is just about the New Testament. What is the state of Old Testament textual criticism (or analysis)?

Misleading the Masses

The number four hundred thousand comes from a remarkable book published by Bart Ehrman in 2005: *Misquoting Jesus: The Story behind Who Changed the Bible and Why*. Ehrman is professor of New Testament at the University of North Carolina in Chapel Hill and has become a prolific writer and popular speaker and teacher. He once embraced evangelical Christian faith but now describes himself as an agnostic. The general tenor of most of his publications and talks makes it clear that he wants to help disabuse people of whatever Christian faith they have as often as he can. Some of his former students have told me that he has said as much in class.

The title of the book is highly misleading. The book is not about anyone misquoting Jesus but about the nature of the similarities and differences among the New Testament manuscripts. When scribes accidentally or intentionally changed an element of the text they were copying, they were not misquoting anyone; they were miscopying a text. But a title like *Miscopying New Testament Texts* would not have sold nearly as many books. Astonishingly, *Misquoting Jesus* made it to the *New York Times* bestseller list for several months after it was released. Yet most of its content discloses nothing that biblical scholars of all theological or ideological stripes have not known for decades. What made it so enormously successful? The answer lies primarily in its packaging and marketing, and in the fact that once its contents started to become known, people who were not scholars realized that here was a dimension of study of the world's most influential book about which they knew nothing or next to nothing. Sadly, this seemed to be just about as true for most believers as for most unbelievers.[2]

In readable language, Ehrman's book presents the basics of the textual criticism of the New Testament—the number and nature of the manuscripts, the process of copying, and the kinds of mistakes that were introduced—but he focuses on the most interesting parts of the discipline. He looks at two twelve-verse segments that are printed in standard translations of the New Testament but have been determined most likely not to have been written by the authors of the books in which the passages are embedded: the so-called longer ending of Mark (16:9–20) and the story of the woman caught in adultery (John 7:53–8:11). Ehrman discusses much shorter but still fascinating variants, such as whether Mark 1:41 originally read that Jesus "showed compassion" or "was angry" when he encountered a man afflicted with leprosy. He explores whether Hebrews 2:9 originally insisted that Christ tasted death for everyone "by the grace of God" or "apart from God." Ehrman points out instances in which scribal changes were likely motivated by theology. Throughout the New Testament, the most common such change involves adding titles for Jesus. Ehrman's doctoral dissertation, published under the provocative title *The Orthodox Corruption of Scripture*, lays out the evidence in detail.[3] Passages that originally said merely "Jesus" were sometimes altered to read "the Lord Jesus" or "Jesus Christ" or even "the Lord Jesus Christ." The changes reinforced orthodox belief about the identity of Jesus but in so doing changed the wording of the originals.

Nothing in all of this is new. Readers of almost any English-language translation of the Bible except for the King James Version (KJV) and the New King James Version (NKJV) can look at the footnotes, or marginal notes, of their Bibles and see mention of a broad cross-section of the most important and interesting of these variants. Unfortunately, many readers don't consult these notes often enough. Of course, more and more people are reading the Bible in electronic form, and many electronic versions of the Bible don't even include such notes.

A key problem with Ehrman's book, however, is with what he does *not* include. It is easy for the uninformed reader to come away from his treatments of the largest or most interesting variants and start to wonder how often there might be other passages that we still don't know about, with similarly large or significant variants that would change the nature of Christianity. What Ehrman doesn't make clear is that the number and nature of manuscripts we have make it extraordinarily unlikely that we shall ever again find variants that are not already known. As Daniel Wallace, professor of New Testament and Greek at Dallas Seminary and founder of the Center for the Study of New Testament Manuscripts, likes to put it, while there are places where we are uncertain of what the original text read, the original reading is almost certainly one of the options recorded in the existing manuscripts somewhere.[4]

With this background, we are ready to analyze the issue of four hundred thousand variants. Here is Ehrman's statement:

> Scholars differ significantly in their estimates—some say there are 200,000 variants known, some say 300,000, some say 400,000 or more! We do not know for sure because, despite impressive developments in computer technology, no one has yet been able to count them all. Perhaps, as I indicated earlier, it is best simply to leave the matter in comparative terms. There are more variations among our manuscripts than there are words in the New Testament.[5]

How easy it would be to conclude from this that there is no word anywhere in the New Testament that we can say with certainty was what the original author wrote! But that is not even remotely the real nature of things.

Less than a page before the paragraph just quoted, Ehrman himself notes that 5,700 manuscripts of portions of the Greek New Testament exist from the centuries before the printing press was invented. In the paragraph immediately preceding the quote, he acknowledges that we have about ten thousand manuscripts of the Latin translation of the New Testament along with manuscripts in other ancient languages such as Syriac, Coptic, Armenian, Georgian, and Slavonic, along with all of the quotations of Scripture passages in the church fathers (or patristic writers), especially from the second through sixth centuries of church history.[6] Although Ehrman doesn't total all the numbers, Wallace does, and the result is that those 400,000 variants, if there are that many, are spread across more than 25,000 manuscripts in Greek or other ancient languages.[7]

Suddenly the picture begins to look quite different. This is an average of only 16 variants per manuscript, and only 8 if the estimate of 200,000 variants is the more accurate one. Nor are the variants spread evenly across a given text; instead, they tend to cluster in places where some kind of ambiguity has stimulated them. Paul Wegner estimates that only 6 percent of the New Testament and 10 percent of the Old Testament contain the vast majority of these clusters.[8] Of course many of the manuscripts are not of the entire New Testament, but of select collections of books, individual books, and, as one gets back to the very earliest fragmentary scraps of texts available, small portions of books. And a statistical average does not enable us to recognize which manuscripts were very carefully copied and which ones had numerous errors creep in. So we need to supplement these statistics with other ones.

The Truth about Textual Variants

The New Testament

The United Bible Societies' fourth edition of the Greek New Testament contains 1,438 of the most significant textual variants in its footnotes and presents the most important manuscript evidence for each existing reading of the disputed text.[9] Using the letters A through D, the committee that produced the edition also ranks its level of confidence in its decision to adopt a particular reading. A companion volume, edited by Bruce Metzger, called *A Textual Commentary on the Greek New Testament*, explains the committee's rationale for their choices and their levels of confidence, with all the variants arranged canonically.[10] The twenty-eighth edition of the Nestle-Aland Greek New Testament includes about seven times as many variants as the UBS fourth edition but then drastically limits the number of manuscripts listed in support of each reading.[11] In Nestle-Aland, however, seldom do the extra variants not found in the UBS seem at all significant. Many of them involve the inclusion or omission of an article or conjunction, the inversion of a couple of words, variant spellings of words, or other minor differences that leave meaning virtually unaffected.

Even beginning Greek students with just a few hours of classroom instruction in textual criticism can begin to understand the process of reasoning used by the committees that produced these critical editions of the Greek New Testament.[12] Decisions are based on both external and internal evidence. External evidence refers to the number and nature of the manuscripts that support each variant reading—their age, location of origin, overall quality, and similarities to other reputable manuscripts. Internal evidence is the evaluation of the kinds of changes a scribe was most likely to make, whether intentionally or unintentionally, as well as what the original author would most likely have written. Confusing syntax, unusual vocabulary, theological oddities, and overly brief comments are all likely to be smoothed out, explained, replaced, or altered in ways that improve intelligibility. Accidental mistakes include misspellings of words; duplicating or omitting a letter, word, or line of text; dividing words that were originally run together without spacing; or placing punctuation in different places—in short, all the mistakes that even typists today make when typing up someone else's writing instead of merely scanning, copying, or cutting and pasting the original text electronically.

When one then peruses the more than 1,400 textual footnotes included in the UBS Greek New Testament, one learns that the *only* disputed passages involving more than two verses in length are the two Ehrman mentions, Mark 16:9–20 and John 7:53–8:11. Almost all modern English translations alert readers to the issues with these two texts. The *ESV Study Bible* (English Standard Version), for example, places in brackets and capital letters a statement between Mark 16:8 and verses 9–20 that reads, "Some of the earliest manuscripts do not include 16:9–20." The text is then surrounded by double brackets: [[and]]. In the study notes at the bottom of the page, the reader learns not only that "some ancient manuscripts of Mark's Gospel" do not contain these verses but also that the verses are missing from "numerous early Latin, Syriac, Armenian, and Georgian manuscripts. Early church fathers (e.g., Origen and Clement of Alexandria) did not appear to know of these verses. Eusebius and Jerome state that this section is missing in most manuscripts available at their time."[13] Quite frankly, we should be delighted to learn this, because what came to be labeled as verse 18 promises that believers "will pick up serpents with their hands; and if they drink any deadly poison, it will not hurt them." There is a tragic history of very fundamentalist Christian snake-handling churches in Appalachia throughout the twentieth century that treated this verse as if it were inspired Scripture, and yet they had numerous fatalities. Even today in one state, West Virginia, snake-handling remains legal and occurs in a few small, usually rural congregations.

Where then did these verses come from?[14] If Mark ended his Gospel at verse 8, then he concluded his narrative without Jesus appearing to anyone. A young man dressed in a white robe merely instructs the women who have found the tomb empty to tell his disciples that he is going ahead of them to Galilee, where they will see him. Verse 8 ends the undisputed portion of Mark 16: the women leave the tomb, saying nothing to anyone, because they are afraid. Scribes undoubtedly thought that Mark could not have intended to end his Gospel that way, without an actual resurrection appearance, and so they composed a more "proper" ending. The odd verse about snakes was probably created on the basis of Paul's experience recorded in Acts 28:3–6, where he was not harmed by a viper's bite while on the island of Malta, and an overly literal interpretation of Jesus's promise to his disciples that they will tread on snakes and scorpions without ill effect (Luke 10:19). But there are far more textual variants within these twelve verses than within any comparable span of text elsewhere in Mark's Gospel. And the style of writing in the Greek significantly differs from the rest of Mark's Gospel.[15] A footnote in the *ESV Study Bible* also tells us that

> a few manuscripts insert additional material after verse 14; one Latin manuscript adds after verse 8 the following: *But they reported briefly to Peter and those with him all that they had been told. And after this, Jesus himself sent out by means of them, from east to west, the sacred and imperishable proclamation of eternal salvation.* Other manuscripts include this same wording after verse 8, then continue with verses 9–20.[16]

All this makes it overwhelmingly likely that Mark did not originally contain these verses.[17]

Scholars debate whether the original ending of Mark was lost or whether he intended to end with what we call verse 8. The open end of a scroll was the most vulnerable part of a manuscript for damage; perhaps Mark literally got "ripped off"! More likely, he intended to end with the fear and failure of the women. His Gospel is the one that most emphasizes the fear and failure of all of Jesus's followers, male and female alike. If early church tradition is correct that Mark wrote to Roman believers experiencing increasing persecution, then this makes good sense since he could have wanted to highlight that Jesus's first followers were no stellar heroes of faith. If God could use them, despite their gaffes, he could use Roman Christians a generation later as well, despite their insecurities and weaknesses. Mark is not concealing information from his audience that they don't already know. They could scarcely have become believers without having heard about Christ's resurrection appearances. But he is catching them up short by stopping where he does, in order to make a point that should, even in a slightly backhanded way, greatly encourage them.[18]

The situation with the story of the woman caught in adultery is quite different. Whereas there are a number of good, generally reliable, relatively early manuscripts that contain the last twelve verses of Mark, almost none of the oldest, most complete, and most reliable manuscripts contain John 7:53–8:11. A few that do include these verses place them elsewhere, such as after John 7:36, at the end of John's Gospel, in the narrative stream of Luke's Gospel (after 21:38), or at the end of Luke's Gospel! Again, there are more textual variants than normal for this length of passage. Obviously it is a story looking for a final form and for a home. On the other hand, there is nothing theologically objectionable here like handling snakes or drinking their venom. Even fairly liberal scholars often think that the account of the woman caught in adultery reflects an authentic episode from the life of Jesus, not least because no other known teacher in his world would likely have been so gracious in this kind of situation. But the account almost certainly was not written by the author of the Fourth Gospel.[19] To quote the *ESV Study Bible* again, "It should not be considered as part of Scripture and should not be used as the basis for building any point of doctrine unless confirmed in Scripture."[20] Preachers, Sunday School teachers, and Bible study leaders who fail to heed this advice risk setting their people up for confusion when books like Ehrman's appear and people have no idea how to respond. Christian leaders need to teach the basics of textual criticism in a responsible way to their congregations.[21]

Why is this discipline no threat to Christian faith? It is because there are no other places in all 25,000+ manuscripts where any other passages like these two appear. Had there originally been more, it is impossible that all record of them could have been expunged from the textual tradition, given how independently from each other many of these documents were copied. The same is true of shorter variants. There are about two dozen in the entire New Testament that involve one to two verses. All the rest affect less than a verse, usually just a few words. Interested readers can flip through the footnotes of their modern English-language translations, locate them, and decide for themselves how crucial they are. All told, a typical English translation of the New Testament will include around 200–300 variants in its footnotes, averaging roughly one per chapter of the various books.[22] The following is a cross-section of illustrations to help the reader get a feel for their nature.

In Matthew 5:22a, the New American Standard Bible (NASB) accurately reflects what was almost certainly the original text of Jesus's words in the Sermon on the Mount: "But I say to you that everyone who is angry with his brother shall be guilty before the court." Of all the major translations, only the KJV and NKJV add "without a cause" after "angry," because the translators commissioned by James I of England to produce the KJV in 1611 had access to only about twenty-five manuscripts, most of them much later and noticeably less reliable than the best manuscripts that have been rediscovered in the centuries since.[23] In this passage, some ancient scribes were clearly trying to make Jesus's teaching a little more manageable. The "harder reading" is usually the earlier reading (unless it becomes nonsensical), and Jesus's seeming condemnation of all anger against one's spiritual siblings is certainly the harder reading of the two.[24]

In the KJV and NKJV, Matthew 6:13 contains the famous doxology at the end of the Lord's prayer: "For thine is the kingdom, and the power, and the glory, for ever ["forever" NKJV]. Amen." All other major translations exclude these words because they are overwhelmingly absent from the earliest and most reliable manuscripts. Well-meaning scribes probably thought the prayer deserved a better ending, and the words may have been composed on the basis of 1 Chronicles 29:11–13.[25] There is absolutely nothing wrong with praying these words, unless a person has decided never to speak a word in prayer that is not a direct quotation of Holy Scripture! They just don't appear to have been in Matthew's original text, so they should not be treated as uniquely inspired.

Ehrman's selection of Mark 1:41 is a good example. Most modern translations follow the KJV here, reporting that Jesus, seeing the leper, was "moved with compassion" (or an equivalent expression). Codex Bezae, an important fifth-century Greek manuscript of what is called the Western text-type, like various old Italic manuscripts, reads instead that Jesus was "indignant." The external evidence in support of the "indignant" reading is not at all strong enough to tip the scales in its favor, but the internal evidence overwhelmingly supports it. What scribe would ever change Jesus's compassion to indignation? Yet it would be easy for scribes to think that Mark was claiming Jesus was upset with the leper, rather than with his disease or its effects in making him a social outcast, and therefore want to change the text to "moved with compassion."[26] As a result, the updated (2011) edition of the New International Version (NIV), along with the Common English Bible (CEB), has used "indignant" and put "moved with compassion" into a footnote as an alternate option, while the Revised English Bible (REB) reads simply "moved to anger."

On the other hand, against Ehrman, Hebrews 2:9 really does have too little external evidence for his suggestion to be the original reading. The manuscripts containing "apart from God" are few, late, in languages other than Greek, or in secondhand quotations. The Greek for "by the grace of God" in the capital letters of the earliest manuscripts, without spaces between the words, is ΧΑΡΙΤΙΘΕΟΥ, while "without God" is ΧΩΡΙΣΘΕΟΥ. Because Jesus sensed the rupture of his communion with the Father on the cross, when he cried out, "My God, my God, why have you forsaken me?" (Mark 15:34), a scribe could easily have misread the text of Hebrews he was copying and yet realized that "without God, he [Jesus] tasted death for everyone" made perfect sense and so didn't catch his mistake.[27]

A famous two-verse variant appears in Luke 22:43–44. In the middle of Jesus's agony in the garden of Gethsemane, we read that "an angel from heaven appeared to him and strengthened him. And being in anguish, he prayed more earnestly, and his sweat was like drops of blood falling to the ground." The NIV offers the following footnote at this point: "Many early manuscripts do not have verses 43 and 44." Many others do. The external evidence is quite split: about half of the oldest and most reliable manuscripts contain these sentences, and about half don't. The vast majority of all the late manuscripts contain them, but their evidence doesn't weigh that heavily in a decision. There is nothing terribly "hard" about this reading, especially when we realize that Luke is employing a simile: Jesus's sweat is *like* drops of blood. The text does not say he actually sweats blood. So it seems more likely that some overly pious scribe wanted to add a supernatural dimension to the story, with the role of the angel as strengthening Christ, than that someone omitted these verses despite finding them in the manuscript he was copying.[28]

By now, readers discovering textual criticism for the first time may well be asking, "If various passages are not likely original, why do translations at times continue to print them?" The answer is that some people take serious offense at anything being left out of a given Bible translation that previous translations have typically included, and Bible translators and publishers want to avoid unnecessary hostility against them![29] The Revised Standard Version (RSV) was one modern translation that often relegated such doubtful verses entirely to its footnotes, but the majority of versions adopt the approach of the NIV: retain the text but alert the readers with a footnote about the extent of the textual uncertainty.

If both the external and internal evidence for a certain variant is weak enough, however, most translations *will* relegate the doubtful words to a marginal reading. The more famous or theologically significant a text is, though, the more they will exercise caution. For example, the NIV, the New English Translation (NET), the New American Bible (NAB), the New Jerusalem Bible (NJB), and the CEB all place Acts 8:37 entirely in a footnote. This verse provides a direct answer to the Ethiopian eunuch's question about what stands in the way of his being baptized. Philip answers that if he believes with all his heart, he may be baptized, and the eunuch replies that he believes that Jesus Christ is the Son of God. The manuscripts that lack this interchange are truly impressive in both quality and number. There is every reason to believe that a scribe added this clarification, because without it the story never explicitly indicates that the eunuch has come to believe.[30] The primary reason that not all translations consign verse 37 to a footnote is because it is such a well-known, significant, and powerful confession of faith. People who overly exalt the KJV regularly criticize modern translations for a variety of (usually unjustified) reasons, and translators are reluctant to give them even more fuel for their attacks.

The examples we have given thus far, like others Ehrman considers, are among the handful of most dramatic and interesting variants. Even among the variants chosen for inclusion in the textual notes of English translations, the typical ones are much smaller and much less significant. In Romans 5:1, for example, there is very strong external evidence for the Greek verb "have" (ΕΧΩΜΕΝ) appearing in the first-person plural subjunctive mood, which would yield a translation such as "Therefore, having been justified by faith, *let us have* peace with God through our Lord Jesus Christ." English translations, in tandem with critical editions of the Greek New Testament, nevertheless almost unanimously adopt the later, widely attested reading ΕΧΟΜΕΝ, a simple indicative-mood verb meaning "*We have* [peace with God . . .]." In this instance, the internal evidence proves decisive. The entire paragraph that spans Romans 5:1–11 is about the results of justification. It is filled with theological statements, not commands or exhortations. One can understand how easily the omega (Ω) could have been inserted instead of the omicron (Ο), given how similar the two look. Moreover, verse 2 contains a verb (ΚΑΥΧΩΜΕΘΑ) that, until accent marks were added centuries later, could have been read as either indicative or subjunctive. In other words, it could have meant either "we boast" or "let us boast." A scribe understanding this word as a subjunctive might well have wanted to change the verb in 5:1 to a subjunctive, too, so that the two words would match in function.[31]

A good way to get a feel for how ordinary and uninteresting are the vast majority of textual variants is to choose a single section of text in one of the biblical books and note all the variants that the UBS Greek New Testament has chosen as worthy of inclusion, remembering that by definition these will be the most significant and "exciting." John 3:16, for example, is one of the best known and loved Bible verses of all. Are there significant textual variants in it or in its context? The UBS presents only three textual issues for all of John 3:1–30. In verse 13, there is some uncertainty as to whether the original read simply, "and no one has ascended into heaven except the one who descended from heaven, the Son of Man," or whether after "Son of Man" should be added either "the one in heaven" or "the one from heaven." In verse 15 ("in order that everyone who believes in him might have eternal life"), some manuscripts substitute a synonymous expression for "in him," a few say "on him," and a number add language from verse 16, yielding "in order that everyone who believes in him might *not perish but* have eternal life." In verse 25, finally, the debate about cleansing that erupted between John's disciples and "a Jew" is in some manuscripts between John's disciples and "Jews," plural. Because of the uncertainty, a few late manuscripts simply omit any reference to the disciples' conversation partner. The first of these three variants finds its way into the NIV footnotes; the other two are neither certain enough nor sufficiently significant to merit any mention.[32]

What about the additional variants that Nestle-Aland's text presents? Now we can identify one that affects John 3:16 itself. Some manuscripts explicitly add the Greek pronoun for "his," probably to make absolutely clear that this is the way the article used with "only" is to be understood ("his only Son" not just "the only Son"). But the idea is already clearly present in the sentence. Backing up to verse 12, there are a few texts that change the Greek tense of the second use of the verb "believe" to emphasize *ongoing* belief and thus match the tense of the first use of that verb in the verse. In verse 8, a few manuscripts repeat "of water and" before "the Spirit" to make the language match verse 5. Nothing else nearby is any more interesting; several items are even less so. What these very minor and poorly attested variants demonstrate most commonly is a desire to smooth out the text or to harmonize the language of one passage with that of another relevant passage on the same topic, often in the nearby context.

Or take another beloved chapter of the Bible, 1 Corinthians 13 on love. Again the UBS offers three textual footnotes. The first is quite interesting and has affected various translations. In verse 3 most have followed the KJV: "and though I give my body *to be burned* and have not love, it profits me nothing." But instead of ΚΑΥΘΗΣΟΜΑΙ from "to burn," key manuscripts read ΚΑΥΧΗΣΟΜΑΙ, which is only one letter different. This then means "and though I give my body *to boast*." That this is so less vivid a reading than "to be burned" suggests that a scribe probably changed it to the more dramatic reading rather than vice versa.[33] Thus the 2011 NIV, NAB, NET, NRSV, and New Living Translation (NLT) all use "boast." The CEB follows this latter approach, too, with its rendering, "hand over my own body to feel good about what I've done."

The other two variants in 1 Corinthians 13 are much less interesting. Some manuscripts do not repeat the subject "love" with the verb "boast" in verse 4. They use the word for love only twice in the verse: "Love is patient, love is kind. It does not envy, it does not boast, it is not proud" (NIV). Some repeat "love" a third time before "does not envy" (ESV), a few instead insert it a third time before "does not boast" (NASB), and some include it in both places (KJV). Finally, one important early manuscript uses a positive phrasing at the beginning of verse 5, so that love behaves in a seemly way, rather than the double negative ("love does not behave in an unseemly way") that all the rest of the manuscript tradition contains.

Turning to Nestle-Aland's additional variants, we find an issue over the tense of an infinitive ("to remove") in verse 2. Should it be aorist (simple action) or present (ongoing action)? In verse 5, one early copyist accidentally wrote, "[love] does not honor others," rather than "does not dishonor" (the difference in Greek is only a two-letter prefix). In verse 10, a few manuscripts add "then" between "but when completeness comes" and "what is in part disappears." In verse 11, many manuscripts add "but" between "I reasoned like a child" and "when I became a man." Verse 12 finds manuscripts divided among "as through a mirror," "through a mirror as," and "through a mirror and." Finally, a few copies of verse 13 invert the order of "faith, hope, and love" and "these three things" in the Greek word order. Have Paul's magnificent teachings on love and spiritual gifts in this chapter been altered by any of these changes? Not one whit![34]

Ehrman has one final claim, however, worthy of comment here. He argues that before Constantine became the first Christian emperor in the early fourth century and legalized Christianity, copies of New Testament books were not made nearly as officially and therefore not nearly as carefully. He postulates that if we had enough evidence, we would discover that the farther back in time one went toward the first century, when the books were first penned, the more diversity among the manuscripts one would find.[35] But this is sheer hypothesis unsubstantiated by any actual data. There is a slightly greater amount of variation among pre-Constantinian manuscripts than afterward, but there is no evidence that the farther one moves back in time from the early fourth century, the more the manuscripts diverge.[36] Nor is it the case that the manuscripts appear so few and far between that we have a "black hole" in our knowledge of the state of the text during this period. A full 102 copies of individual New Testament books or portions of them have been recovered from the second and third centuries.[37] And every single one of them is written with the very careful handwriting of an experienced scribe, not with the more careless scrawls of less literate individuals whom Ehrman postulates would have introduced many more errors in these earliest centuries.[38]

By now the point should be clear. The vast majority of textual variants are wholly uninteresting except to specialists. When one hears numbers like 400,000 variants (if that number is even accurate), one must remember that they are spread across 25,000 manuscripts. A large percentage of these variants cluster around the same verses or passages. Less than 3 percent of them are significant enough to be presented in one of the two standard critical editions of the Greek New Testament. Only about a tenth of 1 percent are interesting enough to make their way into footnotes in most English translations. It cannot be emphasized strongly enough that *no orthodox doctrine or ethical practice of Christianity depends solely on any disputed wording*. There are always undisputed passages one can consult that teach the same truths.[39] Tellingly, in the appendix to the paperback edition of *Misquoting Jesus*, Ehrman himself concedes that "essential Christian beliefs are not affected by textual variants in the manuscript tradition of the New Testament."[40] It is too bad that this admission appears in an appendix and comes only after repeated criticism!

The Old Testament

But what about the Old Testament? Ironically, the text of the Old Testament is not as secure as that of the New, yet skeptics hardly ever talk about it. Maybe this is because it's a quite technical area of study and harder to understand; maybe it's because one has to master several more foreign languages to gain true expertise in the field. Or perhaps it's because they know most Christians (sadly) don't care that much about the Old Testament.

Before the earliest discoveries of the Dead Sea Scrolls in 1947, English translations were based almost exclusively on the Masoretic Text (MT), named after the Masoretes. They were the Jewish scribes who meticulously copied the Hebrew Bible (especially during the sixth through eleventh centuries AD) and, among other things, added the Hebrew vowel points to the consonantal texts they inherited. More than three thousand manuscripts, transcribed extremely carefully from these exemplars, survive from the 1100s through 1440.[41] The oldest existing copy of the MT can be dated to the ninth century AD. A very complete and well-preserved Hebrew Old Testament is Codex Leningradensis (named after Leningrad, or St. Petersburg, Russia, where it has long been housed). This copy dates to 1008.[42]

Although the existing copies of the Hebrew Masoretic Text were copied more than a thousand years after the eras in which the Old Testament documents were first written, scholars have long had access to ancient manuscripts of the Greek translation of the Old Testament known as the Septuagint, produced in roughly 200 BC. The Septuagint is often referred to by the abbreviation LXX (the roman numeral for 70) after the legend that seventy (or seventy-two) scholars, all working in isolation from each other, created identical translations. Some of the manuscripts of the Septuagint are part of the same codices as the ancient Greek New Testaments, showing that they were preserved in Christian circles (and they are not word-for-word identical to each other!). After the birth of Christianity, some distinctively Jewish editions of the Septuagint rendered certain key words and passages slightly differently, often in woodenly literal fashion, to make it harder for Christians to appeal to them as messianic prophecies fulfilled by Jesus.[43]

The differences between the ancient Septuagintal manuscripts and the Masoretic texts can occasionally prove dramatic. The book of Jeremiah, for example, is one-sixth shorter in the LXX than in the MT. Significant differences appear in smaller stretches of Joshua, Ezekiel, 1 Samuel, and Proverbs, while numerous other Old Testament books have interesting minor variations between the Greek and the Hebrew. Some sections within certain books are placed in differing orders, and the manuscripts containing multiple books of the Bible sometimes preserve the biblical books in different canonical sequence.[44] Scholars had long wondered whether all of these differences could be accounted for via loose translation of the Hebrew into Greek or by corruption, whether accidental or intentional, of the Hebrew text. Or could it be that in at least some instances, the LXX *was* a literal translation, but of a different Hebrew original? This last theory proved especially attractive, because the New Testament often quotes a Septuagintal form of an Old Testament passage, even when the LXX is not a very literal translation of the Hebrew (MT).[45]

With the discovery after World War II of portions of every Old Testament book except Esther in the caves near the shores of the Dead Sea, possibly representing the library of a separatist Jewish sect known as the Essenes at a monastic-like site called Qumran, scholars no longer needed to speculate. Overall, the most striking result of comparing these approximately 200 biblical manuscripts, ranging from roughly 250 BC to AD 50, was how similar they were to the Masoretic texts of a millennium or more later. The most stunning example of this was the discovery of an entire scroll of Isaiah with only a handful of extremely minor differences in content (as opposed to orthography or grammar) from the MT copies dating a millennium and a quarter later.[46]

Some copies of biblical texts in this collection, however, disclosed a variety of interesting differences from the MT. Occasionally, the texts of these far more ancient Hebrew manuscripts matched how the distinctive renderings of the LXX would read if translated back into Hebrew.

An excellent example of this appears in Deuteronomy 32:43b. The MT reads, "Rejoice, you nations, with his people, for [God] will avenge the blood of his servants; he will take vengeance on his enemies and make atonement for his land and people." The LXX, however, adds at the end of the verse, "and let all the angels worship him." This is precisely the portion of the verse that Hebrews 1:6 quotes, in the context of the letter's argument that Christ is superior to the angels. Hebrew copies of Deuteronomy from the Dead Sea also contain these extra words.[47] A similar phenomenon recurs in numerous Old Testament texts. So now it is clear that at least some of the differences between the LXX and the MT are because the LXX translators were closely rendering a Hebrew text that differs from that of the MT rather than because the LXX translators were playing fast and loose with their sources.[48]

On other occasions the Hebrew scrolls from Qumran contain passages that were previously unknown from either the MT or the LXX. Probably the most striking example occurs between the end of 1 Samuel 10 and the beginning of chapter 11. The NIV, for example, follows the MT by ending the chapter, after Saul has been made king, with a reference to "some scoundrels" who "despised him and brought him no gifts." Next the narrator adds, "but Saul kept silent" (1 Sam. 10:27). Chapter 11:1 then shifts to a new setting: "Nahash the Ammonite went up and besieged Jabesh Gilead." Apparently realizing they could not resist him, the residents of Jabesh Gilead asked for a peace treaty and promised to become Nahash's slaves. But what led them to give in so readily? This was not characteristic behavior for ancient Israelites. In the copy of 1 Samuel recovered from Qumran, the sentence "but Saul kept silent" is missing. The following appears instead:

> Now Nahash king of the Ammonites oppressed the Gadites and Reubenites severely. He gouged out all their right eyes and struck terror and dread in Israel. Not a man remained among the Israelites beyond the Jordan whose right eye was not gouged out by Nahash king of the Ammonites, except that seven thousand men fled from the Ammonites and entered Jabesh Gilead. About a month later. . . ." (NIV mg.)

Then the text continues as in the MT of 1 Samuel 11:1.

The NIV prints this text in a footnote, being appropriately cautious not to jump to the conclusion that it was in the original text of Samuel. The ESV does not even put it in a textual footnote, though the Study Bible edition does mention it in its notes. But the NRSV introduces it as an unnumbered separate paragraph between 10:27 and 11:1, printing it in exactly the same font as the rest of the main text of 1 Samuel. The footnote in the NRSV reads, "Q Ms [Qumran manuscript] Compare Josephus, *Antiquities* VI.v.1 (68–71): MT lacks *Now Nahash . . . entered Jabesh-gilead*." In his twenty-volume work *The Antiquities of the Jews*, first-century Jewish historian Josephus claims that Nahash had defeated other Israelite armies beyond the Jordan and gouged out their troops' right eyes, which suggests that he was probably aware of texts of Samuel that contained this account.

Perhaps the majority of modern translations are right in concluding that this was a later scribal addition to explain how quickly the Jabesh-gileadites were ready to surrender. But the rationale recounts a bizarre episode, it does not seem to have any overtly theological motivation, and a much simpler explanation could have accounted for the reaction in Jabesh-gilead if someone were just making up a reason. At the very least, this additional paragraph may represent the true historical state of affairs, even if it was not part of 1 Samuel originally. Given the age of the Dead Sea scroll in which it appears, though, it just might have been what the oldest text of 1 Samuel contained.[49]

An example of a similar phenomenon that is easier to resolve appears in Genesis 4:8. This time it is not a Dead Sea scroll that potentially solves a mystery but the combined witness of the three most ancient or important translations of the Hebrew Bible—the LXX, the Latin Vulgate, and the Syriac—along with one Hebrew witness, the version of the Pentateuch (Genesis through Deuteronomy) used by the ancient Samaritans. In the MT, something is clearly missing, because the verse reads, "Now Cain said to his brother Abel. While they were in the field, Cain attacked his brother Abel and killed him." All these other textual traditions, however, agree that what Cain said was "Let's go out to the field." The KJV obviously did not know what to do with this gap, so they tried a translation that would not make it so obvious that something was missing: "And Cain talked with his brother Abel." But that is not nearly as natural a translation of the Hebrew.[50] More-recent English versions have at times done something similar to that of the KJV (e.g., NASB, ESV), but most have filled the gap as the NIV does by adding, "Let's go out to the field," or something very similar (e.g., the Holman Christian Standard Bible [HCSB], NAB, NET, NJB, NLT, CEB, and NRSV).

Occasionally, the MT has a gap that other ancient versions filled in, but in a variety of different ways, suggesting that no one really knew any longer what the original text should be. Thus 1 Samuel 13:1 has long puzzled scholars. The most natural translation of the Hebrew of the MT is "Saul was one year old when he became king, and he reigned over Israel two years." This obviously cannot be correct. The KJV dealt with this problem by translating, "Saul reigned one year; and when he had reigned two years over Israel . . . ," but this is not easily derivable from the Hebrew. The ESV, NAB, NJB, and NRSV assume that something has dropped out of the text but don't supply anything other than ellipses, reading, "Saul was . . . years old when he began to reign, and he reigned . . . and two years over Israel." Josephus says in one place that Saul reigned for twenty years (*Ant.* 10.143) and in another that he reigned for forty years (6.378). Most manuscripts of the Septuagint omit the verse, but a few late ones have Saul beginning to reign at age thirty. Acts 13:21 ascribes to Paul the conviction that Saul reigned for forty years. Combining these last two observations, the HCSB, NIV, updated NASB, NET, NLT, and CEB all opt for "Saul was thirty years old when he became king, and he reigned over Israel forty-two years," or words to that effect, assuming that forty is a round number for forty-two. But no Hebrew text has yet been discovered containing these clarifications.[51]

These examples barely scratch the surface of the topic but already point out a key principle that differentiates Old and New Testament textual criticism. Most scholarly reconstructions of the New Testament text are eclectic: they do not begin with one existing version of the New Testament in Greek but take into account all of the evidence before deciding on a reading in any given context. Old Testament textual criticism, however, almost always begins with the MT and then turns to other versions, whether from the Dead Sea Scrolls or other ancient translations, only if there are problems with the MT.[52] Of course, different scholars and varying Bible translation committees will have different thresholds beyond which the MT is too difficult for them to believe that it was original.[53]

Did Originals Originally Exist?

Because of the extent of the differences among the ancient versions of some Old Testament books, textual critics have at times suggested that we should not talk about one original text—the autograph—but merely the oldest text of a given book. Moreover, both Old and New Testament studies have often postulated stages of composition of various biblical documents, leading some scholars to wonder if we can even identify a final form of a text that was viewed as the author's finished product or as the finished product of one or more editors. If we cannot always isolate a final form, then the distinction between the composition of a book and its transmission becomes blurred.[54]

On the other hand, almost all of the theories of composition, however probable, remain entirely speculative in the sense that no manuscripts have ever been found of the supposed sources that a biblical writer used—whether it is Q (sayings of Jesus common to Matthew and Luke but not in Mark, which may have formed a pre-Synoptic written source);[55] or a version of Job without the opening and closing chapters that place Job's plight and discourses in the context of an unseen heavenly contest;[56] or a copy of 2 Corinthians 1–9 without chapters 10–13 (which was possibly a later Pauline letter combined on the same scroll with an earlier one);[57] or numerous other similar proposals for various biblical books. Even if such documents were discovered, that would not by itself mean they functioned as anything more than sources for the later, finished works that were greatly valued. That we are not always sure which version of a biblical book was viewed as the final, authoritative version does not mean that no such version ever existed. The ancient discussions of such topics always affirm or presuppose that people believed such versions *did* exist (cf., e.g., the debates between the Samaritans and Jews over which was the original and therefore authoritative Pentateuch).[58] So it remains most probable that each biblical book circulated at a given time as a finished, authoritative document and only later began to be copied and/or translated.[59]

This supposition is strengthened by the study of the use of documents kept in libraries in the ancient Mediterranean world. Craig Evans has recently called attention to the important study by George Houston[60] of "libraries, collections and archives from late antiquity," showing that "manuscripts were in use anywhere from 150 to 500 years before being discarded." Evans continues, "The fourth-century Codex Vaticanus (B) was re-inked in the tenth century, which shows that it was still being read and studied some 600 years after it was produced."[61] Most laypeople and scholars alike have usually assumed that a heavily used manuscript would wear out after a decade or two so that there might be dozens of copies (of copies of copies . . .) having to be produced over just a few centuries (exactly the model Ehrman depends on for his theories). *In fact, the original copy of a biblical book would most likely have been used to make countless new copies over a period of several centuries, leading to still more favorable conditions for careful preservation of its contents.* This is precisely what we see at Qumran, with scrolls of Old Testament books being preserved for 200–300 years. So when Bart Ehrman writes "We don't even have . . . copies of the copies of the copies of the originals,"[62] he is almost certainly wrong. Second- and third-century New Testament manuscripts may well be copies of the very autographs, or at least copies of those copies.

A more modest revision of textual critics' goals may, however, be in order. Particularly in Old Testament studies, given the potential gap of centuries between the presumed originals and the oldest copies in existence, even from Qumran, it might occasionally be more appropriate to speak of the "earliest attainable" form of a given document rather than the original.[63] Ironically perhaps, it is more conservative scholars, who tend to date biblical books earlier than many in the guild, who then need to reckon with an even greater interval between composition and extant manuscripts. But it is still important to recall that we have no actual evidence to suggest that the Hebrew text of a biblical book was ever treated without great care by the majority of copyists in *any* era of its transmission. Even when the Dead Sea copies of books deviated noticeably from the MT, they rarely introduced a new reading unknown to us from all the versions and not readily explainable via an accidental error in copying or an intentional change in diverging from an earlier manuscript.[64] One may fantasize about all kinds of wild changes being introduced between the first, complete written form of a given book and the oldest copy we actually have, but it will be just that—fantasy—unless some truly remarkable new discoveries change the state of the discipline.

Comparative Data

How does the wealth of textual evidence for the biblical books measure up with comparable evidence for other works of antiquity? The answer is that they do so astonishingly well. In the ancient Mediterranean world, Homer's *Iliad* and *Odyssey* were by far the next most treasured documents outside of the Christian Bible, and they were put into writing eight hundred years before the New Testament, yet we have fewer than 2,500 manuscripts of those works put together.[65] Few other works exist in copies numbering even to triple digits; the collected works of the early second-century Roman historians, for example, number a little more than 200. Historians today are typically elated when we have a double-digit number of copies of an ancient work, as with 75 copies of the works of the Greek historian Herodotus (fifth century BC), 20 copies of the histories of his contemporary Thucydides, and 27 of the works of the Roman historian Livy (first century BC to first century AD). And the oldest surviving manuscript for any of these authors dates from at least four centuries after the time it was first written, sometimes as many as nine centuries after, versus a gap of only one century, or less, for most of the NT books.[66]

When one turns to the gnostic and apocryphal New Testament texts, about which much has been made in the popular media in recent years, most documents exist in the one and only copy that has been discovered in modern times. Occasionally we have discovered two copies, and in several instances there are radical differences between the two. In other cases, Greek fragments of apparently the same texts have been known for a longer period of time. By far the most famous and important of these texts is the Coptic *Gospel of Thomas*, known from one complete fourth-century manuscript and fragments of three second-century Greek texts.[67] The contrast in the amount of textual evidence for the canonical Christian works could scarcely be greater.

When I wrote the first draft of this chapter in September of 2012, the internet was flush with speculation about a supposedly fourth-century scrap of Coptic text, released and translated by Harvard professor Karen King. King's article made it clear that she thought the text had no bearing on our knowledge about the Jesus of history,[68] but that was not what news reports latched on to. What they hyped was a fragmentary line of text that apparently read, "Jesus said to them, 'My wife . . .'" If the text were not a forgery, if it were genuinely from the fourth century, and if King had given us the best possible translation, we would still need to note that fragmentary fourth-century Coptic texts from the Middle East with unorthodox teaching about Jesus and the disciples are precisely what the large corpus of gnostic texts represents. These documents tell us next to nothing about the historical Jesus, only about the distortions made of him by one heterodox sect that came to full bloom only in the second century after Christ.[69] Within a short time, however, other scholars, especially Durham New Testament professor Francis Watson, gave reasonably conclusive evidence to suggest that the fragment was a forged, modern pastiche of snippets of the *Gospel of Thomas* and that the word King translated as "wife" should be rendered as "woman," detached as it originally was from "my."[70] Yet only a handful of news stories, not nearly as well publicized, disabused the public of the misleading views originally put before them.[71]

When people are willing to jump on discoveries like the *Gospel of Judas* (in 2006)[72] or the fiction of *The Da Vinci Code* (in 2003)[73] and to believe them, while remaining skeptical about whether we have any adequate copies of the Old and New Testaments, then it is clear that they are simply believing whatever they wish were true and have abandoned all vestiges of genuine scholarship or rational inquiry. If we cannot say with confidence that we have the ability to reconstruct a biblical text that is overwhelmingly likely to be very, very close to the original texts of the books of Scripture, then to be consistent we should discard *all* ancient writings on any topic as being far more suspect and plead total agnosticism concerning the original contents of any documents produced before the breakthrough of Gutenberg's printing press in about 1440!

Avoiding the Opposite Extreme

By far the greatest errors in discussions about the nature of the textual evidence for the autographs of the biblical books come from those who fail to appreciate how much of the original texts we can reconstruct with such a high degree of probability. But it is also crucial to help people understand that we do not claim to have a perfectly flawless copy of any book of the Bible anywhere in existence. Chapter 4 (below) discusses in more detail the Christian doctrines of the inspiration and inerrancy of the Bible. Suffice it for now to say that the standard, orthodox theology of the church has never been to claim inerrant *transmission* of God's Word, merely inerrant *originals*.

Some people, however, remain unnecessarily uncomfortable with a scenario in which God did not preserve his Word as perfectly as he first inspired it. The most extreme example of this discomfort is found in the "King James Version Only" movement. Each time the movement seems to be on the verge of death, someone or something revives it, and another generation must face the misguided claims of those who insist that the KJV is based on the most carefully preserved and most reliable of all the ancient manuscripts.[74] Less drastic but still misleading are the anthologies of perspectives that present the rare scholarly defender of the textual criticism on which this view relies as if the scholar actually represents a significant segment of the academic guild.[75]

Several major flaws afflict the arguments of the KJV-only defenders and the scholars co-opted to appear as if they support them. Their most central argument is that the Byzantine text-type of New Testament manuscripts, which the KJV translators followed and which reflects about 80 percent of all the existing texts, must be accurate because that sizable a majority of texts couldn't be wrong. But textual criticism is not a democracy. One does not count manuscripts; one weighs them. The reason so many texts of the Byzantine tradition have been preserved is largely because Byzantium (modern-day Istanbul) was the center of the Eastern Orthodox world for centuries, exactly where one would expect the greatest number of manuscripts to be preserved.[76]

The KJV supporters also claim that the manuscripts that follow in the textual tradition of the Textus Receptus, or "Received Text," flawlessly preserved the New Testament originals. They demonstrably did not. Neither the KJV translators, nor Luther before them, nor Erasmus before him ever used only one New Testament manuscript exclusively, and no two manuscripts of the few dozen used in preparing these English, German, and Greek editions, respectively, ever agreed in every exact detail. Intriguingly, a better case could be made for a remarkably carefully preserved textual tradition with the MT for *the Old Testament*, but KJV-only people actually talk less about that portion of Scripture. Still, even within the manuscripts of the MT, there remain a host of very minor variants.

The KJV-only supporters often allege that all modern translations are "liberal" because they have "removed" passages that support the Trinity, the deity of Christ, or some other cardinal doctrine. The most famous example appears in 1 John 5:7–8. The NIV reads, "For there are three that testify: the Spirit, the water and the blood; and the three are in agreement." A footnote indicates that "Late manuscripts of the Vulgate [add after "testify"] . . . *in heaven: the Father, the Word and the Holy Spirit, and these three are one. And there are three that testify on earth:* . . . (not found in any Greek manuscript before the fourteenth century)." There is a fascinating story behind how the fifteenth-century Catholic reformer, Erasmus, was talked into including the Greek for these italicized words in his edition of the New Testament by a manipulative priest when he had previously found them only in Latin texts, which in turn led to the KJV's including them decades later, but that need not detain us here.[77] The important point to make is that modern translations are not *removing* the words; they are translating from the thousands of Greek texts *before* the fourteenth century, none of which *contains* the words. In this way, compared to the KJV, they are restoring the original text. It is true that *one* traditional proof text for the doctrine of the Trinity is now not available for believers; but there remain plenty of others![78]

The real issue is a very different kind of theological one. Many people simply can't live with even a very slight uncertainty about the exact reading of the original text of a document they treat as inspired, authoritative, and infallible Scripture. So, however implausible their arguments have to be, they insist on defending the notion that God has inerrantly preserved his Word.[79] But think of just what kind of miracle this would need to be for it really to have occurred. Not only would God have superintended the process of a select group of biblical authors penning their documents so that their words reflected precisely what God wanted to have written; God would also have needed to intervene in the lives of all the tens of thousands of copyists over the centuries to ensure that not one of them ever introduced a single change to the texts they were reproducing. Moreover, if no translation other than the KJV is really adequate, what does that say about the sizable majority of all Christians in the history of the church who have never had access to the KJV? Which exactly is the one mysterious Greek manuscript that was somehow kept free from error, since the KJV relied on numerous texts, none of which was absolutely identical to any other? What about all the Christians before and after the KJV was published who have never been able to read a word of English or Greek? Did God not want any of these people to have an equally reliable copy or translation of his word?

A comparison with traditional Muslim beliefs about the Qur'an is instructive at this juncture. In Islam, reading the Qur'an in a translation from the original Arabic is never considered a very satisfactory substitute for learning enough Arabic to be able to recite the original text itself. Never mind whether you can understand it; so long as you can at least memorize and pronounce the words, Allah will be pleased.[80] After variant readings in copies of the Qur'an were discovered at the time of Muhammad's death, and all copies but one were destroyed, Muslim scribes and religious leaders have gone out of their way to carefully safeguard the process of copying their holy book to an extent that Christianity has never undertaken.[81] Most Muslims think this makes the Qur'an superior to the Bible. But I much prefer the Christian commitment to putting God's Word into the hands of as many people in the world in as many of their indigenous languages as possible (even if at times the processes of copying and translation have not been undertaken with as much care as we would wish), in order to facilitate the greatest possible identification with and *understanding* of Scripture. Merely venerating the words of a text in a language one cannot understand, because they are supposedly identical to those given by God in an ancient culture, can hardly by itself make one religion or its holy book superior to another.

In essence, this is what the King James Only movement does. In that sense, it is more Islamic than Christian in methodology! Never mind if one cannot understand the Elizabethan English of the KJV. Never mind if the quest for a pristine original that was translated perfectly literally is a chimera. Never mind the amazingly ethnocentric arrogance behind idolizing one given language into which the Bible has been translated. The KJV-only people want certainty, not 99 percent probability or higher. So they create myths by which they deceive themselves into thinking they have attained the certainty that in fact does not and cannot exist.

Why should anyone expect more certainty in religion than in any other area of life, given that we are finite and fallen human beings? What we should want is confidence based on the greatest probabilities.[82] Every day in countless ways we trust our lives and well-being to beliefs and actions that have proven track records and are extremely likely to work successfully but are not 100 percent guaranteed. The chair that has always held us up can suddenly collapse under us, the gas station that has never run out of gasoline before may suddenly run dry, or the house we thought we would retire in may burn down due to an out-of-control forest fire. But if we failed to act until we could prove beyond the shadow of a doubt that every chair would hold us up, every gas station we stopped at would have fuel, and every home we considered living in was utterly fireproof, we would never sit down, our cars' gas tanks would all be empty, and we would live out-of-doors in tents!

Conclusion

For every practical purpose for which Christians use the Bible, the modern editions of the Hebrew Old Testament and Greek New Testament, like all the standard modern-language translations in use around the world today, can more than adequately function as remarkably close approximations of God's inerrant autographs and can guide us theologically and ethically in every walk of life. The Scriptures have not been inerrantly preserved; to claim otherwise flies in the face of all the evidence and unnecessarily discredits Christianity among those who know better. More important, however, we have massive amounts of support for our convictions that the sixty-six books of the canonical Scriptures accepted by all branches of Christianity have been extraordinarily well preserved. Of course, knowing what the biblical writers most probably first penned does not make a word of their testimony true. But it means that we can move on to the question of their trustworthiness in ways that we couldn't if we weren't even sure what they first wrote.

First, however, we must ask, "Why these sixty-six books?" How can we know that the documents of the Protestant Bible are uniquely inspired and worthy of canonization? Do they all merit inclusion? Should more be added, like the Old Testament Apocrypha of the Roman Catholic canon? Why not include some of the writings of the early church fathers or of the gnostics? Or why not stop with the Hebrew Scriptures, as Jews do? What about the claims of the Muslims or Mormons to have additional scriptures from a much later period of time, often viewed as even more important for the faithful? And do all sixty-six books truly deserve a place in the canon? It is to these questions that we must now turn.

2

Wasn't the Selection of Books for the Canon Just Political?

A recent book by David Dungan reflects a commonly held notion about the formation of the biblical canon with its title *Constantine's Bible: Politics and the Making of the New Testament*. Dungan spells out that notion:

> When the Roman government, in the person of the emperor, powerfully intruded into the church's activities, it irrevocably skewed the whole debate by transplanting it into the state's legal framework, where coercive enforcement of the outcome was routine. After the Edict against the Heretics came out, what nonorthodox Christian would dare publicly to use a non-accepted writing or attack the orthodox collection and propose an alternative selection of scripture?[1]

In other words, Scripture was created by the winning side of the early (fourth-century) Christian battle for control over the belief and practice of the masses.

Bart Ehrman phrases things even more forcefully:

> The victors in the struggles to establish Christian orthodoxy not only won their theological battles, they also rewrote the history of the conflict; later readers, then, naturally assume that the victorious views had been embraced by the vast majority of Christians from the very beginning, all the way back to Jesus and his closest followers, the apostles.

Ehrman then asks the question about the fate of the other books claiming to be written by the apostles that were not accepted as part of the Bible. His answer is that "for the most part they were suppressed, forgotten, or destroyed—in one way or another lost, except insofar as they were mentioned by those who opposed them, who quoted them precisely in order to show how wrong they were."[2]

If these claims are at all accurate, then it really doesn't matter much whether or not the text of the Bible has been well preserved (the point of chap. 1 above). We might still not have a good representation of original Christianity, because the books that could have given us that might have been excluded from the Scriptures. Unfortunately for defenders of this perspective, the real historical truth of the matter is almost exactly the opposite! Good arguments, adopted by a wide swath of liberal and conservative scholars alike, date all of the books accepted into the New Testament to the first century or, in the case of one or two books, perhaps to the very earliest years of the second century.[3] The next oldest Christian writings, the so-called Apostolic Fathers, which date mostly from the first half of the second century, are all largely orthodox in their doctrine.[4] Only beginning in the second half of the second century does literature begin to emerge of a very different kind, and it presupposes the earlier existence and widespread usage of the New Testament documents. The most fanciful and unorthodox documents do not emerge until the third through the fifth centuries, and then only as a small percentage of the totality of the Christian literature written in those centuries. Lost in these debates, too, is the fact that from its earliest days Christianity inherited a body of sacred literature, which only the orthodox and apostolic tradition continued to treasure. To fully discuss the Christian Bible, then, we must begin in pre-Christian times.

The Old Testament Canon

The Hebrew Scriptures (or Old Testament, as they came to be known in Christian circles) formed the Bible for Jesus and his first followers, all of whom were Jewish. Some scholars have tried to argue that these books were also the product of political wrangling,[5] but this is a far more difficult claim to defend, if for no other reason than that many mysteries shroud the origins of the Old Testament. But the percentage of the Hebrew Bible that criticizes the people and the leadership of Israel is far too great for it to have been produced by anyone trying to maintain the status quo for very long![6] Furthermore, no references to competing, unorthodox Hebrew writings *from Old Testament times* (rather than the intertestamental period) exist anywhere, even in documents rebutting them as candidates for canonization. In other words, there is not a shred of evidence to suggest that any works ever rivaled Leviticus or Samuel, Ruth or Ezra, Job or Micah, or any other book in the Hebrew "canon"—the collection of distinctively authoritative, sacred literature—in their day.[7]

Development of the Canon

There are two clear ways ancient Judaism subdivided its Scriptures. Sometimes they were referred to as "the Law and the Prophets," while other times three divisions were created. Eventually the latter became standardized as "the Law, the Prophets and the Writings."[8] Judaism has treated the five books traditionally ascribed to Moses (the Torah, or Law)—Genesis, Exodus, Leviticus, Numbers, and Deuteronomy—as the most foundational and significant core of its Scripture. The later, larger sections of the Old Testament all refer back to the Law to some degree or another as authoritative. For both of these reasons, it is natural to envision these five books as the earliest to be canonized—grouped together as distinctively inspired and normative for the ancient Israelites. But we don't actually know this from any testimony or documentation anywhere.[9]

The Hebrew Bible typically placed the Prophets after the Law, divided into the Former Prophets (Joshua through 2 Kings) and the Latter

Prophets (Isaiah through Ezekiel and Hosea through Malachi). The former prophets are largely historical or narrative in genre; the latter combine together large segments of oracular or prophetic speech, with a small amount of historical narrative interspersed. The latest of the historical characters to appear in these books (e.g., Nehemiah or Malachi) lived in the late fifth century BC, so it is easy to imagine the Prophets as being added to the Hebrew canon sometime in the fourth century BC. The last division, the Writings, is the most amorphous, comprising, in various orders, the books of Job, Psalms, Proverbs, Ecclesiastes, Song of Songs, Ruth, Lamentations, 1–2 Chronicles, Ezra, Nehemiah, Esther, and Daniel. Debates in Jewish circles after the time of Christ about the propriety of books like Ecclesiastes, Song of Songs, and Esther have suggested to many that the Writings were not finalized until the late first century AD (at least as a complete collection of writings rather than merely individual works viewed as authoritative).[10]

But again, we don't actually know any of this! At least as plausible is the view that the canon had recently been closed when the grandson of one Jesus son of Sirach in the late second century BC penned his prologue to his grandfather's proverbial writing later known as Ecclesiasticus. In it, he refers to a highly influential collection of documents as "the Law and the Prophets and the others that have followed in their steps," "the Law and the Prophets and the other Books of the fathers," and "the Law itself and the prophecies and the rest of the Books."[11] That there was no standard name for the third group of books could easily suggest that the fixing of this third division of the Hebrew Bible was relatively recent, from the perspective of this individual.[12] A logical time for this to have occurred would have been just after the Maccabean revolt, when the Syrian forces were expelled from most of Jerusalem in 164 BC. At that time Judas Maccabeus gathered the writings that the Syrian ruler Antiochus Epiphanes had caused to be scattered (and sometimes destroyed) in his pogrom against the Jews (2 Macc. 2:14–15).[13] Persecution and the threat of martyrdom for hiding sacred books usually makes people want to be sure they know what they will die for! That some rabbis continued to debate whether a few books belonged in their Bible long after the canon was settled is no more unusual than that some scholars continue to do so today, two millennia later.

Old Testament Apocrypha and Pseudepigrapha

There *are* numerous other writings from Second Temple Judaism, composed during the period spanning the fourth century BC through the first century AD. One collection of such writings has come to be called the Old Testament Apocrypha—works that would eventually be accepted into Roman Catholic and/or Eastern Orthodox canons.[14] How one counts the actual number of documents depends both on which branch of Christianity one is describing and also on how one counts multiple additions to the books of Daniel and Esther, but there are about fifteen such works or portions of works. These include four books describing the Maccabean period (1–4 Maccabees), historical novels (Judith and Tobit), books of proverbs or wisdom literature (Ecclesiasticus/Sirach and Wisdom of Solomon), and shorter works such as the Prayer of Manasseh and the Letter of Jeremiah.[15] Another sixty or more books from this period have been recovered and are known as the Old Testament Pseudepigrapha because they are typically attributed to some ancient Old Testament patriarch or key figure in Jewish history who lived long before the time of the book's actual writing.[16] Here we encounter numerous apocalypses (esp. those ascribed to Enoch) and testaments (or farewell addresses) ascribed to ancient patriarchs, along with a wide assortment of other writings.[17] With only one or two exceptions, these works were never canonized by anyone.[18] The books at times provide invaluable background to understanding the theological developments within Judaism just before the time of Christ and his apostles,[19] but they are not serious contenders for inclusion in the canon.

The Apocrypha, however, became a point of contention, especially at the time of the Protestant Reformation. Although never accepted as inspired or authoritative by any branch of Judaism, *nor even put forward as candidates for canonization within Judaism*, these writings came to be valued in early Christianity, especially after the time of Constantine. They were prized because they taught on doctrines not found anywhere else in Scripture (like purgatory or praying for the dead), because they were simply inspiring (i.e., an exciting, edifying read, like Judith and Tobit), because texts they contained could be interpreted allegorically and viewed as foreshadowing Jesus, or just because they were good religious literature.[20] Yet despite their widespread usage, including for preaching in churches, no ecumenical (i.e., empire-wide) council ever officially declared them canonical until the Council of Trent in 1546. Only after Martin Luther insisted that Christians return to the Bible of the Jewish Jesus and the Jewish apostles, so to speak, did irate Catholic authorities retaliate by formally canonizing the Apocrypha.[21]

Why did Jews draw a line after the fifth century BC and believe that later literature did not merit canonization? Again, most of the details have been lost to the ravages of time. But we do know that Josephus, a late first-century Jewish historian, believed that Judaism as a whole had come to the conviction that after the last of the writing prophets, like Haggai, Zechariah, and Malachi, prophecy had ceased in Israel (in the formal sense of inerrant words from the Lord) and that Jews were longing for its resumption because it would indicate the imminence of the messianic age.[22] Later rabbis explicitly reaffirmed this belief, and implicit evidence for the cessation of prophecy appears also in Sirach, 1 Maccabees, and 2 Esdras.[23] Given that even the Writings could be lumped with the Prophets and then combined with the Law, to be spoken of simply as "the Law and the Prophets" (e.g., Matt. 5:17), it is quite likely that all of the Hebrew Scriptures were believed to be prophetic in origin. As Moses was thought to be the author of at least the core of the Torah, or Pentateuch, and with his prophetic role being included within the books ascribed to him (see, e.g., Deut. 18:15), it is clear that Moses was likewise thought to exercise the gift of prophecy. A high percentage of the authors who, as Jews traditionally believed, wrote the rest of the Old Testament are also somewhere referred to as prophets, or at least as functioning in a fashion akin to prophets—foretelling and forthtelling God's will.[24] Josephus also appears to suggest that Jews believed that their Scriptures did not contain insuperable contradictions, that they were inspired by God, and that they therefore functioned authoritatively.[25]

Different Canons Elsewhere?

It is sometimes argued that because the earliest complete or nearly complete New Testament manuscripts still in existence (from the fourth and fifth centuries) have the LXX attached to them, and because their versions of the Septuagint contain the Apocrypha, Hellenistic or Diaspora Judaism thus must have had an expanded canon, larger than the Hebrew collection that would give rise to the Masoretic Text (see above, chap. 1). But because these manuscripts are later *Christian* documents, preserved in Christian rather than Jewish circles, this conclusion hardly follows. Given both the intermingling of Hellenism with Jewish thought in Israel and the authority often exercised by Jews in Israel over Jewish communities in the Diaspora, it is hard to imagine there being two separate canons of Scripture in first-century Judaism that differed so dramatically.[26] The actual discussions of the contents of Scripture in ancient Judaism show no trace of an expanded canon that included the Apocrypha.[27]

It is also significant that some portion of every book of the Hebrew canon has been found at Qumran, among the Dead Sea Scrolls, except for Esther, and the most important books appear in considerable number. Given the fragmentary nature of so many of these scrolls, it is quite possible that Esther was once present too; we just don't know. On the other hand, only three books of the Apocrypha are represented among the Qumran fragments. The discovery of the Dead Sea Scrolls does not confirm the exact parameters of the Jewish canon, nor when they were established, but it does point in the direction of the more limited canon of the Hebrew Scriptures much more than to the expanded LXX collection.[28] It is sometimes argued that the (probably) Essene monastics at this site would have considered some of the compositions of their own community as Scripture, especially those of an otherwise unnamed leader called the Teacher of Righteousness. This is possible, of course, but no actual evidence has yet emerged to support this hypothesis.

Particularly telling is that the New Testament explicitly quotes from a broad cross-section of Old Testament documents but never quotes from the Apocrypha. Jude quotes once from a pseudepigraphic work, *1 Enoch*, but not in a fashion that necessarily implies that he understood the work to be part of the Hebrew canon.[29] Paul at times quotes Greek poets and philosophers as well (e.g., Acts 17:28; Titus 1:12), without implying that he thought they were inspired or had authored Scripture. If one expands the database from quotations to allusions, one may speculate about numerous possible references to both apocryphal and pseudepigraphic texts in the New Testament. But good preachers have always alluded to well-known or important literature outside the Bible. One has to look for language that unambiguously shows that a given author is treating a book as canonical before declaring that quotations or allusions to it imply this kind of uniquely authoritative status.[30] It is also noteworthy that none of the apocryphal books claim to be God's Word, as many books of the Hebrew Scriptures do. In addition, many books of the Apocrypha have historical inaccuracies or theological inconsistencies in them.[31]

Craig Allert unwittingly demonstrates how confused these analyses can become. Rightly warning against an overly simplified, cut-and-dried narrative of the formation of the Christian canon, he at times swings the pendulum too far in the opposite direction in overestimating early Christian diversity. In his chapter on the formation of the New Testament canon, in a section titled "Three Principle [*sic*] Theories,"[32] he rightly debunks the notion that the canon emerged spontaneously and the view that the canon was completely closed by the second century AD. Apparently he thinks large numbers of American evangelicals hold one or both of these positions, but the only individuals he cites are the German conservative Theodor Zahn, from a century ago, and the American R. Laird Harris, from half a century ago, and even Harris moderated his views somewhat in the revised 1995 edition of his book.[33]

Somehow Allert gets sidetracked from his topic of the New Testament and includes a section on "A Wider Old Testament Canon?" in this chapter. Immediately after correctly warning that second-century Christian writers using the Greek term for "Scripture" (*graphē*, "writing") weren't necessarily citing works as canonical in the sense of being part of a uniquely authoritative *collection* of "New Testament" documents, Allert cites the use of *graphē* in the *Epistle of Barnabas* to conclude that its author *was* treating various Old Testament apocryphal works as canonical! Some writers in the Apostolic Fathers corpus refer to passages in apocryphal works as prophecy or to their authors as prophets,[34] but early Christians consistently believed that in both Jewish and Christian contexts the phenomenon of prophecy was broader than merely the production of canonical Scripture.[35] Plus, the second century is the period when the earliest theological tendencies emerged that would lead in the fourth and fifth centuries to more full-orbed Roman Catholicism, so it is hazardous to use its literature to determine first-century Christian views. The Reformers' argument against the Apocrypha was never that all patristic writers agreed on the extent of the Old Testament canon. Rather, it was that no *Jews* ever seriously supported the canonization of any of the Apocrypha. As in all areas of Christian thought and practice in which we want to be informed by Jesus and the apostles, we must do our best to recover the *first-century* viewpoints on the biblical books.[36]

More Debatable Issues

There are, to be sure, interesting and diverse phenomena surrounding the formation of the Old Testament canon that are harder to pin down. What order should the books be put in? This may not be a question that was even raised until post–New Testament times when the codex (book) form of preserving documents replaced individual scrolls for each separate writing. The Protestant canon largely followed the order of the LXX, minus the Apocrypha, with the Hebrew canon following the sequence of Law, Former Prophets, Latter Prophets, and Writings. Were there twenty-two books or twenty-four? It depended on whether Judges and Ruth were kept together as one book and whether Jeremiah and Lamentations were kept together as one book. The other twenty would have been Genesis, Exodus, Leviticus, Numbers, Deuteronomy, Joshua, 1 and 2 Samuel kept together as one work, 1 and 2 Kings likewise, 1 and 2 Chronicles likewise, Ezra-Nehemiah as one, Esther, Job, Psalms, Proverbs, Ecclesiastes, Song of Songs, Isaiah, Ezekiel, Daniel, and the twelve Minor Prophets as one book.[37] Another intriguing question is why Daniel and Chronicles were included among the Writings rather than among the Prophets. But none of these issues should distract from the fact that the books in the Hebrew canon had no known competitors within Judaism.

One can similarly debate the dates of almost every Old Testament book.[38] In various scholarly circles it has become fashionable to date many of them very late—well into the Hellenistic period of Israel

(323–164 BC)—much later than the liberal consensus of the past century, which postulated largely exilic and postexilic dates (722–ca. 400 BC), and later still than the time in which the ancient authors whom the early Jews believed wrote these books actually lived.[39] But this debate need not detain us, for the more likely it is that a biblical book was contemporaneous with books of the Apocrypha or Pseudepigrapha, the more significant it is that there was no known campaign to include the latter in the Hebrew canon. The only debates reflected among the rabbis in early post-Christian centuries were whether a few of the twenty-two or twenty-four books (depending on how one counted them) merited inclusion, not whether any others deserved to join them. The Song of Songs was suspect because of its apparent delight in the sexual desires of a young woman and her lover. Ecclesiastes raised questions because of its rather pessimistic outlook on life, while Esther was doubted because it was the only book being considered that never explicitly mentioned God. Occasionally questions were raised about Proverbs and Ezekiel as well.[40]

A Unity of Plot

A final phenomenon merits mention at this juncture. The unfolding story line of the Hebrew Scriptures demonstrates a remarkable continuity. Of course, it is easy to find elements of diversity among the books of the Old Testament. Since they were written by many different authors, over numerous centuries, this is exactly what one would expect. What is harder to explain, if these are merely human books, is the amount of agreement and unity over such a long span of time, with signs of careful interlocking of beginnings, middles, and endings of later biblical books with earlier ones.[41] Genesis begins with the creation of the heavens and the earth and the primeval history of humanity (Gen. 1–11). Because of our ancestors' fall into sin, God singles out one individual, Abram, and promises that his offspring will inherit the promised land of Canaan and that through them all the earth will be blessed (Gen. 12:1–3). The rest of the five books of the Law describe the obstacles that seem to put those promises in jeopardy, but also the ways in which God preserves Abram's descendants and eventually leads them out of slavery in Egypt to that very promised land. En route he gives them laws to obey that will form the heart of prescribed Israelite religion from that time forward. The remaining historical books, or in Hebrew parlance, the Former Prophets, narrate the cycles of obedience and disobedience of God's people in his land. To the extent that they, and especially their leaders, were more obedient to his law than not, he blessed them with prosperity, peace, and safety in the land. To the extent that they were more disobedient than not, God remained patient but eventually handed them over to their enemies—Philistia, Assyria, Babylon, and finally Persia.

The Latter Prophets all contain some combination of condemnation and edification: denunciation of Israel and the surrounding peoples for their sins, announcing the various judgments that God has in store for them but also inserting promises, as we have just seen, of a subsequent restoration of Israel, when the people will again follow their God. Ultimately representatives of all the nations will embrace the God of Israel in an age of messianic deliverance. The Writings that do not take the form of historical narrative depict the worship and lament (esp. Psalms and Lamentations) and wisdom (esp. Proverbs) from many eras of Israelite history, presupposing the Law but also raising countercultural questions about evil (Job), wealth and pleasure (Ecclesiastes), and love and sexual desire (Song of Songs). Those books within the Writings that do take the form of historical narrative present important illustrations of God's dealings with his people during the time periods they depict—Ruth during the Judges, Esther during the period of Ezra-Nehemiah but for those Jews who did not return home from Persia to Israel, and Daniel and Lamentations during the time of Chronicles (and of Jeremiah and Ezekiel) and the Babylonian exile. Indeed, the sweep of history covered by Chronicles, from Adam to the restoration of Israel under Cyrus, sums up the entire Old Testament period in a fashion that could point to an intention to complete the collection of Hebrew Scriptures, as its location at the end of the Jewish canon would then reinforce.[42]

The Hebrew Scriptures thus form a remarkably comprehensive package of the history of ancient Israel, the history of its relationship with God, and the ways in which God wants his people to live. Add the Old Testament Apocrypha, and the chronological and theological unity is disrupted. Historical narratives gain intrusive additions (Esther and

Daniel), books describing different historical time periods with distinctive theologies appear (Maccabees), works of wisdom present a more pessimistic outlook on Israelite behavior (Sirach, Wisdom of Solomon), and historical novels contain patently obvious factual inaccuracies (Tobit and Judith).[43] All of these works have considerable merit as well, but not as plausible candidates for having been divinely inspired.

The New Testament Canon

What, then, of the New Testament? Are the apostolic documents contained in it really just late distortions of the true Jesus, who was really just a good Jewish rabbi or the original gnostic? Hardly. It doesn't matter how you arrange the New Testament books, how you slice them into sections, or how you date them and their putative sources: a thoroughly supernatural Jesus, making numerous implicit and occasionally explicit claims for himself as the uniquely divine but fully human Son of God, permeates every section, from the earliest years onward.[44] And these are the only Christian writings we know of that can confidently be dated to the first century. In another context, one could debate whether, with many conservative scholars, one should date Mark, Matthew, and Luke-Acts all to the 60s and John to the 90s—or with many liberal scholars, Mark to the 70s, Matthew and Luke-Acts to the 80s, and John to the 90s. But for our purposes here, the main point remains unaltered. Under either dating scheme, these writings precede all other early Christian writings with the possible exception of the *Didache*, a late first- or early second-century writing called "The Teaching of the Twelve Apostles" (the Greek word *didachē* means "teaching"), which gives almost entirely orthodox instructions for basic Christian living and on specific topics such as baptism, the Lord's Supper, prayer and fasting, and positions of church leadership.[45]

The seven undisputed Letters of Paul (Galatians, 1 Thessalonians, 1–2 Corinthians, Romans, Philippians, and Philemon) are almost universally dated to sometime between the late 40s and early 60s. One does not even need to go beyond the canonical Gospels to discover agreement on the fundamental contours of Jesus's life and the primary obligations of his followers. In fact, as far as we know, there was never any dispute on the unique nature and authoritative role of the four New Testament Gospels; the book of Acts; these seven Letters of Paul *plus* 2 Thessalonians, Ephesians, and Colossians; and the non-Pauline Epistles of 1 Peter and 1 John. Very little debate ever surrounded the so-called Pastoral Epistles (1–2 Timothy and Titus) either. The seven books that did trigger a little extra discussion (but still significantly less than any excluded book) were Hebrews, James, 2 Peter, 2–3 John, Jude, and Revelation.[46]

Why a Few Books Were Debated

The questions surrounding these disputed New Testament books are still raised by readers today. For example, no one knew for sure who wrote Hebrews. Some in the early church proposed that Paul had written the book, but the style is quite different, and Hebrews 2:3 suggests that the writer was not a firsthand witness to Jesus's resurrection as Paul was (see Acts 9:1–9; 1 Cor. 15:8). Others suggested Barnabas, Luke, or Clement of Rome. Origen's opinion has been cited probably more than anyone else's: "Only God knows." But continuity with apostolic teaching was clearly perceived, and all of the alternatives to Paul who have been suggested, whether in ancient times or more recently, were at some point disciples of Paul.[47]

James raised questions because of its apparent contradiction (see esp. James 2:18–26) with Paul's emphasis on salvation by grace through faith apart from works of the law (see esp. Gal. 3:1–18; Rom. 4:1–12). On closer inspection, however, Paul clearly thinks true believers will live changed lives (Eph. 2:10; Gal. 5:6). And the works that James sees as necessary are Christian acts of mercy that demonstrate God's transformation of believers, not obedience to the law so as to merit God's favor (see esp. James 2:14–17).

Second Peter is written in a dramatically different style than 1 Peter, so ancient Christians wondered if one writer could have penned both epistles. But ancient letter writers regularly dictated their thoughts to scribes, sometimes giving them freedom to write up those thoughts in their own style. If that happened with one or both of these letters, then nothing about authorship can be determined from the nature of their Greek. The Letters of 2–3 John and Jude were simply so short that questions were asked about their timeless, enduring value. But 2 John warns against giving false teachers a platform to promote their doctrine in a Christian congregation, and 3 John praises Demetrius as a model of hospitality and warns Gaius against the self-promoting behavior of Diotrephes. Jude, finally, describes how his audience must "contend for the faith" once delivered to all the saints (v. 3), against false teachers whose errors seem more to be immoral lifestyles than false doctrine. All of these issues in these three little one-chapter letters prove important and timeless enough to warrant their inclusion in the New Testament canon.[48]

Revelation, of course, has puzzled readers throughout church history, because of the very nature of its apocalyptic genre, combined with elements of prophecy and letter writing. With its many allusions to Genesis, however, especially at its end, Revelation forms a fitting literary inclusio, or bookend, with Genesis, creating the beginning and ending of the Christian canon.[49] That is not to say that John was conscious of writing the last book of the Bible when he penned Revelation but that the early church recognized it as a worthy candidate for that role. In John's original context, Revelation 22:18–19 on not adding or subtracting to the words of this book referred only to the book of Revelation itself. But when the church finalized the canon, by including Revelation and ending with it, it was in essence applying John's words to the entire collection of authoritative documents.

Why Some Books Were Not Included

But what of the infamous books that did not make it into the canon? Are there really dozens of early Christian writings that competed for inclusion in the New Testament canon? Not that we know of. Lee McDonald has published in an appendix to his edited volume on *The Canon Debate* the thirty earliest known "Lists and Catalogues of New Testament Collections" from the second through sixth centuries. Exactly fourteen writings outside of the standard twenty-seven-book New Testament are commended at least once, though sometimes in separate categories that indicate the writer's or compiler's doubts about them.

Ten of these fourteen documents appear on only one of the thirty lists: the *Acts of Paul*, *1–2 Clement*, the *Psalms of Solomon*, the *Preaching of Peter*, the *Two Ways*, the *Apostolic Constitutions*, Sirach, the *Didache*, and the *Gospel of Thomas*. The Wisdom of Solomon appears three times, as does the *Epistle of Barnabas* and the *Apocalypse of Peter*, while the *Shepherd of Hermas* is mentioned five times. The only gnostic source in this whole list is the *Gospel of Thomas*, about which we will say more later. The other writings, whether from the Apostolic Fathers or the New Testament Apocrypha, begin to show the occasional deviation from first-century Christian doctrine but in general are far more orthodox than any of the gnostic literature that has become famous in recent decades.[50]

Space prohibits us from proceeding one at a time and considering each of these fourteen works, much less all of the New Testament Apocrypha, gnostic writings, or Jewish-Christian writings that were never put forward by anybody, to our knowledge, as on a par with the twenty-seven books eventually canonized. With rare exceptions, however, several generalizations apply to them. They do not tie in with the Old Testament nearly as explicitly as the canonical New Testament books; indeed, some of them appear to have developed completely outside of any Jewish milieu and even occasionally seem anti-Semitic. Those containing narrative material purport to supplement the Gospels and Acts by recounting teachings or deeds of Jesus or the apostles from periods of their lives that the canonical works do not treat. Probably a main reason for their composition was to satisfy the curiosity of the gullible about those perceived gaps in the New Testament record.[51] Those that are more didactic in form, such as letters, address issues of significance in the church life of their day. Some of them even explicitly claim not to be written with the same degree of authority as the writings of the first generation of Jesus's followers (e.g., Ign. *Trall.* 3.3).

Most tellingly, not a single gnostic or apocryphal document's writer or supporter ever puts one of these books forward as worthy of inclusion in the canon. The very fact that names of first-century followers of Christ were attached to documents from the second through sixth centuries shows that their authors knew they would gain no hearing unless people thought they came from the first generation of disciples.

Yet even then, a hearing is apparently all they wanted; there is no indication that gnostics or any other sect tried to create a rival canon or even sought inclusion of extra books in the orthodox canon. And given the amount of literature that *has* survived or been rediscovered from these circles, we would almost certainly have found evidence of such efforts if they had ever existed. Instead, these later documents formed a heterodox interpretive grid by which to understand preceding revelation.[52]

Criteria of Canonization

By what criteria, then, were the New Testament documents evaluated? Three requirements stand out as predominant: apostolicity, catholicity, and orthodoxy.

Apostolicity. The criterion of apostolicity does not mean that every book was written by an apostle—by one of Jesus's twelve closest followers—but rather that they were written during the apostolic age, before the last of the Twelve (most likely John) had died. Put another way, there is good reason to believe that these books come from the first century, the apostolic era.[53] No book, moreover, is more than one person removed from an apostle or an authoritative eyewitness of the life of Jesus. The Gospels of Matthew and John are attributed to apostles, as are the Epistles of Peter, John, and the book of Revelation (also assigned to John). Mark was a traveling companion of both Peter and Paul, and strong early church tradition ascribes much of Mark's Gospel to the memoirs of Peter. Luke interviewed eyewitnesses of the life of Christ (Luke 1:1–4) and traveled with Paul, who called himself an apostle because of his experience with the risen Christ, even if he recognized that his vision came later than the other appearances, rendering him as one "untimely born" (1 Cor. 15:8 NRSV). James and Jude were both half brothers of Jesus. And as already noted, the author of Hebrews was probably a follower of Paul.

Of course, just as dates have been challenged, so have many of these ascriptions of authorship. But in almost every case, even more-liberal scholarship assigns dates and authors for these books to the first century, so that the criterion of apostolicity as defined above remains satisfied. Even when the critical consensus deems an author unknown or anonymous, it grants that the author likely was well aware of apostolic teaching.[54] Moreover, before the time of Constantine, in the early fourth century, it seems that apostolicity was the dominant criterion and that books virtually imposed themselves on the church because of their sources or origin despite debates over usefulness or orthodoxy.[55]

Catholicity. Catholicity has nothing to do with the *Roman* Catholic Church. "Catholic" as an adjective simply means "universal." The books accepted into the New Testament were never those that were found among only one sect within Christianity or used in one small corner of the Christian world (at first roughly contiguous with the Roman Empire, though soon spreading further afield). The criterion of catholicity means that believers throughout the parts of the world to which Christianity had spread were in agreement on the abiding value of these books and used them widely.[56]

Orthodoxy. Orthodoxy is the criterion that refers to *faithfulness* to the teachings of Jesus and the apostles. It is a criterion that could not have developed if people had not recognized that the heresies afflicting the church in its earliest centuries were parasitic on orthodoxy. That is to say, the heresies developed in response to apostolic doctrine—modifying it, challenging it, trying to refute it, supplementing it, or simply rejecting it. A careful read through any large swath of this literature discloses this parasitic character repeatedly.[57] There is very little chance that the books not included in the New Testament canon, at any significant point in which they differ from those that were included, actually represent earlier or equally viable or prevalent Christian developments than what came to be recognized as orthodoxy.[58]

There is a sense, therefore, in which Dungan and Ehrman are right, but it is a very limited sense. The twenty-seven New Testament books did win out over the others. But sometimes in history (as in sports or any other form of competition), winners actually deserve to win! And the fact that we have so much Christian literature from before the finalizing of the canon, attesting to the "messiness" of the process, proves that Ehrman is flat out wrong in claiming that the church rewrote the history of canonization to tidy things up or that it somehow suppressed the books it rejected. The number of late fourth-, fifth-, and sixth-century lists and catalogs of the canon in McDonald's appendix[59] shows how much diversity remained even after post-Constantinian councils decreed what should be in the New Testament in the fourth century. These lists likewise disprove Dungan's claim that people wouldn't have dared to contradict the state once it had become Christian and had facilitated councils to promulgate authoritative decrees on such matters. Indeed, the subversive nature of so much of the Old and New Testaments is hard to explain if either synagogue or church were simply including what would support their own power base. They would hardly have allowed so much critique of their own sins and errors to stand![60]

Moreover, positions like those of Ehrman and Dungan are internally self-contradictory. On the one hand, they argue against the reliability of the Bible because of countless errors or contradictions within it. On the other hand, they insist that the criterion of orthodoxy was used in a heavy-handed fashion to suppress dissenting viewpoints. They cannot have it both ways. Michael Kruger expresses it well:

> Ehrman raises the provocative question, "What if some other form of Christianity had become dominant, instead of the one that did?" He answers that we would likely have "an entirely different set of books." Our current canon therefore represents a loss of "the great diversity of the early centuries of Christianity." But there is a problem here. If the current form of the canon includes the preferred books of the theological winners and thereby represents a *loss* of great diversity, how, at the same time, can one claim that the canon is composed of contradictory books that reflect great diversity? If the "winners" determined the canon, then why would they pick books from various and contradictory theological camps? One cannot argue that the canon is the "invention" of the proto-orthodox designed to suppress the opposition and then turn around and argue that the canon is a cacophony of diverse theological viewpoints that stand in opposition.[61]

Logically, the most likely position is that the canon is neither self-contradictory nor the distortion of earliest Christianity.

The criterion of orthodoxy, sometimes called noncontradiction, also extended to the Old Testament, the Hebrew Scriptures. The first centuries of Christianity believed that the twenty-seven books ultimately included in the New Testament were the documents that best exhibited the continuity between the prophetic roles of the Old Testament books and their fulfillment in the life and times of Jesus and his first followers. Having already stressed that Jesus and those followers had an existing Bible in their day (what we call the Old Testament), we may fairly ask why the church came to add *any* books to its existing collection, even in a separate section called a New Testament. The primary answer is that the Old Testament canon is a collection of open-ended documents.[62]

Fulfilling the Hebrew Scriptures. Especially as one reads the Latter Prophets, book after book predicts God's imminent judgment on Judah or Israel. But many of them close their texts by looking ahead into the more distant future and predicting God's restoration of his people in conditions of magnificent blessing. Isaiah 40–66 depicts this period in greater detail than other prophets, including prophecies of a Suffering Servant who will take away his people's sins (52:13–53:12). Jeremiah and Ezekiel prophesy a coming new covenant, when God will write his laws on people's hearts and they will serve him with unprecedented obedience (Jer. 31:31–34; Ezek. 36:22–38). God will replace Israel's evil rulers and shepherds with wise and faithful ones, establishing a "covenant of peace" (Ezek. 34). Hosea 14:4–7 promises that God will heal Israel's apostasy and love his people freely, just as the prophet has loved his prostitute-wife Gomer even after her faithlessness. Joel 2:28–32 predicts a coming day when God will pour out his Spirit on all his people, the mighty and the lowly, men and women, old and young, free and slave, rather than having the Spirit merely come temporarily upon select people for special acts of proclamation and service as he had previously done. Amos 9:11–15 prophesies not only the restoration of Israel but also that people from all nations who bear the name of the Lord will be incorporated into the community of Israel.

The closing verses of Micah are so beautiful that they merit citation in full:

> Who is a God like you, who pardons sin and forgives the transgression of the remnant of his inheritance? You do not stay angry forever but delight to show mercy. You will again have compassion on us; you will tread our sins underfoot and hurl all our iniquities into the depths of the sea. You

will be faithful to Jacob, and show love to Abraham, as you pledged on oath to our ancestors in days long ago. (Mic. 7:18–20)

Zephaniah elaborates on these themes and adds others (3:14–20), including saving the lame and gathering the outcast (v. 19). Haggai envisions a servant-king like Zerubbabel who will rule over the nations after God again shakes the heavens and earth (2:20–23). Zechariah concludes with the temple being purified and no more traders or merchants present in it, so that people from every nation may worship the Lord there (14:18–20). Malachi, finally, foresees the coming of Elijah before the "great and dreadful" day of the Lord (3:1), when the Lord will suddenly come to his temple and purify his people (4:5).[63]

In the first century, Jews debated how these and similar prophecies would be fulfilled. Jesus, the Gospels affirm, taught that many of them were being fulfilled in himself and in the events surrounding his ministry, and his first followers echoed these claims, extending that fulfillment to all of biblical prophecy. Some prophecies, however, would require his death, resurrection, ascension, and subsequent return from heaven at an unspecified future time before they would be literally fulfilled. Others were already fulfilled, but metaphorically rather than literally. For example, Jesus saw John the Baptist as playing the role of Elijah, as Malachi had foretold (e.g., Matt. 17:9–13). Luke would later write, therefore, that John came "in the spirit and power of Elijah" (Luke 1:17).[64] Because of these differences from common Jewish expectations of how the story of Israel would be completed, many rejected the claims of Jesus and his apostles.[65]

The point stands, however, that the Hebrew Scriptures remained an open-ended narrative in a way the New Testament did not. Christians, in compiling their uniquely sacred Scriptures, added to the Old Testament what they believed was the divinely intended fulfillment of the story of God's dealings with humanity. Jesus made full forgiveness of sins available for all people. The community of his followers was to model his kingdom ethics before a watching world and proclaim the good news of salvation available in him. History might continue for a long time before believers fulfilled Christ's commission to go into all the world, preaching, baptizing new disciples, and teaching them to obey everything Jesus had commanded them (Matt. 28:19–20a). Yet eventually history would culminate in Jesus's personal, visible return to earth, ushering in judgment day (e.g., Matt. 25:31–46; Mark 14:62 pars.). Then Christ would reign on earth and subdue the nations, so that every knee would bow and every tongue confess that Jesus Christ is Lord, some willingly and others begrudgingly (Isa. 45:22–25; Phil. 2:9–11).

In other words, the story of Israel was scarcely complete when prophecy was believed to have ceased. By creating a Second Testament (from the Latin *testamentum*, "covenant"), Christians were thus explicitly claiming to be supplying the completion of God's revelation to which the First Testament pointed. Since Jews believed that God put his oral covenant with them at Sinai under Moses into written form, we should not be surprised that Jewish (and later Gentile) Christians would envision a similar written collection of documents as the inscripturation of God's new covenant.[66]

Inspiration and self-attestation. Besides the criteria of apostolicity, catholicity, and orthodoxy, many early Christian discussions of a New Testament canon included a criterion of inspiration. This is a much more subjective criterion. What appears as inspired to one person may not to another, and vice versa. Given this fairly obvious observation, it is all the more remarkable that numerous ancient writers, like many theologians ever since, spoke about Scripture's self-attestation. Jews and Christians alike frequently have believed that God's Spirit testifies to his people as to which books are divinely revealed. That testimony comes to communities, not just individuals, and thus fosters international and ecumenical conversations and councils. One can easily find individual passages in nonbiblical books that closely resemble all manner of scriptural texts. One can find great Jewish and Christian literature from across the centuries that is at least as *inspiring* as many of the biblical books. But it is hard to take entire documents from antiquity of the same literary genre as any given book in the Protestant canon of Old and New Testaments, read them straight through from beginning to end, and claim they have as many marks of being as "God-breathed" (*theopneustos*, the quality Paul predicates of Scripture in 2 Tim. 3:16) as the sixty-six books spanning Genesis to Revelation.

Particularly significant is the way any such addition would interrupt, to one degree or another, the tightly knit unity within the diversity of the Jewish and Christian canons. No other books, moreover, read as if the authors might be consciously supplementing Scripture, naturally carrying on its story line, and building on its authoritative foundation without ever explicitly contradicting it.[67]

The Process of Canonization

How then did the process of the growing agreement about the contents of the New Testament canon proceed?[68] The New Testament contains hints of the beginnings of the process but little more. As Jesus prepares his disciples for his departure, he promises to send them the Holy Spirit. Among many roles to be performed, the Spirit will cause the disciples to remember Jesus's teaching (John 14:26), testify further about Jesus (15:26), and lead them into all truth (16:13). These suggestive comments scarcely demonstrate what form that ministry will take, but with 20/20 hindsight it is understandable why the church would look back and envision the inspiration of New Testament books as a central part of that process. In varying ways, the four Gospel authors each write as if continuing the story line of the Old Testament, with Jesus as the fulfillment of Jewish hopes. To what extent any of these authors was conscious of writing something "under inspiration" is a fascinating but probably unanswerable question;[69] Luke 1:1–4 reads as if Luke thought he was simply doing good historical research. On the other hand, Paul's use of oral Jesus tradition suggests a uniquely authoritative source of teaching already in the first generation of the Christian movement. In this broader sense, canonical texts thus began to be recognized and acknowledged very early in the history of the church.[70]

First Timothy 5:18 contains the tantalizing references: "For Scripture says, 'Do not muzzle an ox while it is treading out the grain,' and 'The worker deserves his wages.'" The first quotation comes from Deuteronomy 25:4; the second is from Luke 10:7. Of course, it is possible that Paul is citing only the passage from Deuteronomy as Scripture and then simply quoting Luke or the oral tradition he inherited because Jesus made a comparable point. But the more natural reading is that both sayings are being called Scripture, which also implies that they came from written texts. If Paul wrote 1 Timothy, he did so most likely in the mid-60s, while Luke cannot be dated much earlier than 61 or 62. This would be an astonishingly short time in which Luke's Gospel, presumably along with his Acts of the Apostles, would have been acknowledged by at least one fellow Christian as on a par with the Old Testament.[71] On the other hand, Paul in 1 Corinthians 7:40 discloses that he believes his own writing is guided by the Holy Spirit (though in what way remains completely unspecified), so perhaps he *would* have recognized a work by his "beloved physician" as uniquely inspired.

An even more remarkable phenomenon appears in 2 Peter 3:15–16. Here we read,

> Bear in mind that our Lord's patience means salvation, just as our dear brother Paul also wrote you with the wisdom that God gave him. He writes the same way in all his letters, speaking in them of these matters. His letters contain some things that are hard to understand, which ignorant and unstable people distort, as they do the other Scriptures, to their own destruction.

Here the author, apparently Peter (see 1:1), shows awareness of more than one of Paul's Letters. We don't know how many, but "all" suggests a collection of at least several. In likening them to "other Scriptures," he clearly implies that Paul's Letters also merit that label. Like Paul, Peter was martyred in the mid-to-late 60s, so we have about five years from the last of Paul's undisputed letters (Philippians and Philemon, written about 61–62), during which time multiple Epistles of Paul could have been informally canonized. Of course, one could argue that this collection included only Paul's earliest letters, in which case we could envision those written from around 49–55, but still the interval is very short.[72]

At the same time, 1 Timothy, 2 Timothy, and Titus are the most disputed of all the letters attributed to Paul. Second Peter is the New Testament epistle whose traditional claims of authorship are more disputed than *any* other. Critical scholarship frequently dates these letters to around the end of the first century or even early in the second century. Either way, however, they remain our earliest evidence for the beginning of the canonical process for New Testament literature. To the extent that one of the key reasons for disputing these letters' authenticity is the very claim reflected in these verses (2 Pet. 3:15–16), the argument turns into a vicious circle: (1) Why is traditional authorship doubted? Because canonical consciousness could not have developed so quickly. (2) Why do these letters not demonstrate an almost immediate canonical consciousness after an inspired book is written? Because they couldn't have been written by Peter or Paul! To be sure, there are other arguments against the authenticity of these epistles, but they are not nearly as decisive as many claim them to be.[73]

In the writings of the Apostolic Fathers (first half of the second century), such works as the *Shepherd of Hermas*, the *Epistle to Diognetus*, the *Martyrdom of Polycarp*, the *Didache*, and especially the letters of Clement, Ignatius, and Polycarp all quote and even more often allude to a broad cross-section of the writings that would come to form the New Testament. The nature and context of the quotations and allusions suggest that these early patristic authors viewed such writings as uniquely authoritative and occasionally declared them explicitly to be Scripture, in the sense of being on a par with the Old Testament.[74] By the middle of the second century, two heterodox challenges to apostolic Christianity loomed large. Marcion, bishop of Sinope in Pontus (northern Turkey), pitted what he viewed as the wrathful God of the Old Testament against the loving Jesus of the New Testament, jettisoned the Old Testament, and kept only the Epistles of Paul and an edited version of the Gospel of Luke as his sacred documents. Scholars dispute whether Marcion can rightly be considered a gnostic, but others who were clearly gnostics certainly did craft an alternative to the Jewish belief in the goodness of the world God created. Building on Greek philosophical, and especially Platonic, thought, gnosticism regarded the material world as irredeemably evil. Only the immaterial soul could be redeemed and live forever in disembodied form.[75] These theological threats to the Jewish foundations of Christianity, coupled with periodic outbreaks of increasingly intense persecution of believers by the Roman state, meant that Christians had more than enough motive to clarify which books they deemed sacred and authoritative and for which they would be willing to die if necessary.

In the late second century, the Muratorian Canon listed the twenty undisputed books of the New Testament mentioned above plus Hebrews, making twenty-one.[76] Irenaeus acknowledges twenty-two by including 2 John. With respect to the four Gospels, Irenaeus takes it for granted that all Christians recognize that there can be these and only these, just as there are four corners of the world and four universal winds. This kind of reasoning suggests that there was no significant dispute as to which Gospels were inspired, since even in antiquity such logic would convince no skeptic but impress only those already convinced on other grounds.[77] Tertullian, at the beginning of the third century, mentions twenty-three books for a New Testament, including James and Revelation but not 2 John. Shortly afterward, Origen of Alexandria distinguishes three categories of books—those widely acknowledged, those doubted by some, and others that he rejects as teaching false doctrine. Acknowledged were the four Gospels, Acts, the thirteen letters attributed to Paul, 1 Peter, 1 John, and Revelation. Disputed were Hebrews, James, 2 Peter, 2–3 John, and Jude, along with the *Didache*, the *Epistle of Barnabas*, the *Shepherd of Hermas*, the *Preaching of Peter*, and the *Acts of Paul*. Later, after moving to Caesarea and not finding these latter works accepted there, Origen became even more doubtful about their validity. Rejected altogether were a variety of heretical gospels and acts, especially various gnostic works. Eusebius of Caesarea closely mirrored Origen's later perspectives.[78]

Despite Dan Brown's fiction,[79] *the Council of Nicaea in AD 325, convened by Constantine, had nothing to do with deciding which books belonged in a New Testament canon. Nicaea was all about formulating trinitarian doctrine; the resulting Nicene Creed contained three articles about belief in the Father, Son, and Holy Spirit.* Constantine did commission Eusebius to have fifty new Bibles copied and sent to key locations throughout the empire. Yet there is no record of any debate about which New Testament books to include; this very fact suggests that there was little or no debate among the church leaders present. Eusebius would have included all twenty-seven books, which he had divided into the categories of acknowledged and acknowledged with some doubt.[80]

The first official promulgation of a list with the twenty-seven books of our New Testament canon occurred a generation later, in AD 367, when Athanasius, bishop of Alexandria, wrote his Easter encyclical to the rest of the church and listed precisely the books that Christians still acknowledge today. The Councils of Hippo (393) and Carthage (397), both in North Africa, more formally ratified the recognition of these twenty-seven books.

Rehabilitating Gnostic Texts?

But suppose we did start over from scratch? Given what we know today, are there good reasons for including the gnostic gospels? After all, these are really the only documents consistently discussed by those who question the wisdom of the original decisions about canonical contents. The best way to answer this question is to invite readers to access the texts of these documents, read them, and decide for themselves. To begin with, none of them is a narrative of any large swath of Jesus's life. To call them gospels, therefore, misleads those who have not read them as to their literary genre. Most involve long, rambling discourses attributed to Jesus, supposedly given to one or more of his followers secretly after the resurrection, teaching about the nature of creation and the heavenly worlds, with all sorts of esoteric cosmological speculation.

The *Dialogue of the Savior* is representative of this literature. Quoting an example from it almost at random, we read this conversation:

> Judas said, "Behold, the archons dwell in heaven; surely, then, it is they who will rule over us."
>
> The Lord said, "You will rule over them. But when you remove envy from you, then you will clothe yourselves with the light and enter into the bridal chamber."
>
> Judas said, "How will our garments be brought to us?"
>
> The Lord said, "Some will bring (them) to you [and] others will receive [them], for they are [the ones who bring] you your garments. Who [can] reach that place which is the reward? But they gave the garments of life to the man, for he knows the way on which he will go. For indeed it is a burden to me as well to reach it."

> Mariam said, "Thus about 'The wickedness of each day,' and 'The laborer being worthy of his food,' and 'The disciple resembling his teacher.'" This word she spoke as a woman who knew the All. (*NHL* III.138.11–139.13)[81]

Anyone with even a superficial familiarity with the canonical Gospels will recognize how different a milieu we have here. Instead of discussing the kingdom of God, the Son of Man, and the ethical behavior that God desires (so central to the Synoptic Gospels), or even the presence of eternal life (so central to John), we have issues about heavenly rank and hierarchy, rewards and garments, and special knowledge. The words attributed to Mary (Mariam) show that canonical teaching is already so well known that Jesus's authentic sayings can be referred to the way we might refer to a hymn—just by its first line or a summary statement of its contents.

Or, turning to the so-called *Gospel of Truth* (because of its opening line), we sample a text not attributed to Jesus but simply expounding on gnostic theology:

> The gospel of truth is a joy for those who have received from the Father of truth the gift of knowing him, through the power of the Word that came forth from the pleroma—the one who is in the thought and the mind of the Father, that is, the one who is addressed as the savior, (that) being the name of the work he is to perform for the redemption of those who were ignorant of the Father, while the name [of] the proclamation of hope, being discovery for those who search for him.
>
> Indeed, the all went about searching for the one from whom it (pl.) had come forth, and the all was inside of him, the incomprehensible, inconceivable one who is superior to every thought. Ignorance of the Father brought about anguish and terror. And the anguish grew solid like a fog so that no one was able to see. For this reason error became powerful. It fashioned its own matter foolishly, not having known the truth. It set about making a creature, with (all its) might preparing, in beauty, a substitute for the truth. (*NHL* I.16.31–17.20)[82]

Here appear technical terms from gnostic theology such as the *plērōma* (referring to the "fullness [of the Godhead]") and "the all" (the entirety of the spiritual world). Here salvation clearly refers to the alleviation of ignorance, substituting truth for error, rather than the forgiveness of sins leading to moral transformation and a relationship with the living, knowable God, as in orthodox Christianity.[83]

In fact, there is really only one post–New Testament gnostic or apocryphal text that is worth any serious consideration: the Coptic *Gospel of Thomas*. It is true that Dan Brown's fiction attributes various distorted or completely made up things to the *Gospel of Philip* and the *Gospel of Mary*,[84] but no serious scholar, however liberal, turns to them for historical information about Jesus. It is true that Dominic Crossan has postulated a source behind the *Gospel of Peter* that might contain some information about the crucifixion of Jesus at least as authentic or old as the canonical Gospels,[85] but almost no one has followed him in that assessment. At one time, a number of scholars were duped by Morton Smith's claims to have photographed an ancient manuscript quoting excerpts of a "Secret Gospel of Mark" at the Mar Saba monastery in the Judean Desert, but two independent studies in recent years have reasonably decisively proved the text to be a modern forgery, probably done by Smith himself.[86] There was also a flurry of interest in the mid-2000s with the discovery of the *Gospel of Judas*, known since the second century from its critics, but again only people unaware of the methods of scholarship took it as containing any serious history, inasmuch as it turned Judas into the hero rather than the villain for betraying Jesus.[87] Some Muslims point to a sixteenth-century Italian (and fourteenth-century Spanish) document called the *Gospel of Barnabas* and assert that it contains the true account of Jesus, which conveniently fits the Qur'an's claims about him better than it does the New Testament's claims, but no trace of this document has ever been discovered from an earlier date.[88]

So we return to the *Gospel of Thomas*, the only gnostic text ever found on any ancient canonical list of recommended books, and then only once. The complete text appears only in a fourth-century Coptic manuscript, but three excerpts of it in late second-century Greek fragments show that its composition dates back to at least that period of time. As with all the other gnostic and apocryphal gospels (except for the *Gospel of Barnabas* in the Middle Ages), it is not a narrative covering the full span of the public ministry of Christ, like the canonical

Gospels. In fact, *unlike* the other gnostic and apocryphal gospels, it contains no narrative at all, merely 114 largely unconnected sayings attributed to Jesus. A handful have a brief introduction, with a disciple making a statement or asking a question that triggers Christ's response. But most begin merely with, "and he [Jesus] said," followed by a brief teaching or parable ascribed to him.[89]

Slightly over one-third of the 114 sayings have at least a partial parallel in the canonical Gospels. Sometimes the parallel is fairly close, as when Jesus describes the kingdom of heaven "like a mustard seed, the smallest of all seeds. But when it falls on tilled soil, it produces a great plant and becomes a shelter for birds of the sky" (*Gos. Thom.* 20; cf. Mark 4:30–32 pars.). Even then one can usually detect a slight change in the direction of a gnostic interpretation, such as here with the addition of "tilled"; the soil must be prepared by gnostic teaching. In other cases the parallel is more distant. For example, in *Gospel of Thomas* 43 Jesus says to his disciples, "You do not realize who I am from what I say to you, but you have become like the Jews, for they (either) love the tree and hate its fruit (or) love the fruit and hate the tree." The last half of this saying calls to mind Matthew 7:17–18 and parallel: "Likewise, every good tree bears good fruit, but a bad tree bears bad fruit. A good tree cannot bear bad fruit, and a bad tree cannot bear good fruit." But the parallels are not really that close.[90]

Also a little more than one-third of the sayings in the *Gospel of Thomas* have no canonical parallel at all and are rather obviously gnostic. Saying 56, for example, reads, "Jesus said, 'Whoever has come to understand the world has found (only) a corpse, and whoever has found a corpse is superior to the world.'" In other words, this material world is dead and dying, and the person who recognizes this has already come to transcend it.[91] The canonical Jesus, on the other hand, believes that God's kingdom has broken into this world and can be manifest through the community of his followers as they live holy lives right in the midst of this world, arresting corruption and redeeming it en route, anticipating the resurrection of the *body*, not just the immortality of the soul (e.g., Matt. 5:13–16; Luke 11:20; John 5:24–29).

The remaining sayings intrigue scholars the most because they need not be interpreted in an explicitly gnostic fashion, though they could be so understood. Might even just a few of these be authentic teachings of Jesus that have survived through oral tradition even though they were never recorded in Matthew, Mark, Luke, or John? What, for example, about saying 82 ("Jesus said, 'He who is near Me is near the fire, and he who is far from Me is far from the Kingdom'")? Is this an orthodox linkage of Jesus with God and his kingdom, with God's Spirit portrayed as baptizing with metaphorical fire? Or does it suggest some more hidden and esoteric meaning? Short of the discovery of additional evidence, it may be difficult ever to know for sure.

Some scholars have speculated that the forms in which some of the paralleled sayings in *Thomas* appear actually predate their canonical counterparts. For example, saying 65 presents a noticeably abbreviated form of the parable of the wicked tenants (cf. Mark 12:1–12 pars.). On the assumption that the longer, more allegorical forms in the Synoptics must be elaborated versions of shorter, nonallegorical forms, *Thomas*'s version becomes a prime candidate for being closer to the original version that Jesus spoke. But although Jesus's parables should never be wholly *allegorized*—interpreted as if most details in them carried symbolic freight—it is very likely that the historical Jesus intended some *allegorical* referents behind some of the details of his stories, so that the shortest versions are not necessarily the earliest.[92] The *Gospel of Thomas*'s version also shows that it contains distinctives of later, Lukan editing of Mark, most notably in including "perhaps" in the line about the master's expecting the tenants to show respect for his son.[93]

Indeed, a major reason for concluding that the *Gospel of Thomas* is later than and dependent on the Synoptics, not an earlier independent witness to the historical Jesus, is that parallels to all four Gospels appear in *Thomas*, as well as parallels to all of the standard layers or sources into which those Gospels are divided, and to all of the sections that are usually deemed to be redactional (editorial) additions by the four evangelists.[94] That the author of the *Gospel of Thomas* knew all four canonical Gospels in their completed form is therefore far more likely than that every canonical source, writer, and editor knew and borrowed from *Thomas* at some point.[95] Indeed, Nicholas Perrin has mounted an intriguing case for seeing the sequence of sayings in the *Gospel of Thomas* as created by catchwords linking each saying to the next—catchwords that appear even more commonly if one translates either the Coptic or Greek of the *Gospel of Thomas* back into Syriac, the language of Tatian's Gospel harmony, called the *Diatessaron*, composed in the late second century. Furthermore, certain parallels in the *Gospel of Thomas* to distinctive material in the *Diatessaron* suggest it was composed after the *Diatessaron* and in dependence on it, a century and a half too late for *Thomas* to reflect teachings of Jesus more original or authentic than those in the canonical Gospels.[96] Simon Gathercole, on the other hand, mounts at least as strong a case that *Thomas* appeared in Greek first, perhaps in the mid-second century, but he is equally certain that it is not earlier or more authentic than the Synoptics.[97]

Finally, supporters of the *Gospel of Thomas*, or of gnostic texts more generally, need to be highly selective in what they commend (e.g., Mary Magdalene's exalted role among the disciples). As a group of elitist sects, gnosticism was considerably more sexist and anti-Semitic than any branch of Christianity reflected in the canonical Gospels, which contain internecine Jewish disputes and women's liberation, at least against typical Jewish stereotypes of the day. The *Gospel of Thomas*, on the other hand, has the disciples ask Jesus if circumcision is beneficial or not. Jesus replies, "If it were beneficial, their father would beget them already circumcised from their mother. Rather, the true circumcision in spirit has become completely profitable" (saying 53). There is no room in the *Gospel of Thomas*, apparently, as there is in the New Testament, for Jewish Christians to continue practicing the law as an element of their culture that remains highly meaningful for them.[98] Or consider saying 114:

> Simon Peter said to them, "Let Mary leave us, for women are not worthy of Life."
>
> Jesus said, "I myself shall lead her in order to make her male, so that she too may become a living spirit resembling you males. For every woman who will make herself male will enter the Kingdom of Heaven."

Not surprisingly, feminists wanting to invoke the *Gospel of Thomas* for support, especially because God's Wisdom (Greek, *sophia*, a feminine noun) is personified as a woman, postulate that this last saying of the gospel is a redactional addition to a more liberating original version.[99] But there is no manuscript support for this, so again we have a vicious circle. (1) Why should this saying be deleted? Because it clashes with the supposed feminism of gnosticism. (2) How do we know that *Thomas* 114 doesn't mitigate the claims of a feminist gnosticism? Because we delete it as inauthentic!

The Four Multiply-Supported Books That Were Excluded

What, though, about the four noncanonical works that appeared in *more than one* ancient catalog for possible canonical inclusion? The Wisdom of Solomon, as noted earlier, is an intertestamental work. Precisely because many viewed the Old Testament canon as closed, a few Christians apparently valued it enough to try to argue for its inclusion in the New Testament. It contains little objectionable and a lot of inspiring material, but "it is more a book about wisdom—its benefits, nature, and role in history—than a wisdom book giving practical advice (like Proverbs . . .)." More like Philo of Alexandria in the first century, "This effort at using Greek philosophy and rhetoric in the service of biblical religion makes the author to some extent also a pioneer in inculturation, of adapting the religious message to different thought patterns and modes of expression."[100]

The *Apocalypse of Peter* dates to the first half of the second century and depicts Peter as discoursing with Jesus about the afterlife and being shown detailed visions of heaven and hell. It appears in two quite different forms in Greek and Ethiopic. Much of it is a pastiche of quotations from Old and New Testament texts, while the visions of people's eternal destinies bristle with details that go far beyond anything in previous Jewish or Christian literature. Especially in its portrayal of hell, this document turns grotesquely graphic in depicting punishments and tortures of those who have violated basic scriptural ethics. The only reason it ever received even the little support that it did is probably its association with Peter, given his prominence in the emerging Roman Catholic Church.[101]

The *Epistle of Barnabas* and the *Shepherd of Hermas* are both part of the collection of mostly orthodox second-century writings known as the Apostolic Fathers. As with most of the post–New Testament Christian literature mentioned in this chapter, we do not know the true authors. The *Epistle of Barnabas* employs classic Greek allegorical interpretation to make sense of hard passages in the Old Testament and to claim that many of them testify about Jesus. Very little in the New Testament itself supports this approach.[102] The *Shepherd of Hermas* expresses

> a Jewish-Christian theological perspective by means of imagery, analogies, and parallels drawn from Roman society and culture, . . . [dealing] with questions and issues—for example, postbaptismal sin and repentance, and the behavior of the rich and their relationship to the poor within the church—of great significance and concern to him and that part of the Christian community in Rome to which he belonged.[103]

Suggested dates range from the end of the first century to the late second century, in part because the document may be composite. The Muratorian Canon attributes it to the brother of Pius, bishop of Rome, in the mid-second century. In any case, it does not pass the criterion of apostolicity.

New Scripture in a Much Later Era?

Perhaps we may agree that believers during the first half-millennium of Christianity's existence made good choices, but we may still wonder how to respond to later claims by Muslims or Mormons when they have added large collections of further revelation centuries after the New Testament. Might not the Qur'an (seventh century) or the Book of Mormon (nineteenth century) function as a third testament of sorts? Put otherwise, if the New Testament could not merely preserve but also alter the application of Old Testament teaching because Jesus came to "fulfill" it (Matt. 5:17), why could God not later want to change things again, with still fuller and more perfect revelation?

This phrases the question wrongly. There are very few things that God might not *want* to do (except for that which is immoral or logically contradictory). The question is what God has already disclosed about his purposes, about what he actually *will* do. The New Testament is not open-ended the way the Old Testament is (see "Fulfilling the Hebrew Scriptures" above). In the ministry, death, resurrection, and ascension of Jesus, followed by the sending of the Spirit at Pentecost, Christians claimed that God had accomplished all that was necessary for the salvation and sanctification of the world's inhabitants. All that remained was the church's fulfillment of the Great Commandment (Mark 12:28–31 pars.) and the Great Commission (Matt. 28:18–20) and the return of Christ to usher in final judgment at the end of the age. Tellingly, the only way Muslims and Mormons have been able to justify another collection of divinely inspired literature is to claim either (1) that the existing texts of the New Testament are corrupt and originally taught something quite different (the typical Muslim claim), or (2) that entire books were left out of the canon that God originally gave to his people (the typical Mormon claim). As chapters 1–2 here have demonstrated, there is not a shred of historical evidence to support either of these claims; anyone choosing to believe them must do so by pure credulity, flying in the face of all the evidence that actually exists.

But what if someone found a document known from the Bible as having existed in biblical times? What, for instance, about Paul's earlier letter to the Corinthians, alluded to in 1 Corinthians 5:9? Bypassing all the debates that would inevitably arise about its authenticity, what if it could indeed be shown to satisfy the criteria of apostolicity and orthodoxy and seemed to be as inspired and edifying as any of Paul's canonical writings? The problem would remain that it could not satisfy the criterion of catholicity. If God in his providence allowed it to remain buried somewhere for all these centuries, it is difficult to imagine his wanting it to be in his canon of "revealed" Scripture.[104]

Avoiding the Opposite Extreme

Just as our discussion of textual criticism focused primarily on challenges from the "left" of the theological spectrum but ended, more briefly, with equally deleterious mistakes of the "far right," so too our defense of the historic Christian canon of Scripture must not swing the pendulum too far back from the modern errors and excesses of skeptics and critics by reverting to unnecessary and unsupportable ultraconservative hypotheses. Probably the most important one to mention here is a certain take on what is sometimes called the doctrine of the sufficiency of Scripture.

Second Peter 1:3 declares that God's "divine power has given us everything we need for a godly life through our knowledge of him who called us by his own glory and goodness." In context, Peter makes it plain to what he is referring: everything necessary for escaping the world's corruption (v. 4), with faith that keeps on producing goodness, knowledge, self-control, perseverance, godliness, mutual affection, and love (vv. 5–7).[105] But very conservative Christians sometimes allege that texts like this one mean that a person need not or should not consult secular or non-Christian sources for knowledge about anything that impinges on one's own spirituality. Thus, for example, the so-called biblical counseling movement has often rejected integrating the insights and findings of non-Christian psychology, no matter how unprejudiced and empirically based their studies have been. If we can't find a given principle taught in the Bible, this movement alleges, then we dare not utilize it.[106] Or in studying world religions, we must never expect to find a spiritual truth in a non-Judeo-Christian religion unless it agrees with something clearly promoted in Scripture. In other words, the canon of Scripture is closed, not merely in the sense that we should not be looking for more books to add to it but also in the sense that we should not expect to find religious truth anywhere outside of it.[107]

On closer inspection, no one who makes these kinds of claims ever lives consistently by them. A Jewish, Muslim, or even atheist commentator can at times more faithfully describe what a biblical passage means in its original context than certain evangelical Christian interpreters, because this exegete has studied the original languages, history, and culture more. The difference between the two interpreters may lie in not who is more accurate but who has appropriated the teaching of a given passage into their own lives and who hasn't. Since God reveals himself through both special and general revelation, we should not be surprised to learn truth, even religious truth, from any source anywhere in the history of the world. We just do not expect to learn *saving* truth that is contrary to the Old and New Testaments from those who have rejected the Christian worldview.[108]

Almost no one expects the Bible to teach higher mathematics or neuroscience, or how to write music or play golf. So why should secular psychology, sociology, or literary interpretation be off-limits for Christians? Every theory or methodology that unambiguously contradicts Scripture should of course be rejected, but if God is the source of all truth, then truth from any source is God's truth.[109] Years ago one of my seminary professors, now with the Lord, put it rather strikingly: "The only person who could be wrong all the time is God! That is because he is the only person who knows truth on all topics and therefore could choose consistently to contradict it if he wanted to. But of course he does not. Any mere human being, on the other hand, could be right now and then, even accidentally!"[110]

Christian Smith, in a recent tirade against most American evangelicals, accuses us of what he calls "biblicism." He defines biblicism with nine assumptions and beliefs, most of which are largely unobjectionable but presented in somewhat extreme or simplistic form.[111] Crucial for our purposes here is a tenth and usually unstated principle that Smith finds the first nine generating. He calls this a "handbook model" to truth, which affirms that

> the Bible teaches doctrine and morals with every affirmation that it makes, so that together those affirmations comprise something like a handbook or textbook for Christian belief and living, a compendium of divine and therefore inerrant teachings on a full array of subjects—including science, economics, health, politics, and romance.[112]

This emerges particularly from the notion that Smith calls "complete coverage," that "the divine will about all of the issues relevant to Christian belief and life are contained in the Bible."[113]

Smith defends his claims about the pervasiveness of this approach by listing fifty-one titles of evangelical books from popular evangelical publishers, "almost all of which are currently in print." These include *Biblical Principles for Starting and Operating a Business*, *Cooking with the Bible: Recipes for Biblical Meals*, *Queen Esther's Secrets of*

Womanhood: A Biblical Rite of Passage for Your Daughter, *A Crown of Glory: A Biblical View of Aging*, *The Biblical Guide to Alternative Medicine*, *Bible Solutions to Problems of Daily Living*, *Bible Answers for Every Need*, and many more.[114] There are several problems with such a list. First, Smith does not indicate that he has actually read many (or any) of these books, and a title is often suggested by publishers based on what they think will attract sales rather than what is truly descriptive of the book's contents. Second, ours is indeed an age of do-it-yourself and self-help manuals, so that such titles do attract a large readership. Third, these titles alone betray nothing about whether the books contain valid, general, and somewhat abstract biblical principles thoughtfully applied to the areas of living they cover, or whether they form little more than collections of proof texts—biblical passages taken out of context that superficially reinforce an author's preconceived opinion. Fourth, the handful of titles that I recognize come from books that by no means uniformly illustrate the trend Smith is lamenting. Finally, given the amount of Christian literature I canvass annually, the fact that I do not recognize a substantial majority of Smith's titles suggests that these fifty-one books are hardly dominating or representative of the Christian market.

Nevertheless, at least *some* of the titles do represent books that justify Smith's complaints. As Smith goes on to stress, this can afflict works of a more academic level as well. Occasionally an evangelical systematic theology is written with insufficient reference to the history of Christian thought on the topic or to the philosophical and cultural underpinnings of the major schools of thought throughout that history. The result makes it appear as if the theologian's task is merely to group every passage from the Bible on a given topic together and see what concepts emerge.[115] Wayne Grudem's widely used *Systematic Theology: An Introduction to Biblical Doctrine* unfortunately too often approximates this approach.[116] Grudem has also written an equally large tome titled *Politics according to the Bible: A Comprehensive Resource for Understanding Modern Political Issues in Light of Scripture*, which manages to claim that the Bible offers insights (complete with chapter-and-verse references) on everything from school vouchers to a cure for recessions, to farm subsidies, to CAFE standards for automobile mileage![117] The chapter in the Bible that Grudem cites more often than any other is Romans 13, particularly on submitting to the government (vv. 1–7), at least when the current American governmental policies line up with Grudem's consistently Republican/Libertarian, free-enterprise, pro-democracy convictions. Not surprisingly, he doesn't advocate adopting the status quo when our government's positions don't so align, even though Paul makes no such distinction in Romans 13 as to when to submit and when not to submit.

In cases like these, Smith is right that Christians have begun to abuse the canon of Scripture. The Bible was never written to be a textbook on politics, economics, dating, counseling, aging, or farming. In fact, it was never written to be a *textbook*—a logically arranged introductory primer—*on anything*, even theology. Theology must be derived from the Bible, to be sure, but only after one is sensitive to the full range of principles of interpretation: understanding narrative flow, literary genre, historical-cultural background, timeless versus situation-specific principles, and so on.[118] One must also familiarize oneself with the full range of Christian perspectives on a given topic throughout history and understand what influences besides simply the Bible have helped shape those perspectives.[119]

In other words, if it is wrong to treat the *Gospel of Thomas* or the book of Judith with as much reverence as we do the book of Proverbs or the Epistle to the Romans, it is equally dangerous to claim to provide responsible and healthy counseling without ever studying, critiquing, and appropriating certain insights that *are* valid from Freud, Jung, Skinner, Maslow, Rogers, and various other non-Christian psychologists. If it is wrong to expect to find salvific truth in other world religions where they disagree with biblical truth, it is equally wrong to expect to be able to learn nothing, even just about the human condition, from other religions. If it is wrong to rely on a syncretistic blend of Buddhism, Hinduism, Islam, and Christianity when trying to understand God's designs for the economic order, it is equally wrong not to be conversant with both Adam Smith and Karl Marx, to recognize how different contemporary brands of capitalism and socialism are from pure laissez-faire or pure communist economics, and to realize that only the barest foreshadowings of either economic system existed in biblical times.[120]

Conclusion

To review, the sixty-six books of the Protestant canon of the Bible were well chosen. Jews did not err in including what they did in their Hebrew Scriptures, and Christians living before the Reformation era were not wrong in never formally canonizing the Apocrypha at any ecumenical council. The Council of Trent overreacted to Luther in the sixteenth century. The gap between the number of "votes" in antiquity for even the most disputed books of the New Testament and the amount of support for any other book that did not "make it in" remains sizable. And almost all of the books that were supported on even just one canonical list were theologically orthodox. Only the *Gospel of Thomas*, of all the gnostic literature and (NT) apocryphal writings, was ever proposed, and then only once. The *Gospel of Thomas* merits close scrutiny, but after such scrutiny it becomes clear it does not belong in the canon.

The Bible is uniquely inspired and authoritative, but that does not mean that Christians shouldn't read widely from every perspective on every topic about which they wish to learn. Nor does it mean that we can treat the Bible like a textbook on any topic, even theology, as if immersing ourselves in Scripture alone, with no other resources, will suffice to teach us everything that God has revealed about any area of human inquiry. General revelation *may* supplement special revelation. We *should*, of course, use the Bible to assist us in doing many things besides simply learning correct doctrine, including worship, confession of sin, prayer, praise, lament, apologetics, evangelism, and overall godly living.[121] But these are all a far cry from the approach that treats Scripture as a how-to manual for complex disciplines like psychology, sociology, economics, politics, or any other major discipline typical of university curricula.

In chapter 1 we argued that the Hebrew and Greek texts of Scripture have been extraordinarily carefully preserved over the centuries, even if not flawlessly. In this chapter we have argued that the books in the Protestant canon of Scripture are far more than the product of the winning factions in Christian history. While debates may continue between Protestants, Catholics, and Orthodox with respect to the Old Testament Apocrypha, there are no significant debates left in any major branch of Christianity concerning New Testament books, and there is no reason to turn to the ancient gnostic or New Testament apocryphal texts for credible alternatives.

But what about contemporary English translations of the Bible? To listen to the rhetoric in some of the recent battles over Bible translation, one could easily gather the impression that it is not at all clear whether we have accurate translations of Scripture or, if we do, which ones they are. Chapter 3 takes up this issue.

3

Can We Trust Any of Our Translations of the Bible?

We have already pointed out fallacies of those who argue that the King James Version of the Bible is the only or even the best translation for English-speaking people to use (see "Avoiding the Opposite Extreme," in chap. 1 above). In recent years, however, it is hardly just the KJV supporters who have engaged in translation wars. Supporters of a variety of modern translations of Scripture or of certain philosophies of translation have strenuously insisted that theirs is the only fully legitimate approach to adopt. Others have made the lesser claim that there is one clear choice or preference for those who want to understand God's Word best. More often than not, those who have argued most loudly in these debates are Westerners who have promoted an "essentially literal" translation of the Scriptures.[1] But in modern Bible translation worldwide, the dominant approach is to prioritize translation that is the clearest or easiest to understand for a broad cross-section of the speakers of the language into which the Scriptures are being rendered.[2] Compounding the problem further are people's varying responses to translations that use inclusive language for humanity rather than words like "he," "him," or "man" in a generic sense to refer to both men and women, since many English-language speakers no longer use these words this way.

Little wonder that a biblically illiterate populace, especially those who have never been churchgoers or had any sustained Christian influence in their lives, observe these debates and wonder if *any* translations can be trusted.[3] What are modern-language speakers to do if they cannot read ancient Hebrew, Aramaic, and Greek? And what about languages besides English, in which there often are not nearly the number or variety of translations from which to choose? What good is it even if we can reconstruct the original biblical texts with a high degree of confidence and even if we are persuaded that we have chosen the correct books for the biblical canon, if we then have so many different ways to translate the ancient texts into modern languages? Indeed, if down through the history of Christianity there have been so many different kinds of translations in so many different languages, can we really trust that any of them will be sufficiently reliable to instruct us in detail about the contents of the original Hebrew, Aramaic, and Greek texts?

The writers who have engaged in the most-heated translation wars rarely seem to think about the damage they have done among unbelievers and skeptics who have little understanding of what is being debated. Not a few outsiders have come away with the impression that they can't trust any translation and that the contents of Bibles must be distinctly different from one version to the next.[4] Even Bible publishers must shoulder some of the blame. In their eagerness to reach all kinds of niche markets, they create titles such as *The Busy Mom's Bible* or *Revolution: The Bible for Teen Guys* or *Chunky Bible* (so-called because it is shaped almost like a cube) but fail to print in nearly as prominent lettering the actual version or translation employed. Titles like these, and numerous others, can actually all refer to the identical translation, in this case, the New International Version (NIV). The differences pertain only to the edition's size and shape, covers, front and end matter, sidebars, study notes, or inspirational thoughts or devotions scattered throughout, while the actual text of Scripture remains identical from one edition to the next. But the uninitiated window-shopper has no idea what is going on and may figure that the contents of the Bible itself have been drastically altered in each new packaging.[5]

The main point of this chapter, therefore, deserves to be stated at once and directly. *Except for aberrant translations produced by sects or cults to promote their distinctive doctrines, every Bible on the market today is sufficiently faithful in its translation so that its readers can learn all of the fundamental truths of Christianity accurately.* The same events occur in all versions, the same characters appear, the same commands are given, the same wisdom is imparted, the same prophecies are articulated, the same doctrine promulgated, and so on. The differences are exceedingly minor compared to the overall similarities. This remains true even if one adds in the many other standard translations and versions that have been used throughout church history.[6]

Illustrations of the Similarities and Differences among Translations

Probably the best way to make this point is to illustrate it somewhat randomly—in other words, without deliberately choosing passages in which there is the least variation. The Bible has sixty-six books, so let us create six examples by choosing the eleventh verse from every eleventh book and compare two different major English translations each time, so that we utilize a total of twelve versions.[7] In the very literal KJV, first published in 1611, we read 1 Kings 1:11: "Wherefore Nathan spake unto Bathsheba the mother of Solomon, saying, Hast thou not heard that Adonijah the son of Haggith doth reign, and David our lord knoweth *it* not?" Then we compare the Contemporary English Version (CEV [1995]), which prefers straightforward, readable English over literal translation: "When Nathan heard what had happened, he asked Bathsheba, Solomon's mother: Have you heard that Adonijah the son of Haggith has made himself king? But David doesn't know a thing about it." The word order varies. The Elizabethan English has been transformed into contemporary colloquial equivalents. But in each instance it is obvious that the same question about the same people is being posed by the same prophet to the same woman.

Skip to Song of Songs 1:11 in the American Standard Version (ASV [1901]), even more woodenly literal than the KJV: "We will make thee plaits of gold with studs of silver." A recent easy-to-read translation, God's Word (GW [1995]), has "We will make gold ornaments with silver beads for you." The latter is much more intelligible to almost all English speakers today than the former. But the "plaits" correspond to the "ornaments" and the "studs" to the "beads." There is no doubt that both versions are translating the same Hebrew words, which express the desire of the lover to make beautiful, costly jewelry for his beloved, even though there is obviously a little uncertainty as to precisely the kind of jewelry those Hebrew words denote.[8]

In Micah 1:11, the highly touted "essentially literal" English Standard Version (ESV [2001]) declares, "Pass on your way, inhabitants of Shaphir, in nakedness and shame; the inhabitants of Zaanan do not come out; the lamentation of Beth-ezel shall take away from you its standing place." The widely popular New Living Translation (NLT), first published in 1996, translates for clarity and intelligibility first: "You people in Shaphir, go as captives into exile—naked and ashamed. The people of Zaanan dare not come outside their walls. The people of Beth-ezel mourn, for their house has no support." The NLT is indeed clearer, disclosing that the inhabitants of these Israelite communities are leaving for exile, hiding and/or grieving Judah's defeat, but both translations are potentially accurate renderings of the original text.[9]

In the New Testament, consider Acts 1:11. The well-publicized version produced by the Southern Baptist Convention, known as the Holman Christian Standard Bible (HCSB [2004]), renders it, "They said, 'Men of Galilee, why do you stand looking up into heaven? This Jesus, who has been taken from you into heaven, will come in the same way that you have seen Him going into heaven.'" The most widely used English translation internationally in the Roman Catholic world, the New Jerusalem Bible (NJB [1985]), reads, "And they said, 'Why are you Galileans standing here looking into the sky? This Jesus who has been taken up from you into heaven will come back in the same way as you have seen him go to heaven.'" One barely notices any difference. Denominational origins do not skew the renderings at all here.[10]

The most recent update of the New International Version (NIV [2011, orig. 1978]), designed to maximize both accuracy and clarity by prioritizing both equally, translates 2 Timothy 1:11, "And of this gospel I was appointed a herald and an apostle and a teacher." The most recent update of the New American Standard Bible (NASB [1995, orig. 1971]), a very literal translation, preserves the verse as the subordinate clause it is in the Greek: "for which I was appointed a preacher and an apostle and a teacher."[11] Intriguingly, "preacher" isn't quite as literal a translation as "herald," but both more than adequately convey the meaning of the Greek *kēryx*, "an official entrusted with a proclamation."[12]

Finally, we consider Revelation 1:11. In the New English Translation (NET [1996]), a translation designed for online storyboarding of study notes, we read, "Write in a book what you see and send it to the seven churches—to Ephesus, Smyrna, Pergamum, Thyatira, Sardis, Philadelphia, and Laodicea." It is hard to imagine saying these words much differently, so we are not surprised when we turn to the New Revised Standard Version (NRSV [1989]), possibly the most widely used translation among English-speaking scholars worldwide, and find, "Write in a book what you see and send it to the seven churches, to Ephesus, to Smyrna, to Pergamum, to Thyatira, to Sardis, to Philadelphia, and to Laodicea." Apart from the repetition of the preposition "to" and the use of a comma rather than a dash before the list of churches, there is no difference at all.

By this time, it would be more natural for the reader to ask why we have so many translations in the first place if there are so few differences among them. Part of the answer, of course, is that somewhat greater differences do appear in other verses beyond these few we have just examined. A brief survey of the history of Bible translation is therefore necessary, followed by a discussion of the varying philosophies that have produced them. We will then need to assess the strengths and weaknesses of these philosophies along with looking at more specific passages and how they differ among the various translations.[13]

A Brief History of Translations

As noted earlier, from its earliest days Christianity was concerned to make the Bible accessible for as many people as possible in languages they could easily understand. The first five centuries, therefore, saw translations proliferate in such languages as Syriac, Coptic, Ethiopic, Georgian, Armenian, and the like. When Jerome, in the fifth century, created a very readable and fluent Latin translation, Roman Catholicism was well on its way to becoming entrenched in Western Europe. While the various national forms of Eastern Orthodoxy continued to produce and use translations in their indigenous languages, the Western Church coalesced around Jerome's Vulgate, as it came to be called, from the Latin word for "common." The kind of Latin employed was the common vernacular of the day. The Vulgate would prevail as the most widely used single translation of the Bible for the next millennium.[14]

With the Protestant Reformation, the emphasis on Bible translation resumed. Luther himself produced a standard, widely used German translation in the sixteenth century. A French counterpart of sorts was the *Bible de Genève* of 1535. Catholic leaders also recognized the growing need for Bibles in the first language of its dominant people groups, so versions like the Spanish *Reina Valera* in 1569 and the English Douay-Rheims, finally complete in 1610, also appeared. Unfortunately, the latter was translated from the Latin, so that wherever Jerome's text was less than accurate, the Douay-Rheims version perpetuated the inaccuracies.[15]

Protestant English translations that were not authorized by the established church had emerged from the pens of John Wycliffe, William Tyndale, and others, and later less-opposed translations such as the Geneva Bible and the Bishops' Bible had become widely used. So the translators King James commissioned early in the seventeenth century were hardly starting from scratch.[16] Yet no translation in any language after the Latin Vulgate has proved as influential as the Authorized Version (as the King James Version [KJV] is typically called in the United Kingdom and countries of the former British Empire).[17]

Like the Vulgate, and like most of the other Reformation-era translations, the KJV aimed at reproducing the meaning of the original biblical languages in a style common or ordinary enough that a person of average intelligence or education could readily understand it.[18] Modern-day English speakers unfamiliar with the English of seventeenth-century England may not always realize that it was normal for people in that culture to speak to one another with language such as, "Greetings, how art thou today, fair maiden?" or "Dearest husband, I pray thee, suffer me to fetch thee a garment for thy lap." A good dose of unrevised Shakespeare can illustrate the language of that day quite quickly!

Even into the nineteenth century, British English remained comparatively unchanged. But American vernacular was "corrupting" its Victorian counterpart, and by the end of the century even the British had largely abandoned the old-fashioned "thee" and "thou" and the corresponding verb conjugations ending in -st and -th (e.g., givest, hath). Except in some poetic passages, the Revised Version in Great Britain in 1885 and the American Standard Version of 1901 replaced much of this language with more current usage and updated other archaic vocabulary and idioms as well. Overall, though, they lagged behind changes in the language, preserving the somewhat archaic feel that the KJV had come to represent.

A variety of translations have been produced, many by individual translators, to fill a certain niche in their day, but then they have dramatically waned in use and popularity after a comparatively short time. Some became famous because of who the translator was, such as the translations of the British classicist Richard Weymouth (1902) or the American New Testament scholar E. J. Goodspeed (1923). Others became well known because of an unusual translation philosophy. The Concordant Literal New Testament of 1926 sought to use the same English word every time the same Greek or Hebrew word occurred, almost irrespective of context or how idiosyncratic the results were. J. B. Phillips's translation in 1958 employed colloquial British English, which made it very popular but also controversial, because it was one of the first versions of the Bible that at times paraphrased the text.[19]

The real flurry in the publication and widespread dissemination of English Bible translations has occurred since the end of World War II. Because the ASV's revisions of the KJV had been very conservative and because English continued to change, there was still a need for a Bible translation in understandable mid-twentieth-century English. The Revised Standard Version (RSV) was produced by an ecumenical team of scholars and endorsed by the broadest cross-section ever of the Protestant, Roman Catholic, and Eastern Orthodox communions internationally.[20] First published in 1952, it still retained the occasional "thee" and "thou" in very poetic or famous texts but otherwise was written in more readable English than the ASV, while still remaining a very accurate translation. Because of a few famous places where the translators decided to deviate from the previous English renderings in theologically significant texts, conservative evangelicals sometimes blacklisted it or else just continued to use other translations.

By far the most well-known of these texts was Isaiah 7:14, in which the RSV used "young woman" instead of "virgin" for the famous text about the conception of a child to be called Immanuel—a completely appropriate translation given the possible range of meaning of the Hebrew *ʿalmâ*.[21] After all, the immediate context of Isaiah explains that the child born to this young woman will be a sign that the land (Aram/Syria and Israel/Ephraim) of the two kings who have terrorized Judah will soon be laid waste—before the child even knows how to choose good over evil (v. 16). Nevertheless, because Matthew 1:23 applies this prophecy to Mary's giving birth to Jesus and uses the Greek word for "virgin" (*parthenos*), which the LXX used to render the Hebrew *ʿalmâ* in the Isaiah passage, some archconservatives branded the RSV "liberal"![22]

In the 1960s, work began on the New American Standard Bible, to follow in more up-to-date language the highly literal translation theory of the old ASV, and it was the first translation produced entirely by contemporary evangelical scholars (published in 1971). This was also the era of Ken Taylor's Living Bible Paraphrased (portions appearing incrementally throughout the 1960s and finally finished in 1971), which was a very free rendering of the ASV into contemporary colloquial English and not a translation from the original Hebrew and Greek.[23] Countless teens and young adults of the 1960s and 70s, however, finding the other translations too staid or difficult to follow, devoured the Living Bible and became avid Bible readers as a result. Also around this time, a very simplified English rendering was produced by the American Bible Society and called the Good News Bible (GNB) or Today's English Version (TEV [1976]). In addition, 1978 saw the production of a magnificent work, over a decade in the making, by a multinational team of evangelical scholars, called the New International Version. Seeking the best possible balance between faithfulness to the original meaning of the text and fluency or intelligibility in English, it soon became the best-selling and most widely distributed English language version of the Bible in the world.[24]

In the late 1980s, the Revised Standard Version received an updating and became known as the New Revised Standard Version (published in 1989). Ever so slightly freer with its translation in a few places, its main claim to fame (or notoriety, depending on one's perspective) was that it was the first major translation to introduce some inclusive language for humanity. In other words, when words like "man" or "men" in the original Hebrew or Greek referred to "people" without reference to gender, the NRSV sought for ways to express that in comparably inclusive English. The same was true of a variety of places where the pronouns "he," "him," or "his" were used generically. Already in the late 1960s, American English, especially in the northern half of the country and on the west coast, had begun to prefer terms such as "chairperson" for "chairman," "he or she" instead of merely "he," "people" for "men," and so on. As a result, an increasing number of individuals heard "man" and "he" as gender-exclusive, referring to males only. So to be faithful to the original meaning of God's Word in context, for passages in which these grammatically masculine terms denoted men and women alike, equivalent expressions were sought. The NRSV thus quickly became the version of choice for a large number of English-speaking scholars worldwide.[25]

A brief survey like this can touch only on the most influential versions. The past generation has likewise seen Roman Catholics produce two major English versions, which for the first time consulted the biblical languages exclusively, rather than translating from the Latin versions. Of these two Bibles, the distinctively American one was appropriately called the New American Bible (NAB [1970, updated in 2011]); the most widely used international version was the Jerusalem Bible (JB [1966]), now updated as the New Jerusalem Bible (NJB [1985]). The NAB is very similar to the NIV in its style; the NJB is a little freer but also more flowery.[26] For readers of British English, the New English Bible (NEB [1970]) emerged, with some rather distinctive vernacular, now updated and homogenized somewhat as the Revised English Bible (REB [1989]).[27] A project begun by several Dallas Seminary professors led to the NET (1996), a translation falling somewhere between highly literal and very free.[28] More recently the Southern Baptist-led HCSB (1999) adopted a similar translation philosophy.[29]

Ken Taylor's son, Mark, who succeeded his father as president of Tyndale Publishing House, initiated a major project involving ninety scholars to turn the Living Bible Paraphrased into a bona fide translation, not merely a paraphrase. The result was the NLT (1996). Readers wanting updated language for obsolete or archaic words in the KJV but still wanting the textual base on which the KJV relied (wrongly thinking it was the better one) got the New King James Version (NKJV [1979]). Eugene Peterson produced a paraphrase called The Message (2002), which was much freer than even the Living Bible Paraphrased but still theologically orthodox in all its content. A messianic Jewish translation, preserving Hebrew words for Jewish names and technical terms, is called the Complete Jewish Bible (CJB [2001]). An edition of the NIV with simplified vocabulary for young children is known as the New International Readers' Version (NIrV [1996]). Most recently, a mainline Protestant alternative to the NRSV in even more straightforward language, frequently using contractions like "you're," "didn't," "he's," and so on, is the Common English Bible (CEB [2011]).

With this proliferation of translations, the only versions in the last decade ever to capture more than 10 percent of the Bible market in any given year have been the NIV, the KJV, the NKJV, and the NLT.[30] But one more translation merits mention, which has come close and may one day top 10 percent. When the RSV went out of print, an evangelical publisher, Crossway Books, secured the rights to revise it and republish it as the English Standard Version (ESV), a fairly presumptuous title for a work that was more American than English and not yet standard! "Young woman" was removed from Isaiah 7:14 and replaced with "virgin." "Kiss his feet" in the RSV of Psalm 2:12 became "Kiss the Son" in the ESV. Changes were similarly made in various other passages believed to have reflected a "liberal" bias on the part of the RSV translators. The ESV translators adopted a reasonably formal, exalted literary style, especially in poetry but by no means limited to it.[31] They prioritized the accuracy of meaning, not the clarity or intelligibility of style. Because about 92 percent of the ESV is the unrevised RSV,[32] readers who appreciated the style of the RSV should find the ESV almost as elegant. But their supporters, more so than with any other recent translation, tend to make inaccurately inflated claims about it, especially concerning how literal, elegant, or intelligible the ESV actually is and about how consistently it implements its criteria for translation. A thorough study by Thomas Nass, from the very conservative Wisconsin Evangelical Lutheran Synod, has demonstrated this exaggeration in detail.[33] A very similar set of conclusions appears in an only slightly less meticulous analysis by Australian Reformed scholar Allan Chapple.[34]

Three Main Philosophies of Translation

Are all of these English translations really necessary? Probably not. Has each one reached some niche or subculture that might not have otherwise become excited about Bible reading? Possibly, in which case their production has proved worthwhile even if not absolutely essential. Many other languages in the world have one KJV-like translation, produced early in the history of the arrival of Christianity to the part of the world where that language was birthed, highly literal, in archaic language that is hard to understand today, and often using an inferior textual base. Most of those languages, in turn, now have at least one modern translation following either the optimal or dynamic equivalence translation theories (see below). But in many cases, those are the only options for non-English speakers. It is arguable that before any other new English-language Bible version is produced, translators and publishers should ensure that many more options are available in the other languages of the world, especially those spoken by the largest number of people.

In the foreseeable future for English translations, it would not be surprising if only five continued to vie for any sizable portions of the Bible market share: the KJV, because it is so venerable and has exercised so much influence on the English language over the last 400 years;[35] the NKJV, because it is a much more readable revision of the KJV; the NIV, because of its enormous popularity for the past thirty-five years; the NLT, because it has become the version of choice for those who want something that prioritizes clarity over literal translation and yet is eminently defensible as a legitimate way of translating the Hebrew and Greek; and the ESV, because of the huge advertising campaigns undertaken on its behalf, its usefulness as an essentially literal translation with some poetic elegance, and its use of the best textual basis available. The NRSV will continue to be widely used by scholars, but sales have dramatically decreased in recent years because the mainline churches that most often endorse the NRSV do not always value Bible reading as much as many evangelicals do (who therefore wear out Bibles and need to replace them), and congregations who initially placed large orders for NRSV pew Bibles have yet to feel the need to replace them, because they remain in fairly good but relatively unused condition!

Put differently, once you set aside the KJV and NKJV due to their idiosyncratic textual bases, you have three major options, each beautifully representing one of three major translation philosophies. Every Bible translation aims at various degrees of (a) accurate renderings of the meaning of the original biblical documents and (b) fluency, clarity, and intelligibility for its readers. The options are whether to (a) prioritize accuracy, (b) prioritize fluency, or (c) optimize both by seeking as much of *a* and *b* as can be accomplished simultaneously.[36] Of course, there can also be gradations of these priorities, but in broad generalizations, the NASB, ESV, and NRSV represent *a* (putting meaning ahead of clarity);[37] the NLT, CEV, and GNB represent *b* (putting clarity ahead of meaning);[38] and the NAB, NET, HCSB, CEB, and NIV represent *c* (aiming at the optimal amount of meaning and clarity simultaneously).[39] Other translations could be plotted at points along this spectrum as well.

To use the more technical language of Bible translators, option *a* is often called "formal equivalence," option *b* is often called "dynamic equivalence" (or "functional equivalence"), and option *c* has recently been termed "optimal equivalence."[40] At this juncture it is important to stress that neither *a* nor *b* is anywhere close to the absolute end of the spectrum of possibilities. The most formally equivalent translation possible would be one that sought a single word equivalent in the "receptor language" (the language of the translation) for every single word in the original or "source language" and then used the same word in the receptor language every time the same word in the source language appeared (the concordant approach). But this would lead to nonsensical sentences, even more incomprehensible than interlinear translations.[41] And of course, there never is a perfect one-word-to-one-word correlation between two different languages, but such a hyperliteral translation approach could be illustrated by applying it to the first half of the famous Philippians hymn (Phil. 2:6–8). It would yield:

> who in form of God belonging not prize considered the to be equal to God, but himself emptied form of slave having taken in likeness of men becoming and scheme having been found as man humbled himself becoming obedient until death, death but of cross.

Such an example disproves the myth, all too often repeated, that the more "literal" a translation is, the better it is, because it necessarily captures the meaning more accurately.

The opposite end of the spectrum doesn't have as obvious an absolute endpoint. Maximum clarity could arguably be accomplished by elaborating on any potentially ambiguous word with long commentary that fully explains it. But that is why the literary genre of biblical commentaries has developed. So, among works actually published, if an interlinear is the most literal of what could be called a translation, then at the opposite end of the spectrum is The Message, which is probably the freest of all English language "paraphrases" (restating a text in one's own words) known today. In Philippians 2:6–8, it adds enough interpretive explanation that it more than doubles the length in English of the interlinear rendering:

> He had equal status with God but didn't think so much of himself that he had to cling to the advantages of that status no matter what. Not at all. When the time came, he set aside the privileges of deity and took on the status of a slave, became *human*! Having become human, he stayed human. It was an incredibly humbling process. He didn't claim special privileges. Instead, he lived a selfless, obedient life and then died a selfless, obedient death—and the worst kind of death at that—a crucifixion.

Now compare the ESV, NIV, and NLT on these same verses:

> who, though he was in the form of God, did not count equality with God a thing to be grasped, but emptied himself, by taking the form of a servant, being born in the likeness of men. And being found in human form, he humbled himself by becoming obedient to the point of death, even death on a cross. (ESV)

> Who, being in very nature God, did not consider equality with God something to be used to his own advantage; rather, he made himself nothing by taking the very nature of a servant, being made in human likeness. And being found in appearance as a man, he humbled himself by becoming obedient to death—even death on a cross! (NIV)

> Though he was God, he did not think of equality with God as something to cling to. Instead, he gave up his divine privileges; he took the humble position of a slave and was born as a human being. When he appeared in human form, he humbled himself in obedience to God and died a criminal's death on a cross. (NLT)

By design, these three translations represent what may well be the best examples in English of the three major approaches to Bible translation. The ESV reflects what most linguists call "formal equivalence" or, as a few scholars prefer, "essentially literal." Neither label is entirely satisfactory, however. It is true that formally equivalent translations follow the form, structure, and syntax of the document they are translating considerably more consistently than the other two kinds of translations we have introduced. Yet the rationale is not to follow form for form's sake but to reproduce the original meaning as well as possible. If the original language reads, "Ate John the apple," but the receptor language never employs such word order, even a formally equivalent translation will use "John ate the apple" without hesitation. But if an original text reads, "Magnificent were the undertakings of the mighty," with a word order that is occasionally used and thus intelligible, especially in a literary genre that is poetic or particularly formal, a formally equivalent translation is likely to use exactly those words in that sequence. Other translations, however, may be more concerned to use more common English word order and may read, "The undertakings of the mighty were magnificent."

The expression "essentially literal" is intended to contrast with a "woodenly literal" translation and also with one that fails to recognize idioms or figurative language that make no sense or may even mislead if translated literally.[42] An essentially literal translation like the ESV would never render James 2:1 as "Brothers of me, not in receiving face you all have the faith of the Lord of us, of Jesus of Christ, of the glory," even though that is exactly how you would translate the verse if you were simply rendering each word with its most common meaning, one at a time, in order. English uses the possessive pronoun where Greek regularly uses the genitive case (a specific word-ending on nouns and pronouns) of the personal pronoun, so we would say, "my brothers" and "our Lord." The verb most commonly translated "have" can also mean "hold," which fits much better in this context. It is a second-person plural imperative, but in English if we use a pronoun before a verb (e.g., "You go to the store"), it sounds as though we are making a statement, not giving a command. Also, we don't distinguish between a singular and a plural "you" anyway except in regional colloquial English ("you" versus "you-all," "y'all," "you-uns," or "yous guys"). After "faith," the remaining seven words in the Greek sentence are all in the genitive. The most exegetically neutral way to render a genitive in English is to precede the word having that case ending with an "of," but many passages in numerous contexts do not yield what is meant in the original if an English translator follows that method. The obvious idiom in the sentence is the Greek verb, probably a Semitism based on a similar Hebrew idiom, which is created by combining the verb for "receive" with the noun for "face." Even in English, we can understand how the notion of receiving someone according to their face—judging merely by external appearances—could convey the notion of discrimination or showing favoritism or partiality. Finally, with a majority of commentators, an essentially literal translation like the ESV can understand the string of genitives to be in apposition to one another (renaming the same person), with the first one ("Lord") being an objective genitive—faith *in* the Lord, not faith *of* the Lord. But while "Lord Jesus Christ" is fine English, "Lord Jesus Christ Glory" isn't, nor does "Lord Jesus Christ of glory" communicate much, so the ESV repeats the word "Lord" even though it occurs only once in the Greek.[43]

Thus the complete ESV formulation of James 2:1 is "My brothers, show no partiality as you hold the faith in our Lord Jesus Christ, the Lord of glory." And this is fully in keeping with an "essentially literal" translation. If I seem to be belaboring the point, it is simply to clarify how much freedom is possible and indeed necessary in a translation that can still be called essentially literal or formally equivalent. Many people who have never studied a foreign language are not aware of this, and even many who have done so think that "essentially literal" is much closer to an interlinear rendering than it really is. Indeed, there are plenty of times where the ESV is more "woodenly literal" than the NASB and plenty of times when the ESV is freer in its renderings than the optimally equivalent translations to be discussed below. The various categories are helpful for understanding the overall goals of translators, but we can find many exceptions when we closely examine passages within individual translations.[44]

The NLT subscribes to what linguists label a "dynamically equivalent" translation philosophy. Sometimes people call this "thought for thought" rather than "word for word," but that is not a very helpful description, because we have just seen how even essentially literal translations need to take multiword expressions together in discrete units of thought to determine how to render them most accurately in English. A better way to describe dynamic equivalence is to say that clarity, fluency, and intelligibility are always the highest priorities. Complex sentences are broken down into their most basic constituent elements. Each of these is translated into the receptor language, and then they are reassembled in the structure that is most natural and intelligible in that language.[45] If slight nuances of meaning simply can't be preserved in this process without using an awkward style, lesser known vocabulary, or old-fashioned speech, then the dynamically equivalent translation will choose ease of understanding over a highly precise reproduction of meaning.

Today the NLT is by far the most popular, commonly used, and aesthetically pleasing example of a dynamically equivalent translation of the Bible.[46] It phrases James 2:1 as "My dear brothers and sisters, how can you claim to have faith in our glorious Lord Jesus Christ if you favor some people over others?" James was writing to Jewish Christians in a variety of congregations in the Diaspora, which clearly included men and women. In his culture, addressing a mixed audience of both genders with the word *adelphoi*, when the people were not biological siblings, was a way of acknowledging that they were kin of some kind, in this case, spiritual kin. Today, a speaker addressing a mixed audience with the opening word "Brothers" would elicit confusion. Is the speaker talking just to the men or to everyone? Why is such exclusive language being used? So the NLT appropriately uses "brothers and sisters."[47] Indeed, if a Bible is targeting an audience that has a significant number of people likely to misunderstand gender-exclusive language as referring only to men, then *not to use inclusive language would distort the meaning*.[48]

A little more surprisingly, the NLT turns James's original command into a question. This would not occur in any versions even slightly more literal than a fully dynamically equivalent translation. But in polite or formal situations, we do sometimes "soften the blow" of a command a little by turning it into a question. For example, if it looks like I am not moving into the turning lane at a traffic intersection when I should be doing so, my wife might ask me, "Don't you want to turn here?" Actually, she knows full well that I do but that I have forgetten to do so. She is really telling me that I should get ready to turn, but phrasing it as a question sounds nicer than giving me the abrupt command "Turn here!" The NLT, furthermore, follows most commentators in understanding "the Lord of glory" to mean "the glorious Lord." After all, even after repeating "Lord" to create the expression, "the Lord of glory," the ESV expression is not all that transparent. Finally, to clarify what kind of "partiality" is involved, the NLT also speaks of "favoring some people over others."

The NIV represents the third, mediating translation philosophy. In essence, this approach wants to maximize *both* faithfulness to original meaning *and* clarity. It recognizes that at times one must be sacrificed for the sake of the other, but it makes no assumptions in advance about which one must take priority. In every passage the goal is to be as faithful and clear as possible simultaneously. The HCSB has a similar goal, which Ray Clendenen describes as displaying neither formal equivalence nor dynamic equivalence but "optimal equivalence."[49] This is the philosophy that combines many of the strengths of the other two approaches while avoiding most of their weaknesses. The updated NIV thus translates James 2:1 as "My brothers and sisters, believers in our glorious Lord Jesus Christ must not show favoritism." It agrees with the NLT in its rendering of "brothers and sisters" for the identical reasons. It preserves the command form of the sentence, just as the ESV does. It avoids the slightly awkward expression "to hold the faith" and prefers "favoritism" to "partiality" (both words differing from the ESV). Still, it preserves one noun in English to translate one Greek noun (unlike the NLT).

The HCSB similarly occupies a middle ground between the ESV and NLT as it offers the command "My brothers, hold your faith in our glorious Lord Jesus Christ without showing favoritism."[50] It unfortunately preserves the gender-exclusive "brothers" like the ESV, but it makes "hold the faith" more intelligible with "hold your faith," while still being closer to the ESV than to either the NIV or NLT. Like the NLT and NIV, however, it uses "our glorious Lord Jesus Christ." And "without showing favoritism" is also closer to the NLT and NIV than the ESV's "show no partiality." Other translations that likewise seek equally both clarity and accuracy include the NET: "My brothers and sisters, do not show prejudice if you possess faith in our glorious Lord Jesus Christ"; and the NAB: "My brothers, show no partiality as you adhere to the faith in our glorious Lord Jesus Christ."[51]

Turning to other examples of *formal equivalence* in this passage, we may consult the KJV ("My brethren, have not the faith of our Lord Jesus Christ, *the Lord* of glory, with respect of persons") and the NKJV ("My brethren, do not hold the faith of our Lord Jesus Christ, *the Lord* of glory, with partiality"). For other examples of dynamic equivalence in this passage, we may compare the NJB: "My brothers, do not let class distinction enter into your faith in Jesus Christ, our glorified Lord";[52] and the CEV: "My friends, if you have faith in our glorious Lord Jesus Christ, you won't treat some people better than others." Of course there will often be translations that generally adhere to one of the three approaches outlined here but at times vary from their normal approach. Thus the CEB, usually an optimally equivalent translation, turns very dynamically equivalent in James 2:1 with its "My brothers and sisters, when you show favoritism you deny the faithfulness of our Lord Jesus Christ, who has been resurrected in glory." And except for the older English word "brethren," the NASB, which is usually highly formally equivalent, becomes quite optimally equivalent in James 2:1: "My brethren, do not hold your faith in our glorious Lord Jesus Christ with *an attitude of* personal favoritism."

Do any of these translations fail to communicate James's point? Not in the least. Are any unfaithful to his meaning? Hardly. Do any suggest that the plethora of translations available implies that we can have no confidence about the meaning of the original Greek text? What a ridiculous suggestion! All we need to do is read several of them back to back, and we will have an excellent sense of the variety of possible nuances in the original. One version of the Bible tries to do this for us all under one cover. The Amplified Bible (1965) regularly puts alternate meanings of key words in a given verse in brackets after the expression it chooses for its translation. So for James 2:1, it reads, "My brethren, pay no servile regard to people [show no prejudice, no partiality]. Do not [attempt to] hold *and* practice the faith of our Lord Jesus Christ [the Lord] of glory [together with snobbery]!" There are a variety of problems here, however. Brackets are also used to supply words believed to be needed for greater clarity ("the Lord" and "together with snobbery"). In places the language is still a bit old fashioned ("pay no servile regard to"). And in many contexts, the words suggested as alternate translations are actually alternate meanings of the same word or expression *in different contexts*, which aren't as likely in the context at hand.[53]

Versions to Treat with Caution

There *are* editions of the Bible, however, that we must use with greater caution. The concordant approach described earlier can at best simply not communicate and at worst mislead considerably. For James 2:1 the danger is only that of not being understood: "My brethren, not with partialities be having the faith of our Lord Jesus Christ of glory." But flip back to 1:17–18, and the English becomes bizarre: "All good giving and every perfect gratuity is from above, descending from the Father of lights, in whom there is no mutation or shadow from revolving motion. By intention, He teems forth us by the word of truth, for us to be some firstfruit of His own creatures." One simply can't mechanically insert one standard definition of a word in one language for each usage of that word in another without any consideration of the context![54]

Conversely, a true paraphrase does not worry about whether every word of the Greek or Hebrew is somehow represented (even if only by punctuation) in the translation, or if numerous explanatory words are added in, or if the gist of the thought is communicated in a very fresh way while not actually being a translation at all. The Message, for example, turns James 2:1 into "My dear friends, don't let public opinion influence how you live out our glorious, Christ-originated faith." Public opinion may or may not have anything to do with why someone discriminates or shows favoritism, but it can be one reason. "Christ-originated faith" is not really a possible translation of "faith in Christ." Even if the Greek construction were taken as a subjective genitive rather than an objective genitive (i.e., with Christ as the acting subject rather than the object of believing), it would mean the faith that Christ had, not merely what came from him. "Christ-originated" would require a genitive of source, which then implies that faith or belief is not an active concept in this context,[55] which it most certainly is. But other texts speak of our faith as originating in Christ, so there is nothing theologically unorthodox here. At the head of all the Greek appositional genitives, the word "Lord"—to whom our faith is actually directed, according to James—is missing from this rendering. Yet it is still a fresh and striking way to remind us of key ideas in the text. That is what paraphrases are meant to accomplish. For readers familiar with the Bible, they help well-known texts come alive in new and exciting ways. For those unfamiliar with the Bible, they stir interest in reading and learning more. But paraphrases are never intended to be the only or main Bible a person reads. Serious study, teaching, and preaching must never use them except by way of illustrating aspects of the text's meaning in a memorable way.[56]

Still other translations betray their sectarian origins by actually distorting the meaning of key texts. The New World Translation (NWT [1961]) of the Jehovah's Witnesses renders James 2:1 as "My brothers, YOU are not holding the faith of our Lord Jesus Christ, our Glory, with acts of favoritism, are YOU?" In this instance, there is nothing theologically heretical here, though there are a few curiosities. The Greek *echete* can, by itself, be either an indicative or an imperative, that is, it can either make a statement or give a command. In the context of the illustration of verses 2–4, and in a book with a primary purpose to give commands, it is unlikely that the verb here would be merely an indicative and not another imperative. That may be why the NWT then turned the sentence into a question, as also possible, given James's use of the adverb *mē*, which can be inserted to indicate a question intended to elicit the answer "no." But again, this is not by any means the most natural way of translating this sentence.[57] The other anomaly is the translation "our Glory," the meaning of which is not at all clear. It sounds as if our Lord, who is Jesus Christ, is someone we glory in. This is a genuine Christian concept, but not one that can be derived from the Greek construction here. But given the very limited knowledge of the biblical languages that the NWT translators had, such anomalies are not surprising.[58]

In other places, however, the NWT is simply wrong, having traded legitimate translation for sectarian theology. The most famous example is John 1:1, which reads, "In [the] beginning the Word was, and the Word was with God, and the Word was a god." In general, the NWT runs roughshod over all the detailed principles that dictated when a Hebrew or Greek writer would or would not use an article.[59] When it suits its theological purposes to stress that Jesus was not fully God, the NWT invents the translation "a god." Or again in John 8:58, to avoid the allusion to the divine name of Exodus 3:14, the NWT has Jesus say, "Before Abraham came into existence, I have been." This allows them to maintain that Jesus was the first and greatest creation of God but not God himself.[60] Yet the Greek employs the present tense of the verb "to be," preceded by the emphatic personal pronoun—hence, "I am." The NWT is also inconsistent about including or omitting the article with the Third Person of the Trinity, which it also does not capitalize.[61] Thus, for example, John 14:26 does talk about "the holy spirit," but Ephesians 5:18 ends merely with "but keep being filled with spirit."

The Joseph Smith Translation (JST [1828]), valued by many Mormons (or Latter Day Saints [LDS]), distorts key texts even more drastically. For John 1:1, it states, "In the beginning was the gospel preached through the Son. And the gospel was the word, and the word was with the Son, and the Son was with God, and the Son was of God." This is not a translation in any sense of the word but rather a series of changes and additions to the text. Sometimes such insertions can span several verses, as in Genesis 9:21–24:

> And the bow shall be in the cloud and I will look upon it, that I may remember the everlasting covenant, which I made unto thy father Enoch; that, when men should keep all my commandments, Zion should again come on the earth, the city of Enoch which I have caught up unto myself.

> And this is mine everlasting covenant, that when thy posterity shall embrace the truth, and look upward, then shall Zion look downward, and all the heavens shall shake with gladness, and the earth shall tremble with joy. And the general assembly of the church of the first-born shall come down out of heaven, and possess the earth, and shall have place until the end come. And this is mine everlasting covenant, which I made with thy father Enoch. And the bow shall be in the cloud, and I will establish my covenant unto thee, which I have made between me and thee, for every living creature of all flesh that shall be upon the earth.

Smith, of course, insisted that he received all these extra portions by revelation from God to replace "plain and precious" truths of the Bible that had been removed from the Bible over the centuries (*1 Nephi* 13.26 in the Book of Mormon). But there is no shred of historical evidence that these portions were ever removed from the Bible. On the other hand, as in James 2:1, much of the JST matches the KJV exactly. Here it reads, "My brethren, have not the faith of our Lord Jesus Christ, *the Lord* of glory, with respect of persons." And it is the KJV itself that is the official version of the Bible for the LDS, not the JST.[62] So the need to debunk the JST is not nearly as acute in conversations with LDS friends as the need to highlight the errors of the NWT in interactions with Jehovah's Witnesses.

We return to our main point. Except for these last two translations, which were produced by sectarian groups, all of the translations of Scripture discussed in this chapter (and many others) are more than adequate in representing God's Word and instructing his people in everything necessary for salvation and sanctification. Whenever, therefore, someone asks me which English translation of the Bible I think is the best, I ask them, "Best for what?" Anyone who tries to tell you that one translation is *the* best in all circumstances—for all the reasons someone might consult a Bible—is simply inadequately informed or unduly biased. For careful, detailed study by people who can't or won't study the biblical languages themselves or read commentaries and other resources that have utilized the original languages, a formally equivalent translation is important. For young people, readers of English as a second language, those not necessarily already interested in Scripture and trying to decide if they want to become Bible readers, or longtime Bible readers eager for a fresh reading, a dynamically equivalent translation can make a huge difference. For pulpit ministry in all but very homogeneous congregations, an optimally equivalent translation will be best understood and teach God's Word most accurately to the broadest cross-section of the congregation. If almost everyone is a college graduate and an experienced Bible reader, a formally equivalent translation could be substituted. If few people are college graduates or experienced Bible readers, a dynamically equivalent translation may be necessary. For those preparing to facilitate a group Bible study or in any context where individuals are likely to have read or brought a variety of translations, it is important, if possible, to have compared and contrasted a variety of translations as well.[63] But these are the ideals. When they can't be met, we should be grateful for almost *any* Bible when many in our world wish they had even *one* translation in a language they can read.

Avoiding the Opposite Extreme

The most divisive question about translating the Bible in recent decades has been about the use of inclusive language for humanity. Sadly, the debates have frequently generated more heat than light. Blatantly false rumors have spread; unchecked and highly misleading information has been passed off as sober truth in contexts where major decisions about which translations to support or censor have been made. The highly publicized contexts of some of these events have helped create the misimpression among many people, unchurched and churched alike, that certain translations should be avoided as dangerous, theologically liberal, or otherwise untrustworthy. Those fostering these misimpressions do far more damage to the cause of Christ than they realize and really should cease and desist from such inappropriate maligning of the Word of God.

The lightning rod for much of the translation warfare was Today's New International Version (TNIV [NT 2001; complete Bible 2005]) and its British predecessor, the New International Version, Inclusive-Language Edition (NIVI [1995]). When the NIV was first published in

1978, the Committee on Bible Translation (CBT) that produced it was chartered to generate periodic revisions or updates, especially as the English language continued to change and as scholarship advanced. Minor revisions were incorporated as early as 1984, but as the twentieth century drew to a close, no further editions of the NIV had appeared. Yet the CBT continued to meet for a minimum of a week each year to discuss and vote on proposals for improving both the accuracy and readability of the existing NIV. By the end of the twentieth century, several English translations had emerged that had begun in various places to employ inclusive language for humanity. We have already mentioned some of the most basic and obvious substitutions above—"person" for "man," "brothers and sisters" for "brothers," and so on. The NIV was quickly becoming the most-used gender-exclusive translation apart from the KJV/NKJV and NASB. So a new edition of the NIV was planned, which would incorporate all of the various revisions that had been voted on over the fifteen-plus years since the last update *and* would introduce gender-inclusive language in English where the original Greek and Hebrew referred to both genders.[64]

A small group of Bible scholars and church and parachurch leaders protested the introduction of much of this language. They convinced a few members of the CBT and representatives of its publishing houses to come to a meeting in Colorado Springs to discuss matters. At the end of the sessions, it seemed that those present had agreed on a series of guidelines as to when it was and was not appropriate to utilize gender-inclusive language in English translation.[65] One of the biggest sticking points had been the use of generic "he." How, for example, does one render a proverbial statement of the kind found in Proverbs 17:15? The KJV reads, "He that justifieth the wicked, and he that condemneth the just, even they both *are* abomination to the Lord." The RSV had updated the language to "He who justifies the wicked and he who condemns the righteous are both alike an abomination to the Lord." But there is absolutely nothing to suggest that the proverb is referring only to men and not also to women who acquit the wicked or condemn the righteous. Such sin is reprehensible no matter who commits it.

The NRSV had tweaked the RSV to produce, "One who justifies the wicked and one who condemns the righteous are both alike an abomination to the LORD." All it had done was replace the two uses of "he" in the RSV with the gender-inclusive word "one." The NET used "the one" rather than just "one": "The one who acquits the guilty and the one who condemns the innocent—both of them are an abomination to the LORD." The GWN dealt with the problem by using "whoever": "Whoever approves of wicked people and whoever condemns righteous people is disgusting to the LORD." But what appears in the Hebrew? Only a pair of participles, not separate words for "he" or "one" or "whoever," though all of those are standard and perfectly proper ways to render participles in translation. So the original NIV broke from the syntactical tradition of the KJV and its successors by declaring simply that "acquitting the guilty and condemning the innocent—the LORD detests them both."[66] The NLT followed suit with its rendering: "Acquitting the guilty and condemning the innocent—both are detestable to the LORD." Thus appears the anomaly of a dynamically equivalent translation being more "literal," in this specific verse, than all the formally equivalent translations of its time! The HCSB continued the new pattern of translating: "Acquitting the guilty and condemning the just—both are detestable to the LORD."

The original promoters of the Colorado Springs Guidelines (CSG), as they came to be called, nevertheless claimed that the masculine gender in the singular somehow indicated actual male examples or illustrations, so that meaning was lost and the masculinity of God's Word was muted by not translating these constructions with masculine singular forms in English. A particular priority of theirs was for English translations to retain hundreds of generic uses of "he" or "brother."[67] Yet the actual evidence to support this approach is virtually nonexistent. First, there is no indication that, in an expression of the form, "He who exercises regularly will have a better chance of staying fit," every speaker or listener is actually envisioning a male individual exercising as an illustration of a principle that applies to people of both genders.[68] People who grow up with this kind of language typically understand it at the level of a general principle without necessarily mentally envisioning an individual of either gender actually exercising.[69]

Moreover, the CSG promoters were willing to permit a variety of grammatically masculine forms to be translated inclusively, including generic masculine participles, masculine forms for "some" or "any," and plural forms like "men" or "brothers" used generically.[70] But the Hebrew- or Greek-speaking person who *would* actually think of a male example or illustration when hearing an expression like "he who exercises regularly" would be as likely to do so whether that was worded with the pronoun explicitly in the text or simply implied by a masculine participle or masculine indefinite pronoun. And, at least in the pre-Masoretic Hebrew of the original Old Testament (i.e., without vowel points), such a person would do so only if they heard the Scriptures read aloud, because the same three-letter word הוא could mean either "he" or "she." Only when pronounced according to an interpretive tradition passed on orally would people have distinguished the two forms, leading to a *later* distinction in spelling. But the doctrine of inspiration historically has not affirmed the inerrancy of vowel points, later paleography, or interpretive oral tradition, since none of these would have appeared in the original autographs.[71]

Furthermore, it makes no sense to argue that "men" and "brothers" may be rendered gender-inclusively but not "man" and "brother," especially when the same writer may alternate between the two forms in the same context.[72] Thus 2 Thessalonians 3:6, for example, addresses the "brothers"—the Christian believers in Thessalonica—and then admonishes them to keep away from every idle or disruptive brother. This cannot be a representative male, even for those who might be tempted to imagine one elsewhere, because "every" is used with "brother" and the command is not restricted to shunning males. Not surprisingly, instead of following the CSG guidelines and permitting "brothers and sisters" in the first usage and then reverting to "brother" for the singular form, the ESV uses "brothers" and "brother." At least it is consistent. But now many readers will not recognize the gender-inclusive language in the original at all. The updated NIV is far preferable: "In the name of the Lord Jesus Christ, we command you, brothers and sisters, to keep away from every believer who is idle and disruptive and does not live according to the teaching." Here it is not the form but the sense and referents of the original that is actually communicated.

Finally, the supporters of the CSG are consistently worried about people misunderstanding gender-inclusive language (e.g., when plurals replace singulars, or when second-person forms replace third-person forms), but when someone is concerned about how easily gender-exclusive language is misunderstood today (as referring only to men), they simply reply, "so explain it to them."[73] Yet CSG proponents never deem this a good-enough answer when it comes from supporters of gender-inclusive translations, who are instead told that the dangers must be minimized by the translation itself.[74] The Golden Rule (Matt. 7:12) suggests that a greater level of consistency is needed here!

Within about half a year after the formulation of the CSG, the participants from the CBT recognized that they could not in good conscience be limited by the guidelines to which they had agreed. They realized they had adopted them prematurely and without adequate time for reflection. After discussion by the full committee, they announced their intentions to continue working on the revision of the NIV unshackled by the guidelines. Other participants who still supported the CSG felt betrayed, and this doubtless led them to unleash more vitriolic criticism than they otherwise would have. The publishers of the NIV settled on what they hoped would be an adequate compromise—keeping the 1984 NIV in print but calling the new edition the TNIV (Today's New International Version) and publishing it separately. Bible readers who used the NIV could therefore choose whether or not they wanted inclusive language or exclusive language.[75]

Tragically, many of the supporters of the older NIV were not content with this decision and embarked on a campaign to speak ill of the TNIV whenever they had opportunity. One widely circulated rumor alleged that it included gender-inclusive language for the Godhead—calling *God* "he or she"—when the CBT had never even had any intention to implement such a change. An even more common charge was that the translation reflected a feminist agenda, despite the fact that the Committee was composed of fourteen men and only one woman, complementarians outnumbered egalitarians on it, and its public explanations of the rationale for gender-inclusive language for humanity repeatedly clarified that a feminist agenda had nothing to do with the translation philosophy.[76] The upshot of this smear campaign was that the TNIV never captured enough readers to stay in print. So the decision was made to go back to the original charter for the NIV, produce another revision of it, and then discontinue printing both the 1984 NIV and the TNIV. Of course, with 400 million copies of the earlier NIV in existence worldwide, access to this edition would hardly disappear overnight!

Meanwhile, the ESV was completed. Its translators and supporters overlapped considerably with the original formulators of the CSG and with some of the harshest critics of the TNIV. When they came to Proverbs 17:15, for example, they left the old RSV unrevised, preserving, "He who justifies the wicked and he who condemns the righteous are both alike an abomination to the LORD." For all the rhetoric about being essentially literal, at least in this verse what won out was the heritage of a gender-exclusive translation rather than a commitment to be faithful to the Hebrew.

Of course, no translation is perfect or perfectly consistent with its overall philosophy, because it is created by flawed human beings. More telling is the process by which a translation is made and the freedom given to translators to do their work. Some Bibles have been the product of individual translators, which by nature will have the greatest number of potential problems because no one person alone is as skilled or gifted in Bible translation as when working with the benefit of many advisers. A committee's process is far more laborious, but if done well, the end results will be better because of the collaboration.[77] But after godly, gifted, and trained translators are commissioned to work together, are they then free to render the text in the ways they believe best communicate it in the receptor language according to the translation philosophy that has been adopted?

At the height of the propaganda campaign against the TNIV, an interview with Albert Mohler, the president of the Southern Baptist Theological Seminary, disclosed an alarming attitude, if accurate. As the HCSB was in preparation, *Christianity Today* quoted Mohler as maintaining, "This is an important thing for Southern Baptists to do . . . if for no other reason than that we will have a major translation we can control."[78] That is precisely what *no* Christian should ever want. The Bible should control us; we should never try to control the Bible! Charles Colson sent a letter to the CBT several years ago, complaining about the TNIV's choice of "deacon" to translate *diakonos* in Romans 16:1, explaining that although he understood that this is what the word most probably meant in that context, it just caused too many problems in most churches in his denomination (the Southern Baptist Convention) because most of them did not permit women deacons. In other words, Colson recognized that many of his fellow churchgoers, when their church practice contradicted Scripture, would insist on censoring a translation of Scripture rather than changing church practice to conform to Scripture![79]

Little wonder, then, that the HCSB renders Romans 16:1 as "I commend to you our sister Phoebe, who is a *servant* of the church in Cenchreae" (emphasis added). The translators would presumably not have been allowed to use the word "deacon" even if they had wanted to.[80] In the case of the ESV, the president of the publishing house that distributes the version sits on the translation committee, in part to ensure that he has his say in whatever is decided. The NLT was produced with very little control exercised by the publisher, although employees who were literary stylists but not biblical scholars were allowed a measure of say in the wording that was finally published. The CBT of the NIV is fairly unique in being a self-perpetuating, independent committee bound by its bylaws to employ skilled translators who agree to the doctrinal statement of its founders. But the publishers in turn are equally bound to publish what the committee produces, without any "veto" power. A good working relationship allows each entity to make requests of the other, sometimes with considerable passion. On occasion, nevertheless, there have been good reasons for not heeding these requests, and the relationship has continued amicably. More important, the results of the committee's work have been published uncensored. These policies in no way ensure that the NIV is always better than the other three translations mentioned here, but this kind of information should encourage the Bible-reading public, given the amount of misinformation circulating these days.

What kinds of revisions, then, appear in the updated NIV (2011), especially when compared with the TNIV?[81] If there was any hesitation that a given masculine term in a given context might refer to males only, gender-exclusive language was reinstated. In the occasional context of well-known proverbial statements when no other rendering worked nearly as well, a singular "man" was reinstated (e.g., "The Sabbath was made for man, not man for the Sabbath" [Mark 2:27]). The still-common use of "mankind" as gender-inclusive allowed its deployment in various contexts where other forms proved more awkward or misleading (e.g., "Let us make mankind in our image" [Gen. 1:26]). Occasionally, the generic "he," "him," or "his" was also reinstated when it just seemed too awkward to express the English any differently (e.g., "The craving of a sluggard will be the death of him, because his hands refuse to work. All day long he craves for more, but the righteous give without sparing" [Prov. 21:25–26]).

Two of the most persistent complaints about the TNIV were that, in the effort to use inclusive language, singulars were changed to plurals and third-person forms to second-person ones.[82] In other words, a sentence of the form "He who studies hard does well on the exam," would have often been changed to "Those who study hard do well on the exam," or "You who study hard do well on the exam." The complaint was that, in the first case, readers might think that the proverb applied only to a group of people, not to each individual.[83] Having made such statements to classes for over thirty years, I honestly find this misunderstanding almost impossible to imagine, but I suppose theoretically it could happen.

In the second case, the complaint was that people might think the proverb applied only to one individual, because current English uses the same form for "you" in the singular and the plural.[84] But if critics of inclusive language are really serious about favoring an essentially literal translation as much as they claim to be on this particular issue, *then they should at least as adamantly insist on having some signal in an English translation to differentiate a singular "you" from a plural "you"* in the thousands of verses that do contain one of those two forms in the original languages.[85] Serious misunderstanding *can* take place when people don't recognize that a "you" is plural and think a text is referring to an individual rather than an entire group (or vice versa). For example, 1 Corinthians 3:16 speaks of the church corporately as the temple of God,[86] but most translations, including essentially literal ones, say something like the ESV: "Do you not know that you are God's temple and that God's Spirit dwells in you?" From this English rendering, there is no way to know that both appearances of "you" in the text are plural. The KJV, with its older English, actually did indicate this by using "ye" for the first plural, but this form has long since vanished from normal English usage. That we never hear a complaint about this from critics of inclusive language nullifies most of their criticism on this point. It is clear that their biggest motivation is intolerance toward anything that could possibly empower the evangelical egalitarians rather than concern for what best clarifies the meaning of the text.[87]

Despite the CBT's widespread dissemination of the kinds of changes made in the 2011 NIV and the rationale behind them, organizations like the Council on Biblical Manhood and Womanhood (CBMW) and individuals like Denny Burk produced highly misleading articles about the updated NIV that have poisoned many people's minds against the translation. Claiming to have compared every text in which the TNIV had introduced gender-inclusive language for humanity where it had not previously appeared in the NIV with the way the updated NIV treated each of those same texts, they calculated that 75 percent of the texts changed nothing from the TNIV.[88] Worse still, a resolution came before the floor of the entire Southern Baptist Convention in the summer of 2011 condemning the updated NIV because of this alleged preservation of 75 percent of the gender-inclusive language of the TNIV.[89]

There are three main problems with this appeal to statistics, however. First, the publisher's own count of the number of texts still with gender-inclusive language is only two-thirds (66 percent, or 2,200 out of 3,300), not three-quarters (75 percent). Second, and more important, a sizable majority of the texts that remained gender-inclusive did so in a very different and limited way. In the updated NIV, the CBT had worked hard to remove almost all of the places where the TNIV had substituted a second-person form for a third-person one. The only time "you" was retained was when second-person forms were already in the immediate context of the passage and would have made a switch from "you" to "he" (or "she") awkward or stylistically poor English, thus justifying the use of a second-person form. Very few plurals in place of singulars were retained either, except in rare instances where something was obviously proverbial, very awkward to render with any other form of inclusive language, clearly generic, and easily understandable.

Thanks to the results of sophisticated computerized searches of the London-housed Collins Dictionary database, it was discovered that

84 percent of all the English represented from recent years rendered what in the 1950s would have called for a generic "he" by using what grammarians today call a singular or distributive "they" *with a singular antecedent*.[90] In other words, in grade school, I used to hear teachers say, "He who wants to go to college had better get all the good grades he can"; in high school, I most commonly heard, "He or she who wants to go to college had better get all the good grades he or she can"; but today by far the most common way of expressing such a thought is "Whoever [or "anyone who"] wants to go to college had better get all the good grades *they* can." The singular noun or pronoun at the beginning of the sentence makes it clear that the speaker is referring to a generic *individual*, neither just a man nor just a woman, but not merely a group either. The "they" then avoids the cumbersome "he or she" and the gender-exclusive "he" but unambiguously refers back to the individual person represented by "whoever" or "anyone." Nor is this the first time in history that such a way of dealing with generic singulars has prevailed. Singular "they" was far more common before the mid-eighteenth century, when generic "he" began to dominate the language.[91]

In spoken English, these constructions have become nearly universal. In written English, their use is growing with each passing year. It may be the best English-language solution to our problem. So the updated NIV commonly makes use of this device to deal with gender-inclusive Hebrew and Greek forms. Neither the CBMW nor Denny Burk said anything about these translational changes, although they had been made aware of them. It is clear that those who put forward the resolution condemning the NIV at the Southern Baptist Convention had no idea about this new translation procedure. It is also clear that none of the authors of the documents censoring the updated NIV was aware of the history of English-language usage of these forms. The SBC resolutions committee, however, had already rejected the proposal because they *had* researched the matter some. But a procedural loophole allowed an individual pastor to bring the resolution to the floor of the convention, with minutes left in the multiday event and after nearly half of the delegates had already left. The resolution passed by a two-to-one margin, the media reported it widely,[92] and as a result few people know the real nature of the updated NIV unless they have actually read sizable chunks of it!

Third and even more serious is the thoroughgoing misuse of statistics by these critics of gender-inclusive language. Unlike votes in an American election, multiple occurrences of a certain grammatical feature do not all merit being counted equally. Earlier we stated that weighing rather than counting manuscripts is the appropriate procedure in textual criticism. The same is true with matters of translation revision. For example, the 2011 NIV's 330 uses of "ancestors" rather than generic "forefathers" mislead no one and hardly counterbalance all the singular and third-person forms that it reinstated. The 2011 NIV's critics recognize this fact about statistics when it comes to complaints that *they* face. If we were to harp on the fact that the ESV has removed the words "man" and "men" from the RSV 671 times,[93] the ESV translation committee would rightly object that most of the time they were following the guidelines they established when they believed this was acceptable and that the vast majority of these changes came in texts that would mislead the fewest people.

These and like-minded critics also inadequately stress that the vast majority of all the passages in the Bible that teach about gender roles in church and home were unchanged from the NIV to the TNIV to the updated NIV. The two or three passages that had minor changes introduced, even while still fully allowing for either complementarian or egalitarian interpretations, were given attention completely out of proportion to all the passages left unchanged. Although *the updated NIV changed most of the kinds of inclusive language the critics had originally complained most strongly about and most of the specific texts that had received the harshest criticism*,[94] this counted for nothing because of an indiscriminate count of verses that remained unchanged—no matter how inconsequential the language was in those contexts. And if one *were* to adopt the "all problems are created equal" approach, then the ESV deserves the severest of censure for preserving (unlike the KJV) many thousands of references to "you" where the English reader simply cannot distinguish between singulars and plurals. That this would be a ludicrous criticism of the ESV shows how equally vacuous the criticisms of the updated NIV really are. Beyond any reasonable doubt, such inconsistencies show that these critics of the updated NIV could never have given it a fair hearing in the first place. Instead, their writings became forums for showcasing their anti-egalitarian agendas.[95] Otherwise, where are the articles and resolutions condemning the ESV and HCSB (and all other post-RSV translations, for that matter) for the thousands and thousands of uses of "you" when it is impossible in English translation to tell the difference between singulars and plurals, since those *are* so easily misread? By the very logic of the NIV's critics, these texts likewise constitute egregious and unacceptable mistranslations of the inspired Word of God, the kind of censure that was repeatedly hurled at the NIV!

One final argument pertaining to these translation issues involves a false dichotomy. Imagining that "we had both a time machine and a language translation machine," Wayne Grudem asks about Psalm 23:

> Should our goal as translators be to use the time machine to bring David to New York City in 2011, give him the language translation machine so that he could understand and speak English, and then ask him to rewrite Psalm 23, but speaking as people would speak in New York City in 2011? Should we tell him, 'David, just rewrite your psalm and use twentieth-first [*sic*] century expressions'?
>
> No, *as a translator of Psalm 23*, I would want to use the time machine to *travel back* to ancient Israel around 1000 BC when David was writing Psalm 23. I would want to use my language translation machine to translate David's words into English and put them in ordinary English word order.[96]

Grudem then quotes the ESV for Psalm 23:1–3 as what the results would sound like. Verse 1 reads, "The Lord is my shepherd; I shall not want."

But the choice can in reality never be an "either-or"; it can only be a "both-and." On Grudem's model, into what kind of English should time travelers render the Greek or Hebrew that they learn in the ancient world? Elizabethan English? Victorian English? Pre–World War II American English? Modern Australian English? Colloquial English from the American South? Urbanese? Or the English that is most commonly used by the broadest cross-section of speakers internationally in the second decade of the twenty-first century? Until this decision is made, time travelers can produce no English translations at all. They must return to the world from which they have come. And if the answer that is chosen to our question is that they should utilize the most common English used by the broadest cross-section of English speakers today, then something more like the NIV, NET, NAB, HCSB, or CEB than like the ESV, NKJV, or KJV is what results. Today we do not normally say "I shall not want" when we mean "I will not lack anything." People unfamiliar with the history of translating Psalm 23:1 often have never even heard "want" used in order to mean "lack," and they are far more likely to say "will" than "shall," at least in the United States. What is more, part of the argument *for* the ESV is that it preserves the more elegant style of more formal, old-fashioned English, especially in poetry (such as Ps. 23), and therefore should *not* always be written in ordinary English.[97] So Grudem's imaginary time traveler isn't really coming back to ordinary twenty-first-century America at all.

With so much misinformation and faulty logic about Bible translations being disseminated, is it any wonder that unbelievers, and even some Christians, are convinced that one simply can't trust Bibles written in modern languages? Should it cause surprise when individuals who once claimed to be evangelical Christians adopt another version of Christianity or abandon their professions of faith altogether and give as a primary reason for doing so the translation wars among Christians? Those who relentlessly engage in these wars, maligning certain major versions of the Bible as unreliable in order to support their own theological and political agendas, would do well to ponder such outcomes.

Conclusion

We cannot emphasize our main point strongly enough. All the major, nonsectarian Bible translations are more than adequate for teaching God's people everything God wants them to know that really matters. The KJV, despite its slightly faulty textual base, is a highly reliable, formally equivalent translation, made intelligible to modern people by the NKJV. The NASB is outstanding even if often somewhat woodenly literal. The RSV never deserved the broadsides it received: it was a very good translation. And both the NRSV and ESV are excellent revisions of it, even if they disagree on how often to use inclusive language for humanity. The NLT has brought countless first-time Bible readers to faith in Christ or to a deepened faith and a love of Bible reading that they did not previously have or might never have had. The HCSB is an excellent optimally equivalent translation that deserves more attention than it has received and a broader share of the Bible "market." The updated NIV may have attained the best combination of accuracy and clarity of all the translations. If gender-inclusiveness is going to be used anywhere (which even the ESV and HCSB employ in hundreds of texts), the updated NIV is probably the most balanced and nuanced in communicating the biblical authors' intentions about whether just men or both men and women were in view in a given passage. Many other good yet less commonly used translations could be added to this litany of praise. And of course there is plenty of room for successive revisions of all translations to improve even on the existing versions.

We have thus traversed the terrain from textual criticism to the formation of the canon to the translation of the Scriptures. In each case we have debunked the claims of overly conservative Christians but have been even more interested in insisting that, despite various loose ends, we (1) *can accurately reconstruct the text of* (2) *the properly chosen books of the biblical canon*, (3) *which have been accurately translated. Liberal and skeptical charges to the contrary are simply wrong and wrongheaded.* But given the loose ends we have acknowledged, is it still fair for evangelical Christians to speak of the inerrancy of the Bible? The next chapter must turn to this question.

4

Don't These Issues Rule Out Biblical Inerrancy?

Evangelical Christians who trace their spiritual roots to the aftermath of the fundamentalist-modernist controversy in America in the 1920s often cherish and vigorously defend the doctrine of *biblical inerrancy*. Other branches of evangelicalism, especially in parts of the world not heavily influenced by American missionary efforts, tend to speak of *biblical authority, inspiration,* and even *infallibility*, but not inerrancy.[1] Sometimes these other Christians mean virtually the same thing, but in other instances they are consciously rejecting "inerrancy" as too narrow a term to apply to the Scriptures.[2] People unfamiliar with the details of the debates often assume that the positions we have staked out on the text, canon, and translation of Scripture in the previous three chapters necessarily preclude inerrancy. Intriguingly, this misunderstanding can emerge among either those who are noticeably more conservative *or* those who are noticeably more liberal in their views of Scripture than mainstream evangelicals.

In recent years, books by writers such as Carlos Bovell, Christian Smith, and Kenton Sparks have poured scorn on the historic Christian doctrine of inerrancy while still identifying with various dimensions of evangelical faith.[3] The kinds of harmonizations of apparent contradictions among the Gospels that I have suggested in my own writings are dismissed as contrived, artificial, and unpersuasive.[4] Yet at the same time, from the far right of the evangelical spectrum, authors such as Norman Geisler, William Roach, Robert Thomas, and David Farnell attack my writings along with similar ones by such evangelical stalwarts as Darrell Bock, D. A. Carson, and Craig Keener as too liberal, threatening inerrancy, or denying the historicity of Scripture. This charge is supported by highlighting how these scholars use approaches other than traditional harmonization, especially form and redaction criticism, to resolve apparent contradictions.[5] And all of this debate emerges just from the Gospels, to say nothing of the rest of the Bible!

In the broader academic guild, but also sometimes among grassroots laypeople, it is often assumed that scholars who teach at confessional institutions such as evangelical Christian colleges or seminaries cannot maintain their intellectual integrity because they must subscribe to certain confessions of faith in order to teach at these schools. It is believed that the theological positions they are required to affirm restrict their freedom to follow the evidence of their research wherever it might lead them.[6] Two main replies to this charge are in order. First, the very fact that over the centuries various scholars have left confessional institutions for others with broader or no confessional frameworks demonstrates that honest scholars will follow the results of their investigations even when it places them outside the doctrinal boundaries of a particular community. The vast majority of these departures have been voluntary, but the most highly publicized tend to be the much less common firings of professors who believed they were staying within their communities' parameters yet discovered that key power brokers within those communities disagreed and succeeded in ousting them. Second, the vast majority of scholars who accept positions at confessional institutions do so only after and because they have come to believe in good conscience, on the basis of their study, that they agree with the doctrinal views of those schools.

But what about the specific doctrine of the inerrancy of Scripture? Isn't this a special case that must be viewed differently? If a person must agree that the Bible is without error in order to hold a position with a school, church, or parachurch organization, doesn't this put a virtual straitjacket on their research? The answer depends almost entirely on whether or not there is good evidence for biblical inerrancy. Most people would not complain today if a scientific organization required that its members believe in a heliocentric solar system (i.e., with the planets orbiting around the sun), because there is very good evidence for that conviction. On the other hand, conscientious membership in the Flat Earth Society would put a noose around genuine scientific research. Flat Earth Society members disagree with the heliocentric conviction, but their numbers constitute an infinitesimal percentage of the people in the world who have investigated the issue at all seriously. Is belief in biblical inerrancy more like belief in a heliocentric solar system or more like belief in a flat earth? The numbers of scholars on each side of the debate and the nature of the evidence to which they point suggest that neither analogy is sufficiently close. We would need a more contested scientific issue to create a closer analogy, perhaps the notion of multiverses rather than a single universe, which challenges a long-held scientific and philosophical concept but is strenuously supported as fact in certain circles.[7] Inerrantism would thus relate to the single universe as errantism does to the multiverse.

Kinds of Inerrancy

There are two quite different approaches, moreover, that can lead to an affirmation that Scripture is without error. One approach is inductive, the other deductive. The *inductive approach* begins with the phenomena of the Bible itself, defines what would count as an error, analyzes Scripture carefully from beginning to end, and determines that nothing has been discovered that would qualify as errant. The *deductive approach* begins with the conviction that God is the author of Scripture, proceeds to the premise that by definition God cannot err, and therefore concludes that God's Word must be without error.[8] In principle, the inductive approach is no different from what I do when reading a student's research paper. Over the years I have read a lot of good research papers that have no factual errors in them, reason cogently without any logical fallacies, and express opinions that, while not necessarily provable, are supported with enough evidence to make them probable. I typically assign these papers an A grade. They are void of anything that normally is termed an error of content (though there usually are a few typos or errors of grammar). Completely apart from the inspiration of God, humans can write long stretches of text without erring or making mistakes if they do thorough research and check their material carefully.[9] Materials that are carefully proofread can avoid even errors of form. Our criticism of works that do contain numerous errors proves that we believe a higher standard is attainable. How much more would we expect this to be the case with sacred literature!

The deductive approach to inerrancy reasons from the conviction that God is the author of Scripture. At least two major forms of the deductive approach are well known. One is held by those with a more *evidentialist* approach to Christian apologetics or defenses of the faith. The other is held by those with a more *presuppositionalist* bent. The *evidentialist* classically argues that there are good philosophical arguments for the existence of God and good historical arguments that Jesus was divine. It can further be shown that the canonical Gospels' portrait of Jesus is historically reliable, at least with respect to those main contours and emphases that recur frequently in multiple layers of the tradition. One of these emphases is Jesus's consistent belief in a fully reliable, authoritative, God-given Scripture (what Christians call the Old Testament) and the Spirit's role in guiding Jesus's followers into further revelation (not necessarily identical to but including at least much of the New Testament). If one professes to follow Jesus as one's divine master, then, one will acknowledge the Scriptures as reliable. When the early church canonized the New Testament, it was treating the twenty-seven books it added to the Old Testament as on a par with that earlier revelation. Thus the vast majority of Christians throughout the history of the church and across the world have believed in the Bible's complete trustworthiness as a collection of uniquely God-breathed (*theopneustos*; 2 Tim. 3:16) literature.[10]

The *presuppositionalist* approach believes that one or more of the foundational premises in the evidentialist's argumentation must simply be posited rather than defended. Perhaps the existence of God is what philosophers call "properly basic." It cannot be proved, but once it is affirmed, the nature of our existence and human history can be better explained by theism than by atheism.[11] Some presuppositionalists believe that one must first assume that the Bible is God's Word, giving it the benefit of the doubt when there are apparent contradictions or problems, looking at the solutions people have produced throughout history, and accepting the best of them—and *then* the Scriptures will disclose a more coherent worldview than the holy books or tenets of any other religion or ideology.[12] Whether following evidentialism or presuppositionalism, this deductive approach ultimately views inerrancy as a corollary of inspiration, not as something to be demonstrated from the texts of Scripture itself. If the Bible is God-breathed (2 Tim. 3:16), and God cannot err, then the Bible must be inerrant.

A Working Definition

With all these options, it should be clear that we need a working definition of inerrancy. One of the most influential and helpful definitions in recent decades emerged in the collection of essays formulated as commentary on the Chicago Statement on Biblical Inerrancy that was signed by 334 mostly American evangelical scholars and church leaders in 1979.[13] One essayist was Paul Feinberg, longtime professor of systematic theology and philosophy at Trinity Evangelical Divinity School. His definition reads, "*Inerrancy means that when all facts are known, the Scriptures in their original autographs and properly interpreted will be shown to be wholly true in everything that they affirm, whether that has to do with doctrine or morality or with the social, physical, or life sciences*" (emphasis original).[14] There are four key parts to this definition.

First is "when all facts are known." This clause acknowledges the finite nature of our knowledge of the relevant information that might bear on an assessment of Scripture's truthfulness. It is not, as some scholars have asserted, a loophole that allows interpreters to be confronted by large numbers of seemingly intractable problems and simply punt by affirming that "a solution to every difficulty will be found some day."[15] In fact, there are no problems in Scripture anywhere that have not yielded at least plausible solutions. The problem is that some solutions seem more probable than others, and past problems have been solved by further scholarship and discoveries, so there is no reason not to imagine that still better answers to a handful of problems may yet emerge in the future. Meanwhile, large volumes by evangelical scholars have demonstrated how the vast majority of all the supposed contradictions or errors in Scripture have been dealt with in reasonably compelling fashion, especially if one grants the biblical authors at least as much benefit of the doubt as classical historians have typically granted other documents of the ancient Near East and the ancient Mediterranean worlds.[16]

Second comes "the Scriptures in their original autographs." As we have already seen, no such autographs (to our knowledge) still exist. Given the length of time manuscripts were kept in existence, however, it is by no means impossible that someday we might find one or more of the original scrolls of various biblical books (see in chap. 1, "Did Originals Originally Exist?"). It is not impossible that one of the second- or third-century fragments we already possess, preserving snatches of one or more New Testament books, is a direct copy of an autograph, though there would be virtually no way ever to demonstrate this, given their provenance. What then is the value of affirming the inerrancy of documents that most likely no longer exist? Much in every way! For precisely all of the reasons discussed in chapter 1, the critical reconstructions of the Hebrew, Aramaic, and Greek texts of the various biblical books likely approximate the contents of the missing autographs quite closely. The chance that the original scrolls contained something no longer present in any of the manuscript traditions or that the manuscripts uniformly added something wholly lacking in the originals is small with respect to the Old Testament and almost nonexistent with respect to the New. If we had no reason for confidence in the degree of care with which the texts were copied, the inerrancy of the autographs would matter little. But precisely because we do have such confidence, we can assert that we have something exceedingly close to the unerring texts of original Scripture.[17]

Third appears the phrase "properly interpreted." Numerous competing theological and exegetical positions over the centuries have appealed to the inerrancy or trustworthiness of Scripture for their support;

in reality these were debates over hermeneutics. For example, despite high-profile claims to the contrary,[18] cogent exegetical support can be marshaled from Scripture for both complementarian and egalitarian interpretations of gender roles in home and church. In the most contested passages, the issue boils down to the interpretive methods one employs rather than whether one does or does not believe in the full inerrancy of Scripture.[19] The same is true for many debates that involve the literary form or genre of various biblical passages or even entire books, as chapter 5 will discuss. "Inerrancy" can be wielded as a blunt tool to hammer into submission people whose interpretations of passages differ from ours, when in fact the real issue is not whether a passage is true or not but what kind of truth it teaches.

Fourth, we read, "in everything that they affirm, whether that has to do with doctrine or morality or with the social, physical, or life sciences." Three comments are important here. First, "in everything that they affirm" intentionally contrasts with what a text does not affirm. A parable does not affirm that its characters ever really lived; it is true not as a factual story but as a symbolic or illustrative analogy between human events and God's dealings with humanity.[20] A biblical author declaring that "the sun rose" need not be affirming a geocentric universe any more than we are when we continue to use the same phrase; the writer was simply using the conventional way of speaking that corresponds to what we observe phenomenologically without the aid of scientific equipment.[21]

Second, despite repeated efforts to limit the truthfulness of the Bible to areas of faith and practice, or doctrine and ethics, Scripture's affirmations about all the topics treated are too intertwined to separate beliefs and morals from all other matters, including especially history and science.[22] As we have just remarked, this hardly means that every statement that at first glance appears to declare that something happened in history or that something reflects a scientific reality must necessarily be interpreted that way. But if, after applying the best principles of interpretation we can uncover, our conclusions are that a text *is* intending to communicate that something happened or that a scientific phenomenon does function in a certain fashion, then inerrantists will accept those affirmations as true.

Finally, the reference to science does not imply one particular explanation of the origins of the universe. Thus Genesis 1 can be and has been interpreted by inerrantists as referring to a young earth, an old earth, progressive creation, theistic evolution, a literary framework for asserting God as the creator of all things irrespective of his methods, and a series of days when God took up residence in his cosmic temple for the sake of newly created humanity in his image.[23] Once again, this is a matter for hermeneutical and exegetical debate, not one that is solved by appealing to the shibboleth of inerrancy.

Too Many Caveats?

Critics of the full trustworthiness of Scripture have often complained that inerrancy "dies the death of a thousand qualifications."[24] This is a curious charge, given that a definition like Feinberg's actually contains only *four* qualifications (even granting the figure of speech involved in 1,000)! Most major Christian doctrines have at least this much complexity, yet one almost never hears fellow evangelicals lamenting that the doctrine of the Trinity or of Calvinist (or Arminian) soteriology or of premillennial (or amillennial or postmillennial) eschatology dies the death of a thousand qualifications! The terms preferred by some, such as "infallibility" or "verbal plenary inspiration," are in fact less common and potentially more misleading, whereas the meaning of "inerrancy" is morphologically straightforward: without error.

What complicates matters is not the meaning of inerrancy but the debate over what constitutes an error. We live in a scientific world that values high degrees of precision in countless walks of life, from the time on the clock to the speed of athletes, numbers in statistical reports, and verbatim reporting of people's words; hence by default we frequently impose modern standards of accuracy on ancient texts in hopelessly anachronistic fashion. Imagine being told one day that your job performance was going to be assessed based on standards that wouldn't be invented until the forty-second century, or shortly before. You'd be outraged. But often without realizing it, we impose on ancient documents twenty-first-century standards that are equally inappropriate.

To this day, we use round numbers; ancient cultures did so regularly. Variations in spelling and grammar remain; ancient writers employed far more. A grammatical or spelling "error" in any culture refers simply to nonstandard writing or usage of words; it is not as if there is some divinely mandated correct way to turn oral speech into letters or to arrange words to make a coherent thought. The doctrine of inerrancy was never designed to pass judgment on the linguistic skills of a given writer.[25]

The reporting of people's words is a particularly significant example of where the ancients employed noticeably less precision than we moderns do.[26] The languages of the ancient world had no symbol for quotation marks nor felt any need for them. A perfect example appears in Genesis 18:12–13. When Sarah heard the prediction that she would bear a son in her old age, she laughed and said to herself, "After I am worn out and my lord is old, will I now have this pleasure?" (v. 12). The narrator of Genesis then describes the Lord asking Abraham, "Why did Sarah laugh and say, 'Will I really have a child, now that I am old?'" (v. 13). Not a single Hebrew word of Sarah's reported speech about herself in verse 13 remains the same from verse 12, but it is obvious that the narrator intends us to recognize the same question in both verses.[27] In fact, when one historian borrowed from existing sources, it was considered good literary style and an appropriate way of owning information for oneself *not* to reproduce all the words verbatim but to integrate the speech of others into one's own narrative via selection, explanation, abbreviation, and paraphrase.[28] The question the reader must ask of two different accounts of the same event or even of the same speech is not whether identical wording is used or the same material included but whether anything in the one account cannot be true at all if everything in the other account is true.

Another mistake many people make is to confuse inerrancy with literal interpretation. Even the expression "literal interpretation," as it was employed by the Reformers, meant taking the words of Scripture according to their most straightforward, intended meaning, not ignoring figurative language.[29] To interpret "the trees of the field will clap their hands" (Isa. 55:12) as implying that trees have actual hands they can bring together would not have been considered literal interpretation, just misguided and silly! To miss the intention behind a figure of speech is both to misinterpret it and to affirm the truth of a proposition that may well be false. Entire passages and even whole books of the Bible may employ literary forms or genres that are misunderstood if taken completely historically. Apocalyptic literature affords a classic example.[30] To take John's visions in Revelation as photographs of coming, future events not only commits us to believing in real dragons (12:3–13:11) and prostitutes so big they can sit atop seven hills (17:9) but also misses the symbolic intention of apocalyptic visions. To affirm the inerrancy of Revelation 13:1–10 does not commit us to believing that a dragon or a beast actually exists as depicted in these verses. Instead, it means that the realities to which they point—Satan and a coming antichrist—really exist, and that John really did have a God-given vision in which these individuals were represented by the creatures described.[31]

Indeed, defenders of inerrancy do not reflect often enough on what it means to say that nonhistorical genres are wholly truthful.[32] What does it mean to say that a psalm of lament or the love poetry of the Song of Songs or the mandates of James in his letter are inerrant?[33] Of course, each of these genres contains propositions, whether expressed or implied.[34] If David pours out his sorrowful heart to God because he is being pursued by his enemies, inerrancy means that he really was on the run and that he genuinely had the emotions he attributes to himself. But more profoundly, it means that lament is a viable and important form of communication with God when God's people find themselves and those they care about in distressing circumstances.[35] If the male lover in the Song of Songs waxes rhapsodic about the beauty of his beloved, inerrancy means that he truly found her beautiful. But more significantly, it justifies erotic love poetry as a legitimate form of romance with a person one hopes to marry.[36] When James asks rhetorically if the kind of faith that refuses to help the materially neediest spiritual brother or sister in one's midst can be saving faith, employing the Greek adverb that implies a negative answer, inerrancy means that it really is not possible to be saved without our faith leading to good deeds, especially in the sharing of our material possessions.[37] The doctrinal implications underlying the rhetorical question thus lead to the mandate to give financially for those who have less.

At the same time, inerrancy does not preclude the hermeneutical need to distinguish between situation-specific and timeless commands or models in Scripture. Applying Old Testament texts in the New Testament age requires believers to filter each passage through the grid of its fulfillment in Christ (Matt. 5:17–20).[38] Believers should not bring bulls or goats with them to church to be slaughtered to atone for sin, even though the laws for animal sacrifice occupy a large portion of Leviticus 1–9. Christ has paid it all, as our once-for-all sacrifice for sin (e.g., Heb. 9:24–28); we obey the Levitical commands by trusting wholly in Jesus's full and final atonement. Determining whether or not tattoos are appropriate for Christians requires more than just turning to Leviticus 19:28b and seeing that they are prohibited there. We read verses 27–28 in their entirety and discover related commands: "Do not cut the hair at the sides of your head or clip off the edges of your beard. Do not cut your bodies for the dead or put tattoo marks on yourselves. I am the Lord." Studying the historical background discloses that all of these practices were part of various ancient idolatrous, pagan rites of worship that the Israelites were not to emulate.[39] God's people today should likewise refrain from getting a tattoo as part of a pagan religious ritual, but a tattoo proclaiming "God loves you" might be an excellent evangelistic tool as a conversation starter. Even in the New Testament, an explicit command may or may not be appropriate for all times and cultures. When ancient Christians greeted one another with a holy kiss, they were following a culturally common and non-erotic practice of greeting friends.[40] If kisses in certain modern cultures are not a common greeting and are likely to arouse romantic feelings, then some cultural equivalent such as a warm handshake or appropriate kind of hug should be substituted. These are all issues of proper hermeneutics and contextualization, not the direct application of a belief in inerrancy.

To clarify the distinction between an inerrantist and an errantist approach, consider this illustration of how two different interpreters may arrive at the same conclusion but by two very different means. The first commentator might confront 1 Timothy 2:12, with Paul's command to women not to teach or exercise authority over a man, and find "it impossible to regard the statements disqualifying women from public speech and roles of leadership as either true or normative."[41] In other words, even before embarking on careful exegesis, this first commentator rules out the possible conclusion that men and women might have distinct roles in the church. This first scholar views verse 12 as containing primitive commands for a patriarchal culture with morally unacceptable standards that cannot be permitted today and should not have been permitted then. It is assumed that if Paul were in our churches today, he would make the same restrictions as he did in the first century, but we simply cannot follow him. This type of reasoning is *not* consistent with a belief in verbal plenary inspiration or inerrancy, because it does not allow for Paul's instruction ever to have been appropriate. A second commentator, such as an evangelical egalitarian, might argue that Paul restricted women because they did not have adequate opportunities for religious instruction in first-century Ephesus and so were not adequately qualified to lead congregations. It was an appropriate limitation in Paul's world because of the circumstances. Today Paul would not impose such a restriction on women as a whole because circumstances have sufficiently changed.[42] The upshot of both commentators' logic is that qualified women are free to teach or exercise authority over men in contemporary churches, but only the second commentator has arrived at that conclusion by a line of reasoning consistent with belief in the full authority and trustworthiness of Scripture.

A Historical Perspective

As we noted above, many Christians have adopted the language of "verbal plenary inspiration" to mean what others have meant by "inerrancy."[43] The adjectives "verbal" and "plenary" are easily misunderstood as meaning that God *dictated* every word of every book of Scripture, but this is not what they were intended to communicate. "Verbal" was used to guard against the idea that only the concepts behind the words of Scripture came from God, not the actual writings as we have them. "Plenary" was utilized to prevent people from accepting only certain biblical books or certain portions of certain books as trustworthy and authoritative, rather than every part of every document.[44]

Throughout church history, influential theologians and preachers have used a wide variety of terms to express a high view of Scripture. They have called it inspired, God-given, God-breathed, infallible, indefectible, wholly reliable, trustworthy, true, and without any mixture of error. They have stressed that the Bible is not merely to be believed; it is also to be obeyed. They have stressed that one must keep both parts of 2 Timothy 3:16 together—"All Scripture is God-breathed" *and* as a result "is useful for teaching, rebuking, correcting and training in righteousness." Verse 17 describes the purpose of this second clause: "so that the servant of God may be thoroughly equipped for every good work." Not everyone has used every adjective that can be predicated of the Bible in exactly interchangeable ways. For example, some definitions of infallibility consciously differ from full inerrancy by limiting their belief in Scripture's complete truthfulness to matters of faith and practice.[45] But the meaning of "infallible" is simply "unable to deceive," without any distinction between various kinds or topics of deception. So it is not clear that this is a helpful terminological distinction.

In short, if one tries to demonstrate that every major orthodox Christian thinker before the rise of modern biblical criticism spoke of the Scriptures as inerrant or adopted the four components of Feinberg's definition, one will fail.[46] But it is difficult to find very many influential Christians throughout the first seventeen centuries of church history—that is, until the Scientific Enlightenment—who did not affirm in a fairly sweeping way the unique truthfulness, reliability, and trustworthiness of the sixty-six books of what came to be the Protestant Bible (debates about the Old Testament Apocrypha notwithstanding).[47] David Bebbington's widely used definition of evangelicalism, moreover, shows that such a view of Scripture is one of the four most central tenets of the faith that marks off those who are true to historic Christianity versus more liberal revisionists who have turned the faith into something quite different.[48] As we have already observed, *what it means to say that the Bible is wholly true varies widely from one genre to the next, but the concept of a deeply flawed or errant Scripture is a virtual oxymoron and largely the invention of recent times.*

Further Objections to Inerrancy

An approach to the nature of Scripture that has emerged from time to time throughout church history and that is commended today particularly by Kenton Sparks is that of divine accommodation.[49] This approach challenges the logic of "the Scriptures are inspired and *therefore* inerrant." Why could God not accommodate himself to fallen, sinful humanity and reveal himself through errant documents? An honest answer would be that he *could* have done so, but this would lead to the neo-orthodox view of the Bible—that it is not the Word of God per se but becomes the Word of God whenever God through his Spirit uses it as a witness to himself.[50] The important question is not whether God could have inspired an inerrant Scripture but whether or not God *chose* to do so.

Often theologians have drawn analogies with Jesus as the personal Word of God. God allowed himself, in the person of Christ, to take upon himself all the limitations of humanity for the sake of us humans. Wouldn't God likewise adopt all the limitations of human communication in his written words?[51] But, as we have seen, even uninspired human writings don't necessarily contain errors, so why must divinely inspired writings contain them? Furthermore, orthodox Christianity has consistently viewed Jesus as sinless, free of moral error. So he did *not* take upon himself *all* the limitations of fallen humanity. Even Adam and Eve before the fall were sinless and yet perfectly human. The true analogy in discussing the divine and human natures of the Bible would thus be to see it as adopting all the writing styles, figures of speech, linguistic conventions, forms of historical investigation, and literary genres that are found in other human documents but without making factual errors, teaching faulty theology, intentionally misleading readers about the nature of God's will, and so on.[52]

Christian Smith stresses the pervasive interpretive pluralism in evangelical exposition of the Scriptures as a reason for rejecting inerrancy. What good would an inerrant Bible be, he wonders, since there is so little that even evangelical interpreters can agree on? Smith cites a long list of books published by evangelical presses that present two, three, four, or five views on various theological topics, all written by evangelicals with a high view of Scripture who nonetheless take differing views on such issues as the atonement, divorce and remarriage, hell, women in ministry, eternal security, divine foreknowledge, the Lord's Supper, the millennium, and numerous other subjects.[53] Smith concludes "that on important matters the Bible apparently is not clear, consistent, and univocal enough to enable the best-intentioned, most highly skilled, believing readers to come to agreement as to what it teaches."[54] Not surprisingly, he has recently converted from evangelical Christianity to Roman Catholicism, in which the dictates of a magisterium settle various issues for the faithful in hopes of excluding some of this diversity.

Several replies are in order. First, much more goes into determining what people will believe about contentious doctrines than merely a careful reading and analysis of Scripture. People are heavily influenced by the denominations or networks of churches in which they have spent the most time. Years ago, as a young adult, I did a thorough study of the Scriptures on the topic of baptism and then read numerous works that were touted as the best theological defenses of believer's baptism and of infant baptism. I expected that the results of my study would show the evidence to be evenly divided. Surprisingly, it was not; the biblical evidence seemed almost entirely on the side of believer's baptism. The best of the studies on infant baptism acknowledged this but then argued that in the first generation of Christianity, the issue of children born to Christian parents simply was not that common a problem because almost every new believer was converting as an adult. Only after the New Testament was largely complete did the issue of infant baptism arise. Since the Bible doesn't directly address the question, Christians arrived at differing conclusions derived from broader theological principles. But it was not because the biblical data were equivocal.[55]

In other instances, debates arise because there just isn't a lot in Scripture on a particular topic. Mention of the thousand years of the "millennium" appears only in Revelation 20, in a highly symbolic book that may be the hardest to interpret of all sixty-six in the Bible. Finding debate on this should hardly cause surprise.[56] In the case of more central issues, such as Christ's atonement, the debates are most likely resolved by acknowledging a substantial measure of truth in each of the positions, which complement rather than contradict one another.

Does Jesus's death conquer the devil, appease God's wrath, or produce healing for believers? Even one of the contributors to the book Smith cites for this debate argues that the answer is all three.[57] In still other cases, not all of the options debated have been widely held throughout church history. With respect to divorce and remarriage, Roman Catholics have with rare exceptions historically held to no divorce or remarriage at all. Until the second half of the twentieth century, Protestants almost universally permitted divorce and remarriage only in the cases of marital unfaithfulness (Matt. 19:9) or an unbelieving spouse wishing to leave (1 Cor. 7:15–16).[58] The view that permits divorce but not remarriage is largely an anomaly limited to twentieth-century fundamentalism and a few precursors and heirs. In church history, the view that permits divorce for a fairly broad variety of reasons is found almost exclusively since about 1970 and arguably reflects simple biblical disobedience.[59] Because evangelicals, until quite recently, have been almost exclusively Protestant, there really is only one *major* evangelical perspective on this issue.

More important than any of these responses to Smith is the doctrinal agreement that remains despite all the diversity he has highlighted. Surf the web almost at random and locate the doctrinal or confessional statements of any ten major evangelical denominations or associations of churches; ten more from independent evangelical missionary organizations; and ten more from other forms of parachurch ministry, such as campus ministries, family ministries, or ministries of compassion and social justice. Of course, one will find differences among them, but it is striking to see as well how much agreement there is concerning the authority of the Bible, the doctrine of the Trinity, the attributes of God, the mighty acts of God in history, the person and work of Jesus Christ, the personhood of the Holy Spirit, the nature of humanity created in God's image, the universal sinfulness of humanity, the inability of humanity ever to merit God's righteousness and save itself, the possibility of salvation through the death and bodily resurrection of Jesus, salvation by grace through faith alone, Christ's ascension to heaven, his sending of the Spirit at Pentecost, and his coming visible return on some future day to judge the living and the dead. There will be agreement on Christ's sinlessness, on the need for growth in Christian holiness following rebirth, on the impossibility of full glorification until the age to come, and on the distinction between the local and the global church but also on the importance of Christian fellowship in corporate gatherings of God's people; on the need for prayer, Bible study, evangelism and mission, deeds of mercy and service to humanity; and on the importance of some form of baptism and the Lord's Supper and of having duly chosen and recognized church leaders.[60] The list could go on in considerable detail; it is a pity Smith did not balance his catalog of diversity with another catalog demonstrating the theological unity that exists even outside of his new home in Catholicism.

Finally, if one compares the diversity that remains within evangelicalism with the diversity of Christendom worldwide, one sees just how relatively monolithic evangelicalism really is.[61] There is more than enough exegetical and theological agreement among believers in biblical inerrancy, when compared with the diversity of views among errantist Christians, to make inerrancy a very worthwhile concept. The errantist must pick and choose which parts of Scripture to treat as inspired and therefore as truthful, which is either hopelessly subjective or requires some extrabiblical norm or criterion.[62] But which of many competing criteria do we then choose? That which liberates women or the poor? That which highlights God as in process? That which focuses on God's love rather than his justice or judgment? Or that which does not involve the miraculous or supernatural? One could make a list as long as Smith's list of multiple-view books! And what authority enables a person to decide among these competing criteria? One can affiliate with a religious communion like Roman Catholicism, Eastern Orthodoxy, or Mormonism that has a magisterium with an earthly leader who can function as the final arbiter of truth, but is commitment to a church whose leaders frequently change and who may repudiate past beliefs really preferable to an unchanging book or collection of books deemed to be divine in origin? When the pope, patriarch, or prophet goes astray, he needs to convince only a small group of his closest followers, who might then let him cling to power and wreak havoc for far too long. When evangelical Protestant leaders working *from Scripture* cannot convince a majority of the communities they serve of the truth and biblically based nature of their views, they will be ousted from their positions of leadership. Do we want something more akin to a democracy or to a monarchy in our churches? As for *liberal* Protestantism, when the Bible, even in all its diversity, cannot be appealed to as the final and most important arbiter, then the stage is set for anarchy and as a result, ironically, the reintroduction of totalitarianism.[63]

Carlos Bovell leaves the door open for some new form of inerrancy but resists current formulations, especially the Chicago Statement. He sees it as too tied to a propositional view of revelation and to a correspondence theory of truth. He suspects progress could be made if one followed Kevin Vanhoozer's appropriation of speech-act theory, identifying the locutions, illocutions, and perlocutions of the various literary genres of Scripture.[64] The *locution* is the meaning of an utterance within its context; its *illocution* is what it intends or accomplishes by its being spoken; and its *perlocution* is the way it is received and the results or effects that reception creates. To illustrate, the locution of my friend's outburst in a stuffy summer room without air conditioning, "It sure is hot in here," is an assertion about the temperature. Its illocution is likely a plea for a window to be opened or a fan turned on. Its perlocution is whatever I do or don't do as a result of his outburst. The truth of a speech act requires an utterance to accomplish what it sets out to do.[65] Vanhoozer's work is indeed very attractive, but it is scarcely at odds with the Chicago Statement. All illocutions and perlocutions require locutions on which they are based. And the truth of locutions depends on their underlying propositions and on whether those propositions correspond to various external realities.[66]

Debates about Harmonization

Maybe the biggest issue in all the methodological debates involves the practice of harmonization. In my thirty years of membership in the Society of Biblical Literature, the world's largest scholarly organization of professors of the Bible from just about any tertiary-level institution, whether confessional or nonconfessional in its perspective, there are two words that I have heard more than any others used as conversation stoppers. If a speaker wants to dismiss a more conservative scholarly perspective on an issue, all that is needed is to say something like "Well, that's just *apologetics*" or "That's a *harmonizing* approach." To actually mount a theological argument for a historic Christian position is enough to merit severe censure, never mind that members regularly argue for countless unorthodox Christian views. And to claim to be a responsible biblical historian while harmonizing seemingly discordant data in the Scriptures, or between the Bible and extracanonical information, dooms one to rejection and ridicule.[67]

The irony is that such charges are almost never pressed by scholars with firsthand experience in classical historiography. The standard scholarly works on the life of Alexander the Great, for example, rely on a variety of ancient sources. The oldest still in existence come from Plutarch and Arrian, who wrote in the late first and early second centuries AD. Each claims to rely on multiple older written sources, but no such source has been preserved. Both sketch reasonably compatible outlines of the broad contours of Alexander's life and exploits, especially once he succeeded his father Philip as king of Macedon. Yet there are numerous places where these two Greek biographers appear to contradict each other. At times classical historians believe they have good reason for charging either Plutarch or Arrian with making mistakes, but more often than not the differences are accounted for because of the ideological emphases, principles of selection, styles of narrative, influences from oral tradition, and so on. In other words, all of the approaches evangelical biblical scholars use to explain apparent discrepancies among parallel passages in Scripture are used by classical historians to analyze other ancient histories and biographies from antiquity. Classical historians have even adopted "additive harmonization," which solves an apparent contradiction between parallel accounts by affirming that someone said or did what both sources claim the person said or did. Thus Plutarch (*Alex*. 16.7–8) declares that in the battle with the Barbarians at the Granicus River, thirty-four of Alexander's soldiers were killed, nine of whom were footmen for whom Alexander had bronze statues erected in their memory. Arrian (*Anab.* 1.16.4) says that brazen statues were erected after this battle for twenty-five territorial troops (a more elite corps) who fell. It seems hardly coincidental that 25 + 9 = 34. Presumably Alexander wanted to honor each of his fallen soldiers in some way for a valiant battle.[68]

The same range of methods appears in the major works from which historians reconstruct a life of Julius Caesar. A striking analogy to the problem of the four Gospels appears with the four extant accounts of Julius's crossing the Rubicon River and committing himself to the civil war that would lead to his becoming emperor and turning the Roman Republic into his empire. No one knows for sure the exact date or location of this crossing. Not all of the details in each account readily square with one another; one even contains a narrative of the miraculous. Still, classicists have no doubt that the event was historical (and of historic significance).[69] One could turn to Josephus's *Jewish Antiquities* and his *Jewish War* for still further examples, all the more telling because the same author wrote both and did not believe that he was contradicting himself![70]

We must therefore allow for a full range of methodological possibilities when comparing and contrasting parallel historical accounts in the Bible, such as Samuel and Kings versus Chronicles, or one Gospel versus another, as well as when considering seemingly divergent theological emphases from one biblical author to the next. There is no question that some writers have proposed strained harmonizations in their quest to resolve problems of apparent contradictions. The most famous in the past generation was Harold Lindsell's suggestion that Peter denied Jesus six times (despite each Gospel's mentioning only three), in order to account for minor differences among some of the narratives.[71] Perhaps the most ludicrous in the history of the church was the affirmation of Osiander, a sixteenth-century Reformer, that Jesus raised Jairus's daughter twice, because some of the details differ between Matthew's and Mark's accounts (Matt. 9:18–26; Mark 5:21–43).[72] But strained and even silly harmonizations do not discredit the method altogether, any more than inappropriately claiming major theological disagreements based on minor narrative variations discredits the entire discipline of redaction criticism, the study of the distinctive theologies of the four Gospel writers.[73] Nor are such artificial uses typical of the overall method of harmonization.[74]

Indeed, recent studies of oral tradition and social memory have demonstrated that the processes involved behind ancient historiography and biography were far more complex than almost any major school of thought acknowledges.[75] Prior to a written document's being considered sacred, oral tradition preserved intact, in multiple forms, the most crucial elements of given episodes while feeling free to vary what was included, omitted, highlighted, explained, or abbreviated from one recounting to another. Public checks and balances by leaders in the communities that treasured these traditions, along with their constant reuse, deeply embedded certain features in the core of the tradition. The analogy to the modern children's game of telephone[76] is about as far from what actually happened in antiquity as one could imagine![77] To be sure, historians and biographers wrote for ideological reasons; no other form of history or biography was ever invented until about two hundred years ago. Sometimes the ideologies could lead to inappropriate distortions of history, but at other times the very ideologies being commended required that people tell their stories accurately.[78]

Even additive harmonization deserves a larger place in the study of biblical history than it typically receives. Countless short sayings of Jesus not tied inextricably to one context in the Gospels were doubtless reused in multiple settings, not only by the evangelists, but also by Jesus himself.[79] If Jesus *didn't* repeat himself frequently, he would have been the only itinerant teacher in the history of the world not to do so! Recognizing how often scriptural narratives group material together topically or thematically actually goes hand in hand with acknowledging Jesus's reuse of similar material in numerous contexts. Many texts printed as parallels in typical Gospel synopses probably are not true parallels. At the same time, arguing that there was more than one "Last Supper" to account for the differences among the Gospels in their narratives of that event obviously *would be* special pleading!

It is curious how emotionally charged the attacks against harmonization can become. Maybe this is because various scholars are unwilling to seriously countenance the possibility that one of their cherished contradictions in Scripture might actually be resolved. Perhaps they recognize the greater authority that does attach to the Bible if it is without error, and they are not prepared to submit to that authority. It is hard to know. Sparks, for example, attacks my harmonization of the apparent tension between John and the Synoptics on the day of Jesus's Last Supper with remarkably jaundiced language, imputing to me (and to the biblical authors, if my view is right) all kinds of motives to which he has no access. John has frequently been said to date Jesus's crucifixion to the day on which the lambs were slaughtered in preparation for the evening meal that began the weeklong Festival of Passover and Unleavened Bread, whereas the Synoptics have the crucifixion a day later. To deal with this problem, one of several common suggestions throughout church history has been that a closer look at key passages in John discloses how he actually agrees with the Synoptics. I have explained the details repeatedly elsewhere, so I need not repeat myself here.[80] But allow me to reuse what I have written only once previously to illustrate the emotive language that Sparks employs in dismissing my view as not worthy of serious consideration:

> In just the three pages in which he rejects my views, for example, Sparks asks, "Why did John *go out of his way* to dissociate Jesus's final meal from the Passover?" He states that I fail to explain "why John would . . . *push so very hard* to associate the crucifixion with the Passover, juxtaposing it *in blatant fashion* with the correct day and time of the slaying of the Passover lambs." He points out what he calls "one of the *most glaring* problems" of my thesis. He considers my approach to be "based *largely on conjecture* and with *so many dangling* questions." He again insists that "John's Gospel *is everywhere at pains to insure* that [Jesus's last meal] is not [the Passover]." Finally, Sparks quotes E. J. Young's wise words against proposing strained and forced harmonizations rather than admitting we have no solutions to problems. Sparks concludes, "I cannot but agree with Young's sentiment. Harmonizations so historically and rationally *strained* as those offered by . . . Blomberg cannot pass as *serious* scholarly readings of the biblical text, mainly because the authors present their *very improbable* reconstructions as if they are likely or even highly probable." (all emphasis added)[81]

I agree with Young's principle but disagree with Sparks's application of it to my argument.[82] The three texts that are debated are John 13:1–2; 18:28; and 19:14. I offer no unsupported conjectures but point out actual historical and textual features to support the suggestions that the supper of John 13:2 is the Passover mentioned in verse 1, that the meal in 18:28 is the lunchtime meal the morning after the nighttime Passover feast (esp. in light of 13:39), and that the day of Preparation for the Passover mentioned in 19:14 means the day of Preparation for the Sabbath in Passover week (in light of 19:31 and 42), not the day before the Passover began. One may or may not find my arguments persuasive; that is the stuff of what exegetes debate. But there are no "glaring problems," mere "conjectures," or "dangling questions" that I have failed to address. Nor does Sparks ever give any actual evidence to support his charges of "strained" harmonization and very "improbable reconstructions." His discussion is entirely ad hominem. The evidence that does exist, outside of the debated meanings of these specific verses, which suggests that John wanted to associate Jesus's crucifixion with the day and time of the slaughter of the Passover lambs, boils down to a single clause in a single verse: the portion of John 19:14 that says it was "about noon" (lit., "the sixth hour").[83]

Would a largely Gentile audience for the Fourth Gospel pick up from this brief comment a reference to a temple ritual that is otherwise left unmentioned? And if the point is about the theological meaning rather than the historical timing of his death, why does John make this comment in conjunction with Jesus's sentencing rather than his expiring on the cross? Where exactly is John's "blatant" juxtaposition of information that Sparks alleges to have found? Where do we actually see John as "pushing so hard"? Where do we see him "going out of his way" to dissociate Jesus's Last Supper from the Passover? Why would he narrate the prediction of Judas's denial and Jesus's betrayal in exactly the same context as in the Synoptics if that were his goal? Again, my point is not so much to argue for the exegesis that persuades me the most but rather to inquire as to what is at stake for Sparks that he has to use this emotionally charged and factually inaccurate language here and throughout his writings as he attacks inerrancy and biblical reliability.[84] This is a prime example of the heightened emotions that frequently arise in debates about harmonization.

Avoiding the Opposite Extreme

Perhaps part of the answer to this question involves the inability or unwillingness of certain critics to distinguish between inerrantists who are nuanced in their interpretations and sensitive to the complexities of the biblical text and those who use inerrancy as if it were a blunt tool designed to bludgeon those who opt for different exegetical conclusions than theirs and force them into conformity with a certain interpretive tradition. In 1999, for example, Robert Thomas and David Farnell edited a collection of essays, largely representing perspectives of the Master's Seminary in California, titled *The Jesus Crisis*. Several of the contributors, but especially Thomas and Farnell themselves, sternly rebuked fellow evangelicals for utilizing such tools as form and redaction criticism and opting for solutions to apparent discrepancies in the Gospels *other* than merely additive harmonization.[85] In one passage, Thomas even referred to such scholars, including me, as experiencing a "satanic blindness."[86] Over the years Thomas has penned a raft of books and articles criticizing mainstream evangelicals and inerrantists for their views on hermeneutics, critical methodology, and any eschatology other than an old-line dispensationalism.[87] A list of those censured reads like an all-star lineup of inerrantist scholars (see chap. 4, note 5); I should be honored to be included in the list!

In his most recent book on inerrancy, Norman Geisler joins William Roach to criticize the work of a variety of scholars ranging all the way from Bart Ehrman, self-confessed agnostic and ex-evangelical who would strongly disavow biblical inerrancy, to Darrell Bock, Dallas Seminary professor and one of the world's leading inerrantist New Testament scholars. Apparently unable to distinguish between genuine contradictions of inerrancy and legitimate in-house inerrantist debates on exegetical, hermeneutical, or methodological questions, Geisler and Roach tar all those they criticize with the same brush. Whether those criticized recognize it or not, Geisler and Roach count them as having denied or threatened inerrancy.[88] If Farnell, Thomas, and Geisler and Roach were to be consistent and chastise every Old or New Testament commentator whose views match those they demonize, they would scarcely find a biblical scholar left in the Evangelical Theological Society who would pass muster in their eyes. Little wonder that a Sparks or a Bovell finds no hope in this kind of inerrantism. Sadder still are the numerous examples of people I have met who, like Ehrman, have given up on the faith altogether because they were taught that if a person found one error in Scripture, the entire Christian faith might as well be abandoned.[89] There are several intellectually viable perspectives between inerrantism and agnosticism/atheism,[90] so that it is academically irresponsible and spiritually detrimental to the Christian mission to claim otherwise.[91]

But it cannot be stressed strongly enough that the Thomases and Geislers of the world do not speak for the vast majority of evangelicals and inerrantists around the globe. Thomas was a point person in founding the Master's Seminary and breaking away from Biola University and its Talbot Theological Seminary in protest against their retreat from fundamentalism. Yet today Biola has the largest and most influential apologetics program in the world, and they are inerrantist to boot. Geisler was livid when the ETS failed to produce the required two-thirds vote to force open theists Clark Pinnock and John Sanders to resign from the society in 2003. (In Pinnock's case there was not even a one-third vote.)[92] For years prior to that, Geisler had made life miserable for Murray Harris, staunch defender of the bodily resurrection of Jesus, publicly speaking and writing against him without fairly representing his views, trying to get him fired from Trinity Evangelical Divinity School and defrocked from the Evangelical Free Church of America, simply because Harris's understanding of Jesus's resurrected body did not precisely match Geisler's.[93] But an ETS-commissioned team of theological experts and longtime ETS members (Roger Nicole, Millard Erickson, and Bruce Demarest) exonerated Harris of Geisler's charges against him.[94] So Geisler finally resigned from the ETS but continues to write as if he has some responsibility or authority to challenge the results of its in-house proceedings.[95] The mass exodus he hoped to lead in protest against the ETS utterly failed to materialize, so he began referring to the ETS in his public speaking as the Formerly Evangelical Theological Society! Geisler accuses countless evangelicals of helping to erode inerrancy, and he feels a responsibility to "expose"[96] us as out of sync with mainstream inerrantism (not unlike calling Ronald Reagan and the two George Bushes too *left* wing to have been true Republicans!), but one needs to look at Geisler's own theological pilgrimage. Consider just the series of institutions at which he taught in sequence, each time moving on in part due to dissatisfaction with insufficiently conservative positions held by colleagues, even though each school was yet further to the "right," theologically and politically, than the previous one: Trinity Evangelical Divinity School, Dallas Seminary, Liberty University, Southern Evangelical Seminary (which he founded), and Veritas Seminary (which he cofounded).[97] Now exactly who is moving in what direction?

Conclusion

A solid block of mainstream biblical scholarship, by no means all evangelical, (1) recognizes that the biblical texts have been preserved remarkably well, (2) realizes the sensible choices involved in the creation of the biblical canon, and (3) knows that all major translations adequately represent the Scriptures in modern languages. When it comes to the accuracy of Scripture, however, the most that can be said is that there is an increasingly large group of scholars outside of evangelicalism who affirm, on the basis of historical investigation, that a fair amount of the Bible can be believed, especially with respect to the historical Jesus, even though they are not the scholars who for the most part receive media attention.[98]

Clearly more is at stake on this topic. One can concede that we have highly reliable texts and translations of Scripture and that no other books seriously rival the biblical ones for inclusion in the canon and yet still not adopt anything like historic Christian faith. After all, just having good translations of accurate copies of the right books of the Bible doesn't make their *contents* truthful. When we turn to questions of Scripture's reliability and trustworthiness, most people, even if only intuitively, recognize that if the Bible is even substantially accurate, the logical corollary that follows is that they must surrender their lives to belief in Jesus and obedience to God's Word. I am continually impressed today, as throughout my life, with the number of people who claim to have intellectual objections to the historic Christian faith (and some of them genuinely do), but if I converse with them long enough, their biggest barriers are existential ones.[99] They want to remain in charge of their own beliefs and behaviors and not submit to any ultimate authority outside of themselves. So it is not surprising that the historic Christian view of the full trustworthiness of Scripture comes under so much attack.

Far more subtly, one way to maintain some measure of personal power and autonomy is to appoint oneself watchdog for the larger Christian community or some considerable segment of it. If one can wield institutional authority to exclude those who disagree with the finer points of one's own articulation of biblical truth, so much the better![100] Given the extent of all human finitude and fallenness, I prefer to exercise caution and commend to others considerable restraint in this arena lest we be found to be fighting against God (Acts 5:39) and have to answer to him for our actions on judgment day.[101]

The rhetoric and passion seem to become even more intense when one turns to the question of acceptable literary genres in the Bible. Must Genesis be interpreted as affirming a historical Adam and Eve? Are the books of Job and Jonah factual or theological fiction? Can Isaiah be viewed as a composite of two or three documents? Might Daniel have been written in the second century BC because it prophesies so explicitly about events that span several centuries all the way up to the desecration of the Jerusalem temple in 167 BC? Can any parts of the Gospels or Acts be properly labeled myth or legend, and what would those labels mean? Can the pseudonymity of New Testament Epistles ever be consistent with inerrancy? Chapter 5 turns to these kinds of questions.

5

Aren't Several Narrative Genres of the Bible Unhistorical?

The so-called aggressive atheists of our day love to lampoon the book of Jonah. Confidently asserting that they could never believe in the story of someone swallowed by a great fish and regurgitated alive three days later, they dismiss the Bible as full of fairy tales—or better, fishy tales![1] A second Old Testament book often dismissed as entirely unhistorical, even by sober scholars, is Job, with its extreme examples of suffering and reward, its stylized and repetitive speeches by Job and his friends and God himself, and its underlying subtext of the contest between Satan and Yahweh.[2] Classic examples of the "assured results" of biblical criticism that often perplex the beginning theological student also include the claims that Isaiah is really made up of two or three different collections of prophecies written centuries apart from each other and that Daniel, purporting to describe the sixth-century BC prophet's predictions about the future of Israel, was actually written just after the fulfillment of all of his most specific prophecies in the middle of the second century BC.[3]

Many college students taking a one-semester introduction to the Old Testament or even a course surveying the whole Bible initially encounter problems of historicity as soon as they discuss the opening chapters of Genesis. Can anyone today seriously believe that the world was created in six twenty-four-hour periods of time only six thousand years ago, that there was a historical Adam and Eve created directly by God as completely sinless, and that their disobedience in eating the fruit of a literal tree of the knowledge of good and evil has made all subsequent humans inherit "original sin"?[4] Once Genesis 1–3 is called into question, is there any reason to accept the rest of Scripture as anything more than pious myth or legend?

Turning to the New Testament Letters, what about the common claims that more than half of the Epistles were not written by the individuals whose names appear as their authors in their opening verses?[5] What about the mysterious book of Revelation, which appears to recount John's Spirit-given visions of events surrounding the end of the world? Are these also to be interpreted as snapshots of genuine future events?[6]

The issue addressed in this chapter is that of the literary form or genre of biblical books or their components. The Old Testament contains books of history, wisdom, law, and prophecy. The New Testament books represent the genres of gospel, acts, epistle, and apocalypse. Each of these can be subdivided into numerous more specific subgenres, and each requires principles of interpretation appropriate to the literary form involved.[7] This is just as true with narrative stories as with any other large genre. Virtually everyone in the history of the church has recognized that at least small parts of the Bible that are written in narrative form do not intend to recount things that actually happened. When Jesus is the narrator of such stories, about half of the time the Gospel writers call them "parables," a well-known form of illustrative storytelling among ancient rabbis.[8] So it is perfectly appropriate to ask questions of form or genre for books like Job and Jonah or sections of books like the opening chapters of Genesis. If there is good historical or exegetical support for identifying such texts as something other than ancient history writing, then *not* to interpret them as such would misrepresent the original intentions of their authors and violate the standard grammatical-historical hermeneutic of interpreting Scripture.[9]

How do these observations square with the church's historic belief in biblical inerrancy, discussed in chapter 4? If we return to the Chicago Statement (a carefully crafted document from the late 1970s, signed by 334 scholars near the beginning of the decade-long work of the International Council on Biblical Inerrancy), we discover numerous statements relevant to these issues. Article 8 includes the clear statement "We affirm that God in His Work of inspiration utilized the distinctive personalities and literary styles of the writers whom He had chosen and prepared."[10] Article 13 elaborates at some length:

> We deny that it is proper to evaluate Scripture according to standards of truth and error that are alien to its usage or purpose. We further deny that inerrancy is negated by Biblical phenomena such as a lack of modern technical precision, irregularities of grammar or spelling, observational descriptions of nature, the reporting of falsehoods, the use of hyperbole and round numbers, the topical arrangement of material, variant selections of material in parallel accounts, or the use of free citations.[11]

The key clause here is "standards of truth and error that are alien to its usage or purpose." The standard of truth in a parable is the spiritual point or points that its author intends to make. It is irrelevant whether or not there ever was a man robbed and left for dead by the side of the Jerusalem-to-Jericho road who was bypassed by both a priest and a Levite but lavishly aided by a Samaritan. Jesus intends to teach his followers that they should emulate the compassion of the Samaritan *in this story*, not allowing religious duty to become an excuse for not performing acts of mercy, and to recognize even enemies as neighbors.[12] To insist that there was an actual Good Samaritan would impose a standard of truth alien to a parable's purpose. On the other hand, the person who decides that an enemy cannot be a neighbor[13] is denying the truthfulness of this text, even if that person believes the account of the Good Samaritan represents a true, historical event!

Therefore, the question that must be asked of every proposal about the literary genre or form of a given biblical text is whether or not the case being made is persuasive. Although I know of no recent parable scholarship that defends the view, laypeople sometimes wonder if the story of the Rich Man and Lazarus in Luke 16:19–31 is not a parable but a historical account of two men who had recently died when Jesus told his story.[14] It is often pointed out that this is the only story told by Jesus in which characters are named (Lazarus and Abraham) and in which the afterlife is described. The context of the passage (coming right on the heels of three unambiguous parables in 15:1–16:13) and the literary form (a short illustrative narrative with a master figure, contrasting subordinates, and a surprise reversal of expectation) make it overwhelmingly likely that the passage is indeed parabolic fiction.[15] But no one ever charges that only those interpreters on one side of this debate believe in inerrancy. The question is simply one about the most likely literary form of the passage.

Old Testament Examples

Genesis 1 and Creation

We must apply the identical methodology to the kinds of questions raised at the beginning of this chapter. Does belief in biblical inerrancy commit one to believing in the creation of the universe only six thousand years ago? Interestingly, even scientific creationists (who think there is evidence in nature for a young earth) typically require at least ten thousand years to have elapsed since creation.[16] They have to interpret the genealogies in any or all of Genesis 1–11 as listing key ancestors in various family trees, with dozens of individuals omitted. They rightly appeal to the language used for fathering or "begetting" as loose enough to refer merely to one who was an ancestor of someone else. They observe gaps in various biblical genealogies when compared with their equally biblical parallels (the classic example is Matt. 1:1–17 versus Luke 3:23–38). They may note similar phenomena among other ancient Near Eastern genealogies.[17] But once they take the biblical text in this "unnatural" but quite plausible way, in order to harmonize it with their scientific findings, then the door is open for anyone else to do the same thing.[18]

Believers in inerrancy have in fact held to a wide variety of positions on Genesis 1, all of which are in keeping with a much older earth, as the vast majority of all scientific investigation suggests.[19] Some have proposed progressive creation, in which the "days" of Genesis 1 correspond to long periods of time. This is sometimes also called the day-age theory. Some of these interpreters have added that God then punctuated these aeons with the direct creation of each new entity or creature as described in the text. Some opt for forms of theistic evolution in which God creates the universe with all the mechanisms built in to give rise, in his perfect timing, to each new development of the creative "week."[20] Others posit a gap of billions of years between the original creation of the universe (Gen. 1:1) and the organizing activity of God to bring order out of the chaos implied in Genesis 1:2. Still others view the chapter as utilizing a much more literary framework, given the poetic form that dominates the Hebrew text, along with the parallels between what is created on the first and fourth, second and fifth, and third and sixth days. For these interpreters the author's intention is almost entirely to narrate the "who" rather than the "how" of creation. Nestled among polytheistic societies that had different gods for different parts of nature, the Israelites were unique in claiming there was one Lord God, Yahweh, who created all that exists and was not to be equated with *any* of the gods of the other peoples and their faiths.[21] Finally, John Walton has recently made an intriguing case for seeing Genesis 1 as depicting God coming into this world as a sovereign taking up residence in a temple, thereby shifting the focus from original creation altogether.[22]

Evangelical interpreters should be free to debate the respective strengths and weaknesses of all these suggestions and to adopt whichever they find most historically and exegetically compelling. Throughout the ages Jews and Christians have suggested a variety of approaches; the claim that everyone before the rise of modern science took this chapter completely literally is simply false.[23] Belief in inerrancy, at least as defined by the Chicago Statement, does not preclude any of the interpretive options presented here. What *is* inconsistent with scriptural inerrancy is the claim that there is no God behind creation at all. Equally excluded are pantheism (that God is everything and therefore not distinct from creation) and polytheism (that different gods are responsible for different parts of creation). Indeed, even a form of monotheism that would attribute creation to an entity other than the God of Scripture would be excluded.

Genesis 2–3 and the Fall of Humanity

How does inerrancy affect interpretation of Genesis 2–3? Must there have been a historical Adam and Eve who consciously violated the express commandments of God? Many scholars, including a few evangelicals, think not. After all, two characters in a story whose names come from the Hebrew words for "man" and "life" sound very much like what one would expect from an archetypal narrative designed to communicate all humanity's fall into sin.[24] Some who disagree reply that *ʾādām* becomes a proper name at the very latest by Genesis 4:25, when the article ("the") in Hebrew no longer precedes it. Furthermore, his name appears in genealogies with other names that are to be understood as referring to real people, while Jesus and the apostles in the New Testament, including in theologically crucial passages about the nature of humanity (esp. Rom. 5:14; 1 Cor. 15:22, 45; and 1 Tim. 2:13–14), refer back to him as if he were a real person.[25]

Part of the issue here lies in carefully thinking through the implications of each theory. Nothing in principle should prevent the person who upholds inerrancy from adopting a view that sees *ʾādām* ("man" or Adam) and *ḥawwâ* ("life" or Eve) as symbols for *every* man and woman, created in the image of God but sinful by virtue of their own rebellious choices in succumbing to Satan's[26] lures. But the question that remains for *all* interpreters, except for those who deny almost the entire fossil record that suggests humanlike creatures have existed for millions of years, is how *Homo sapiens* got to be this way. The thoroughgoing atheist or naturalist has no compelling explanation for why it is that humanity alone, of all the creatures of the world, has a God-consciousness, or even a self-consciousness or self-reflective ability. Why do only human beings label certain behaviors as moral and others as immoral (even when they are not always agreed as to what belongs in each category)? Why do we treat one another as accountable and therefore punishable for evil and injustice?[27] When we think about the heroic efforts of people in times of war, terrorism, or natural disaster, including the self-sacrifice that even nonreligious people often make, and then further reflect on the horrific crimes unleashed by various human beings, including religious ones, we recognize the astonishing capacity for good and evil in our species. When we are honest with ourselves, we recognize the potential for both good and evil in ourselves as well.

Naturalistic evolution has not even come close to a satisfactory explanation of these phenomena. We may well euthanize the most dangerous of apes or killer whales, but we do not try them before a jury of their peers. The very concept of accountability for the destruction they wreak does not even remotely resemble how we hold our fellow human beings accountable for illegal or immoral activity. If we reject a more "literal" reading of Genesis 2–3 as providing the explanation of human nature, we must then ask how reading these chapters less literally and more symbolically better accounts for the origin of human nature as we know it.

One answer, nicely articulated by a British evangelical commentator of a generation ago, Derek Kidner, observes that Adam and Eve are set in a context similar to the Neolithic or first metalworking cultures of about 8,000–10,000 years ago, seen especially in the descriptions in Genesis 4:19–24, rather than in a setting of the earliest known toolmakers and artists or their most remote ancestors. "On this view, Adam, the first true man, will have had as contemporaries many creatures of comparable intelligence, widely distributed over the world."[28] But if God singled out two such creatures on which to place his unique image, or even specially created Adam and Eve with this additional feature, making them his vice-regents over creation, and demonstrating that there is no natural bridge from animal to humanity, he may then have bestowed his image on their contemporaries "to bring them into the same realm of being," as Kidner puts it. He suspects "there may be a biblical hint of such a situation in the surprising impression of an already populous earth given by the words and deeds of Cain in 4:14, 17."[29] At any rate, "what is quite clear . . . is . . . that mankind is a unity, created in God's image, and fallen in Adam by the one act of disobedience; and these things are as strongly asserted on this understanding of God's word as on any other."[30]

C. J. Collins supplements this approach with some ideas from C. S. Lewis, who imagined God as imprinting his image on a mammal evolved enough so that it now had the physiology to be able to experience "a new kind of consciousness which could say 'I' and 'me,' which could look upon itself as an object, which knew God, which could make judgments of truth, beauty and goodness, and which was so far above time that it could perceive time flowing past."[31] Collins concludes that "nothing requires us to abandon monogenesis altogether for some form of polygenesis; rather, a modified monogenesis, which keeps Adam and Eve, can do the job."[32] In any event, Genesis 2–3 cannot be pure fiction. But how literally or figuratively we are to take the accompanying details that support the historical core of the text remains fully debatable, even for inerrantists. The genre of much of Genesis 1–11 remains a puzzle; historical narrative as the ancients would have recognized it begins in earnest only with the call of Abram in Genesis 12.[33] John Goldingay labels chapters 2–3 a "historical parable,"[34] George Coats speaks of a "primeval saga,"[35] while Kenneth Matthews thinks it is simply unique.[36] Other ancient Near Eastern texts are at best only partially parallel; as with Genesis 1, it is likely that when the ancient Israelites wrote their history in forms reminiscent of other cultures' myths, it was done deliberately to subvert those myths and attribute to the God of Israel what other peoples claimed was the purview of their own deities.[37]

The process for distinguishing the genres of Genesis 1–11 and 12–50 remains important for an analysis of any part of the Bible. In every instance, one must ask how close a particular passage is to the central story line of Scripture. Without Abraham and the patriarchs, we have no unconditional covenant with his offspring. Without Moses and the exodus, we have no giving of the law or paradigm for God's liberating activity to come. Without Israel's conquering (in part) the promised land, the entire Deuteronomic covenant makes little sense. The main story line of the judges in the early league of Israelite tribes, followed by the kings of the united and divided monarchies, the exiling of Israel and Judah, and their repatriation—this story line forms the narrative framework of the Old Testament, into which everything else is fitted. Historical reliability, again by the historiographical standards of each era, is far more significant for these core events than for more peripheral ones, which have less bearing on God's history of salvation for humanity.[38]

The Book of Job

What, then, might fit into a more peripheral category of narrative? Perhaps the story of Job does. Apart from the land of Uz, which we are unable to locate, there are almost no historical particulars to tie the book to any other events in Old Testament history.[39] Conservative scholars have sometimes found cultural details old enough to suggest a time concurrent with the patriarchal narratives of Genesis, but we really have no way of knowing the period with any degree of confidence.[40] Commentators on various points of the theological spectrum agree that the specific subgenre is largely unparalleled within ancient literature, despite the existence of other theodicies or discussions of the problem of evil.[41] People do not normally speak to each other at any time, much less intimate companions in times of acute suffering, with the stylized poetry of the speeches of Job and his friends. If they do, their words are not memorized on the spot to be preserved for posterity. It almost defies imagination that one person should suffer such extreme loss, one misfortune at a time, each in a neat sequence, as happens to Job in the rhythmically narrated parallelism of the opening chapter. That he would gain all of this and more back at the end of his misery is even less lifelike. And even after God speaks to Job at the end of the book, he never discloses to him the cosmic contest between Satan and God that explains Job's afflictions. So how would any human narrator ever come to know about it?[42]

Of course, one can posit direct dictation from God to some later author, but if so, it flies in the face of the way God inspires most of the rest of the Bible (see, e.g., Luke 1:1–4).[43] What, after all, is at stake in questions about Job's historicity? The point of the story is that human suffering is a universal phenomenon, sometimes it is acute, and we all ask why it occurs. Many of us have acquaintances (or perhaps sometimes *are* the acquaintances) who spout pious theology wrongly applied and (like Job's friends) wind up hurting rather than helping those in need of comfort. The lesson of the book of Job is that our finitude and fallenness frequently render us incapable of understanding God's ways in such contexts. But God is still sovereign and in all things working "for the good of those who love him" (Rom. 8:28). Given Job's limited knowledge of the cosmic drama unfolding behind the scenes, he is right to protest that he has been treated unfairly. He has done nothing to deserve such acute distress, while most of the world gets off far more lightly despite having been far less godly. The friends' tit-for-tat theology of rewards and punishments for good and bad behavior fits some contexts but not Job's, and they are wrong to turn it into a one-size-fits-all generalization. God himself declares that, apart from his special revelation to Job, it is Job, rather than his friends, who has spoken rightly about God (Job 42:7).[44] All this is the spectacular contribution of Job to Scripture, and not a shred of it changes even if the entire book is parabolic rather than historical! The Jewish philosopher Maimonides recognized this as long ago as the twelfth century.[45] To say that the book of Job is wholly true and without error is to affirm the theology I have just summarized and much more that follows from it. And this is scarcely a trivial affirmation, given the number of people today and throughout history who have concluded that the worst of human suffering demonstrates that the God in which the Judeo-Christian tradition believes couldn't possibly exist. But none of this theology requires Job to have ever existed any more than the teaching of the parable of the Good Samaritan requires the Samaritan to have been a real person.[46]

As a matter of fact, however, many interpreters chart a plausible middle ground between the two alternatives of literal history and complete fiction. There is little precedent for the latter in the ancient Near East; rather, epic and legend are usually built around historical characters. Tremper Longman, an inerrantist, sees the story of Job as being about a genuine, righteous sufferer from Uz (we *do* know of towns with this name, even if we don't know if any of them corresponded to Job's Uz), which was later elaborated, especially via the highly literary nature of both the prose and the poetry in the book. References to Job in Ezekiel 14:14, 20 and James 5:11 prove inconclusive because they could be referring to either historical or literary characters. Longman concludes that we dare not be dogmatic, but he notes that the view of the book as a *māšāl* (Hebrew for "parable" and numerous other forms of figurative speech) goes all the way back to the ancient Jewish midrashic and talmudic literature (*b. Baba Batra* 15a; *y. Soṭah* 5.8/20c; *Gen. Rab.* 57.4).[47]

The Book of Jonah

Surely, however, someone might argue, Jonah must be completely historical, because Jesus himself likens his death and resurrection to Jonah's experience with the great fish: "For as Jonah was three days and three nights in the belly of a huge fish, so the Son of Man will be three days and three nights in the heart of the earth" (Matt. 12:40; cf. Luke 11:30). Actually, this does not follow at all. A contemporary preacher could predict that Christians may have to face spiritual warfare of great magnitude, "just as Frodo and his companions faced life-threatening opposition and dark powers throughout their journey to Mordor." Anyone at all familiar with J. R. R. Tolkien's *The Lord of the Rings*, or the trilogy of epic films made from it, would instantly recognize that the preacher was not affirming that any of Tolkien's characters ever existed. But they would also recognize the aptness of the comparison.[48]

Of course, Jesus goes on immediately to add that "the men of Nineveh will stand up at the judgment with this generation and condemn it; for they repented at the preaching of Jonah, and now something greater than Jonah is here" (Matt. 12:41; cf. Luke 11:32). And in one sentence 2 Kings 14:25 does refer to Jonah son of Amittai as a prophet in the days of Amaziah king of Judah. It makes no sense to say that mythical people will be a part of the final judgment, so someone believing in the complete truthfulness of Scripture should want to acknowledge that Jonah preached to the Ninevites and that many of them repented.[49] Lest this itself seem impossible, it has often been pointed out that the time in which this would have taken place (in the 760s or 750s BC) was when the Assyrian Empire was at its weakest. The land suffered plagues and a solar eclipse, and its people could therefore have been doubting their own gods and been open to a message about a more powerful God,[50] even if their collective repentance was short-lived and not passed on to subsequent generations.

But if Jonah really preached repentance to the Ninevites (Jon. 3–4), must we accept the historicity of the fish story (Jon. 2)? This chapter is quite detachable and self-contained. Remove Jonah 1:17–2:10, and you have the sailors' throwing Jonah overboard and the sea growing calm. They had been trying to reach land; even if they were unsuccessful, it is possible they were close enough once the storm had subsided for Jonah to swim to shore. We could then move directly to 3:1, where the word of the Lord comes to Jonah again. Had we never heard about the great fish, we would never imagine anything missing. To be clear, I am not saying this is what originally happened; I am merely highlighting the structure of the book and the lack of tight connections between the miracle and the rest of the narrative.[51]

For many at this point, the main problem is obviously the miraculous event. For those who exclude all supernatural activity, Jonah 2 cannot record sober fact. We will address the question of miracle more fully in the next chapter. Yet for many readers, the problem is not miracles per se but this specific kind of seemingly outlandish, grotesque, and perhaps unnecessary miracle. This is not a physical healing or exorcism, bringing great benefit to its recipient. Generically, it seems more akin to fairy tales than even to other miracle stories in the Bible. The entire book is full of humor, especially parody, irony, and satire. In almost every way, Jonah does the opposite from what one would expect of a true prophet of God, while pagan sailors offer sacrifices to Yahweh and revival breaks out in the capital city of the enemy empire. Even then Jonah begrudges God's grace to humans made in his image while resenting the death of a mere plant (because it afforded him shade)! Not surprisingly, suggestions about the overall genre of Jonah have proliferated—from allegory to parable, novel, midrash, comedy, didactic story, or satiric parody.[52] Still others find it sui generis—a genre of its own, unparalleled elsewhere[53]—or even a deconstruction of traditional historical genres.[54] On the other hand, this little book contains almost nothing about the miracle of the fish itself; all the focus in Jonah 2 is on Jonah's prayer while captive in the fish. As Desmond Alexander elaborates,

> The account of Jonah's unique rescue is not embellished with vivid descriptions of either the fish or Jonah's stay within. Indeed, the fish is mentioned in only two verses (1:17; 2:10), and even then very briefly.

> The author's portrayal of this most peculiar event is very low key; it has certainly not been included in order to heighten the dramatic quality of the narrative. This being so, why should the author have invented it, if it did not really happen?[55]

One way of defending the historicity of Jonah 2 that has frequently appealed to conservative scholars is to cite various news reports in more recent centuries of people who survived being attacked and swallowed by large fish, especially sharks, and subsequently being spit back out again. The three most commonly cited, however, do not inspire great confidence in their accuracy. The first comes from Europe in 1758,[56] so that it is impossible to confirm the report. The second involves a story from an English whaling ship in the 1890s that was later disavowed.[57] The most recent comes from Japan in 1987 but was reported only in a sensationalist tabloid, so its veracity is suspect.[58] To be sure, it is fascinating that a recent *National Geographic* article about shark attacks on humans, written without the slightest hint of any interest in the biblical book of Jonah, includes some curious gastronomical information. Sharks like to taste objects that they don't recognize and then spit them out if they don't like them. When they swallow large objects, their entire digestive systems slow down so much that they may not eat again for over a week.[59] And it has long been known that the mouths, GI tracts, and stomachs of several large fish (unlike whales, as mammals) can engorge and disgorge something as large as a human body. But at some stage, even if just in keeping Jonah alive and breathing, the biblical story intends to recount a miracle that could not have happened without God's special intervention, so it is uncertain how much help these scientific observations are.[60]

Ernst Wendland, writing as an evangelical, charts a sane middle ground between viewing the book as pure history and claiming it to be pure fiction. After a painstaking analysis of the work's structure and discourses, Wendland concludes that Jonah is fundamentally a historical account that dramatizes, for didactic and hortatory purposes, events that actually happened to the prophet of the same name in 2 Kings 14:25.[61] James Bruckner's observations turn out to be even more helpful:

> It is even possible to hold to the doctrine of the inerrancy of the original manuscripts of Scripture and regard Jonah as a unique parable about a real prophet (2 Kings 14:25). In any case, no other prophetic book is so focused on the prophet and filled with such parable-like writing.
>
> As much as I believe the events described in the book, we should resist the use of the "whale" question as a litmus test for orthodoxy. Such a question obfuscates the Word of God in Jonah and preempts a reader's discovering God's message for today. That message must not be eclipsed by our modern preoccupations with physical phenomena.[62]

Or to repeat the words of the Chicago Statement, we must not "evaluate Scripture according to standards of truth and error that are alien to its usage or purpose."

Two or Three Isaiahs?

What about a different kind of flashpoint or red-flag issue? Can a biblical book be composite? Inerrantist commentators have frequently recognized that 2 Corinthians may be the combination of more than one discrete letter of Paul,[63] just as nonevangelical scholars have occasionally argued for the unity and integrity of the letter.[64] Here again, the issues are ones of genre, alleged parallels in other literature, and the internal evidence that points to quite different contexts for different parts of the epistle as we know it. But could God have inspired two or more authors, sequentially, to collaborate on what is now preserved as a single work of Scripture? Better put, by what criterion could we possibly affirm that God could *not* do this? If John 21:24–25 most naturally reads like the imprimatur a *group* of John's followers stamped on his testimony, and such evidence leads to various theories of one or more stages of redaction of a work initiated by that disciple, nothing about the truthfulness of the contents of the work is necessarily impugned at all (even if some scholars have jumped to unwarranted conclusions from such redactional analysis).[65]

Undoubtedly the most famous and thorny proposal about composite authorship in the biblical canon involves the prophetic book of Isaiah. All but the most conservative scholars today are convinced that it combines two or three basic works, separated by centuries, and represented by chapters 1–39 and 40–66 (possibly to be subsequently separated into 40–55 and 56–66).[66] Many, when confronted with similarities in content in sections of these allegedly separate works, then propose even more elaborate theories of later redactions of the two or three basic books. A key stumbling block for many has been the sudden appearance of the actual name of a Persian king, Cyrus, in Isaiah 44:28 and 45:1 and 13, in prophecy about the restoration of Israel after the Babylonian captivity in the sixth century BC. The historical prophet Isaiah lived in the eighth century BC, and the first half of the book that bears his name is dominated by the context of the Assyrian conquest of Israel in his day and age. Chapter 40, moreover, follows almost as abruptly as possible after chapters 1–39, with its call for comfort to God's people and promise of repatriation after the Babylonian exile, although the earlier Assyrian exile had only just begun.[67]

It is of course proper to point out that one of the historical books in the Old Testament also prophesies the coming of a future king by name (Josiah, in 1 Kings 13:2, nearly three centuries before he reigned). Distinctive themes, most notably the unique title for God as the "Holy One of Israel," unite all major sections of the canonical Isaiah, while New Testament writers refer back to all three portions of the book when they cite words prophesied by "Isaiah" (e.g., Matt. 3:3 quotes Isa. 40:3; Matt. 8:17 quotes Isa. 53:4; John 12:38 quotes Isa. 53:1; Rom. 10:20–21 quotes Isa. 65:1–2).[68] On the other hand, there is often no way to decide whether those writers had in mind the prophet himself or merely the name of the book (even "the prophet Isaiah" could be shorthand for "the book of the prophet Isaiah").[69] Later prophets and/or editors could easily have intentionally created a certain thematic unity with earlier writings whose work or spirit they believed they were following. And 1 Kings 13:2 is the only other example of so specific a prophecy in the entire Bible; those who cannot imagine the historical Isaiah predicting Cyrus by name will simply view the early reference to Josiah in 1 Kings as a later redactor's gloss.[70]

The arguments on each side can be expanded. Despite claims to the contrary, some who argue for a composite Isaiah do so not because they can't believe that God could inspire a prophet to name an important king more than 150 years before his reign. They simply observe that detail after detail in the later chapters of Isaiah is written in the past or present tenses. In other words, they are not even couched as predictions but as circumstances in which the author of these chapters has lived. This observation, though, is complicated by the fact that the Hebrew perfect tense often can be used to refer to future events. Still, the most natural or "literal" reading of texts like these leads to the conclusion that their author is writing in the sixth century BC, in which case it cannot be the prophet Isaiah.[71] On the other hand, the conditions are just vague enough that perhaps we must not settle on one specific exile for a referent.[72]

Of late, applications of literary and canonical criticism to Isaiah are stressing the unity of its final form, without denying the critical consensus concerning its tradition history, which makes one wonder whether that consensus is being undermined without scholars recognizing it. If elaborate intertextual devices for the unity of the final form of Isaiah can be identified, why can they not be attributed to a single original author as well as to a single final redactor?[73] There is some evidence that "Cyrus" could in fact be a dynastic name (like "Pharaoh" in Egypt) rather than a personal name, which would temper the uniqueness of Isaiah's prophecy somewhat.[74] Babylon already was a significant power in the eighth century BC, so it is not too surprising that a prophet could foresee that it might one day conquer Assyria. And nothing anywhere in Isaiah gives any hint of the actual time lag between eighth- and sixth-century events; we know this gap only with 20/20 hindsight. Perhaps we should think of a historical Isaiah as prophesying much the way Jesus and the apostles did about Jesus's return—allowing for the possibility of a considerable interval but without any suggestion that it could not happen much more quickly.[75]

It seems that each side in this debate may have dismissed the other's arguments too readily. I do not find any conclusive evidence that enables me to exclude either option. It is striking that the name Isaiah appears sixteen times in chapters 1–39 in conjunction with the events and prophecies narrated and never again in the rest of the book.[76] *There is no claim within the text of Isaiah 40–66 for Isaianic authorship of these chapters.* The New Testament evidence is suggestive in the direction of the unity of the book but inconclusive. Ultimately, what one decides about its composition or formation need not have anything to do with biblical inerrancy at all.[77]

Daniel and Apocalyptic Literature

Our last Old Testament example is from the book of Daniel. In English Bibles it is included among the prophets; in the Hebrew canon it is part of the Writings (see chap. 2 above). It, too, is composed of two reasonably discrete sections, chapters 1–6, which depict events in the life and times of the sixth-century BC prophet Daniel; and chapters 7–12, which form a miniature apocalypse—dreams and visions about the future of Israel and other nations, including judgments of God depicted in highly stylized and symbolic form. Empires are likened to different beasts or to their horns (chaps. 7–8). Even more striking than the appearance of Cyrus by name in Isaiah is the barrage of events described in Daniel 11:2–35, culminating in a king who so profanes the Jewish temple that his sacrilege is spoken of as "the abomination that causes desolation" (v. 31). Since the middle of the second century BC, it has been possible to correlate almost all of the details of this passage with specific, momentous events in Jewish history, much of it during the intertestamental period, especially in the time of Alexander the Great (esp. 334–323 BC) and his successors (323–167 BC). The "abomination that causes desolation" (Dan. 11:31) is then naturally identified with Antiochus Epiphanes's desecration of the temple in 167 BC.[78] But immediately after this event, Daniel's predictions become so vague and general that it is no longer possible to equate them with specific past history with any confidence (vv. 36–45).[79]

Understandably, the critical consensus has concluded that Daniel 11:2–35 contains prophecy *ex eventu*—after the events. The author has written up his account of his people's history in the guise of prophecy sometime in the mid-second century.[80] Other Jewish apocalyptic writing, most notably the "animal apocalypse" of *1 Enoch* 85–90, also probably written in the second century BC, does exactly the same thing.[81] Once again, the question is one of understanding the function of the literary genre or form at hand. No ancient reader was fooled or deceived by this convention. It was understood as a way of affirming God's sovereign hand of guidance throughout the whole process, his ongoing purposes for his people even in difficult times, and his coming vindication of his elect and his plans for them.[82]

On the other hand, the presence of the book of Daniel at Qumran and its use by the sectarian literature from that Dead Sea community could suggest a third-century BC date or earlier. The Hebrew and Aramaic of Daniel seems more akin to fourth- or fifth-century BC Hebrew and Aramaic than to the forms of those languages that prevailed in the second century.[83] None of this gets us all the way back to the sixth century BC, but it would preclude all of Daniel 11 from being prophecy after the fact. As far back as the Talmud in the middle of the first millennium AD, the rabbinic tradition alleged that the "men of the great synagogue"—traditionally viewed as contemporaries of Ezra and Nehemiah in the fifth century BC—had a role to play in Daniel's editing.[84] This would match the observations just made about the language.

Once again, plausible cases can be made for additional options. Chapters 1–6, when taken as actual events of Daniel's day, in fact generate more historical conundra than do chapters 7–12, which line up nicely with subsequent events at least through the mid-second century.[85] Perhaps two works associated with the prophet Daniel and his successors, written at two different times, were combined.[86] Tremper Longman believes Daniel 11 reflects sixth-century BC prophecy but, similar to one suggestion made above about Isaiah, the prophet was not given enough revelation from God to recognize the length of time embraced by the prophecy.[87] With each of these examples, the point here is not to defend one particular solution as better than all others but to highlight how the doctrine of inerrancy remains unaffected throughout. Once we determine, as best we can, what a passage affirms, according to the conventions of its style, form, and genre, a commitment to inerrancy implies acceptance of the truth of those affirmations. But a commitment to inerrancy does not exclude a priori any given literary style, form, or genre that is not inherently deceptive.

Ernest Lucas's conclusions merit extended citation at this juncture:

> Faced with the fact that all Daniel's visions focus on the time of Antiochus Epiphanes, Collins (1993: 26) gives expression to the theological issue:

> "There is no apparent reason . . . why a prophet of the sixth century [BC] should focus minute attention on the events of the second century [BC]." One response to this is to argue that the reason is that, by giving the prediction so far ahead of time, God assures the people of the second century that he is indeed in control of history, including the situation in which they find themselves. One cannot deny that this has some plausibility. However, an evangelical scholar, Goldingay (1977: 45), can argue that this is not consistent with the picture of God revealed elsewhere in Scripture. As he puts it, "He does not give signs and reveal dates. His statements about the future are calls to decision now; he is not the God of prognosticators. He calls his people to naked faith and hope in him in the present, and does not generally bolster their faith with the kind of revelations that we are thinking of here. He does sometimes grant evidences to those who cannot believe without them, and thus we dare not exclude the possibility that this was the case with the book of Daniel. But the presumption is by no means in favour of this possibility." The argument here is not conclusive either way. Both Collins and Goldingay appeal to what they see to be the balance of (theological) probability. *Those who conclude otherwise should at least acknowledge that there is theological integrity on both sides of the argument.* (emphasis added)[88]

New Testament Examples

Matthew as Midrash?

The stakes seem higher when one turns to New Testament examples, and therefore a more thorough case study is in order. In the early 1980s, Robert Gundry published a detailed and learned commentary on the Gospel of Matthew, in which he identified the Gospel as akin to Jewish midrash.[89] More specifically, he had in mind those kinds of midrash that are often called the *rewritten Bible*. For example, the intertestamental book of *Jubilees* retells much of the story of Genesis, but with numerous additional details. It is hard to know if these come from Jewish tradition or other ancient historical sources or are simply the embellishments of the author of *Jubilees*. Perhaps he was imaginatively adding details to help each story come alive the way many preachers today will flesh out biblical stories, adding scenery, local color, dialogue, motives, and the like. At any rate, as carefully as Jews memorized, recited, studied, and discussed the Torah, there is no question that when they read a book like *Jubilees*, they would recognize the parts that corresponded to their Bible and distinguish them from the later additions.

Gundry treated Matthew's use of Mark and an expanded version of Q (see "Did Originals Originally Exist?" in chap. 1 above) exactly along these lines. Assuming that Matthew's readers would have known the story of Jesus according to Mark and according to Q, which Gundry believed were historically accurate, he could then conclude that they would have recognized the potentially unhistorical elaboration that Matthew added and would not have viewed the redactional parts of Matthew's Gospel the same way they did the traditional parts. Gundry composed an entire, detailed "theological postscript" that came at the end of his commentary, explaining why his view was consistent with inerrancy. On his view, Matthew tried to deceive no one, he employed an established Jewish genre of writing, and his audience would have understood exactly what he was doing, not imagining his embellishments to be making the same kinds of truth claims as his core material from Mark and Q.[90]

Because Gundry was a member of the Evangelical Theological Society (ETS), which requires its members annually to reaffirm belief in biblical inerrancy, a lively discussion began, leading to a variety of presentations and publications critiquing Gundry's approach and assessing whether or not it truly was compatible with inerrancy.[91] Norman Geisler spearheaded a movement to have Gundry ousted from the organization, believing his views to be incompatible with the doctrine. At an open forum on the topic at the annual convention of the ETS, the majority of the speakers spoke in favor of retaining Gundry's membership, even while almost all of them disagreed with his specific approach to Matthew. They argued that it was not the role of the society to censure a member or try to censor his publications if he had made a good case for how his views could be consistent with inerrancy. Rather, scholars who disagreed with his approach to Matthew should present their arguments via all the normal academic outlets of papers and publications. If there was little of scholarly merit to Gundry's proposals, they would gain few supporters, and there would be little long-term effect.[92]

Geisler, however, turned the event into a political campaign, circulating advertisements, calling friends who would not otherwise have come to the ETS meetings, and in general drumming up support for attendance at a business meeting where the issue was to be brought to a vote. As a result, triple the number of members appeared than those who had actually participated in the previous discussion. Gundry's views were simplistically presented, highlighting only the most egregious parts of his proposals,[93] and the membership present voted by just over the necessary two-thirds majority to expel Gundry from the society. Apart from the politicization of the event, it is likely that Gundry would have remained a member in good standing. After all, no less a conservative stalwart than D. A. Carson had written a significant review of Gundry's work, explaining that the questions at stake were hermeneutical ones, involving the question of literary genre, to be addressed via scholarly debate rather than by political action. His words need to be heard again in a new generation that is far more likely to encounter fairly skewed summaries of Gundry's work and never read it firsthand:

> It must first of all be pointed out that evangelicals will entirely miss the mark if they simply cry "Inerrancy!" and accuse Gundry of abandoning the camp. One may reasonably argue that Gundry is cutting a new swath, or that traditional formulations of the doctrine of Scripture should now be tightened up; but as such formulations stand, Gundry in no way contravenes them. Intelligent response to Gundry will have to wrestle with questions of literary genre, source criticism, redaction criticism, the significance of word statistics and the like. The doctrine of Scripture is relevant only insofar as the perspicuity of Scripture is at stake; and here, it must be remembered, Gundry has attempted to forestall criticism by addressing that matter himself.[94]

To this day, thirty years later, not a single critic of Gundry who believed his view *was* inherently contradicting inerrancy has offered what Carson defines above as "intelligent response"—wrestling in detail with the exegetical and historical methods and their applications that Gundry utilized.[95] It was not as if Gundry himself had been engaging in any politicking, trying to drum up support for some campaign of his own. Carson was not at all persuaded that Gundry's approach to

Matthew was correct. Indeed, the last two sentences of his review are particularly pointed: "This commentary combines rigorous brilliance and indefensible methodology, startling insight and fatal flaw. The book is eloquent testimony to the rigor of a front rank scholar whose vision has focused too narrowly, and whose resulting theses are disastrously ill-founded."[96] It is all the more significant, then, that Carson insisted Gundry had the freedom within the framework of inerrancy to make the case he had made and see what scholarly evidence others might marshal for or against his case.

Geisler and Roach may well be correct that the framers of a later document known as the Chicago Statement on Biblical Hermeneutics had situations like Gundry's in mind when they penned, "We deny that generic categories which negate historicity may rightly be imposed on biblical narratives which present themselves as factual."[97] But if so, the wording of this document failed to meet the challenge, because it cannot be applied until there is agreement on which narratives "present themselves as factual." Approximately half of all Jesus's parables are presented without any contextual matter (like the use of the word "parable") to indicate that they are not presenting themselves as factual. Internal evidence and formal similarity to texts inside and outside the canon that are specifically labeled as parables allow us to intuit their nature. Similarly, it was internal evidence and formal similarity of Matthew to Jewish midrash, buttressed by the external evidence of divergent parallel accounts in Mark and Luke, that led Gundry to his position. However mistaken he may have been, if one admits there is a single parable in the Gospels not explicitly called a parable, then one cannot use the Chicago Statement on Hermeneutics, any more than the Chicago Statement on Inerrancy, to exclude Gundry's position.[98]

Pseudonymous Epistles?

Another highly charged topic involves the question of authorship of the various New Testament Epistles. Unlike the Gospels and Acts, which have no actual claims for authorship embedded in a specific verse or passage contained in them, all of the Epistles from Romans through Philemon include in their opening sentences the name "Paul" as the sender of the letter. The letters of James, 1 and 2 Peter, and Jude likewise include those three men's names in their initial verses, indicating authorship. Nevertheless, outside of evangelical circles, roughly half of contemporary New Testament scholars believe that Colossians, 2 Thessalonians, James, 1 Peter, and Jude were not written by the authors to which they have traditionally been ascribed. Perhaps as many as three-fourths of New Testament scholars reject the Pauline authorship of Ephesians and the Pastoral Epistles (1–2 Timothy and Titus), and an even higher percentage rejects Petrine authorship of 2 Peter. Second Peter is also the one canonical letter whose authorship claim was disputed in the ancient church as well.[99]

The reasons for these verdicts need not detain us here. Usually there are questions of literary style, of historical setting or context, and of theological differences from other less disputed epistles. These have been debated at length, and credible defenses of traditional views of authorship have been offered.[100] The question of interest here is whether or not one can affirm pseudonymous authorship (i.e., a false ascription of authorship as we tend to define authorship in the twenty-first century) to a biblical document and still legitimately claim to believe in Scripture's inerrancy. A generation ago, scholarship favoring pseudonymity routinely explained that this was not a device designed to fool anyone.[101] Plenty of other examples exist in ancient Jewish, Greek, and Roman circles for attributing a document to an author whom people would have known was no longer living, doing so as a way of crediting them for being a key resource or inspiration for the ideas contained in the newer work. Far from being deceptive, it was a way of *not* taking credit for the contents of a book when one's ideas were heavily indebted to others of a previous era.[102] Today the prefaces, forewords, and notes enable authors to acknowledge their indebtedness to others; the ancient world simply had different literary conventions. Other plausible motives for pseudonymity were from time to time suggested as well.[103]

We have at least partial parallels in the modern world. Ghostwriters pen autobiographies on behalf of less literate celebrities of various kinds, and one may or may not find their names actually appearing in the book's front or back matter somewhere. Busy scholars may delegate projects to research students or assistants yet put their own names on the works as primary authors without having done very much of the work themselves.[104] An author's memoirs or unfinished work may be fleshed out posthumously by later editors and still attributed largely or entirely to the original writer. We should scarcely be surprised if people in other times and places had their own equivalents to these practices.

On the other hand, it is an open question whether ancient Jews or Christians ever deemed the practice of pseudonymity acceptable *for canonical Scripture*. What evidence we have within Christian circles, beginning from the mid-to-late second century, suggests that Christians did not *knowingly* support pseudonymous works for inclusion in the New Testament.[105] Indeed, when the *Apocalypse of Peter* (see chap. 2 above) came to be recognized as pseudonymous, it fell out of consideration for canonicity. But this occurred in the mid-to-late second century, when many things were changing in Christianity. Specifically, in many respects it was losing sight of its Jewish roots, and developments that would pave the way for the emergence of Roman Catholicism were beginning to flourish. Attitudes of the largely Gentile church on any topic in the late second century scarcely guarantee that Jewish Christians in the first century would have had the identical attitudes.[106]

Interestingly, article 18 of the Chicago Statement on Inerrancy contains the following positive pronouncement: "We affirm that the text of Scripture is to be interpreted by grammatico-historical exegesis, taking account of its literary forms and devices, and that Scripture is to interpret Scripture."[107] This affirmation reinforces everything we have been discussing. We must take account of Scripture's "literary forms and devices." Yet the very next sentence stands in potential tension with this affirmation: "We deny the legitimacy of any treatment of the text or quest for sources lying behind it that leads to relativizing, dehistoricizing, or discounting its teaching, or rejecting its claims to authorship."[108]

Of course, there are two ways to read this denial. If "dehistoricizing" means regarding as unhistorical something that is intended to be taken as historical, then naturally that would be inconsistent with inerrancy. If "rejecting its claims to authorship" means denying that an author wrote a document when the document intends to say that the person wrote it, then again one would be contradicting inerrancy. But one does not dehistoricize when one interprets a parable as a parable.

So, too, if it were the case that "the literary forms and devices" of a certain epistle included pseudonymity, then alleging that the person's name appearing at the beginning of the letter may not have been the real author's name *would not be rejecting its actual truth claims*.[109] We do not accuse Samuel Clemens of error because he wrote under the pen name Mark Twain. We do not censure Herman Melville because the first words of his *Moby Dick* read, "Call me Ishmael." We understand the literary conventions involved. If first-century Christian attitudes to pseudonymity were similar, then we have no right to object to them. If we were instead to insist that the name attached to a biblical letter at its outset must be its "author" as we understand the term, then we would no longer be undertaking grammatico-historical exegesis but anachronistically inserting a later culture's standard into a world that had not yet developed such a standard.[110] And if framers of the Chicago Statement on Inerrancy protest that their intention was never to allow for pseudonymity,[111] then they have conceded that the key to interpreting a document (theirs included) is discerning the author's intention, not merely reading the words on a page of text. So neither the Chicago Statement nor any other a priori definition of inerrancy has the right to take precedence over the quest for the actual authorial intention of the biblical books! To say we know what first-century Christian attitudes to pseudonymity were outstrips the actual evidence, because no comparative material from the first century has yet come to light addressing the question one way or another.

Intriguingly, in both the most conservative evangelical and the most radically liberal scholarship during the past generation, the pendulum has swung away from seeing pseudonymity as intentionally harmless. Without any new evidence actually having been discovered to justify it, Bart Ehrman can now write a book on the topic called *Forged: Writing in the Name of God*.[112] While still believing in pseudonymity, has he become convinced by certain evangelical studies arguing that pseudonymity was *never* acceptable and so therefore declares several of the biblical books to have been forged? That would be the irony of ironies! And he plays right into the hands of the fundamentalist scholars who want to blacklist any evangelical who dares to suggest an acceptable form of pseudonymity. "See," they say, "those evangelicals are as bad as an archskeptic like Ehrman!"[113] Both sides wind up labeling people and methods as completely out-of-bounds while failing to interact with the actual evidence and failing to acknowledge what we simply don't know. Barring some future discovery related to *first-century* opinions, we cannot pontificate on what kinds of claims for authorship would or would not have been considered acceptable in Christian communities, and especially in Jewish-Christian circles when the New Testament Epistles were written. As a result, we must evaluate every proposal based on its own historical and grammatical merits, not on whether it does or does not pass some preestablished criterion of what inerrancy can accept.

Meanwhile, a major international symposium on pseudepigraphy in early Christian epistles, held in Munich in 2007, saw numerous reasonably centrist biblical scholars once again make the case for this literary device as not necessarily intended to deceive or fool anyone. With the Old Testament apocryphal book the Wisdom of Solomon, mimesis (*mimēsis*) may well have been the primary motive: "Entering the mind and thought of the famous, wise king of the past was a literary model for people to imitate. No one would have thought Solomon was actually speaking the words in this text."[114] Among the nonbiblical Dead Sea Scrolls are *no* documents that use the name of a contemporary author; they are all either anonymous or pseudonymous. Eibert Tigchelaar posits multiple motives for pseudonymity, including literary genre, imitation of an earlier biblical work, and various possible psychological and sociological correspondences between the real author and the ancient individual in whose name he wrote.[115] David Aune conveniently summarizes several detailed foreign-language works that analyze six different kinds of ancient pseudepigraphy: (1) works that are partly authentic but have been supplemented by later authors, (2) works written largely by later authors but relying on some material from the named authors, (3) works that are more generally influenced by the earlier authors who are named, (4) works from a "school" of writers ideologically descended from the named authors, (5) originally anonymous works later made pseudonymous for one of these previous reasons, and (6) genuine forgeries intended to deceive.[116] With only one of these six categories involving any intent to deceive, scholars on both the far left and the far right are simply wrong to claim that there is some inherently immoral quality to the practice. In fact, when it comes to postbiblical Jewish apocalypses, every known example is pseudonymous. That, however, makes the New Testament book of Revelation stand out immediately, since it contains in its text the name of its author, John, not once but four times (Rev. 1:1, 4, 9; 22:8). This repetition somewhat emphatically distinguishes Revelation from all other apocalypses of its day.

Revelation and Apocalyptic Literature

We have already mentioned some of the characteristics of apocalyptic literature (see "Too Many Caveats?" in chap. 4 above). When we turn to the book of Revelation, Fee and Stuart's sage advice in their widely used evangelical handbook, *How to Read the Bible for All Its Worth*, remains the soundest: consistently literal interpretation is sometimes the *last* thing we would ever want to do if we are going to be true to the apocalyptic genre, the historical-cultural background, and the use of words and their symbolic meanings in this literature.[117] Here we have made real progress in the last generation. There are now top-notch evangelical commentaries, from introductory to advanced levels, that agree on most of the main points that Revelation makes and how its symbolism is to be understood.[118] Yet sadly, these are ignored by a wide majority of the populace, who remain enamored with the best-selling popular-level prophecy guides, most of whose authors have no training as biblical scholars. Many of these writers also like to sell fictional novels about the end times, and almost all of them try to correlate all of the details of Revelation with current events.[119] The Christian world seems to suffer regularly from collective amnesia, as each successive interpretation turns out to be wrong, but we nevertheless jump on the bandwagon of the next similar proposal just as readily as we did the last. Perhaps we desperately *want* the world to be near its end so that we don't need to wrestle with the complex problems that plague our planet today. Unfortunately, we generally hold no one accountable for their past failed prophecies and with renewed fervor latch on to each new, exciting proposal that Christ's coming is imminent.[120]

Avoiding the Opposite Extreme

I have already mentioned some of the opposite extremes in the course of this chapter thus far: forcing all narrative genres into historical ones, excluding pseudonymity a priori, and trying to impose a consistently literal interpretation on apocalyptic literature. But I must add one particularly egregious, recent example, involving another potentially apocalyptic passage.

Matthew 27:51–53 is in some respects one of the strangest New Testament texts of all. Tucked into the larger narrative about Jesus's resurrection and the events that followed, but appearing for the most part only in Matthew, is a passage that announces, "At that moment the curtain of the temple was torn in two from top to bottom. The earth shook, the rocks split and the tombs broke open. The bodies of many holy people who had died were raised to life. They came out of the tombs after Jesus' resurrection and went into the holy city and appeared to many people." Mark 15:38 agrees that the curtain was torn from top to bottom, and an earthquake could certainly have caused such damage,[121] but no other Gospel anywhere mentions anything about other people being raised at this time. All kinds of questions clamor for answers: Who were these people? Why were they raised and no others? To whom did they appear? How long were they seen? When did the appearances stop? What happened to these people after that?[122] Inasmuch as the resurrection of Jesus is such a central theme in the New Testament, as is his appearance to *many* eyewitnesses, why is no further mention ever made of *these* individuals? Not a shred of data inside or outside of Matthew enables us to answer any of these questions.

One passage in Paul, however, has led commentators fairly consistently to suggest the meaning of the episode. Just as 1 Corinthians 15:20 declares that "Christ has indeed been raised from the dead, the firstfruits of those who have fallen asleep," so also Matthew's inclusion of this reference to resurrected saints seems likewise to have been motivated by the desire to maintain that Jesus's bodily resurrection from the dead guarantees the coming bodily resurrection of *all* God's people from throughout human history.[123] But does that mean that Matthew

27:52b–53 must reflect simple history? Or could the text, too, narrate symbolically what Paul phrases more prosaically?

In a magisterial, detailed defense of the historicity of the bodily resurrection of Jesus, Michael Licona ever so briefly raises this question.[124] In subsequent writings he has clarified that he really is not at all sure what to conclude, but he thinks the idea merits serious exploration.[125] For this, opponents successfully mounted a campaign against Licona[126] and were partly responsible for Licona's departure from Southern Evangelical Seminary and from the North American Mission Board of the Southern Baptist Convention. Albert Mohler, president of the Southern Baptist Seminary in Louisville, fell into the same trap of censuring Licona,[127] and even a New Testament scholar as sharp as Danny Akin, president of Southeastern Baptist Seminary, at least briefly jumped on the bandwagon, insisting that Licona could never teach full-time for him.[128] All of this would be just plain silly if it were not so tragic and if people's careers and livelihoods didn't hang in the balance.

These censors need to read carefully the works of Carlos Bovell and others like him (see citations in chap. 4 above). They need to learn about the personal pilgrimages of some of the most aggressive anti-Christian writers today, who for years were evangelicals, and to discover why they abandoned the faith.[129] Then they need to sit down and listen respectfully to a representative cross-section of the thousands of ordinary laypeople nationwide who are "deconverting" from Christian faith at a record-breaking pace today.[130] If they did so, they would hear several important, recurring themes. One of these is that the form of Christianity in which these church-leavers and faith-leavers were brought up and/or nurtured did not allow for serious discussion of the hard questions of the faith in a safe environment and drew small circles around what was deemed acceptably "Christian." When these former believers discovered how so much of the Christian world was broader and had good intellectual arguments for their positions, they could not remain fundamentalists in good conscience. But those who had bought into the all-or-nothing mind-set of their teachers ("If you depart from [our definitions of] inerrancy, you are on an inevitably slippery slope to unbelief") naturally decided they had then better become atheists or, at best, agnostics.[131] (Fortunately, not all fell so far; some landed in other bona fide versions of the Christian faith.) Closely related to this pattern is the one of individuals watching how ultraconservative Christians treat with very little Christian spirit those with whom they disagree and then deciding that they want nothing to do with Christianity. Surely those who have caused "one of these little ones—those who believe in me—to stumble" (Matt. 18:6) will have much to answer for on judgment day!

Conclusion

As tragic as these situations are, far worse, far more culpable, and even more common are the situations in which professors intentionally seek to lead others, especially young university students, to abandon their faith via one-sided and distorted presentations of "scholarship." Many religious studies instructors do their best to ensure that these students are never exposed to the thousands of articles, essays, and books of evangelical biblical scholars worldwide who have mounted credible cases for the reliability of Scripture. If any of these works are discovered, they are written off as something less than "serious scholarship" (though still claiming to be a Christian and an evangelical at that, Kenton Sparks's rhetoric proves frighteningly similar).[132] Apparently separation of church and state in public universities does not extend to barring attacks *against* Christianity in the classroom (with a vitriol not unleashed on any other religion). Such attacks seem more than welcome in most state universities and not a few private ones; the only prohibition is that one can't speak *on behalf of* a given religion, or at least Christianity. Far too many people in the public square have with impunity perverted our constitutional freedoms *of* religion into freedom *from* religion!

As we noted in our introduction, there is good, well-argued scholarship for the historical reliability of most of the narrative portions of Scripture (i.e., those that are written in a form that suggests they intend to narrate history). In a handful of the places where it seems hardest to defend the classic, historical interpretations of various texts, it is worth asking if we have missed something. Not all writings of a narrative genre intend to record history; we need to treat each on a case-by-case basis.

This chapter has discussed a handful of the most famous debates of our day, where books or passages might fall into a different genre, and also added other high-profile examples from the genres of prophetic, epistolary, and apocalyptic literature.

By nature, I am skeptical of any proposals that seem to have eluded all readers until the last couple of centuries. Where I learn that there were ancient debates over certain issues, I am more open to considering alternative interpretations. I have deliberately not taken a stand myself on any of the problems as I discussed them in this chapter. Because readers seem invariably curious, I will happily disclose where I come down at the moment, given the varying amounts of study I have devoted to each. I would support an old-earth creationism and opt for a combination of progressive creation and a literary-framework approach to Genesis 1.[133] I lean in the direction of Kidner's approach to Genesis 2–3 but am open to other proposals. I suspect that Jonah really intended to recount a miracle that really did happen, but with Job I gravitate more toward Longman's mediating approach. Despite the overwhelming consensus against it, I still find the arguments for the unity of Isaiah under a single primary author, even if lightly redacted later, more persuasive (or at least less problematic) than most do. I remain pretty much baffled by Daniel 11; it is the issue I have researched by far the least. My inherent conservatism inclines me in the direction of taking it as genuine predictive prophecy, but I listen respectfully to those who argue for other interpretations and continue to mull them over. I reject Gundry's approach to Matthew as highly unlikely. I have yet to be persuaded by Licona's initial views of Matthew 27:51–53 but would love to see additional comparative research undertaken. I think good cases can still be mounted for the traditional ascriptions of authorship of the New Testament Epistles, allowing for perhaps some posthumous editing of 2 Peter.[134] And I refuse ever to be suckered back into the views of my young adult years, when I actually believed that the end times would play out as Hal Lindsey claimed they would![135]

But my conclusions on each topic are not the point of this chapter. The point is that all of these examples raise the issue of the genre of a certain book, section, or passage of Scripture. *The truth claims of the Bible, appropriately cherished by inerrantists, can never be determined apart from our best assessment of the literary forms and genres involved.* The Chicago Statement could have stressed this more, but it is reasonably well highlighted. Thus institutions or organizations that claim to abide by it must allow their inerrantist scholars the freedom to explore the various literary options without fear of reprisal. Ironically, when individuals draw the boundaries of inerrancy more narrowly than this, it is *they* who have unwittingly denied inerrancy, at least as it is defined by the Chicago Statement! It would be good to remember the Golden Rule here also (Matt. 7:12). Would such critics want others to condemn their own scholarship with the animus and misconstruals they offer others?[136] Those who find certain proposals about literary genre unconvincing should reply in all of the appropriate scholarly forums, and let the most convincing position win—through scholarship and not through campaigns to oust people from various positions. After all, it may just well be that in some instances the most credible defense of the reliability of a certain part of the Bible will emerge only when one recognizes it as a somewhat different form or genre than what most have taken it to be.

Other examples could have been added to those discussed in these chapters, but these have received at least as much press as any others. The issues of Jonah and the raising of the saints in Matthew 27 require us to turn, finally, to one more key issue—that of the supernatural and the miraculous in Scripture. Can twenty-first-century Bible readers truly believe that the range of miraculous events reported in the Bible really happened? Hasn't science disproved all this? Aren't *all* these stories actually ancient myths or legends? Were they ever even meant to be taken literally? If the bodily resurrection of Jesus forms the heart and core of Christian faith, how can anyone maintain their intellectual credibility and still believe in historic Christianity? To these and related questions our final main chapter turns.

6

Don't All the Miracles Make the Bible Mythical?

Renowned historian Gerd Lüdemann, professor at the University of Göttingen, is more candid than most in explaining why he cannot accept the bodily resurrection of Jesus as historical fact: he is firmly convinced that modern science has proved that dead men cannot rise.[1] His view is a holdover from the mid-twentieth century, before quantum physics and Heisenberg's principle of uncertainty made many scientists somewhat more cautious about pontificating on what could or could not happen, especially when talking about the supernatural.[2] Philosophers of science are also increasingly stressing that the miraculous by definition lies outside the bounds of science because it cannot be tested or experimentally reproduced in a laboratory.[3] Miracles, in other words, should not be defined as the violation of the normal laws of nature or of the universe but as involving their temporary suspension or transcendence. Lüdemann, of course, is by no means the only contemporary historian or biblical scholar who still holds to what philosophers call antisupernaturalism. But increasingly, this is not the first or primary argument critics give for dismissing many of the miracle stories of Scripture.

David Hume's famous philosophical arguments against miracles from eighteenth-century Scotland are still adopted in certain circles, but increasingly they too have been recognized as fallacious.[4] It simply is not the case that a naturalistic explanation of events is always more probable than a supernaturalistic one. In an amazing compendium of the best attested and documented miracles of the modern era from every continent, Craig Keener has collected hundreds upon hundreds of well-documented accounts of instantaneous healings of people with chronic and severe illnesses or injuries, which have occurred after concerted Christian public prayer and without any relapse. And it is not just healings but also the occasional resurrection or other miracle over nature (including instantaneous weather changes after prayer, multiplication of food, walking on water, and turning water into wine), which enables him to conclude that parallels to virtually all New Testament miracles have occurred at some point in recent years. Keener has also compiled a catalog of some of the most verified miracles throughout Christian history, indicating the strict criteria that they must meet, so that he has probably eliminated many genuine miracles from consideration in so doing.[5] In a lengthy appendix he adds contemporary exorcisms into the mix, expanding his compilation considerably.[6]

Psychologists sometimes rightly point out documented cases of mind over matter that could make certain kinds of healings psychosomatic. These could potentially apply to exorcisms as well. Powerful, respected individuals commanding or praying for others to be healed may give some mentally troubled individuals the permission to begin to heal on their own in ways that science and medicine barely understand. But this form of naturalistic explanation cannot explain miracles involving inanimate objects, resurrections from the dead, or healings that have occurred immediately and spontaneously after concerted Christian prayer undertaken without the knowledge of the person suffering an illness.[7]

Critics sometimes point out that miracles are alleged to occur in other world religions today as well, so that such testimony does not prove the truth of the Christian religion. Several points must be made in reply. First, we are not looking for absolute proof but for suggestive evidence of the miraculous. Second, the fact that the claims regularly occur in religious contexts at least calls into question atheism as the most logical worldview to adopt, even if it doesn't guarantee that Christianity is the most logically consistent of the religious worldviews (though it *may* be via a different line of argumentation—recall "Kinds of Inerrancy" in chap. 4 above). Nevertheless, and third, there is no other major world religion in which miracles occupy so central a role.[8] And *no founders of any other major religion outside of the Judeo-Christian tradition have miracles attributed to them in their earliest and most fundamental documents.*[9] Finally, both satanic counterfeit and human manufacture can account for at least a considerable amount of the alleged miraculous activity found outside of the Judeo-Christian tradition. In other words, we do not have to deny the legitimacy of all accounts of the miraculous elsewhere in order to highlight how credible and consistent the biblical and Christian accounts are. This is a key point that Christians often fail to acknowledge, thus leaving them susceptible to the charge of using a double standard in evaluating claims of the miraculous. Given God's temporary use of pagan individuals in the Scriptures—such as Melchizedek, Balaam, Nebuchadnezzar, and Cyrus—for positive but nonsalvific purposes, it is even possible that he might occasionally choose to accomplish good through miracles effected by those who are neither Jews nor Christians.[10] Nor do we need to accept everything that Christians or so-called Christians have alleged; charlatans unfortunately emerge in every religious tradition.

Experiential Evidence

My own experience is more limited than some, but my family and I have had firsthand, personal exposure to or involvement with several experiences for which science has no explanation but that fit Christian faith hand in glove. My aunt who passed away at the age of 88 in 1993 had a multiply-fractured ankle poorly reset in her thirties and experienced so much pain that by her late sixties she was on constant, heavy medication. One evening just before midnight, following the instructions of a preacher on a television show she was watching,[11] she prayed for healing for her ankle and went to bed. The next morning the pain was gone, and she lived another twenty years without its recurrence and without ever taking another pain pill for that particular problem.

As an elder in a local church, I regularly participated in prayers for healing in which we anointed people with oil according to the instructions in James 5:13–18. On two occasions, patients with previously diagnosed cancerous tumors went to their doctors shortly afterward, and the medical experts could find no trace of any tumors ever having existed.[12]

My wife, during her nurse's training at a teaching hospital one evening, watched a team of emergency personnel rush into a room in which she was trying unsuccessfully to make an elderly heart patient comfortable. The head nurse commended my wife for having come to get her, even though she had left her patient unattended in so doing, and confirmed that the patient was indeed having a heart attack. My wife replied that she had never left the room. Later the two women searched the floor, asking everyone they could if anyone resembling my wife had been on the wing, and the answer was uniformly negative. Given that she had fiery red, curly hair, there could not have been many such individuals, and even if such a look-alike had been on the floor, she would have had no reason to tell the head nurse that the patient my wife was attending in that room had suffered a heart attack.[13]

My wife was also an observer and one of those who prayed during an exorcism at our church before a service one evening. An unkempt young woman came off the street and into the lobby and began having what looked like epileptic seizures. While our pastor was waiting for the arrival of the emergency personnel who were summoned, the woman started speaking in a deep, bass, growling voice and recoiling when the pastor prayed in Jesus's name over her. He commanded what he assumed was a demon or demons to come out of the woman, to which the unearthly voice several times shouted, "No, I won't." As others around prayed more fervently, our pastor spoke even more forcefully and with great annoyance. Suddenly the demon left, and the woman grew limp. By the time the paramedics arrived, she was calm and conscious, without any signs of illness.[14]

A few years before my mother moved out of the house she had lived in for over fifty years and into a retirement community, she was starting to go out her back door and walk to the alley behind her garage one cold winter's day, to put out garbage for the trash collector. Unlike any experience she had ever had in her life, and although she was entirely alone in her house, she heard an audible voice telling her, "Take your cane." Startled, but assuming it was God, she grabbed her cane. Just before closing the backdoor behind her, she heard the voice again say, "Now take your cell phone." Again, nothing like this had ever happened to her before, nor has it happened since. As she was walking on the sidewalk through the backyard, she realized that there was a thin layer of ice she hadn't seen from the house, and the cane became quite important to keep her from falling. After emptying the trash, she realized that she was poised precariously between larger sections of snow and ice, so that she didn't want to try to navigate the walk even with the cane. So she used her phone to call for help and was able to get back to the house with assistance. My mother acknowledged that she would have been quite frightened otherwise, having recently had knee surgery, if she had tried to get back on her own, and she felt sure there was a good chance she would have fallen.[15]

Once a friend and former student contacted me, told me she had dreamed that I had a particular affliction, and accurately described a recent injury I had experienced. She said that God wanted to give me a message of encouragement and assurance that he was in charge of the situation, that he still loved me deeply, and that things would soon get better. She assured me that she had not previously been aware of my circumstances, and I had no reason to suspect that she would have been aware of them.

Not long after that, another friend and student of mine at the time, having heard of my malady (a debilitating repetitive stress injury), came to my office and gave me information about a medical technique only recently developed, utilized by only three doctors in the Denver Metro area, which he promised would be my "miracle cure," even though he knew it would sound silly for him to call it that. But he was right: five or six brief treatments of "active release techniques" accomplished in a few weeks what more than a year of conventional physical therapy, chiropractic, and acupuncture combined had failed to do.[16]

All these kinds of experiences, I have discovered, are actually not uncommon among Christian believers. If I expanded my set of examples beyond family members to include experiences of close friends who are so trustworthy that I cannot believe they made up their stories, I could add even more astonishing examples, but I have not sought their permission to tell their stories. Several, I know, would not want attention drawn to themselves.

Near-death experiences of individuals who have lost all vital signs for a prolonged period of time but are eventually resuscitated fit into another category of recurring, documented events.[17] Too many individuals to discount them all have reported experiences of something akin to the Judeo-Christian heaven, or simply of being outside of their body and looking down on it and/or other nearby locations. They have accurately described incidental objects that they saw or snatches of conversation overheard that they would have had no way of knowing about if their souls (or some conscious part of themselves) had not been alive during that time.[18] The recent autobiographical narrative of Eben Alexander, a neurosurgeon who reports spending a week in heaven while in the kind of coma that does not permit any form of thought, describes the most dramatic of thousands of near-death experiences (NDEs) yet.[19] This does not mean all NDEs are real, since some have been plausibly explained as physiologically produced, or that they all completely accurately depict the life to come, since obviously no one gets very far into that world if they are then restored to this one. But such experiences must be taken into account before anyone rules out biblical miracles or the supernatural realm as impossible.[20]

Skeptics may reply to stories of unexplained healings and other miracles with questions: "Why then does God, if he exists and is the cause of these events, not intervene more often? Aren't these events rare enough to still cast doubt on whether any God exists?" Not at all. If they were more common, they would begin to cease to be considered miraculous. Most likely, individuals would attempt (even more than they already do in some circles) to try to manipulate God into producing them on demand.[21] Even the occurrence of just one extraordinary event that naturalism cannot explain demonstrates that naturalism is not a comprehensive worldview that can account for all that happens in the universe. Extrapolating from a 2006 Pew Forum survey, Keener conservatively estimates that as many as 200 million people alive today have personally experienced or witnessed an extraordinary event, unaccounted for by the current state of scientific understanding, and in direct response to Christian prayer.[22] Even though that is only one in every 35 people on the planet, the sheer quantity pokes so many holes in atheistic naturalism as to turn it into a sieve! The Bible gives many explanations for why God does not choose to intervene miraculously most of the time in human affairs: the value God places on our free will, the maturity we can gain through suffering, God's ability to work through human weakness so much more than through our strength, the comfort that God simultaneously provides and wants us to pass on to others, the dependence on Jesus that suffering creates if we allow it to, the people who come to the Lord or grow in their walk with him through seeing us sustained by a power that we could not have manufactured, and so on.[23] No Christian should have to identify the precise reason God did not work a miracle in a certain context in order to continue to believe in God's existence. But atheism has to be able to account for *every* scientifically inexplicable event apart from God for it to be *necessarily* true. *Thus it takes at least as much if not more faith, not founded in empirical evidence, to be an atheist than it does to be a Christian.*[24]

Myths or Legends?

While scientists and philosophers do at times still cling to outmoded defenses of naturalism, among biblical scholars there is a much greater openness to the miraculous than there was even a generation ago. It is widely accepted that Jesus facilitated healings and exorcisms explainable in his world only as miracles, though exactly how he did this is more debated.[25] But the most prevalent twenty-first-century reason for labeling the biblical narratives of the supernatural, including the resurrection of Jesus, as fiction is neither a scientific naturalism nor a Humean skepticism. Rather, it is the claim that they resemble other ancient myths or legends too closely for them to be taken as historical narrative.[26] Here we return to the question of genre discussed in the previous chapter. As I noted regarding the command to Peter to catch a fish (Matt. 17:27; see chap. 5, note 113), once in a great while a passage that has often been labeled a miracle story isn't even a narrative of any kind of action at all. We don't know what Peter did after Jesus commanded him to go to the lake to fish. Occasionally, too, we may discover reasons for thinking that a passage we first thought to recount a miracle may have been intended to be more poetic and less literal instead (see below). But in the vast majority of instances, the alleged parallels with ancient fiction are dramatically exaggerated.

The classic Greco-Roman myths of the exploits of various gods and goddesses over parts of nature, with their older ancient Near Eastern predecessors, typically depict those deities as acting entirely like humans do—disclosing the good, the bad, and the ugly![27] Their interactions with one another regularly involve rivalry and competition for power or jurisdiction over some part of the world or some aspect of nature. They may disguise themselves as mere mortals, but they never become completely incarnate, in contrast to the New Testament accounts of God taking fully human form in Jesus.[28] Most of ancient mythology purports to explain how various natural phenomena came into being—the sun appearing to traverse the sky each day; the cycle of the four seasons; the processes of the planting, growing, and harvesting of crops; and so on. This is utterly unlike the miracles attributed to Jesus and the apostles, Moses and Elijah, or any other biblical character.

Some myths report that humans become gods when they die, especially if they have been great rulers, military conquerors, or wise sages; such deification occurs not within a framework of a monotheistic religion like Judaism or Christianity but in polytheism, which allows for many gods.[29] The births of special people may be attributed to the result of a union between a god and a human woman, but these are not virginal conceptions; they involve stories of the actual copulation of one (counted as a god) who appears to be a human male with one who is genuinely a human female.[30] Stories of resurrections are actually comparatively rare and can take various forms, including resuscitations and pure metaphors. *But nowhere in any ancient mythology or folklore do we ever find even the claim that an indisputably human individual who died within the living memory of others was raised bodily*, much less seen in physical form on many different occasions by hundreds, who then boldly and widely spread the word about their experiences among their contemporaries.[31]

Even the miracle narratives that are somewhat parallel to the New Testament exploits of Jesus and the apostles are primarily post-Christian in origin. The most famous of these appear in Philostratus's accounts of the life of the first-century philosopher Apollonius of Tyana in Cappadocia. According to his third-century biographer, Apollonius showed great wisdom as a child, performed healings as an adult, correctly predicted the future, exorcised demons, appeared to his followers after he died, and ascended bodily into heaven.[32] The one really striking parallel to the New Testament appears with the story of Apollonius raising a young woman who had died "in the hour of her wedding." Apollonius stopped the funeral procession to touch her in her open casket and to whisper to her, after which she sat up, spoke, and was helped out of her coffin (*Life of Apollonius of Tyana* 4.45). We think immediately of similar details in Jesus's raising of the son of the widow at Nain (Luke 7:11–17). But one can trace a process whereby Apollonius, a wise philosopher who perhaps was involved in a few healings, became larger than life in the writings of his later biographers.[33] A similar process occurred with respect to those who recounted the life and accomplishments of Alexander the Great.[34]

These processes, moreover, occurred slowly, over centuries, not within the lifetimes of eyewitnesses of the exploits of the individuals being exalted. To his credit, Lüdemann stresses how early the belief in the bodily resurrection of Jesus developed, almost certainly within a year or two of his death at most.[35] In 1 Corinthians 15:3 Paul stresses how the confessional material about the resurrection that is included in verses 4–7 is what he has passed on to the Corinthians "as of first importance" or "at the first" (NIV mg.). Probably both renderings are accurate. The language of passing on what he received was technical language for the faithful transmission of oral tradition. It is even possible to understand Paul's syntax, given the Greek word order, as meaning, "For I delivered to you what I received at the first," that is, at the beginning of his Christian life. In any event, what Paul learned was probably taught widely enough throughout the empire to have made it from Jerusalem to Damascus as fundamental catechetical material for new converts by the time Paul was instructed by Ananias there (Acts 9:17–19). But that means Paul is talking about what he was taught during the period of time mentioned in Acts 9:19, which must be dated to within two or three years of the crucifixion.[36]

In other words, this is no late, gradually developing myth or legend but a widely held belief from the earliest days of the Christian church onward.[37] The claim that this is metaphorical language founders on the uniform use of resurrection language in Judaism to refer to a real person coming back to life in bodily form.[38] Lüdemann acknowledges all this but still opts for some form of the "subjective-vision" hypothesis.[39] But nowhere in the history of the world have mass hallucinations (i.e., multiple identical visions) ever occurred apart from some actually existing object (a painting, statue, shrine, or oracle, etc.) that provokes the visions.[40] (One of the most common forms throughout Christian history, if indeed they are to be deemed hallucinations, are statues or paintings of the Virgin Mary that appear to weep and shed tears.)[41] And no early Christian writing ever suggests that such an object had anything to do with belief in Jesus's resurrection.

That the closest parallels to the New Testament miracles all postdate the life of Jesus suggests that if anyone borrowed from anyone else, it was not Christianity from paganism but rather the Greco-Roman religions from Christianity. The more the Jesus-movement grew and spread, the more others would have tried to compete by modeling their holy figures to some degree on the stories of Jesus with which they became familiar. Another excellent example involves Mithraism. Mithras worshipers were an offshoot of Zoroastrianism and regularly portrayed their god as a bull-slayer. Supposedly, the bull's blood gave life to the cult members. As in other mystery religions, they participated in certain ritual initiations involving cleansing in water and cultic meals involving bread and water. From time to time some scholars have suggested that the Christian sacraments of baptism and the Eucharist derived from these practices, even though closer parallels existed at an earlier date in Judaism, the religious world from which Christianity most directly descended. The closest parallels in Mithraism, moreover, did not emerge until the third and fourth centuries AD. Only then, for example, did Christians begin to celebrate the birth of their "god"

(Jesus) on December 25 to coincide with the Roman holiday of Saturnalia, which had become combined with Mithras worship no earlier than the late second century. This day simply became a convenient day off work for Christians to worship Jesus and be left alone to do so.[42] Elsewhere I have observed:

> The Mithras cult was exclusivist (open only to men), militaristic (involving codes of honour and purity regulations to prepare men for war), and closely dependent on Roman imperial support for survival. Claims that Christianity or its picture of Jesus was born out of Mithraism reflect almost no historical understanding of chronology, lines of influence, or true similarities and dissimilarities between the two religions.[43]

And if one protests that Mithraism believed in a virgin birth, it needs to be pointed out that the bull-slaying god was born by springing forth from a rock. Presumably the rock had not previously had sex with anyone or anything, but that is a considerably expanded use of the term "virgin"!

With rare exceptions, therefore, when a skeptic alleges that Christian miracles derived from pagan parallels, one or both of two points refute the suggestion almost immediately. First, frequently a closer inspection of the alleged parallel discloses that only a small portion of the account bears any resemblance to the New Testament passage in question. For example, a view debunked more than a century ago has revived in some circles that compares Jesus to the ancient Egyptian god Horus, complete with claims of a parallel virgin birth, crucifixion, and resurrection. Whoever actually checks what was claimed about Horus, however, discovers he was a falcon, born of the goddess Isis after she had sex with her resurrected and previously dismembered husband, the god Osiris. Horus was never even alleged to be crucified and resurrected. Osiris was alleged to be resurrected—every year in conjunction with the fertility cycle as spring followed winter. Even just the Wikipedia articles on Horus and Osiris are sufficient to debunk the claim that Jesus was fabricated on their model, but it is amazing how many blogsites and web-surfers repeat it without ever checking the facts. Such claims demonstrate that the people involved are eager merely to discredit Christianity rather than to discover truth.[44]

Second, far more often than not, even the partially similar "parallels" are post-Christian in origin, too late to have had any influence on the rise of first-century belief in the miracles of Jesus or of his disciples.[45] Erkki Koskenniemi, whose work on Apollonius demonstrates how much Philostratus invented about him in the third century, sums up matters even more pointedly: "I [have] challenged the view that Gentile miracle-workers were a common phenomenon among the Greeks and Romans and that they were a model for Jesus as he was presented in the Gospels. Scholars were never able to name these many alleged men," except for Apollonius. Instead, the closest parallels to the New Testament miracle stories, when any exist at all, are consistently Old Testament miracle stories and especially their interpretations in Second Temple Judaism.[46] It is time, therefore, to turn to precisely those miracles.

Old Testament Miracles

Limitations of space prevent discussion of every miracle in the Hebrew Scriptures, but we can do our best to consider every major category and representative illustrations.

Refuting Other Myths

In comparing Old Testament miracles with other ancient Near Eastern literature, the apparent parallels *are* fairly consistently earlier than their biblical counterparts. This fits a recurring emphasis in the Hebrew Scriptures to show that Yahweh, God of Israel, is Lord over some part of the world that Israelites were tempted to credit to some other deity, due to the influence of their polytheistic neighbors. An excellent example emerges with the cluster of miracles attributed to Elijah and Elisha in 1 Kings 17–2 Kings 13. Leah Bronner identifies the following eight primary motifs associated with Baal during the time of the divided monarchy: control over fire, rain, corn and olive oil (food and cooking staples), fertility to have children, physical healing, life after death, and ascent into the clouds and rivers.[47] The miracles of these two successive prophets of Israel closely match these motifs: calling down fire from heaven (1 Kings 18:36–39; 2 Kings 1:9–15); predicting prolonged drought followed by heavy rain at its end (1 Kings 17:1; 18:41–45); multiplying flour, bread, and oil (1 Kings 17:13–16; 2 Kings 4:1–7, 42–44); bringing the only sons of the women of Zarephath and Shunem back to life (1 Kings 17:17–24; 2 Kings 4:8–37); the resurrection of a man whose corpse touched the bones of Elisha (2 Kings 13:20–21); Elijah's ascending into heaven without dying (2 Kings 2:1–12); and his making an axhead float after it fell into a river (2 Kings 6:1–7). Not every miracle in the Elijah and Elisha cycles of the Kings narrative is accounted for in this way, lest one imagine deliberate fabrication to counter Baal worship, but a sizable majority of them fit. Clearly these are not randomly invented sensationalizing stories but events deliberately designed to demonstrate that Yahweh and not Baal is God (1 Kings 18:24, 39).[48]

The creation story in Genesis 1 affords a second illustration of this lesson. What Israel's neighboring cultures attributed to the creative activities of a multiplicity of gods, Genesis attributes to one God over all the cosmos. Where there are parallels with reference to specific details between Genesis and the older creation stories of neighboring cultures, as Conrad Hyers nicely phrases it,

> this is not a matter of borrowing, as one might borrow an egg here and a cup of sugar there, or even a new recipe. The aim is not to appropriate a superior form, or to make an eclectic compromise, or even to improve upon pagan cosmologies. It is rather to repudiate the divinization of nature and the attendant myths of divine *origins*, divine *conflict*, and divine *ascent*. (emphasis original)[49]

Indeed, the role of the miraculous in competitions between religions is crystal clear in the plagues on the Egyptians in Exodus 7–11. The first two miracles performed by Moses are replicated by Pharaoh's magicians: throwing down his staff to become a snake and turning the Nile into blood (7:12, 22). When Moses announces the plague of frogs, the magicians can imitate that miracle as well (8:7). When he brings the plague of gnats, however, they are unable to copy it and reply, "This is the finger of God" (8:19). Moses's God will vanquish the supposed gods of the Egyptians.

Intriguingly, Moses was commanded to perform *three* signs in sequence in Exodus 4:1–9. First, he was to throw down his staff to become a snake. Second, he was to put his hand in his cloak, pull it out leprous, and then put it in again and draw it out healed. Finally, he was to pour out water from the river to become blood on the ground. Yet when the moment arrives, nothing is ever said about Moses putting his hand into his cloak twice for the miracle of becoming leprous and then being healed. Moreover, God commands Moses to smite the entire Nile. Someone inventing a myth would presumably not create this double mismatch. So the accounts are more likely historical. In addition, the original commands fit Egyptian logic. With disease and healing as the purview of the gods, the miracles involving leprosy would be more persuasive than the staff becoming a snake. With the Nile, which the Egyptians also deified, as the life-giving water for the nation, the authority to damage the river in this way would be more powerful still.[50] All the plagues as a package would have been the most compelling of all. In a polytheistic culture, any one or a small group of them could be attributed to Yahweh's superiority over one or a small group of the Egyptian pantheon. Taken together, they show the utter impotence of the whole horde of deities arrayed against Israel.[51]

Other Patterns and Purposes

Do a sizable majority of the biblical miracles fit into meaningful patterns like these just surveyed? They scarcely all respond to rival religious beliefs as clearly as those just mentioned. Do they at least fulfill meaningful purposes worthy of God's special intervention? It is easy to read quickly through those parts of Scriptures in which the greatest number of miracles are clustered and come away with the perception that their authors have just randomly introduced a host of fabulous narratives in order to convince the credulous. If we don't take the Babylonian myths or the stories of the Olympian gods as sober fact, are there any reasons to treat the Old and New Testament accounts of the miraculous any differently? Indeed, there are several good reasons to do so. A brief survey of the major miracle stories or forms of miracle stories in Scripture will disclose that they function in several very consistent ways that differ from their pagan counterparts.

The so-called translation of Enoch directly to heaven (Gen. 5:24) finds a partial parallel in a Mesopotamian tradition that Utuabzu, adviser to Enmeduranki, the seventh antediluvian king, ascended to heaven. Other Sumerian folklore affirms that the seventh king before the flood received special divine mysteries. Later ancient Near Eastern speculation, including in the Jewish Pseudepigrapha, added many accounts of the great piety of these men. Gordon Wenham comments, "In contrast to these extra- and post-biblical views Gen 5:22–24 is very restrained. It may well be that while acknowledging the truth that Enoch was very devout and did not see death, these verses are trying to counteract these ancient speculations about great men of the past."[52]

Sarah's postmenopausal ability to conceive (Gen. 21:1–5), like Hannah's and Elizabeth's experiences in later centuries (1 Sam. 1:9–20; Luke 1:8–25), provides an important male child for the line of prophets and for the recipients of God's promises as his plan of salvation for the world is unfolding. All three conceptions partially foreshadow the unparalleled miracle of Mary's pregnancy without any human sexual intercourse. J. Gresham Machen's more than eighty-year-old compendium of alleged Jewish and Greco-Roman parallels to a virginal conception remains more than adequate to show how distant those parallels really are.[53] Traditional Jewish monotheism would have abhorred the notion of a story about God replacing a human male in the act of conception:

> It is one thing to say that when Jesus was actually conceived by the Holy Ghost in the womb of the virgin Mary, that fact could be harmonized by divine revelation with the awful transcendence of God; and it is quite a different thing to say that a Jew, beginning with the transcendence of God, would ever have been able, without compulsion of fact, without the enlightenment of revelation, to arrive at the wonderful representation that appears in Matthew and Luke.[54]

Only rarely was Isaiah 7:14 understood to refer to anyone other than a child born in Isaiah's day, at least in pre-Christian Judaism, so it did not likely provoke the invention of a miracle story to provide fulfillment of its prophecy.[55]

As for theories of pagan derivation, are any of the supposed parallels really close enough to be probable sources for the Gospels' accounts? Perseus was said to have been conceived by Zeus and Danaë "by means of a rain of gold which descended upon her in her seclusion." Philip of Macedon was supposedly kept from Olympias on their wedding night because a giant serpent was stretched out next to his wife, from which "union" Alexander the Great was born. Each new king in ancient Egypt was alleged to have sprung from a human mother and the highest god, Amon-Ra, who had sex with the young woman, who was most decidedly not a virgin. Or should we turn to the account of Romulus and Remus, twin founders of Rome, being born after a virgin maidservant of an Italian princess mated with a giant phallus that had sprung from the hearth of her home? Luke's laconic line that the Holy Spirit "will overshadow" Mary (Luke 1:35) is remarkably restrained and dignified in comparison, with no parallel details whatsoever![56]

Particularly in the Old Testament, a variety of miracles involve God judging his people in order to purify them, to teach them that his commands are not to be trifled with and that they must serve no other deities. One thinks of the punishments of Nadab and Abihu for offering "unholy fire before the Lord" (Lev. 10:1–3), Korah and his followers for rebelling against Moses and the Lord (Num. 16), and some of the residents of Beth-Shemesh for opening and looking into the ark of the covenant (1 Sam. 6:19). Less commonly, miracles bring judgment on God's enemies and/or Israel's oppressors. In the first category we think of Sodom and Gomorrah or the Canaanites at the time of the conquest, pagan peoples whose immorality was among the most debased of human history (cf. Gen. 15:16).[57] In the second, we recall God's miraculous interventions during Israel's self-defense against foreign attack (e.g., 2 Kings 19:35; 2 Chron. 20:1–30).

Still other miracles involve theophanies. The Pentateuch contains several references to an angel of the Lord who morphs into "the Lord" himself as the story unfolds (Gen. 16; 22; Exod. 3; Num. 22). The most famous and influential theophany of the Old Testament consists of God appearing to Moses in the burning bush and revealing himself by name, "I AM WHO I AM" (Exod. 3:14)—probably a reference to himself as the eternally existing one. The fire and the shrub recall God's earlier self-revelation in the smoking firepot and blazing torch of Genesis 15:17, while "trees and objects related to trees (rods and in this case a bush) are often found in places made sacred by God's presence. Of course, trees represent life, and God is the author of life. Trees are at the center of Eden and thus holy places are often marked by a tree (Gen. 12:6, 13:18)."[58] Similar imagery for the divine reappears as the cloud (resembling smoke) by day and the fire by night lead the Israelites during their wilderness wanderings (Exod. 13:21; cf. 19:18 and 24:15–18).

The parting of the waters of the Red Sea (Exod. 14) forms the ultimate reversal of creation—separating what God initially brought together to form dry land (Gen. 1:9). But the dry land does indeed appear, providing salvation for the Israelites.[59] Because the miracle is only temporary, however, its aftermath leads to judgment on their enemies as the waters return and swallow up Egypt's chariots and horsemen. This forms a payback of sorts for the Egyptians' intent to drown all the newborn Israelite males in the Nile (Exod. 1:22)[60] and again teaches the Israelites that Yahweh is incomparable among the so-called gods (15:11). The parting of the Red Sea is a clear example of what frequently recurs throughout Scripture: the combination of providential timing and unprecedented power with certain natural elements. Thus Exodus 14:21 attributes the miracle to divine agency using, in part, normal means of nature: "All that night the Lord drove the sea back with a strong east wind." Similar combinations recur with the sequence of the plagues unleashed on Pharaoh (7:14–11:10),[61] with the timing of drought and rain during the ministry of Elijah centuries later (1 Kings 17–18), and in the New Testament, with the death of Herod Agrippa I (Acts 12:23). In this last case, we have the intriguing confirmation by the Jewish historian Josephus, who likewise sees both divine punishment and a physiological disorder as the cause (*Ant.* 19.343–50). The examples could be multiplied.

The reliability of the entire exodus story has, of course, been frequently called into question because of the lack of direct archaeological evidence. The problem is compounded by the debate over its date, whether it should be placed in the thirteenth or fifteenth century BC.

But we do have hieroglyphic paintings from Egypt from the fifteenth century that depict foreign slaves making mud bricks under the supervision of Egyptian overseers, and we have archaeological evidence for the sudden appearance or growth of towns in many places in Israel at about the right time, if we opt for the later date for the exodus. It is not realistic, moreover, to expect anything to remain of the shelters of impoverished people like the Israelite slaves in Egypt living in the marshy delta of the Nile, or of their temporary wilderness wanderings in the Sinai utilizing even less permanent structures. And no Pharaoh would have wanted to acknowledge the loss of a slave community due to their flight by recording or commemorating it in any way! There are, to be sure, sites in Israel where we might have expected evidence of occupation or signs of larger settlements, but it is actually amazing that so much *has* remained over the millennia.[62] We should always remind ourselves that the absence of evidence is never the evidence of absence!

The provision of manna, quail, and water from rock during the forty years in the Sinai Peninsula appears to utilize natural phenomena but on a more massive scale and with more providential timing than can be accounted for naturalistically. Closely tied into Yahweh's rescue and provision for his people is the law that he gives them, also in Sinai. Central in the law is the need to care for the poor, the foreigner, and the downtrodden or oppressed (e.g., Exod. 22:21; 23:9; Lev. 19:9–10, 33–34; Deut. 14:29; 16:11–14; 24:17–22; 26:12–13). Because the Lord has saved them from such conditions, they must treat each other and even the outsider similarly. They must show gratitude to the God who sustains them. Tragically, more often than not they rebel and lapse into idolatry. In the wilderness, the paradigm of this is the incident with the golden calf (Exod. 32). They receive a second chance, however, and the priesthood is established both to administer the sacrifices that symbolize their forgiveness by God and to create a leadership structure for a community that is obviously not yet ready for a more "democratic" model. The miracle of Aaron's rod that budded clearly confirms him as the chief priest (Num. 17:8), but does it do anything else? Since a dead, wooden staff sprouts to life, it quite likely reminds the people that only God can impart life to that which is dead.[63]

Anyone who denies that there is humor in the Bible needs to reread the account of Balaam's donkey in Numbers 22! As with Satan speaking through the serpent in Eden, we should think of this as God talking through this beast rather than a miracle that gives a donkey human speech. Balaam knows that animals do not speak; when he is shocked at his donkey's behavior, it is not because it speaks. This suggests that he realizes it is the voice of God. For our purposes, the important point is that "strange actions by animals were often regarded as omens in Mesopotamia. As a specialist in this sort of divination, he ought to have realized the deity had a message for him."[64] For God's people, "the point of the dialogue is that, when God opens the mouth, even a donkey can speak, so the Israelites need not fear this foreign seer."[65]

The miraculous crossing of the Jordan after the forty years of wandering in the wilderness (Josh. 3) creates an inclusio with the crossing of the Red Sea at the beginning of their journeying. Joshua 3:9–10 gives the most foundational meaning of the miracle: recognizing the presence of the Lord among them and guaranteeing his promise to drive out the people of the nations before them. Interestingly, the only other place besides here in the Old Testament that uses the expression "This is how you will know" is Numbers 16:28, in which God authenticates Moses by working the miracle of judgment against Korah and his rebellious colleagues, a judgment that Moses has just predicted. In Joshua 3, Joshua is similarly authenticated as Moses's successor.[66] Yet, parallel to the Israelites' flight from Egypt through the Red Sea and Elijah's and Elisha's later water-related miracles, the crossing of the Jordan also represents Yahweh's subduing of the rain-swollen Jordan and a demonstration of his sovereignty over Baal, who was believed to unleash the spring rains every year.[67]

The famous "battle" of Jericho reflects no ordinary skirmish. Although scholars have at times suggested naturalistic explanations for the collapse of Jericho's walls, the text describes the people of Israel as performing something more akin to a ceremonial ritual with their perimeter marching and trumpet blowing.[68] As Richard Hess phrases it, "A ceremony will overcome Jericho's walls. Elsewhere in the Ancient Near East among pre-battle rituals there is no comparison to it."[69] The design is clearly to demonstrate the Lord's sovereignty rather than the

Israelites' skills as warriors. The same theme recurs throughout all of Israel's battles, all of which are actually defensive rather than offensive after the initial settlement of the land (even if individual skirmishes within larger wars were started at times by the Israelites).

Sometimes what appears to be a miracle may be better interpreted otherwise, especially in light of ancient Near Eastern parallels. It has often been speculated that Joshua's address in Joshua 10:12–13, reflecting the synonymous parallelism so characteristic of Hebrew poetry, was intended as figurative language of some kind: "'Sun, stand still over Gibeon, and you, moon, over the Valley of Aijalon.' So the sun stood still, and the moon stopped, till the nation avenged itself on its enemies."[70] More specifically, Walton, Matthews, and Chavalas observe:

> The Mesopotamian celestial omens use verbs like *wait*, *stand* and *stop* to record the relative movements and positions of the celestial bodies. When the moon or sun do [*sic*] not wait, the moon sinks over the horizon before the sun rises and no opposition occurs. When the moon and sun wait or stand, it indicates that the opposition does occur for the determination of the full moon day. The omens in the series known as Enuma Anu Enlil often speak of changing velocities of the moon in its course to effect or avoid opposition with the sun. Likewise in verse 13 the text here reports that the sun did not hurry but instead stood in its section of the sky. It should be noted that the text does not suggest the astronomical phenomena were unique, but instead, verse 14 says plainly that what was unique was the Lord accepting a battle strategy from a man ("the Lord listened to a man"). Such an opposition on an unpropitious day would have deflated the Amorites.[71]

This is a far more satisfactory interpretation than needing to imagine God stopping the rotation of the earth on its axis for a while and simultaneously suspending the normal antigravitational forces that would have otherwise caused everything not securely affixed to the planet to fly away into outer space! As in our earlier discussions, it is not that God could not do this if he so desired. It is rather that it would require a whole series of subsidiary miracles of a magnitude and nature utterly unparalleled in Scripture, without any other evidence in the whole of world history for support, and to which no other biblical writer ever again refers![72] Hezekiah's experience with a moving and stopping shadow of the sun in 2 Kings 20:9–11 is best understood as a miracle involving the movement of the shadow (all that the Bible ever describes), not of the entire solar system.[73]

Gideon's fleeces (Judg. 6:36–40) form another unique pair of miracles in the Bible and do not appear in a context highlighting his faith. Indeed, precisely because Gideon is *not* adequately depending on God, in the very next episode that Judges narrates, the Lord makes him pare back his army so that he cannot take credit for the victory he is about to be given (chap. 7). Daniel Block observes that only the generic name "God" appears in 6:36–40 and concludes, "Apparently Gideon has difficulty distinguishing between Yahweh, the God of the Israelites, and god in a general sense. The remarkable fact is that God responds to his tests. He is more anxious to deliver Israel than to quibble with this man's semi-pagan notions of deity."[74] At any rate, after the giving of the Holy Spirit to permanently indwell God's people (Acts 2), it is doubtful if fleeces are ever intended to be an appropriate way of discerning God's will.

Our overview could continue at some length, but two more particularly puzzling passages will suffice to complete our survey. What are we to make of the witch or medium at Endor's conjuring up Samuel in a séance with Saul (1 Sam. 28:7–25)? Although "a straightforward reading of the biblical account suggests the possibility that mediums may possess the capacity to contact dead persons and establish lines of communication between the living and the dead,"[75] it is better to envision it as a diabolical manifestation that surprised even the medium, who made her living by the dark arts. If Satan can masquerade as "an angel of light" (2 Cor. 11:14), it is not difficult to imagine a demon temporarily appearing like Samuel. After all, nothing good comes out of the experience; all Saul learns is about his coming defeat and the death of his two sons and himself in the battle with the Philistines (1 Sam. 28:19).[76]

Finally, 2 Samuel 6:6–7 has understandably troubled many readers. Uzzah, a young Israelite man, takes hold of the ark of the covenant to keep it from falling off an ox-drawn cart when the oxen begin to stumble. But verse 7 announces that "the Lord's anger burned against Uzzah because of his irreverent act; therefore God struck him down, and he died there beside the ark of God." For a reader lacking familiarity with the rest of the biblical narrative, Uzzah's action seems far from irreverent. Yet Exodus 25:12–14 makes clear that the ark is always to be carried with poles inserted through its rings, and numerous other passages in the Old Testament depict the care with which the Israelites characteristically obeyed this command. (In addition to twenty-five references in Exodus 25–40, see Numbers 4:15 ["they must not touch the holy things or they will die"]; 1 Kings 8:7–8; 1 Chronicles 15:15; 2 Chronicles 5:8–9.) Uzzah, on the other hand, had accompanied the ark as it began its journey from Baalah to Jerusalem, and he would have known full well that they were not to transport the ark on a cart (2 Sam. 6:2–4). Apparently this violation of procedure was designed to free up all the men from anyone having to carry the poles so that they could dance in celebration instead (v. 5). The entire passage, therefore, depicts far too cavalier an attitude toward what was at the time the holiest object in all of Israelite religion.[77]

Summary

What have we seen in this walk through a large percentage of the Old Testament miracles? All of them fall into one or more of only a handful of categories: events that demonstrate Yahweh's superiority to his rival deities precisely in the areas in which those deities were believed to hold particular sway; interventions at critical, often life-threatening moments to save God's people and judge their enemies, thus fulfilling God's promises to Abraham and his descendants; judgment within Israel itself when there was clear rebellion at very vulnerable stages of its existence and when division or immorality would prove highly destructive; and the authentication of a new development within God's unfolding plan for his people, showing that it was truly from God.[78]

Miracles in the Gospels

Can New Testament miracles be similarly grouped into a handful of categories? Do recurring patterns make them equally purposeful, or are they simply sensationalizing tales as in much of the New Testament Apocrypha? Because the New Testament stories are usually better known than their Old Testament counterparts, and because they have been studied far more often and in much more detail, we may proceed more rapidly and selectively here.[79]

Reasons for Miracles

The most common category involves miracles of physical healing, including exorcisms and, very occasionally, resurrections. In the Gospels, some of these miracles occur in response to faith in Jesus or, conversely, fail to occur due to insufficient faith: witness the sequence of passages in Mark 5:21–6:6a in which Jairus's faith contributes significantly to the resurrection of his daughter (5:36 pars.), and the hemorrhaging woman's faith leads to her healing (5:34 pars.). But then Jesus can work only a few miracles in his hometown, Nazareth, due to the people's lack of faith (6:5–6a par.). Presumably compassion is a key motive behind these miracles as well, but only three times does a passage explicitly declare this (Mark 6:34 pars.; 8:2 par.; Matt. 20:34).

On the other hand, and giving the lie to the prosperity or "health-wealth" gospel, there is no consistent pattern of greater faith increasing the likelihood of experiencing a miracle.[80] Just as often as Christ works a sign or wonder in response to faith, he also effects a miracle to produce faith where it is too small or nonexistent. We see this in the varying accounts of the stilling of the storm (Mark 4:40–41 pars.), in the healing of the nobleman's son in John 4:48, and in the interaction between Jesus and Thomas after the resurrection (John 20:25–29). Particularly in John's Gospel, Jesus can imply that a person's affliction was the result of some sin. Thus, after healing the lame man by the pool of Bethesda (John 5:1–9), Jesus tells him, "See, you are well again. Stop sinning or something worse may happen to you" (5:14). Later, however, when the disciples try to extrapolate from this experience and determine whether a man blind from birth had somehow sinned (in utero?) or whether he was being punished for the sins of his parents, Jesus explains that neither is true. In this instance, the man's condition merely magnifies the coming glory that God will receive when Jesus performs the healing (John 9:1–3).[81]

A disproportionately large number of the recipients of Christ's miracles are those who would have been ostracized to some degree by the orthodox Jewish leaders. It may be a Gentile centurion's servant (Luke 7:1–10 par.), a Samaritan leper (Luke 17:11–19), or a demon-possessed Gerasene who inhabited the local cemetery (Mark 5:1–20 pars.). A disproportionate number of the miracles recorded in the Gospels also occur on the Sabbath—the one day of the week on which Jesus would consistently be charged with violating Pharisaic interpretations of what constituted work he should not perform. In no instance did his Sabbath healings cure people whose lives were even remotely in danger, a legal stipulation that would allow for Sabbath healings. Sometimes the Gospel writer seems to go out of his way to tell us how chronic the problem had been (Luke 13:11; John 5:5; 9:1). Jesus's critics undoubtedly imagined that waiting one more day after someone's years of suffering was a small price to pay for obeying God's law, but Jesus roundly disagreed.[82]

None of these themes, however, represents the most central reason Jesus performed miracles. Several explicit statements in the Gospels make this clear. After being accused of casting out demons by the power of the devil, Jesus highlights the fallacies of such a position (Luke 11:14–19 par.). Then he adds, "But if I drive out demons by the finger of God, then the kingdom of God has come upon you" (v. 20).[83] When asked by some of John the Baptist's followers, after their master had been thrown into prison, whether he is the Messiah, Jesus replies, "Go back and report to John what you have seen and heard: the blind receive sight, the lame walk, those who have leprosy are cleansed, the deaf hear, the dead are raised . . ." (Luke 7:22 par.). *In other words, the miracles point to Jesus's messiahship. If the kingdom has arrived, then its king must be present. If the Messiah has come, then the messianic age must be at hand.*[84] The specific kinds of miracles prophesied in Isaiah 35:5–6 were being fulfilled. Similar conclusions about Jesus's identity can be derived from Mark 2:10–11, as Jesus provides forgiveness of sins while healing the paralyzed man lowered to him through a hole dug in the flat roof,[85] and from Jesus's words just before the raising of Lazarus, in which he declares himself to be "the resurrection and the life" (John 11:25).

Miracles Other than Healings

There is, in fact, notably less variety in the kinds of miracles Jesus works than in the diversity of Old Testament signs and wonders. Apart from healings, including exorcisms and resurrections, we find only the following: calming the storm (Mark 4:35–41 pars.), feeding the five thousand and the four thousand (Mark 6:32–44 pars.; 8:1–10 par.), walking on the water (Mark 6:45–52 pars.), the transfiguration (Mark 9:2–8 pars.), cursing the fig tree so that it withered quickly (Mark 11:12–14, 20–25 par.), the two miraculous catches of fish (Luke 5:1–11; John 21:1–14), and turning water into wine (John 2:1–11). When one understands the cluster of associations that each of these wonders would have evoked among their largely Jewish audiences, they fit very consistently with the rest of Jesus's ministry and do not appear as anomalies.[86]

The Gospel writers agree that the result of stilling the storm was to make the disciples ask who this Jesus was who could make even wind and waves obey him (Mark 4:41 pars.). In other words, like the exorcisms, like his kingdom teaching and ministry more generally, the miracle confronted its observers with the question of Jesus's identity. In the Old Testament, Yahweh retained the authority to calm storms (cf. Jon. 1–2; Pss. 104:7; 107:23–32); Jesus must somehow be sharing in that unique power.[87] The Lord likewise treads on the waves (Job 9:8)—hence, Jesus's walking on the water. His words to the terrified disciples, "Take courage, it is I" (Mark 6:50 pars.), are rendered by the evangelists with the same Greek construction used in the LXX of Exodus 3:14 (*egō eimi*) for the divine name ("I AM").[88] The transfiguration similarly discloses a normally hidden glorious side of Christ, as he appears with Moses and Elijah in their heavenly forms. This is a literal mountaintop experience, to prepare the disciples for the ever-increasing horrors of the road to the cross, which Jesus follows unrelentingly from here to the end of the Gospel. They have received at least a glimpse of his glory and of what they themselves can expect one day on the other side of suffering. The transfiguration further foreshadows the resurrection, which is in turn the firstfruit of our coming resurrections as believers.[89]

The feeding miracles recall the provision of manna for the Israelites in the wilderness and the multiplication of the loaves by Elisha. They identify Jesus as a new Moses and a new Elisha—a new and greater prophet, miracle worker, and deliverer of his people. That he performs the miracle so similarly on two occasions invites us to examine who the two different groups of 5,000 and 4,000 were, who received the miraculously provided loaves and fishes. In the feeding of the 5,000, crowds from Galilee have followed Jesus around the lake as he crossed over by boat (Mark 6:31–33 pars.), so they presumably are largely Jewish in makeup. For the feeding of the 4,000, Jesus has just been in the Decapolis (7:31) and is now in a more remote location than for the feeding of the 5,000 (8:3–4). The passage occurs in the middle of a larger sequence of passages in which Jesus is almost always outside Israelite territory (7:24–9:32). So in this case, we may assume that the crowds are overwhelmingly Gentile in makeup. John 6 depicts Jesus preaching in the Capernaum synagogue shortly after the feeding of the 5,000 and interpreting the meaning of the miracle: he is the Bread of Life, the spiritual sustenance of his followers (6:35, 48). Together the two feeding miracles demonstrate him to be this Bread for Jews and Gentiles alike.[90]

The miraculously large catches of fish and the turning of water into wine represent the inexplicable provision of a superabundance of food and drink. Although the two fish catches appear in separate Gospels, together they create a remarkable inclusio around Peter's time as a disciple during Jesus's earthly life. The first miracle authenticates Jesus to Peter when he is called as an apostle and leads to his ministry of fishing for people (Luke 5:1–11). The second miracle accompanies Peter's "recall" or reinstatement after he has denied Jesus three times; it shows Peter that his master is willing to be as generous in his provision for him now as he was at the outset of their ministry together (John 21:1–23).[91] The miracle of water into wine depicts in reality what Jesus speaks of in metaphors when he insists that new wine cannot be put into old wineskins. Not by coincidence does John tell us that the water Jesus turned into wine was in six stone jars used for the Jewish rites of purification (John 2:6), especially in an account otherwise so sparse of detail that the miracle itself is never narrated, only the discovery of its results. Jesus is clearly portraying the newness of his ministry, showing that what he is offering cannot be contained in the old rituals of Judaism.[92] There would be plenty of continuity with Judaism but significant changes as well, especially with respect to the laws of ritual purity.

To understand the cursing of the fig tree, one must recognize that fig trees in the Old Testament frequently stood for Israel (esp. Mic. 7:1; Jer. 8:13). Jesus told a parable in Luke 13:6–9 about a barren fig tree, symbolizing the fruitlessness of the current regime in Israel, which could anticipate complete destruction in the near future if it did not repent by accepting Jesus. This symbolism fits the cursing of the fig tree between Bethany and Jerusalem equally well. Particularly in Mark, it is sandwiched around the account of Jesus clearing the temple, a distinctively Markan literary device for highlighting the interrelatedness of two key events.[93] The temple clearing even more obviously indicated the present corruption of the sacrificial cult and threatened imminent destruction, a threat that was fulfilled in the razing of the temple by the Romans in AD 70.

Miracles in Acts

The most striking feature of the miracles in the Acts of the Apostles is how closely they replicate miracles of Jesus or fulfill Old Testament prophecy.[94] Jesus's ascension (Acts 1:9–11) completes his forty days of resurrection appearances and gives the eleven apostles a glimpse of the glory that Peter, James, and John experienced at the transfiguration. Speaking in unknown languages at Pentecost fulfills the explicit prophecy of Joel 2:28–32, as Peter makes clear in his subsequent address to the onlookers gathered (Acts 2:16–21). Jesus healed individuals who were paralyzed and lame; Peter and Paul are now empowered to do the same (3:6–10; 9:32–35; 14:8–10). But whereas Jesus could simply command signs and wonders to occur, the disciples pray and issue commands *in his name* to show where the true power resides.[95]

Just as the Old Testament and the Gospels disclose the occasional miracle of judgment, so too Acts depicts Peter's pronouncing God's death sentence on Ananias and Sapphira. The parallels with the judgment of Achan in Joshua 7 have often struck commentators, particularly with the only two uses in biblical narrative of a Greek verb meaning "to swindle" occurring in these two contexts (Josh. 7:1 LXX; Acts 5:2–3). In both cases, God unleashes unusually harsh discipline on key families for the identical sin at precisely those times when his fledgling covenant communities are very vulnerable, poised for great works but also susceptible to extinction early in their history.[96] We may surely speak of this as typological fulfillment, even if Luke does not directly mention the precursor in Joshua. For an example of a miraculous judgment on one of God's enemies that also utilizes natural means, akin to certain Old Testament judgments, consider the narrative about the death of Herod Agrippa I (Acts 12:21–23) mentioned earlier in this chapter.

Whereas one of Jesus's miracles of destruction withered a tree, and another one somewhat less directly caused the death of a herd of pigs (the exorcism of the Gerasene demoniac), the remaining miracle of destruction in Acts involves the temporary blindness of the sorcerer who served Sergius Paulus, the proconsul in Paphos, on the island of Cyprus. That one of his names was "bar-Jesus" ("son of Joshua") means he was ethnically Jewish, so that it was all the more inappropriate for him to be engaging in this occupation prohibited by the Torah. But the punishment fits the "crime," since sorcerers cast (usually temporary) spells on others to harm them in some way.[97]

Of course, it did not fit God's plan for Jesus to be miraculously released from his imprisonment, because his mission was to die. If tradition can be believed, most of Jesus's apostles followed him in martyrdom, but not immediately and not without some miraculous escapes from prison (Acts 5:20–24; 12:6–11; 16:25–34). Saul's conversion formed a spiritual escape from a prison Saul did not know he was in; the physical miracle that occurred was his encounter with the risen Lord on the Damascus Road (9:1–10), which he would later interpret as on par with the resurrection appearances to the Twelve (1 Cor. 15:8). Peter and Paul, like Jesus during his lifetime, are also enabled to raise the dead, not to eternal life but to a new lease on earthly life (Acts 9:36–42; 20:7–12). Acts 16:16–18 and 19:13–16 recount exorcisms closely akin to those Jesus performed, even down to the specific detail of the demons expressing knowledge of the identities of their spiritual opponents.[98]

Two striking passages in Acts depict Peter and Paul as working miracles more indirectly. People brought the sick out to the streets in hopes that even Peter's shadow might fall on them (5:15). This could have reflected just the kind of superstition Jesus encountered with the lame man wanting to get into the pool of Bethesda when the water was stirred (John 5:7). Yet the juxtaposition of Acts 5:16, in which others from the countryside brought their sick and demon-possessed and "all of them were healed," suggests we are meant to understand that Peter's shadow, at least on this occasion, became a means for physical healing as well. Then in 19:11–12, we read that "God did extraordinary miracles through Paul, so that even handkerchiefs and aprons that had touched him were taken to the sick, and their illnesses were cured and the evil spirits left them." We are reminded of the woman who touched Jesus in Mark 5:27–30 and parallels, when Jesus recognized that power had gone out from him. At times God graciously honors people's faith even when it is mixed with superstitions, especially when it demonstrates his supremacy over rival powers.[99]

Provisional Conclusions

By now the point of this survey should be clear. Throughout both Testaments, the miracles are scarcely random. They are not an arbitrary collection of wonders sprinkled throughout an ordinary narrative in order to give it an extraordinary quality. They are part and parcel of the biblical revelation from start to finish, even if certain periods of time saw more intense clusters of wondrous events. People can choose not to believe that they could have happened, but in light of the massive amount of documented parallels in today's world, this would be a leap of faith in spite of the evidence, not the logical outgrowth of scientific or philosophical reasoning. Treating them as mythical or legendary has only a slightly greater likelihood of being a correct assessment, especially given the astonishingly early testimony to the resurrection. And critics, like the apostles, have recognized that the resurrection is the central fact of Christian history on which the credibility of our faith depends.[100]

The Resurrection and History

Of course, it is still commonplace to find biblical scholars protesting that the resurrection, by its very nature, lies outside the bounds of historical research. But this seems far-fetched. If the testimony is strong enough, voiced by credible witnesses whose lives were changed for the better from that moment onward, why should the same criteria not come into play as for any other allegedly historical event?[101] Perhaps the ultimate *explanation* for the resurrection appearances (the activity of God) lies outside the bounds of historical investigation, but that the appearances occurred and were not merely subjective and visionary appears to be an eminently legitimate historical claim. Additional issues reinforce this conclusion.

Most notably, why would four largely independent resurrection accounts all have invented women as the first and primary witnesses in the face of antiquity's general disparagement of the validity of female testimony? How did the first followers of Jesus, who were all Jews, get past the clear teaching of their law that a crucified person was cursed by God (Deut. 21:23)? How did they convince themselves it was acceptable to worship on the first day of the week when the immutable Torah insisted on the seventh day as the Sabbath, unless something of enormous significance objectively datable to one Sunday morning actually occurred? How could they boldly proclaim Jesus as Lord and Christ from that moment onward, frequently putting their lives at risk, with a holy, transformed character that they had not previously exhibited?[102] These questions are rarely even addressed by those who question the truth of the resurrection accounts, much less given any plausible explanations.

Avoiding the Opposite Extreme

In the early nineteenth century, as American settlers became more and more aware of the vast expanse of the continent that opened up before them to the west, many began to wonder if God was doing some special new work in this fledgling nation to usher in the last days of human history, to bring a renewed awareness of the presence of his Spirit, and to once again manifest all the gifts of the Spirit as described by Paul in Romans 12:6–8; 1 Corinthians 12:8–10, 28–30; and Ephesians 4:11. Many Christians particularly longed for the reestablishment of prophecy as direct words of the Lord both about the future and to guide his people in the present. When a young man by the name of Joseph Smith Jr., in upstate New York, was seeking revelation from the Lord in the 1820s, all the major denominations that he encountered firmly taught that the seemingly more-supernatural gifts of the Spirit—including prophecy, the discerning of spirits, tongues, their interpretation, and various workings of miracles—had ceased with the close of the biblical canon and the end of the apostolic age.[103] One of the major attractions of the religion he founded, the Church of Jesus Christ of Latter-day Saints, or Mormonism, was its claim that all these gifts had been restored in his church.

However, after a few precursors in other parts of the country and the world, a major manifestation of these gifts did occur during the Azusa Street Revival in Southern California in 1906. This birthed modern Pentecostalism and the denominations it would spawn, including especially the Assemblies of God, the Foursquare Gospel movement, the Church of God (Cleveland, TN), the Church of God in Christ, the Association of Vineyard Churches, and Calvary Chapels. In the 1960s and 1970s, neither Roman Catholicism nor the major Protestant denominations escaped the influence of spiritual awakening, thanks to the appearance of these gifts, though in each case only a minority of worshipers and congregations were affected. Today Pentecostalism and the charismatic movement (the expression sometimes reserved for Pentecostal-like phenomena in contexts other than recognized Pentecostal churches) constitute the fastest growing branch of any religion in the world; in some parts of the Majority World it is the dominant expression of Christianity.[104] One wonders whether Mormonism would ever have come into being if the Azusa Street Revival had occurred eighty-six years earlier and somewhere near Palmyra, New York, where Joseph Smith was living!

Unfortunately, with every religious movement come abuses and quackery. With the advent of television and the proliferation of televised ministries, especially of Pentecostal or charismatic preachers and their congregations, the potential for even more abuse becomes natural, whether in harangues for money, deceptive claims of miracles, or overly authoritarian ministries. But we should never throw the proverbial baby out with the bathwater. Millions of Christians worldwide worship weekly with one or more of the supernatural gifts present, without undue attention drawn to them, and with men and women coming to Christ, growing in Christ, and experiencing spiritual power and healing—and, occasionally, dramatic physical healing as well.[105] To dismiss all of this as of human manufacture, or worse, as diabolical counterfeits, is a presumption of monstrous proportions.

Yet, although their numbers are not nearly as large as they were even just a generation ago, there are still plenty of cessationists, who argue that the supernatural gifts have ceased.[106] This, of course, requires them to distinguish two kinds of gifts where the first Christians would almost certainly have looked at *all* the gifts as supernatural. The cessationist view is based on some fanciful exegesis of passages, introducing distinctions that cannot stand up to close scrutiny.[107] Often cessationism requires its advocates to acknowledge that God can still work miracles today, but that what we see happening just shouldn't be called the spiritual gift of miracles—virtually a distinction without a difference![108] Most serious of all, it risks putting one on the threshold of committing what Jesus labeled the unforgivable sin—attributing the visibly undeniable power of the Holy Spirit to the devil (Mark 3:29).

We dare not swing the pendulum to the opposite extreme and insist that every church or every believer have one or more of the so-called supernatural gifts. As 1 Corinthians 12:11 makes crystal clear, God through his Spirit distributes his gifts as he desires. The metaphor of the diverse parts of the body makes it equally clear that he does not want all Christians to look alike. The rhetorical questions in verses 29–30, repeating the Greek negative adverb *mē*, prove that the desired answer to Paul's questions is negative: *no* one gift is given to all believers.[109] Thus any church or ministry insisting that all people exercise any one gift in order to be saved or even in order to be mature believers is simply contradicting Scripture. But the church of Jesus Christ worldwide would take huge steps forward toward unity with the appreciation of diversity if noncharismatics would obey 1 Corinthians 14:39 ("Be eager to prophesy, and do not forbid speaking in tongues") and charismatics would heed verse 40 ("But everything should be done in a fitting and orderly way").[110] In each culture, "orderly" means what will not lead outsiders who visit a service to conclude that the worshipers are out of their minds (14:23)!

Conclusion

Miracles should not be excluded a priori from historical research. Neither science nor philosophy gives us valid reasons for doing so. Enough contemporary events have been documented that resemble the New Testament miracles closely enough to make it credible to believe that they also happened. The only serious objection to the biblical miracle accounts is the one of literary form. Do they closely enough resemble bona fide myths or legends to be classified similarly? The closest parallels to New Testament accounts consistently prove to be post-Christian in origin; very few pre-Christian pagan miracle stories are at all similar. Old Testament miracles, on the other hand, often postdate their ancient Near Eastern parallels. Here the closest parallels come in contexts suggesting that the biblical counterparts are attributing to Yahweh what other people groups ascribed to numerous different gods. The purpose of the miracle stories is to counter the suggestion that any god but the Lord of Israel exists; only real events, not just mythical stories, could accomplish this. Other Old Testament miracles consistently fall into one of just a handful of categories, making it unlikely that the biblical narratives comprise random, fictitious accounts of the supernatural inserted into blander stories for sensationalizing purposes.

New Testament miracles most centrally point to the arrival of God's kingdom and therefore of God's king, Jesus the Messiah. The miracles in the Gospels and Acts closely parallel each other and often find their meaning when one recognizes Old Testament backgrounds as well. It does little good to believe in miracles in Bible times but not to be open to them—or to any of Paul's more supernatural gifts of the Spirit—today. Those who still defend cessationism risk quenching the Spirit (contra 1 Thess. 5:19) and inappropriately closing themselves and others off from the full range of blessings God might have for them and from potentially the greatest amount of effective service for his kingdom. *Without swinging the pendulum to the opposite extreme and embracing the various abuses of the charismata or trying to imitate the Spirit's work in one's own strength, cessationists really should cease trying to limit God in how he chooses to work in his world today*. It is, in essence, a form of antisupernaturalism for all the postapostolic eras of Christianity. The position is inconsistent with belief in a living and active God, amounts to a practical deism, and smacks of humans trying to usurp God's sovereignty by dictating what his people can and cannot do with respect to spiritual giftedness.[111]

Conclusion

As we noted in our introduction, we could go in a wide variety of directions when addressing questions about the reliability of the Bible. (1) We could discuss the trustworthiness of the history it records. (2) We could debate the coherence of the theology it promotes. (3) We could examine the morality it espouses. (4) We could examine countless minutiae to see if they create true contradictions with other parts of Scripture or with information from outside of Scripture. Many good books have done all of these things.[1] Instead, I have chosen six issues on which I have detected substantial changes in the average layperson's understanding and in the popular media's presentation over the past thirty to forty years. Thus we have titled the book, *Can We Still Believe the Bible? An Evangelical Engagement with Contemporary Questions*. Ironically, what has become best known in our culture over the past generation, both inside and outside of Christian circles, is the flurry of skepticism that certain narrow segments of scholarship and pseudoscholarship have unleashed. This is ironic because in each instance *the less-quoted majority of scholars*[2] *have increasingly come to recognize that the evidence is actually stronger for the trustworthiness of Scripture in each of these areas, as long as that trustworthiness is appropriately defined by the standards of antiquity*. Sadly, some of Christianity's very conservative, high-profile power brokers have played directly into the hands of the most skeptical wing of scholarship by giving the skeptics more attention than they deserve and by branding almost all scholars who reject their own ultraconservatism as just as "liberal" as the archskeptics! Worse still, some people are discouraged from holding the faith altogether, buying into the misconception that they cannot be true Christians at all unless they hold these ultraconservative viewpoints.

We have thus discussed the charges that the textual transmission of the biblical books was so corrupt that we cannot even be sure how close to the original documents our current Bible is. We have examined claims that the biblical canon is up for grabs, that the only or main reason we have the sixty-six books that all branches of Christendom agree on is because the early church leaders, who decreed which documents should be treated as uniquely sacred, were the victors in battles with others who wanted to create a very different Bible. We have looked at allegations that the proliferation of modern-language translations, especially in English, suggests that we really don't have the ability to declare any given translation sufficiently reliable for Christian thought and life. The true state of affairs in each of these areas is quite the opposite: (1) We have an extraordinarily high probability of being able to reconstruct the original texts of the biblical books, much higher than for any other documents of antiquity. (2) Especially with respect to the New Testament books, where there is no disagreement among the major branches of the Christian church as to what the canon should contain, claims about the accuracy and value of apocryphal or noncanonical counterparts are dramatically exaggerated. (3) Modern-language translations, including in English, are demonstrably very reliable.

In addition, we have scrutinized the historic Christian doctrine of the inerrancy of Scripture to see what it does and does not claim about the uniquely trustworthy nature of the Bible. We observed that it does not require us to hold the ancient texts to any higher standards of accuracy than would have been imposed by the societies from which they emerged. To do otherwise is sheer anachronism. We considered a sampling of some of the most well-known illustrations of biblical books or passages where Christians without access to comparative literature from the ancient world may have too often taken a text to be historical that was never intended to be so taken. In other words, defending Scripture's reliability in these instances might require our recognition of a different genre of prose narrative rather than straightforward history.

The results, in turn, may make inerrancy even *more* defensible than it was previously.

Finally, we turned to the issue of the miraculous. While for many this is the ultimate defeater in taking the Bible seriously, the amount of documented evidence for miracles similar to those of the Bible, especially from the last century or so, is so overwhelming that it actually counts as strong evidence *for* the credibility of Scripture. If someone seriously and dispassionately examines this evidence and still rejects it in toto, it is hard not to conclude that the prejudice at work is just irrational. This does not mean that we accept all claims of the miraculous in our world or in previous eras; indeed, we should want to employ very strict criteria before ever accepting them in any context. But when those criteria are fully met, to then continue to claim that there must be a naturalistic or scientific explanation that we just haven't discovered yet constitutes a *faith claim* with less rational foundation than the faith that believers must exercise to be Christians!

These are among the most important reasons that I believe in the uniquely God-given nature of the Bible more than ever after forty-three years of being a Christian and after forty-two years of studying it from just about every perspective ever invented! To be sure, if I seriously believed that holding any of the following positions were necessary for me to be a Christian (or at least an evangelical), it would be much harder for me to remain a Christian (or at least an evangelical): (1) *the inerrant preservation of Scripture*; (2) *"biblicism"* as Christian Smith defines it (see "Avoiding the Opposite Extreme" in chap. 2 above); (3) an *essentially literal and gender-exclusive translation* as the only or best kind of Bible translation; (4) the *anachronistic usages of "error"* that ultraconservatives employ (see chap. 4 above); (5) treating all narrative material in the Bible as monolithically representing the same kind of dispassionate chronicle, *without reference to Scripture's diverse literary genres and forms*; or (6) believing that the *spiritual gift of miracles* (or any of the biblical gifts of the Spirit, for that matter) *have ceased.*

The great news, however, is that none of these six restrictions that some would place on faith is even remotely necessary. Worldwide and throughout history, only a minuscule percentage of Christians have ever adopted this entire package of wrongheaded perspectives, and a large number have never adopted any of them. Even among those accepting the label "evangelical," and even among those who affirm inerrancy (the latter largely limited to the United States and to parts of the world heavily influenced by certain branches of American evangelicalism), there is no necessary reason why any of these six restrictions must be adopted. To claim otherwise is to put unnecessary obstacles in front of people struggling with whether or not to become and/or stay Christians (or evangelicals or inerrantists). The stumbling block of "Christ and him crucified" (1 Cor. 2:2) must *never* be excised from faith. If it is so excised, one no longer has *Christian* faith.[3] But with issues that do not jeopardize people's salvation, our model should be that of Paul in 1 Corinthians 9:19–23—being "all things to all people so that by all possible means [we] might save some." Focusing on cruciform Christian living will also go a long way toward preventing the heavy-handed exercise of power in excluding from our academic institutions and societies or from our churches and Christian organizations those with less narrow views than our own on nonsalvific doctrines.

A study of the heresies that the early church had to address in its first several centuries quickly discloses that there are two ways one can distort the truth. The best known, then and throughout church history, has been to redefine central doctrines too broadly—to become too "liberal." Less well remembered are the heresies caused by redefining central doctrines too narrowly—to become too "conservative."[4] In addition, it is always easier to look at those who are completely outside our Christian communities, who make no profession of faith, and especially those who prove most hostile in attacking the faith, and direct the burden of our polemic against them. It is much harder, more awkward, more uncomfortable, and sometimes even more dangerous to turn to those inside of our Christian communities who profess faith but spend most of their time drawing the boundaries of faith more narrowly than Scripture itself does. Harder still is it to confront those who attack everyone who does not agree with them, because such confrontation typically just leads to another round of even worse attacks. Most evangelical churches of any size, unfortunately, have a few such people, and they can make life miserable for the many. Unfortunately many Christian schools, colleges, seminaries, campus ministries, missions organizations, and other parachurch groups have a few as well, even if only among the more generous donors who use their influence inappropriately to attach strings to their giving. And yes, the academic guild and scholarly societies have their unfair share also. At some point, known only to God, people whose careers are characterized by trying to tear down the work of fellow Christians cross a threshold and thereby demonstrate that they aren't true believers at all (1 Cor. 3:16–17).[5]

Some will perhaps read this book and charge *me* with being too harsh on fellow evangelicals (and perhaps not harsh enough on non-Christian critics and skeptics).[6] I invite such readers to replicate an experiment I undertook over a decade ago, by asking a key question: "When do Jesus and the apostles get really mad?"[7] In other words, read the New Testament carefully from Matthew to Revelation, noting every time the text is surprisingly harsh and every time it is surprisingly mild in how it treats those who do not closely align themselves with Jesus's or the apostles' views. After such an investigation, it becomes quite apparent that two very consistent patterns emerge. Jesus and the apostles are surprisingly harsh with the Pharisees and Sadducees in the Gospels and Acts and with the Judaizers in the Epistles and Revelation. In other words, receiving the most censure are fellow members of the same religious community who *occupy positions of Christian leadership* and have created overly restrictive doctrinal boundaries and should know better. Conversely, those who are on the fringes of the community or clearly outside the community are treated surprisingly gently, being wooed with love and mercy, in the hope that they will repent or return. I wonder how often evangelical Christians in today's world have completely inverted these priorities, kowtowing to the overly conservative, judgmental insiders and blasting away at the non-Christian world for not adhering to Christian morality. Yet how can we expect non-Christians to pursue Christian morality when they do not have God's Spirit within them, the Spirit who alone makes such obedience possible?[8]

We can still wholeheartedly believe the Bible in the twenty-first century, even after honestly engaging contemporary questions. To any who are doubting the faith or who know they don't believe, my first question is to ask for the specific reasons. Some answer that it is because God has never miraculously (i.e., incontrovertibly) made himself known to *them*. Here several responses come to mind. First is to ask how much of life would come to a standstill if one believed only in things that one has experienced firsthand. A second is to point to the roughly two billion people on our planet who claim to have experienced the God of the Bible or the 200 million who have been privy to some kind of miracle (see chap. 6 above). God never compels belief; he always allows those who want to doubt to do so and does not coerce them into faith against their will. But "blessed are those who have not seen and yet have believed" (John 20:29). The amount of testimony from those who have experienced the supernatural, whose lives have been changed for the better, and/or who have contributed good to society over the last two thousand years *within a Christian context*—such accumulating testimony dramatically outweighs what has been experienced and accomplished by any other ideology *and* dramatically outweighs the evils done in the name of Christ as well.[9]

Those who don't recognize this should study history more carefully and thoroughly, including the history of ordinary people never deemed "newsworthy." If possible, they should travel the world to see what is happening every day in Christian communities in every corner of the globe. Seasoned journalist and once hardened skeptic Brian Stewart is just one recent example of many who have turned or returned to the Christian faith after seeing Christian ministry in the aftermath of natural disasters, in the middle of civil wars, despite famines and drought or rampant disease—in short, in the worst examples of "hell on earth," where hardly anyone else tries to make a difference for good.[10] Yes, horrible things are done in Jesus's name, and the media give hugely disproportionate attention to them. But nearly two billion people quietly work in unsung fashion, often behind the scenes, acting out their Christian faith week after week, year after year, particularly in the Majority World, particularly in very deprived circumstances materially, faithfully serving Jesus as Lord and making the world just a little better.[11]

Many who have deconverted, however, or who have never seriously explored biblical faith in the first place, have been pushed away by the bad behavior of a handful of self-identified Christians. If any such people are reading this book, I apologize to you vicariously for any abuse you have received at their hands. Even if you have never encountered

Christians who are quite different from these abusive ones, I assure you that millions of loving Christian communities of many different sizes and shapes around the globe have people who are as distressed as I am about this state of affairs. Please don't reject Jesus because of the awful things some of his people have done. Please don't reject the church as a whole, even if you may need to leave or avoid a few specific, toxic congregations.

Many people have been hurt by life circumstances. Their understanding of Christianity has been so truncated that they have come to believe that following Jesus will exempt them from the worst of human suffering. They don't understand why God seemingly fails to answer their prayers for health or wealth. Whether victims of the explicit "prosperity gospel"[12] or of more implicit and subtle forms of this thinking, they have not fully absorbed the repeated scriptural theme of God working best through human weakness. They need to immerse themselves in the biographies and autobiographies of some of the unsung heroes of Christian history, the "cloud of witnesses" whose faith in God and service for Christ have flourished in spite of (or perhaps even because of) chronic illness, injury, or disability.[13]

Other individuals just haven't encountered sufficiently convincing reasons for biblical faith. To them I ask, "Have you consulted *all* the major Christian perspectives on whichever topics trouble you? Or are you just rejecting one or a handful of Christian options, perhaps even because some Christians told you there weren't any other options?" Those advisers may or may not be right, but we should care enough to at least check out such claims.[14] Finally, a surprisingly large number of Christians I have met over the years, have heard about from others, or have read about have described a period of time in their lives during which they were atheists or adherents of some other worldview, ideology, or religion. With astonishing regularity, they subsequently reported that the real reason they had formerly rejected Christianity was their unwillingness to relinquish ultimate control and authority over their lives. Sometimes they realized their true motive at the time, and sometimes they realized it only with 20/20 hindsight. Christianity, by definition, means turning one's life over to Christ. Given this frequent admission of motives, it is only logical to assume that a large number of those who currently claim some *other* reason as to why they do not believe may really just be trying to control their own lives too. Ours is an age of radical autonomy and independence that dislikes submission to any kind of authority.[15]

At some point in their lives, almost as large a number of those who deconvert or never convert acknowledge that they simply wanted to adopt a lifestyle that they knew was not Christian. Thinking that it would allow them to avoid being accountable to God, they therefore denied Christian belief.[16] But if God exists, he exists independently of whether any given person *believes* that he exists. If, as the historic Christian creeds say, God will one day "judge the living and the dead," he will do so regardless of whether we continue to believe he will or not. How prepared will we be for that possibility if it turns out that historic Christianity is true rather than false?

These experiences recall an issue I raised in the introduction. Does one approach the Scriptures (or any other influential document or collection of documents in the history of world civilization) with a hermeneutics of consent or a hermeneutics of suspicion? Christians have not done well in trying to read literature from other religions empathetically, and atheists and adherents of other world religions today increasingly approach the Bible with preexisting hostility. When I was in my late twenties and early thirties, I read large portions of the sacred documents of the world's major religions; I read the Qur'an and the Book of Mormon twice carefully, cover to cover. I did my best to understand what the authors of each wanted to inculcate in their original contexts and why. I wanted to be open to truth from wherever it might emerge. Each document had many admirable qualities and things with which I could agree, but none touched my heart or convinced my mind the way the Bible did. From a theological perspective, the Christian should want to credit God through his Spirit with the ultimate wooing power that brings people to himself and to an appreciation of Holy Scripture (e.g., John 6:44). But people have the freedom to quench the Spirit with their attitudes (1 Thess. 5:19), God's Spirit will never force himself on anyone, and God eventually stops courting those who consistently refuse all his overtures (Rom. 1:24, 26, 28). Conversely, one may be utterly convinced that God has testified to them of the truth of a sacred text of a particular religion, but if they cannot give viable intellectual answers to the problems that others perceive with that same text, one has to wonder if they have misjudged the source of their convictions.

Some conservative evangelicals write or speak as if the only legitimate form of Christianity is inerrantism. Only a tiny minority throughout church history has held this conviction, and it often proves counterproductive. As we have already seen, it was this attitude drummed into Bart Ehrman's early years in evangelical circles that helped convince him to become a full-fledged agnostic within a remarkably short period of time after he abandoned inerrancy (see chap. 1 above). Millions of evangelicals worldwide and throughout history have not accepted the belief that every last word of Scripture is without error, yet they are living (or have lived) faith-filled, Christ-directed, God-honoring lives. Other Christians, often not identifying themselves as evangelicals, have embraced the conviction that the Bible is not inherently the Word of God but that God regularly uses it to accomplish his work in the world so that it *functions* as divine revelation on those occasions when the Spirit speaks to and works in believers' lives through it. Often this position is referred to as neo-orthodoxy.

Still other Christians believe that God accommodates himself to human beings to such an extent that his revelation is inextricably intertwined with the fallible thoughts of fallen human beings, and we have to do the best we can today to distinguish the two.[17] "Inclusivist" (or nonrestrictivist) Christians affirm that God can bring people to himself through the sacred writings of more religions than just Christianity.[18] That view may be wrong, but holding it doesn't automatically condemn one to hell! I may think that thirty of the fifty used cars in a dealer's parking lot are in good enough condition for me to drive them cross-country and arrive safely at my destination when in fact only one (or some other number less than thirty) of them can actually get me there. Yet it is not my belief concerning the roadworthiness of the other cars that determines if I make it to where I want to go, but whether or not I purchase and drive a car that is in good enough condition to get me there. "Inclusivist" Christians could be wrong, but they would not be "lost" as long as *they* are trusting in Christ and following him rather than any of the faulty ideologies that they think might also prove effective.

There are still other approaches to the Bible that Christians can hold without jeopardizing their salvation, even if they might have less than optimal effects on other areas of doctrine and life.[19]

My point here is that readers who are not convinced by my defense of inerrancy should not think that I am one of those people who argue in an all-or-nothing fashion. If I became convinced of a handful of fairly trivial errors in the Bible, I would opt for an infallibilist position (see chap. 4 above) instead. If I felt that some of these errors were more serious, I would fall back on neo-orthodoxy. If that became too much of a stretch, I would explore accommodationism or even more liberal Christian epistemologies. I have known too many godly and committed believers in each of these camps over the years ever to countenance jettisoning all Christian options simply because I found one unconvincing or inadequate. I have never understood why some who deconvert jump directly from fundamentalism all the way to atheism without even exploring the many intermediate positions. But, as this book should make clear, I do not think one has to settle for anything short of full-fledged inerrantist Christianity so long as we ensure that we employ all parts of a detailed exposition of inerrancy, such as that found in the Chicago Statement on Biblical Inerrancy (1979; see chap. 4 above), and not just those sections that are most amenable to our personal philosophies or theologies.[20] This also means that we interpret the Chicago Statement, like the Bible, in terms of what is actually written, and not merely what one of its authors might have wanted to write or might have wanted it to mean.

Another way of getting at this issue is to ask, "How much of the Bible must be historical for Christianity to be true?" Paul makes it clear that without the bodily resurrection of Jesus, our faith is futile and we are of all people "most miserable" (1 Cor. 15:12–19 KJV). Elsewhere he boils things down to what may be the earliest known confession of Christian faith—confession of Jesus as Lord, as our divine Master—and belief in the resurrection (Rom. 10:9–10). Early Christian confessions of faith like the Apostles' and Nicene Creeds collect key biblical affirmations and organize them in trinitarian sequence—beliefs about Father, Son, and Holy Spirit. Intriguingly they jump directly from Jesus as "born of the Virgin Mary" to his suffering, death, burial, resurrection, and ascension. Much more of the Gospels' accounts of the events in Christ's life are accepted by the majority of Gospels scholars than just his birth and death, but the early Christian fathers obviously recognized where the nonnegotiables lay. As we have already seen, there is a core plot running through the Old Testament—from creation to human sin, to the call of Abram, to the lives of the patriarchs and Moses, to the exodus, to the settling of Israel, to the ministries of judges and kings, and to the experiences of exile and restoration—without which the coming of the Messiah makes little sense. But the more one moves away from this backbone toward the extremities of the biblical story line, the more there is room to say, "This need not be historical for Christianity to remain true." I may be convinced that there are good reasons for seeing a certain segment as historical, but I must distinguish between the more essential and the more peripheral parts when I assess how significant someone else's doubts about that segment are. As we have seen, almost nothing is at stake if Job never existed, whereas everything is at stake if Jesus never lived.

Too often Christians present the gospel as if the biblical story primarily culminates in rewards and punishments. There is a sense in which this is true, of course, but it is far too easily misunderstood. Without foreclosing on important debates about predestination or the work of the Spirit in people's lives, it is important to stress that all major branches of Christian theology agree that God's sovereignty never cancels out human freedom and responsibility.[21] Those who in this life choose to maintain their independence from God get their wish confirmed in the next. There are plenty of metaphorical passages about the afterlife in Scripture, but one that can be taken entirely literally is 2 Thessalonians 1:9, in which unbelievers are said to be "shut out from the presence of the Lord and the glory of his might." More prosaically, they will be excluded from God and all things good.[22] But why would anyone ever seriously want to choose this, when the glories and grandeur of a new heaven and a new earth (Rev. 21–22)—beyond our ability even to comprehend or describe—are freely available? It is, to use C. S. Lewis's famous analogy, like children content to play with mud pies in a slum rather than going for a holiday by the sea.[23] But some, thinking they can control their lives in the mud, sadly prefer that to the uncertainty of following someone else to new and uncharted territories, however wonderful they promise to be.

The aggressive atheists sometimes like to draw a laugh from their audiences by saying that, if it turns out that heaven and hell do exist, at least they won't have to spend eternity with the worst of the self-centered, money-grubbing, audience-haranguing televangelists. Other unbelievers, badly hurt by the most legalistic and dour of conservative churchgoers, might likewise feel relieved about not having to continue to interact with those who have injured them. Two replies prove crucial here. First, if those televangelists or legalists truly are Christian, then they, like all other believers, will receive perfectly glorified, sinless resurrection bodies (1 Cor. 15:35–58). All their offensive character traits will be purged; all believers will be completely loving. On the other hand, in the worst case scenario, those hurtful people may turn out not to be true Christians at all. In that case, the atheists' worst nightmare will come true: they *will* spend eternity with these self-centered people. Unbelievers will also be purged, not of sin but of living in an environment with all the goodness and grace that came from everyone and everything outside of themselves, which had prevented them from being as bad as they might otherwise have been.[24] Dawkins, Hitchens, Harris, and their ideological kin should really be much more careful about what they wish for!

Some will now reply that I am simply using scare tactics. That is hardly my intention, though I would make the following observations. If the building *is* starting to burn down, we usually appreciate rather than criticize those who set off the fire alarm. If there *is* a terrorist about to shoot up a shopping mall, we are forever grateful to the person who quickly ushers us out a side door and away from the threat.[25] More important, my motivation for belief is far more the enjoyment of God and all the community of the redeemed of all time, in unimaginable eternal happiness, than the mere avoidance of hell. And that enjoyment, however imperfect, begins now in this life, as we are freed for service to the world, to do everything in our ability, empowered by God's Spirit, to improve its conditions, spiritually and materially. If this book helps even a few more people experience the joy of that freedom, then it has been well worth the effort to produce it.

Unlike the illusory freedoms we think we have when we manage our own affairs, the freedom that God offers us in Christ truly does make possible what is the very best for us now and throughout an eternity to come. As the advertisers like to say, "We really can have it all!" But only on God's terms and in his timing (Rev. 21–22).[26] The most magnificent parts of the Bible, which we can still believe in the twenty-first century, are its last two chapters, which should be read again and again. Too often our views of heaven are much too impoverished.[27] We have been offered new heavens and a new earth, with the fulfillment of our greatest dreams and without any evil marring them ever again. We have been offered it through Jesus, whom we come to know and understand best through the Christian Scriptures. And these Scriptures are trustworthy. We can still believe the Bible. We *should* still believe the Bible and act accordingly, by following Jesus in discipleship.

NOTES

Introduction

1. See esp. Alvin Plantinga, *God, Freedom, and Evil* (New York: Harper & Row, 1974; Grand Rapids: Eerdmans, 1977); Richard Swinburne, *Providence and the Problem of Evil* (Oxford: Oxford University Press, 1998); C. S. Lewis, *The Problem of Pain* (London: Geoffrey Bles, 1940; New York: Macmillan, 1944).

2. For an excellent survey of the half-dozen major Christian options, see John Sanders, *No Other Name: An Investigation into the Destiny of the Unevangelized* (Grand Rapids: Eerdmans, 1992). Cf. also William V. Crockett and James G. Sigountos, eds., *Through No Fault of Their Own? The Fate of Those Who Have Never Heard* (Grand Rapids: Baker, 1991).

3. Christian answers have fallen into three broad categories: restrictivist, inclusivist, and universalist. Restrictivists believe all who reject Christ are lost. Universalists believe all who reject Christ will eventually be saved, though opinions vary on how or after what experiences this will occur. Inclusivists allow for some who have not consciously put faith in Christ for their salvation, but this by no means includes all such individuals (and again opinions vary widely on the conditions under which this can occur). Among self-identifying evangelicals, all three groups can be found, though the universalist is by far the smallest category. But see Gregory MacDonald, *The Evangelical Universalist*, rev. ed. (Eugene, OR: Wipf & Stock, 2012). For an excellent anthology of two different evangelical restrictivist views, one evangelical inclusivist view, and one nonevangelical universalist view, see Dennis L. Okholm and Timothy R. Phillips, eds., *Four Views on Salvation in a Pluralistic World* (Grand Rapids: Zondervan, 1996).

4. See esp. Helmut Merkel, *Die Pluralität der Evangelien als theologisches und exegetisches Problem in der Alten Kirche* (Bern: Peter Lang, 1978). Cf. also Robert M. Grant, *The Earliest Lives of Jesus* (New York: Harper & Row; London: SPCK, 1961). The earliest known harmony is Tatian's *Diatessaron*, in the late second century.

5. For a representative sampling of these problems, see Gleason L. Archer, *Encyclopedia of Bible Difficulties* (Grand Rapids: Zondervan, 1982). Archer's responses have sometimes been superseded by better ones, but the issues he highlights are a good collection of the kinds of problems many Bible readers have observed. The best approach to discovering the breadth of credible scholarly responses is to consult the more detailed evangelical commentaries on the given biblical book in which the particular issue appears. Updated at least annually and highlighting the best of these (and other) academic resources for biblical studies, helpful

lists appear in the Old and New Testament department bibliographies in the *Denver Journal*, http://www.denverseminary.edu/resources/the-denver-journal/.

6. See further Gregory C. Chirichigno, *Debt Slavery in Israel and the Ancient Near East* (Sheffield: JSOT Press, 1993); Jennifer A. Glancy, *Slavery in Early Christianity* (Oxford: Oxford University Press, 2002); J. Albert Harrill, *The Manumission of Slaves in Early Christianity* (Tübingen: Mohr Siebeck, 1995); and Rodney Stark, *For the Glory of God: How Monotheism Led to Reformations, Science, Witch-Hunts, and the End of Slavery* (Princeton: Princeton University Press, 2003), 291–366.

7. Esp. compare and contrast John Piper and Wayne Grudem, eds., *Recovering Biblical Manhood and Womanhood: A Response to Evangelical Feminism* (Wheaton: Crossway, 1991); with Ronald W. Pierce and Rebecca Merrill Groothuis, eds., *Discovering Biblical Equality: Complementarity without Hierarchy* (Downers Grove, IL: InterVarsity, 2004). See also James R. Beck, ed., *Two Views of Women in Ministry*, rev. ed. (Grand Rapids: Zondervan, 2005).

8. Evangelicals were also at the forefront of various nineteenth- and early twentieth-century feminist movements, but the fundamentalist-modernist controversy in the 1920s led to retrenchment in several instances. For a very evenhanded treatment of women's ministries throughout church history, see Ruth A. Tucker and Walter L. Liefeld, *Daughters of the Church: Women and Ministry from New Testament Times to the Present* (Grand Rapids: Zondervan, 1987).

9. See further Richard S. Hess, "The Jericho and Ai of the Book of Joshua," in *Critical Issues in Early Israelite History*, ed. Richard S. Hess, Gerald A. Klingbeil, and Paul J. Ray Jr. (Winona Lake, IN: Eisenbrauns, 2008), 33–46. More broadly, cf. C. S. Cowles, Eugene H. Merrill, Daniel Gard, and Tremper Longman III, *Show Them No Mercy: Four Views on God and Canaanite Genocide* (Grand Rapids: Zondervan, 2003).

10. See esp. Richard Dawkins, *The God Delusion* (London: Bantam, 2006; New York: Mariner, 2008); Christopher Hitchens, *God Is Not Great: How Religion Poisons Everything* (New York: Hachette, 2007); and Sam Harris, *The End of Faith: Religion, Terror, and the Future of Reason* (New York: Norton, 2004).

11. For a brief sampling of and response to these distortions, see Richard S. Hess, "Appendix 2: Apologetic Issues in the Old Testament," in *Christian Apologetics: A Comprehensive Case for Biblical Faith*, by Douglas Groothuis (Downers Grove, IL: IVP Academic; Nottingham, UK: Apollos, 2011), 662–76.

12. For two excellent compendia, see John H. Walton, Victor H. Matthews, and Mark W. Chavalas, *The IVP Bible Background Commentary: Old Testament* (Downers Grove, IL: InterVarsity, 2000); and Craig S. Keener, *The IVP Bible Background Commentary: New Testament* (Downers Grove, IL: InterVarsity, 1994).

13. See esp. William Webb, *Slaves, Women and Homosexuals: Exploring the Hermeneutics of Cultural Analysis* (Downers Grove, IL: InterVarsity, 2001).

14. Dawkins, *God Delusion*, 268–316; Hitchens, *God Is Not Great*, 97–122. For considerably greater detail, see John W. Loftus, *Why I Became an Atheist: A Former Preacher Rejects Christianity* (Amherst, NY: Prometheus, 2008), 265–395.

15. The exceptions are the ex-evangelicals. But typically they do not become atheists because a dispassionate study of the evidence gradually leads them to change their mind. As Loftus indicates (*Why I Became an Atheist*, 24), three factors are often involved: a personal crisis of some kind, the absence of love and care from the Christian community they were depending on, and a serious investigation of a different worldview they had never examined in any detail previously.

16. See esp. Peter Stuhlmacher, *Historical Criticism and Theological Interpretation of Scripture: Toward a Hermeneutics of Consent* (Philadelphia: Fortress, 1977; Eugene, OR: Wipf & Stock, 2003).

17. E.g., Mark A. Powell, *What Is Narrative Criticism?* (Minneapolis: Fortress, 1990; London: SPCK, 1993), 23–25. Powell explains, "Even if we are atheists, we will have to become Christians for a while if we are to read Bunyan or Dante. Readers are free, of course, to critique the point of view a narrative espouses. An initial acceptance of that point of view, however, is essential as preliminary to such criticism, for without such acceptance the story can never be understood in the first place" (24).

18. A remarkable compendium for OT studies is Kenneth A. Kitchen, *On the Reliability of the Old Testament* (Grand Rapids: Eerdmans, 2003). For the NT, see esp. Jack Finegan, *The Archeology of the New Testament: The Life of Jesus and the Beginning of the Early Church*, rev. ed. (Princeton: Princeton University Press, 1992). Less comprehensive but still very thorough and completely up to date is Eric M. Meyers and Mark A. Chancey, *From Alexander to Constantine: Archaeology of the Land of the Bible* (New Haven: Yale University Press, 2012).

19. See esp. Christopher J. H. Wright, *The Mission of God: Unlocking the Bible's Grand Narrative* (Downers Grove, IL: IVP Academic, 2006). Much more briefly, cf. Craig L. Blomberg, "The Unity and Diversity of Scripture," in *New Dictionary of Biblical Theology*, ed. T. D. Alexander and Brian S. Rosner (Leicester, UK: Inter-Varsity; Downers Grove, IL: InterVarsity, 2000), 64–72, and the literature cited there.

20. See esp. David B. Hart, *Atheist Delusions: The Christian Revolution and Its Fashionable Enemies* (New Haven: Yale University Press, 2009); and Jonathan Hill, *What Has Christianity Ever Done for Us? How It Shaped the Modern World* (Oxford: Lion; Downers Grove, IL: InterVarsity, 2005).

21. The classic examples being, of course, the Crusades, which occurred periodically from the eleventh to the fifteenth century.

22. E.g., Harris, *End of Faith*; Valerie Tarico, *The Dark Side: How Evangelical Teachings Corrupt Love and Truth* (Seattle: Dea, 2006). The classic examples here are the Marxist-Communist totalitarian regimes (several of them spanning much of the twentieth century) of Lenin and Stalin in the Soviet Union, Pol Pot in Cambodia, Mao Zedong in China, Fidel Castro in Cuba, and the Kim dynasty in North Korea.

23. Augustana College, Rock Island, IL, 1973–77. Until 1962 the college had housed a Lutheran seminary. A long-tenured and highly beloved president, Conrad Bergendoff, had been a masterful champion of the highest levels of academic achievement within a framework of informed but devout Christian faith. Under Thomas Tredway, the president inaugurated during my student days, attention was given almost exclusively to the academic goals. The religion department (no longer the department of Christianity as under Bergendoff) was most eager to expose students to virtually every perspective except the historic, pietistic Lutheranism (or its equivalent in other denominations) that had characterized the school before the mid-1960s.

24. None was more instrumental in this respect than George Kalemkarian, volunteer director of a chapter of Campus Crusade for Christ at my college and extraordinarily well read in biblical and theological scholarship for an engineer, none of whose degrees were in divinity or religious studies. Credit must also go to Ron Weimer, pastor of the Grace Brethren Church in Davenport, Iowa, for considerable tutelage in my high school years, along with Hugh Rohr, Tom Dudenhofer, and Dick Kemple, successive Campus Life / Youth for Christ directors for the Rock Island High School club.

25. Cf. D. A. Carson, *The Gagging of God: Christianity Confronts Pluralism* (Grand Rapids: Zondervan, 1996), 78–79n66.

26. For a convenient introduction, see John J. Collins, *Introduction to the Hebrew Bible* (Minneapolis: Fortress, 2004), 47–61.

27. Esp. Philip R. Davies, *Memories of Ancient Israel: An Introduction to Biblical History—Ancient and Modern* (Louisville: Westminster John Knox, 2008); Thomas L. Thompson, *Biblical Archaeology and the Myth of Israel* (London: Random House;

New York: Basic Books, 1999); John van Seters, *In Search of History: Historiography in the Ancient World and the Origins of Biblical History* (Winona Lake, IN: Eisenbrauns, 1997).

28. Esp. Paul N. Anderson, in several writings, such as *The Fourth Gospel and the Quest for Jesus: Modern Foundations Reconsidered* (London: T&T Clark, 2006), 192.

29. N. T. Wright, *Jesus and the Victory of God* (London: SPCK; Minneapolis: Fortress, 1996), 13–124. Cf. esp. James K. Hoffmeier and Dennis R. Magary, eds., *Do Historical Matters Matter for Faith? A Critical Appraisal of Modern and Postmodern Approaches to Scripture* (Wheaton: Crossway, 2012).

30. See esp. R. S. Sugirtharajah, ed., *The Postcolonial Bible* (Edinburgh: T&T Clark, 1998); Fernando F. Segovia and R. S. Sugirtharajah, eds., *A Postcolonial Commentary on the New Testament Writings* (London: T&T Clark, 2007).

31. Cf., e.g., the similarities and differences between the contents of the first and second editions of Joel B. Green, ed., *Hearing the New Testament: Strategies for Interpretation* (Grand Rapids: Eerdmans, 1995; 2nd ed., 2010).

32. Esp. in Robert W. Funk, Roy W. Hoover, and the Jesus Seminar, *The Five Gospels: The Search for the Authentic Words of Jesus* (New York: Macmillan, 1993); and Robert W. Funk and the Jesus Seminar, *The Acts of Jesus: The Search for the Authentic Deeds of Jesus* (San Francisco: HarperSanFrancisco, 1998).

33. Washington Junior High School, Rock Island, IL, 1968–69.

34. Esp. in the NT, with the appearance of the initial volumes of the *Novum Testamentum Graecum: Editio Critica Maior* series, produced by the Institut für neutestamentliche Textforschung (Stuttgart: Deutsche Bibelgesellschaft, 1997–), which catalogs every known variant for a given book, verse by verse.

35. E.g., Robert W. Funk, *Honest to Jesus: Jesus for a New Millennium* (San Francisco: HarperSanFrancisco, 1996), 116–20.

36. See Philip Jenkins, *Hidden Gospels: How the Search for Jesus Lost Its Way* (Oxford: Oxford University Press, 2001); Darrell L. Bock, *The Missing Gospels: Unearthing the Truth behind Alternative Christianities* (Nashville: Nelson, 2006); Andreas J. Köstenberger and Michael J. Kruger, *The Heresy of Orthodoxy: How Contemporary Culture's Fascination with Diversity Has Reshaped Our Understanding of Early Christianity* (Wheaton: Crossway, 2010); C. E. Hill, *Who Chose the Gospels? Probing the Great Gospel Conspiracy* (Oxford: Oxford University Press, 2010).

37. See esp. Eugene A. Nida and Charles R. Taber, *The Theory and Practice of Translation* (Leiden: Brill, 1969); John Beekman and John Callow, *Translating the Word of God* (Grand Rapids: Zondervan, 1974); J. de Waard and Eugene A. Nida, *From One Language to Another: Functional Equivalence in Bible Translating* (Nashville: Nelson, 1986); Johannes P. Louw and Eugene A. Nida, *Lexical Semantics of the Greek New Testament* (Atlanta: Scholars Press, 1992); Stanley E. Porter and Richard S. Hess, eds., *Translating the Bible: Problems and Prospects* (Sheffield: Sheffield Academic Press, 1999); Glen G. Scorgie, Mark L. Strauss, and Steven M. Voth, eds., *The Challenge of Bible Translation: Communicating God's Word to the World* (Grand Rapids: Zondervan, 2003); and Stanley E. Porter and Mark J. Boda, eds., *Translating the New Testament: Text, Translation, Theology* (Grand Rapids: Eerdmans, 2009).

38. The latest and most prominent round of questioners include Kenton L. Sparks, *God's Word in Human Words: An Evangelical Appropriation of Critical Biblical Scholarship* (Grand Rapids: Baker Academic, 2008); idem, *Sacred Word, Broken Word: Biblical Authority and the Dark Side of Scripture* (Grand Rapids: Eerdmans, 2012); Peter Enns, *Inspiration and Incarnation: Evangelicals and the Problem of the Old Testament* (Grand Rapids: Baker Academic, 2005); Carlos R. Bovell, *Inspiration and the Spiritual Formation of Younger Evangelicals* (Eugene, OR: Wipf & Stock, 2007); idem, *Rehabilitating*

Inerrancy in a Culture of Fear (Eugene, OR: Wipf & Stock, 2012); and Christian Smith, *The Bible Made Impossible: Why Biblicism Is Not a Truly Evangelical Reading of Scripture* (Grand Rapids: Baker Academic, 2012).

39. See esp. V. Philips Long, *The Art of Biblical History* (Grand Rapids: Zondervan, 1994); V. Philips Long, David W. Baker, and Gordon J. Wenham, eds., *Windows into Old Testament History: Evidence, Argument, and the Crisis of "Biblical Israel"* (Grand Rapids: Eerdmans, 2002); Jens B. Kofoed, *Text and History: Historiography and the Study of the Biblical Text* (Winona Lake, IN: Eisenbrauns, 2005); Richard A. Burridge, *What Are the Gospels? A Comparison with Graeco-Roman Biography* (Cambridge: Cambridge University Press, 1992); Craig S. Keener, *Acts: An Exegetical Commentary* (Grand Rapids: Baker Academic, 2012), 1:90–382.

40. For the OT, see esp. the magisterial series Forms of Old Testament Literature, 17 vols., ed. Rolf P. Knierim, Gene M. Tucker, and Marvin A. Sweeney (Grand Rapids: Eerdmans, 1981–2005); for the NT, see Craig L. Blomberg, "Genre in Recent New Testament Commentaries," in *On the Writing of New Testament Commentaries: Festschrift for Grant R. Osborne on the Occasion of His 70th Birthday*, ed. Stanley E. Porter and Eckhard J. Schnabel (Leiden: Brill, 2012), 72–90, and the literature cited there.

41. See esp. Craig S. Keener, *Miracles: The Credibility of the New Testament Accounts* (Grand Rapids: Baker Academic, 2011), 1:211–599.

42. See, e.g., Colin Brown, *Miracles and the Critical Mind* (Grand Rapids: Eerdmans; Exeter, UK: Paternoster, 1984; Pasadena: Fuller Seminary Press, 2006); R. Douglas Geivett and Gary R. Habermas, eds., *In Defense of Miracles: A Comprehensive Case for God's Actions in History* (Downers Grove, IL: InterVarsity, 1997); C. John Collins, *The God of Miracles: An Exegetical Examination of God's Action in the World* (Wheaton: Crossway, 2000).

43. See further Alan R. Millard, James K. Hoffmeier, and David W. Baker, eds., *Faith, Tradition, and History: Old Testament Historiography in Its Near Eastern Context* (Winona Lake, IN: Eisenbrauns, 1994); Ronald H. Nash, *The Gospel and the Greeks: Did the New Testament Borrow from Pagan Thought?*, 2nd ed. (Phillipsburg, NJ: P&R, 2003).

44. For these phenomena in the context of both conversion and deconversion, see Scot McKnight and Hauna Ondrey, *Finding Faith, Losing Faith: Stories of Conversion and Apostasy* (Waco: Baylor University Press, 2008).

45. E.g., see the stories in Edward T. Babinski, *Leaving the Fold: Testimonies of Former Fundamentalists* (Amherst, NY: Prometheus, 2003). This work contains a variety of accounts, not merely of those who became atheists, but also of those who simply converted to a different religion or a different form of Christianity. Babinski uses the term "fundamentalists" to refer to those who would have often self-identified as "conservative evangelicals."

46. Cf. Kelly J. Clark, *Philosophers Who Believe: The Spiritual Journeys of 11 Leading Thinkers* (Downers Grove, IL: InterVarsity, 1993); Ronald A. Knott, ed., *College Faith: 150 Christian Leaders and Educators Share Faith Stories from Their Student Days* (Berrien Springs, MI: Andrews University Press, 2002); idem, ed., *College Faith 2: 150 Christian Leaders and Educators Share Faith Stories from Their Student Days* (Berrien Springs, MI: Andrews University Press, 2004); and idem, ed., *College Faith 3: 150 Christian Leaders and Educators Share Faith Stories from Their Student Days* (Berrien Springs, MI: Andrews University Press, 2006).

Chapter 1: Aren't the Copies of the Bible Hopelessly Corrupt?

1. Bart D. Ehrman, *Misquoting Jesus: The Story Behind Who Changed the Bible and Why* (San Francisco: HarperSanFrancisco, 2005), 89.

2. For a simple introduction to textual criticism and a response to Ehrman written at the most straightforward, introductory level,

see Timothy P. Jones, *Misquoting Truth: A Guide to the Fallacies of Bart Ehrman's "Misquoting Jesus"* (Downers Grove, IL: InterVarsity, 2007).

3. Bart D. Ehrman, *The Orthodox Corruption of Scripture: The Effect of Early Christological Controversies on the Text of the New Testament* (Oxford: Oxford University Press, 1993).

4. E.g., Daniel B. Wallace, "Challenges in New Testament Textual Criticism for the Twenty-First Century," *Journal of the Evangelical Theological Society* 52 (2009): 95.

5. Ehrman, *Misquoting Jesus*, 89.

6. Ibid., 88–89.

7. J. Ed Komoszewski, M. James Sawyer, and Daniel B. Wallace, *Reinventing Jesus: What "The Da Vinci Code" and Other Novel Speculations Don't Tell You* (Grand Rapids: Kregel, 2006), 82.

8. Paul D. Wegner, *A Student's Guide to Textual Criticism of the Bible* (Downers Grove, IL: InterVarsity, 2006), 37, 39.

9. Barbara Aland, Kurt Aland, Johannes Karavidopoulos, Carlo M. Martini, and Bruce M. Metzger, "Preface to the Fourth Edition," in *The Greek New Testament*, 4th ed. (Stuttgart: Deutsche Bibelgesellschaft; New York: United Bible Societies, 1993), v.

10. Bruce M. Metzger, *A Textual Commentary on the Greek New Testament*, 2nd ed. (Stuttgart: Deutsche Bibelgesellschaft; New York: United Bible Societies, 1994).

11. Barbara Aland et al., eds., *Novum Testamentum Graece*, 28th ed. (Stuttgart: Deutsche Bibelgesellschaft, 2012).

12. See, e.g., Craig L. Blomberg with Jennifer Foutz Markley, *A Handbook of New Testament Exegesis* (Grand Rapids: Baker Academic, 2010), 1–35.

13. Hans F. Bayer, "Mark," notes in *ESV Study Bible*, ed. Wayne A. Grudem (Wheaton: Crossway, 2008), 1933.

14. For a plausible and thorough account, see James A. Kelhoffer, *Miracle and Mission: The Authentication of Missionaries and Their Message in the Longer Ending of Mark* (Tübingen: Mohr Siebeck, 2000).

15. See esp. Travis B. Williams, "Bringing Method to the Madness: Examining the Style of the Longer Ending of Mark," *Bulletin for Biblical Research* 20 (2010): 397–417.

16. Bayer, "Mark," 1933.

17. David A. Black, ed., *Perspectives on the Ending of Mark: Four Views* (Nashville: B&H, 2008). This work is highly misleading in assembling essays by two authors who believe in the authenticity of Mark 16:9–20 and two who do not, as if the scholarly debate were evenly divided between the two positions. Black and Maurice A. Robinson, who write the first two essays, may in fact be the only two scholars of their stature in the world who hold the position that Mark wrote these verses!

18. Cf. Andrew T. Lincoln, "The Promise and the Failure: Mark 16:7–8," *Journal of Biblical Literature* 108 (1989): 283–300.

19. See esp. Gary M. Burge, "A Specific Problem in the New Testament Text and Canon: The Woman Caught in Adultery (John 7:53–8:11)," *Journal of the Evangelical Theological Society* 27 (1984): 141–48. For a recent survey of the complete breadth of scholarship on this passage, see Chris Keith, "Recent and Previous Research on the *Pericope Adulterae* (John 7:53–8:11)," *Currents in Biblical Research* 6 (2008): 377–404.

20. Andreas J. Köstenberger, "John," notes in *ESV Study Bible*, 2039.

21. Daniel B. Wallace, "Challenges in New Testament Textual Criticism for the Twenty-First Century," *Journal of the Evangelical Theological Society* 52 (2009): 99.

22. The NASB is unusually sparse with its notes: I counted 87 such footnotes in the entire NT. The HCSB is unusually full: I counted 106 such footnotes in 1 Peter through Revelation alone.

23. Jack P. Lewis, *The English Bible from KJV to NIV: A History and Evaluation*, 2nd ed. (Grand Rapids: Baker, 1991), 42.

24. David L. Turner, *Matthew*, BECNT (Grand Rapids: Baker Academic, 2008), 178.

25. Grant R. Osborne, *Matthew*, ZECNT (Grand Rapids: Zondervan, 2010), 231.

26. R. T. France, *The Gospel of Mark: A Commentary on the Greek Text*, NIGTC (Carlisle, UK: Paternoster; Grand Rapids: Eerdmans, 2002), 115, 117.

27. Metzger, *Textual Commentary*, 594, adding another possibility that the change was intentional to show that "everything" in Hebrews 2:8 does not include God (cf. 1 Cor. 15:27).

28. Metzger, *Textual Commentary*, 151.

29. As an extreme example, in the museum at the headquarters of Biblica (formerly the International Bible Society) in Colorado Springs, one can see an original 1978 NIV with a bullet hole through it, which was returned to the society by an irate KJV supporter!

30. Darrell L. Bock, *Acts*, BECNT (Grand Rapids: Baker Academic, 2007), 348.

31. Thomas R. Schreiner, *Romans*, BECNT (Grand Rapids: Baker Academic, 1998), 258.

32. See further Metzger, *Textual Commentary*, 174–75.

33. Claude Perera, "Burn or Boast? A Text Critical Analysis of 1 Cor 13:3," *Filología neotestamentaria* 18 (2005): 111–28. When scribes assumed that the texts they were copying had minor errors in them and made changes to what they assumed those texts originally read, it was much more likely that they would "correct" a very bland, puzzling reading to a much clearer, more powerful one than that they would change the text in the other direction.

34. Daniel B. Wallace ("Lost in Transmission: How Badly Did the Scribes Corrupt the New Testament Text?" in *Revisiting the Corruption of the New Testament: Manuscript, Patristic, and Apocryphal Evidence*, ed. Daniel B. Wallace [Grand Rapids: Kregel, 2011], 40) distinguishes four kinds of variants: "spelling differences and nonsense errors," "minor differences that do not affect translation or that involve synonyms," "differences that affect the meaning of the text but are not viable," and "differences that both affect the meaning of the text and are viable." Suffice it to say that very few of the Nestle-Aland variants not found in the UBS Greek NT fall into this final category.

35. Ehrman, *Misquoting Jesus*, esp. 45–69. Cf. Bart D. Ehrman and Daniel B. Wallace, "The Textual Reliability of the New Testament: A Dialogue," in *The Reliability of the New Testament*, ed. Robert B. Stewart (Minneapolis: Fortress, 2011), 14–27.

36. Wallace, "Lost in Transmission," 51–52. Cf. Ehrman and Wallace, "Textual Reliability," 30–41.

37. See the breakdown by book of the NT in Larry W. Hurtado, *The Earliest Christian Artifacts: Manuscripts and Christian Origins* (Grand Rapids: Eerdmans, 2006), 20–21.

38. Craig A. Evans, speaking at "The Word" conference at Grace Chapel, Englewood, CO, November 3, 2012, noted that he has personally examined originals or facsimiles of all the pre-Constantinian manuscripts of the Gospels, and not one is written in the informal scrawls that often indicated sloppy copying by barely literate scribes. Contra Ehrman, *Misquoting Jesus*, 38–41.

39. D. A. Carson, *The King James Version Debate: A Plea for Realism* (Grand Rapids: Baker, 1979), 56.

40. Cited by Daniel B. Wallace, "Has the New Testament Text Been Hopelessly Corrupted?," in *In Defense of the Bible: A Comprehensive Apologetic for the Authority of Scripture*, ed. Steven B. Cowan and Terry L. Wilder (Nashville: B&H Academic, 2013), 161.

41. Ellis R. Brotzman, *Old Testament Textual Criticism: A Practical Introduction* (Grand Rapids: Baker, 1994), 58.

42. Wegner, *Student's Guide to Textual Criticism*, 158–59.

43. These are the translations of Aquila, Symmachus, and Theodotion. For a full introduction to the LXX, see Karen H. Jobes and Moisés Silva, *Invitation to the Septuagint* (Grand Rapids: Baker Academic; Carlisle, UK: Paternoster, 2000). For these three translations, see 37–44 of Jobes and Silva.

44. For full details, see Emanuel Tov, *Textual Criticism of the Hebrew Bible*, 3rd ed. (Minneapolis: Fortress, 2012), 286–324.

45. See esp. Martin Hengel, *The Septuagint as Christian Scripture: Its Prehistory and the Problem of Its Canon* (Grand Rapids: Baker Academic, 2004).

46. James C. VanderKam, *The Dead Sea Scrolls Today* (Grand Rapids: Eerdmans; London: SPCK, 1994), 126.

47. For full details, see Gareth L. Cockerill, "Hebrews 1:6: Source and Significance," *Bulletin for Biblical Research* 9 (1999): 51–64.

48. It is also clear that the translational approaches vary from book to book, so that no overall generalizations can be made. For both points, see Ernst Würthwein, *The Text of the Old Testament*, trans. Erroll F. Rhodes, 2nd ed. (Grand Rapids: Eerdmans, 1995), 66–71.

49. See, e.g., Ralph W. Klein, *1 Samuel*, WBC (Waco: Word, 1983), 102–5.

50. See further Kenneth A. Mathews, *Genesis 1–11:26*, NAC (Nashville: Broadman & Holman, 1996), 272–73.

51. For all these possibilities, see David T. Tsumura, *The First Book of Samuel*, NICOT (Grand Rapids: Eerdmans, 2007), 330–33. Tsumura offers yet another translation, "a certain year of age was Saul when he became king, and just for two years he ruled over Israel," taking the two years to be the first two years of his much longer reign before God rejected his kingship.

52. Individual scholars may, however, reverse this process for one or more specific OT books, as, e.g., J. Daniel Hays does for Jeremiah in "Jeremiah, the Septuagint, the Dead Sea Scrolls and Inerrancy: Just What Exactly Do We Mean by the 'Original Autographs'?," in *Evangelicals and Scripture: Tradition, Authority and Hermeneutics,* ed. Vincent Bacote, Laura C. Miguélez, and Dennis L. Okholm (Downers Grove, IL: InterVarsity, 2004), 133–49.

53. As a last resort, scholars opt for "conjectural emendation," assuming a change to have occurred that is not attested in any of the manuscripts in any of the ancient languages. The more minor the change (e.g., the substitution of a single Hebrew consonant for one that looks similar), the more plausible the proposal. Many scholars suggest that the procedure should *never* be adopted in NT textual criticism because of the wealth of manuscript evidence available. Almost all scholars agree that it occasionally *must* be adopted in OT textual criticism because there is no other way to create a text that makes sense. In between these two parameters remain very different degrees of enthusiasm for the practice.

54. E.g., Eugene C. Ulrich, "The Canonical Process, Textual Criticism, and Latter Stages in the Composition of the Bible," in "*Sha'arei Talmon": Studies in the Bible, Qumran, and the Ancient Near East Presented to Shemaryahu Talmon*, ed. Michael A. Fishbane, Emanuel Tov, and Weston W. Fields (Winona Lake, IN: Eisenbrauns, 1992), 267–91.

55. That something like Q once existed remains probable, but large numbers of the theories erected on the hypothesis of its use as a source for Matthew and Luke prove far less likely. For an overview of Q studies, see Leslie R. Keylock, "The Sayings of Jesus: Source (Q) in Recent Research—A Review Article," *Trinity Journal* 26 (2005): 119–30.

56. And perhaps also without the speeches of Elihu and/or the poem on wisdom in chap. 28. For all of these proposals, see David J. A. Clines, *Job 1–20*, WBC (Dallas: Word, 1989), lvii–lix.

57. For the full range of options and their respective merits, see, e.g., Frank J. Matera, *II Corinthians: A Commentary*, NTL (Louisville: Westminster John Knox, 2003), 24–32.

58. See, e.g., Emanuel Tov, "Rewritten Bible Compositions and Biblical Manuscripts, with Special Attention to the Samaritan Pentateuch," *Dead Sea Discoveries* 5 (1998): 334–54.

59. Eckhard J. Schnabel, "Textual Criticism: Recent Developments," in *The Face of New Testament Studies,* ed. Scot McKnight and Grant R. Osborne (Grand Rapids: Baker Academic; Leicester, UK: Apollos, 2004), 75.

60. George W. Houston, "Papyrological Evidence for Book Collections and Libraries in the Roman Empire," in *Ancient Literacies: The Culture of Reading in Greece and Rome*, ed. William A. Johnson and Holt N. Parker (Oxford: Oxford University Press, 2009), 233–67.

61. Craig A. Evans, *Jesus and His World: The Archaeological Evidence* (Louisville: Westminster John Knox, 2012), 75.

62. Ehrman, *Misquoting Jesus*, 10.

63. I adopt the expression from Eldon J. Epp, "It's All about Variants: A Variant-Conscious Approach to New Testament Textual Criticism," *Harvard Theological Review* 100 (2007): 275–308, esp. 282–87.

64. The NIV, e.g., includes forty-five textual footnotes in which it deems a distinctive reading from the Dead Sea Scrolls worthy of mention, but in only nine of those instances (1 Sam. 1:22; 2:20; 11:1; 2 Sam. 22:36; Pss. 38:19; 107:29; Isa. 7:14; 23:3; and 49:12) is the reading from the Scrolls not supported by one or more other ancient translations (or a parallel biblical passage). Apart from the paragraph addition between 1 Samuel 10 and 11 (discussed above), none of the other variants affect more than a verse or a sentence. Of the nine listed above, only in four instances did the NIV find the evidence strong enough to prefer the DSS reading (1 Sam. 2:20; 2 Sam. 22:36; Ps. 107:29; and Isa. 49:12).

65. Komoszewski, Sawyer, and Wallace, *Reinventing Jesus*, 72.

66. Ibid., 71.

67. Beate Blatz, "The Coptic Gospel of Thomas," in *New Testament Apocrypha*, rev. and ed. Wilhelm Schneemelcher (London: James Clarke; Louisville: Westminster John Knox, 1991), 1:111. The copying of *Thomas* seems to have been noticeably less careful than the copying of NT texts. See Tim Ricchuiti, "Tracking Thomas: A Text-Critical Look at the Transmission of the Gospel of Thomas," in *Revisiting the Corruption of the New Testament*, 189–228.

68. Karen L. King, "The Gospel of Jesus's Wife: A New Coptic Gospel Papyrus," Harvard Divinity School, 2012, © 2013 President and Fellows of Harvard College, http://www.hds.harvard.edu/faculty-research/research-projects/the-gospel-of-jesuss-wife.

69. For an excellent introduction, see Birger A. Pearson, *Ancient Gnosticism: Traditions and Literature* (Minneapolis: Fortress, 2007). Cf. also Alastair H. B. Logan, *The Gnostics: Identifying an Early Christian Cult* (London: T&T Clark, 2006).

70. See esp. Francis Watson, "The Gospel of Jesus' Wife: How a Fake Gospel Fragment Was Composed," Mark Goodacre's Homepage, 2012, http://markgoodacre.org/Watson.pdf.

71. An important exception was the major British newspaper *The Guardian*. See Andrew Brown, "Gospel of Jesus' Wife Is Fake, Claims Expert," *The Guardian*, September 21, 2012, http://www.guardian.co.uk/world/2012/sep/21/gospel-jesus-wife-forgery.

72. See further Stanley E. Porter and Gordon L. Heath, *The Lost Gospel of Judas: Separating Fact from Fiction* (Grand Rapids: Eerdmans, 2007).

73. Dan Brown, *The Da Vinci Code: A Novel* (New York: Doubleday, 2003).

74. Key works in the recent phase of the movement include Edward F. Hills, *The King James Version Defended*, 4th ed. (Des Moines: Christian Research Press, 1984); Wilbur N. Pickering, *The Identity of the New Testament Text*, 3rd ed. (Eugene, OR: Wipf & Stock, 2003); Gail Riplinger, *Which Bible Is God's Word?*, rev ed. (Ararat, VA: A. V. Publications: 2007); and Joey Faust, *The Word: God Will Keep It! The 400 Year History of the King James Bible Only Movement* (Wasilla, AK: Fundamental Publishing, 2011). For an overview and rebuttal, see James R. White, *The King James Only Controversy: Can You Trust the Modern Translations?*, rev. ed. (Minneapolis: Bethany House, 2009).

75. E.g., Maurice A. Robinson, "The Case for Byzantine Priority," in *Rethinking Textual Criticism*, ed. David A. Black (Grand Rapids: Baker Academic, 2002), 125–39. Cf. idem, "The Long Ending of Mark as Canonical Verity," in *Perspectives on the Ending of Mark*, 40–79.

76. Carson, *King James Version Debate*, 48–52.

77. For full details, see Raymond E. Brown, *The Epistles of John*, AB (Garden City: Doubleday, 1983), 775–87.

78. See, e.g., throughout Millard J. Erickson, *God in Three Persons: A Contemporary Interpretation of the Trinity* (Grand Rapids: Baker, 1995).

79. See the presentation of this perspective and a rebuttal of it in Daniel B. Wallace,

"The Majority-Text Theory: History, Methods and Critique," *Journal of the Evangelical Theological Society* 37 (1994): 185–215, esp. 101–4.

80. Josef van Ess, "Verbal Inspiration: Language and Revelation in Classic Islamic Theology," in *Qur'an as Text*, ed. Stefan Wild (Leiden: Brill, 1996), 177–94.

81. Wallace, "Lost in Transmission," 35–36. Cf. Paul D. Wegner, "Has the Old Testament Text Been Hopelessly Corrupted?," in Cowan and Wilder, *In Defense of the Bible*, 134–36.

82. Cf. Komoszewski, Sawyer, and Wallace, *Reinventing Jesus*, 66–68.

Chapter 2: Wasn't the Selection of Books for the Canon Just Political?

1. David L. Dungan, *Constantine's Bible: Politics and the Making of the New Testament* (Minneapolis: Fortress, 2007), 120–21.

2. Bart D. Ehrman, *Lost Scriptures: Books That Did Not Make It into the New Testament* (Oxford: Oxford University Press, 2003), 2.

3. See, e.g., Raymond E. Brown, *An Introduction to the New Testament* (New York: Doubleday, 1997); Mark A. Powell, *Introducing the New Testament: A Historical, Literary, and Theological Survey* (Grand Rapids: Baker Academic, 2009).

4. For introduction and texts, in both Greek and English, see Michael W. Holmes, ed. and trans., *The Apostolic Fathers: Greek Texts and English Translations*, 3rd ed. (Grand Rapids: Baker Academic, 2007).

5. Classically, Morton Smith, *Palestinian Parties and Politics That Shaped the Old Testament*, 2nd ed. (London: SCM, 1987).

6. R. Walter L. Moberly, "The Canon of the Old Testament: Some Historical and Hermeneutical Reflections from a Western Perspective," in *Das Alte Testament als christliche Bibel in orthodoxer und westlicher Sicht*, ed. Ivan Z. Dimitrov, James D. G. Dunn, Ulrich Luz, and Karl-Wilhelm Niebuhr (Tübingen: Mohr Siebeck, 2004), 251–52.

7. Some scholars speak of a book being canonical once it is deemed uniquely authoritative, but discussions of the "canon" or "canonization" of the Bible usually refer to when it was included within a *collection* of such uniquely authoritative books. For the distinction, see esp. Stephen B. Chapman, "The Old Testament Canon and Its Authority for the Christian Church," *Ex auditu* 19 (2003): 125–48. Chapman calls these the "norm" and "list" approaches to canon, respectively.

8. Stephen B. Chapman ("'The Law and the Words' as a Canonical Formula within the Old Testament," in *The Interpretation of Scripture in Early Judaism and Christianity: Studies in Language and Tradition*, ed. Craig A. Evans [Sheffield: Sheffield Academic Press, 2000], 26–74) argues for a third descriptor, "the Law and the Words," in which some of the books that later formed the discrete section of Writings may have been included with the Prophets in a second section supplementing Torah.

9. Thus Stephen B. Chapman (*The Law and the Prophets: A Study in Old Testament Canon Formation* [Tübingen: Mohr Siebeck, 2000]) proposes a process in which Torah and Prophets emerged as equally authoritative at least by the sixth century BC.

10. For a brief sketch of this probable three-part development, see Stephen G. Dempster, "Torah, Torah, Torah: The Emergence of the Tripartite Canon," in *Exploring the Origins of the Bible: Canon Formation in Historical, Literary, and Theological Perspective*, ed. Craig A. Evans and Emanuel Tov (Grand Rapids: Baker Academic, 2008), 87–127.

11. Roger Beckwith, *The Old Testament Canon of the New Testament Church and Its Background in Early Judaism* (Grand Rapids: Eerdmans, 1985), 110.

12. Ibid., 142.

13. Arie van der Kooij, "Canonization of Ancient Hebrew Books and Hasmonaean Politics," in *The Biblical Canons*, ed. J.-M. Auwers and H. J. de Jonge (Leuven: Leuven University Press and Peeters, 2003), 27–38. Cf. Bruce K. Waltke, "How We Got the Hebrew Bible: The Text and Canon of the Old Testament," in *The Bible at Qumran: Text,*

Shape, and Interpretation, ed. Peter W. Flint (Grand Rapids: Eerdmans, 2001), 32.

14. A standard English edition is Bruce M. Metzger and Roland E. Murphy, eds., *The New Oxford Annotated Apocrypha*, rev. ed. (Oxford: Oxford University Press, 1991). While the Roman Catholic church has officially designated which books fall into this collection, the different Orthodox groups (Greek, Syrian, Ethiopian, Russian, etc.) have not all accepted the same number of apocryphal works.

15. For the standard, classic introduction, see Bruce M. Metzger, *Introduction to the Apocrypha* (Oxford: Oxford University Press, 1957).

16. The Greek word *pseudepigrapha* means "false inscriptions."

17. The most complete English edition is James H. Charlesworth, ed., *The Old Testament Pseudepigrapha*, 2 vols. (New York: Doubleday, 1983–85).

18. E.g., *1 Enoch* is considered canonical by the Ethiopian Orthodox communion.

19. See esp. Gerbern S. Oegema and James H. Charlesworth, *The Pseudepigrapha and Christian Origins* (London: T&T Clark, 2008).

20. See esp. the sections on "Significance" at the end of each chapter on individual apocryphal books in Daniel J. Harrington, *An Invitation to the Apocrypha* (Grand Rapids: Eerdmans, 1999). Cf. Martin Hengel with Roland Deines, *The Septuagint as Christian Scripture: Its Prehistory and the Problem of Its Canon* (Edinburgh: T&T Clark, 2002), 122–23.

21. See further David A. deSilva, *Introducing the Apocrypha: Message, Contents, and Significance* (Grand Rapids: Baker Academic, 2002), 23–25.

22. This view has been challenged, but the challenges have been successfully rebutted. See Benjamin D. Sommer, "Did Prophecy Cease? Evaluating a Reevaluation," *Journal of Biblical Literature* 115 (1996): 31–47.

23. Andrew E. Steinmann, *The Oracles of God: The Old Testament Canon* (St. Louis: Concordia, 1999), 190.

24. Cf. esp. R. Laird Harris, *Inspiration and Canonicity of the Scriptures*, rev. ed. (Grand Rapids: Zondervan, 1969; repr., Eugene, OR: Wipf & Stock, 2008), 154–77. An important complementary perspective links the OT canon formation to the concept of covenant. The Law established God's covenant. The Prophets called people to a proper relationship to it. The Writings expanded on what obedience to it meant. See esp. Meredith G. Kline, *The Structure of Biblical Authority* (Grand Rapids: Eerdmans, 1972).

25. Paul D. Wegner, Terry L. Wilder, and Darrell L. Bock, "Do We Have the Right Canon?," in *In Defense of the Bible: A Comprehensive Apologetic for the Authority of Scripture*, ed. Steven B. Cowan and Terry L. Wilder (Nashville: B&H Academic, 2013), 402.

26. E. Earle Ellis, *The Old Testament in Early Christianity: Canon and Interpretation in Light of Modern Research* (Tübingen: Mohr Siebeck, 1991; Grand Rapids: Baker, 1992), 33–36; Eckhard J. Schnabel, "History, Theology and the Biblical Canon: An Introduction to Basic Issues," *Themelios* 20, no. 2 (1995): 16–24, esp. 17–20.

27. For details, see Johan Lust, "Septuagint and Canon," in Auwers and de Jonge, *Biblical Canons*, 41–42.

28. James VanderKam and Peter Flint, *The Meaning of the Dead Sea Scrolls: Their Significance for Understanding the Bible, Judaism, Jesus, and Christianity* (London: T&T Clark, 2002), 154–81.

29. Jude 14 declares, "Enoch, the seventh from Adam, prophesied" about the false teachers when he spoke of God's coming judgment, in the company of his myriads of angels, to destroy and punish the wicked. This does not mean Jude believed *1 Enoch* to be inspired, because, as far as we know, no other Jews did so believe. Rather, he could well have imagined that this text unwittingly reflected a divine truth, much as Caiaphas was said to have prophesied unknowingly in John 11:51. Nor need Jude have believed that the historical Enoch actually wrote these words. The phrase "seventh from Adam" actually comes from *1 Enoch* itself (60.8)

and thus helps to identify Jude's source; it need not be an affirmation of authorship. What Jude *does* believe is that the quoted verse of *1 Enoch* reflects a true statement. In fact, its teaching fundamentally agrees with Zechariah 14:5.

30. Schnabel, "History, Theology and the Biblical Canon," 20.

31. For both of these points, see Wegner, Wilder, and Bock, "Do We Have the Right Canon?," 403–4.

32. Craig D. Allert, *A High View of Scripture? The Authority of the Bible and the Formation of the New Testament Canon* (Grand Rapids: Baker Academic, 2007), 40.

33. Harris, *Inspiration and Canonicity of the Scriptures*.

34. Allert, *High View?*, 44–48.

35. The fullest study remains David E. Aune, *Prophecy in Early Christianity and the Ancient Mediterranean World* (Grand Rapids: Eerdmans, 1983).

36. "Thus, for Christians the question of the extent of the OT canon will never be a purely historical question, but is bound up with the question of the source of teaching authority in the church. If teaching authority depends solely upon the prophets and Jesus and his apostles, only one canon is possible. If teaching authority extends beyond Scripture to tradition, then the canon is defined by the tradition one accepts" (Steinmann, *Oracles of God*, 196).

37. Beckwith, *Old Testament Canon*, 235–45.

38. See any standard OT introduction; e.g., Tremper Longman III and Raymond B. Dillard, *Introduction to the Old Testament*, 2nd ed. (Grand Rapids: Zondervan, 2006).

39. E.g., Philip R. Davies, *Memories of Ancient Israel: An Introduction to Biblical History—Ancient and Modern* (Louisville: Westminster John Knox, 2008). For a more thorough and balanced overview of recent scholarship relevant to OT history, see Megan Bishop Moore and Brad E. Kelle, *Biblical History and Israel's Past: The Changing Study of the Bible and History* (Grand Rapids: Eerdmans, 2011).

40. For full details and for the rabbinic defense of the canonicity of all five books, see Beckwith, *Old Testament Canon*, 274–337.

41. In detail, see throughout John Sailhamer, *Introduction to Old Testament Theology: A Canonical Approach* (Grand Rapids: Zondervan, 1995). For the New Testament, see esp. Thomas R. Schreiner, *Magnifying God in Christ: A Summary of New Testament Theology* (Grand Rapids: Baker Academic, 2010). For both testaments, see esp. idem, *The King in His Beauty: A Biblical Theology of the Old and New Testaments* (Grand Rapids: Baker Academic, 2013). Much more briefly, cf. Craig L. Blomberg, "The Unity and Diversity of Scripture," in *New Dictionary of Biblical Theology*, ed. T. D. Alexander and Brian S. Rosner (Leicester, UK: Inter-Varsity; Downers Grove, IL: InterVarsity, 2000), 64–72.

42. Stephen Dempster, "Canons on the Right and Canons on the Left: Finding a Resolution in the Canon Debate," *Journal of the Evangelical Theological Society* 52 (2009): 47–77, esp. 75–76.

43. See Carey A. Moore, *Judith: A New Translation with Introduction and Commentary*, AB (Garden City: Doubleday, 1985), 46–49; idem, *Tobit: A New Translation with Introduction and Commentary*, AB (New York: Doubleday, 1996), 9–11.

44. See esp. Larry W. Hurtado, *Lord Jesus Christ: Devotion to Jesus in Early Christianity* (Grand Rapids: Eerdmans, 2003).

45. On which, see esp. Kurt Niederwimmer, *The Didache: A Commentary*, Hermeneia (Minneapolis: Fortress, 1998).

46. See further F. F. Bruce, *The Canon of Scripture* (Downers Grove, IL: InterVarsity, 1988), 158–69.

47. See, e.g., William L. Lane, *Hebrews 1–8*, WBC (Dallas: Word, 1991), xlvii–li.

48. For an excellent, recent introduction to all these non-Pauline Epistles and the issues they raise, see Karen H. Jobes, *Letters to the Church: A Survey of Hebrews and the General Epistles* (Grand Rapids: Zondervan, 2011).

49. See esp. David Mathewson, *A New Heaven and a New Earth: The Meaning and*

Function of the Old Testament in Revelation 21.1–22.5 (London: T&T Clark, 2003).

50. Lee M. McDonald, "Lists and Catalogues of New Testament Collections," in *The Canon Debate*, ed. Lee M. McDonald and James A. Sanders (Peabody, MA: Hendrickson, 2002), 591–98.

51. Hans-Josef Klauck (*Apocryphal Gospels: An Introduction* [London: T&T Clark, 2003], 223) approvingly cites (and translates) Walter Bauer's summary of the relevant motives: "a pious yearning to know more, a naïve curiosity, delight in colourful pictures and folktales."

52. See esp. C. E. Hill, *Who Chose the Gospels? Probing the Great Gospel Conspiracy* (Oxford: Oxford University Press, 2010), 234. For an anthology of introductions to the most important works, see Paul Foster, ed., *The Non-Canonical Gospels* (London: T&T Clark, 2008).

53. John C. Peckham, "The Canon and Biblical Authority: A Critical Comparison of Two Models of Canonicity," *Trinity Journal* 28 (2007): 242.

54. See, e.g., throughout M. Eugene Boring, *An Introduction to the New Testament: History, Literature, Theology* (Louisville: Westminster John Knox, 2012).

55. Charles E. Hill, "The New Testament: Deconstruction ad Absurdum?," *Journal of the Evangelical Theological Society* 52 (2009): 101–19.

56. Cf. Lee M. McDonald, *The Origin of the Bible: A Guide for the Perplexed* (London: T&T Clark, 2011), 228.

57. Made possible esp. by Edgar Hennecke, *New Testament Apocrypha*, ed. Wilhelm Schneemelcher, 2 vols. (Louisville: Westminster John Knox, 1990–91); and Marvin W. Meyer, ed., *The Nag Hammadi Scriptures* (New York: HarperOne, 2007).

58. See esp. Andreas J. Köstenberger and Michael J. Kruger, *The Heresy of Orthodoxy: How Contemporary Culture's Fascination with Diversity Has Reshaped Our Understanding of Early Christianity* (Wheaton: Crossway, 2010). Cf. Henk Jan de Jonge, "The New Testament Canon," in Auwers and de Jonge, *Biblical Canons*, 319.

59. McDonald ("Lists and Catalogues," 596–97) includes ten post-Constantinian lists, each demonstrating the small but continuing diversity of items.

60. Stephen B. Chapman, "The Canon Debate: What It Is and Why It Matters," *Journal of Theological Interpretation* 4 (2010): 292–94.

61. Michael J. Kruger, *Canon Revisited: Establishing the Origins and Authority of the New Testament Books* (Wheaton: Crossway, 2012), 146.

62. Cf. Hengel, *Septuagint as Christian Scripture*, 125–27.

63. See further Willem A. VanGemeren, *Interpreting the Prophetic Word* (Grand Rapids: Zondervan, 1990), esp. 70–99.

64. For the full range of NT uses of the Old, see G. K. Beale and D. A. Carson, eds., *Commentary on the New Testament Use of the Old Testament* (Grand Rapids: Baker Academic, 2007).

65. For the breadth and diversity of ancient Jewish messianic expectations, see James H. Charlesworth, ed., *The Messiah: Developments in Earliest Judaism and Christianity* (Minneapolis: Fortress, 1992).

66. Stephen G. Dempster, "An 'Extraordinary Fact': *Torah and Temple* and the Contours of the Hebrew Canon," *Tyndale Bulletin* 48 (1997): 191–218. For the NT, see throughout David Trobisch, *The First Edition of the New Testament* (Oxford: Oxford University Press, 2000).

67. On what he calls the criterion of self-authentication and its interaction with the more objective criteria discussed earlier, see Kruger, *Canon Revisited*, 88–122.

68. For more details concerning the process sketched here, see esp. Bruce M. Metzger, *The Canon of the New Testament: Its Origin, Development and Significance* (Oxford: Oxford University Press, 1987). Cf. also David G. Dunbar, "The Biblical Canon," in *Hermeneutics, Authority, and Canon*, ed. D. A. Carson and John D. Woodbridge (Eugene, OR: Wipf & Stock, 2005), esp. 315–60.

69. But see the suggestive comments by D. Moody Smith, "When Did the Gospels

Become Scripture?," *Journal of Biblical Literature* 119 (2000): 3–20.

70. James D. G. Dunn, "How the New Testament Canon Began," in *From Biblical Criticism to Biblical Faith: Essays in Honor of Lee Martin McDonald*, ed. William H. Brackney and Craig A. Evans (Macon, GA: Mercer University Press, 2007), esp. 135–37.

71. George W. Knight III cuts against the grain of the critical consensus with this conclusion. But he notes that in 1 Corinthians 9:14 Paul alludes to this same saying later recorded in Luke 10:7, treating it as just as authoritative as the Law of Moses (1 Cor. 9:9), and that in 7:10 and 10:23–25, Jesus's words "are as authoritative for Paul as any word of OT scripture" (*The Pastoral Epistles: A Commentary on the Greek Text*, NIGTC [Carlisle, UK: Paternoster; Grand Rapids: Eerdmans, 1992], 234).

72. For a balanced assessment, see Douglas J. Moo, *2 Peter, Jude*, NIVAC (Grand Rapids: Zondervan, 1996), 215–17.

73. See further Thomas R. Schreiner, *1, 2 Peter, Jude*, NAC (Nashville: Broadman & Holman, 2003), 255–76.

74. For a full cross-section of uses, see Clayton N. Jefford, *The Apostolic Fathers and the New Testament* (Peabody, MA: Hendrickson, 2006), 107–44. For a specific focus on one of the earliest fathers and his use of the Gospels in this fashion, see Charles E. Hill, "Ignatius, 'the Gospel,' and the Gospels," in *Trajectories through the New Testament and the Apostolic Fathers*, ed. Andrew Gregory and Christopher Tuckett (Oxford: Oxford University Press, 2005), 267–85.

75. See esp. Birger A. Pearson, *Ancient Gnosticism: Traditions and Literature* (Minneapolis: Fortress, 2007).

76. Attempts have recently been made to date this document as late as the fourth century, but they fail to persuade. See esp. Joseph Verheyden, "The Canon Muratori: A Matter of Dispute," in Auwers and de Jonge, *Biblical Canons*, 487–556.

77. Hill, *Who Chose the Gospels?*, 38. Justin Martyr already in about 160 had referred in the plural both to memoirs of the apostles and to memoirs of those who followed them, making at least four (and nicely lining up with Matthew and John, and Mark and Luke, respectively). His student, Tatian, also harmonized exactly these four around 180. See Jordan D. May, "The Four Pillars: The Fourfold Gospel before the Time of Irenaeus," *Trinity Journal* 30 (2009): 67–79.

78. Bruce, *Canon of Scripture*, 192–95, 197–203.

79. Dan Brown, *The Da Vinci Code: A Novel* (New York: Doubleday, 2003). One of the true scandals of the modern academy, apparently almost entirely unaddressed in the guild, involves the number of instructors in religious studies promoting, in their classes, Dan Brown's wholly fictitious claims about what took place at Nicaea as if they were actually based on some historical fact. Yet in the past decade, one of the most recurring questions I have been asked by students on university campuses where I have spoken is how the Council of Nicaea determined the NT canon. When I explain to them that this wasn't what Nicaea was about, they stare in disbelief or reply that one of their professors taught them that it was.

80. Bruce, *Canon of Scripture*, 203–5.

81. Helmut Koester, Elaine H. Pagels, and Harold W. Attridge, "The Dialogue of the Savior," in *The Nag Hammadi Library*, ed. James M. Robinson (Leiden: Brill; San Francisco: Harper & Row, 1977), 235.

82. George W. MacRae, "The Gospel of Truth," in Robinson, *Nag Hammadi Library*, 37–38.

83. Cf. Riemer Roukema, *Gnosis and Faith in Early Christianity: An Introduction to Gnosticism* (London: SCM; Harrisburg, PA: Trinity, 1999), 143–44.

84. Brown, *Da Vinci Code*, 323–25.

85. John Dominic Crossan, *The Cross That Spoke: The Origins of the Passion Narrative* (San Francisco: Harper & Row, 1988; Eugene, OR: Wipf & Stock, 2008).

86. See esp. Peter Jeffery, *The Secret Gospel of Mark Unveiled: Imagined Rituals of Sex, Death, and Madness in a Biblical Forgery* (New Haven: Yale University Press, 2007). Cf. also Stephen C. Carlson, *The Gospel Hoax:*

Morton Smith's Invention of "Secret Mark" (Waco: Baylor University Press, 2005).

87. Even Bart D. Ehrman (*The Lost Gospel of Judas Iscariot: A New Look at Betrayer and Betrayed* [Oxford: Oxford University Press, 2006], 172–73) forcefully argues that the *Gospel of Judas* contains nothing of value for understanding the historical Jesus.

88. For more on this document, see Oddbjørn Leirvik, "History as a Literary Weapon: The Gospel of Barnabas in Muslim-Christian Polemics," *Studia theologica* 54 (2001): 4–16; and Jan Joosten, "The Gospel of Barnabas and the Diatessaron," *Harvard Theological Review* 95 (2002): 73–96.

89. For a good introduction and the text in translation with brief commentary, see Richard Valantasis, *The Gospel of Thomas* (London: Routledge, 1997). For greater detail, see Petr Pokorný, *A Commentary on the Gospel of Thomas: From Interpretations to the Interpreted* (London: T&T Clark, 2009). Most likely better than both of these will be the forthcoming commentary by Simon J. Gathercole.

90. Nor is it entirely clear what the point is—perhaps that Jesus's Jewish opponents claim to follow God but reject his Son, or perhaps, like Matthew 12:33, a response to those who always find something to complain about without realizing that they have to take the bad with the good. See Uwe-Karsten Plisch, *The Gospel of Thomas: Original Text with Commentary* (Stuttgart: Deutsche Bibelgesellschaft, 2008), 117.

91. Cf. further Bertil Gärtner, *The Theology of the Gospel of Thomas* (London: Collins, 1961), 159–60.

92. Craig L. Blomberg, *Interpreting the Parables*, rev. ed. (Downers Grove, IL: InterVarsity, 2012).

93. Ibid., 335–36, and the literature cited there.

94. See esp. Mark Goodacre, *Thomas and the Gospels: The Case for Thomas's Familiarity with the Synoptics* (Grand Rapids: Eerdmans, 2012), 66–108; Simon J. Gathercole, *The Composition of the Gospel of Thomas: Original Language and Influences* (Cambridge: Cambridge University Press, 2012), 127–224.

95. Craig L. Blomberg, "Orality and the Parables (with Special Reference to J. D. G. Dunn's *Jesus Remembered*)," in *Memories of Jesus: A Critical Appraisal of James D. G. Dunn's Quest for the Historical Jesus*, ed. Robert B. Stewart and Gary R. Habermas (Nashville: B&H, 2010), 112–14.

96. See throughout Nicholas Perrin, *Thomas and Tatian: The Relationship between the Gospel of Thomas and the Diatessaron* (Leiden: Brill, 2003). Cf. also idem, *Thomas, the Other Gospel* (London: SPCK; Louisville: Westminster John Knox, 2007).

97. Gathercole, *Composition of the Gospel of Thomas*, 17–125.

98. Plisch (*Gospel of Thomas*, 136) observes, "The peculiar argument rejecting physical circumcision in the second sentence is quite unique and has no parallel in the New Testament or related Early Christian literature."

99. E.g., April D. DeConick, *The Original Gospel of Thomas in Translation: With a Commentary and New English Translation of the Complete Gospel* (London: T&T Clark, 2006), 297.

100. Harrington, *Invitation to the Apocrypha*, 57.

101. C. Detlef G. Müller, "Apocalypse of Peter," in Schneemelcher, *New Testament Apocrypha*, 2:625.

102. Joseph Lienhard (*The Bible, the Church, and Authority: The Canon of the Christian Bible in History and Theology* [Collegeville, MN: Liturgical Press, 1998], 17) generalizes nicely: "If Marcion took the Old Testament perfectly literally and threw it out of the Church, Barnabas took it exclusively figuratively and took it away from the Synagogue."

103. Holmes, *Apostolic Fathers*, 442.

104. See further Eric D. Barreto, "The Canon: Open or Closed? Closed: A Historical Commitment," *Word & World* 29 (2009): 421.

105. Thus a fully orthodox and biblical definition of the sufficiency of Scripture is one like Timothy Ward's: "Because of the

ways in which God has chosen to relate himself to Scripture, Scripture is sufficient as the means by which God continues to present himself to us such that we can know him, repeating through Scripture the covenant promise he has brought to fulfillment in Jesus Christ" (*Words of Life: Scripture as the Living and Active Word of God* [Downers Grove, IL: InterVarsity, 2009], 113).

106. For an unambiguous example, see John F. MacArthur Jr., "Rediscovering Biblical Counseling," in *Introduction to Biblical Counseling*, ed. John F. MacArthur Jr. and William A. Mack (Nashville: Nelson, 1994), 19: "I have no encouragement for people who wish to mix psychology with the divine resources and sell the mixture as a spiritual elixir. Their methodology amounts to a tacit admission that what God has given us in Christ is not really adequate to meet our deepest needs and salve our troubled lives." David Powlison ("A Biblical Counseling View," in *Psychology and Christianity: Five Views*, ed. Eric L. Johnson, 2nd ed. [Downers Grove, IL: InterVarsity, 2010], 255) complains that "a persistent misunderstanding of the biblical counseling view asserts, 'You don't believe Christians can learn anything from secular psychology.'" But in light of high profile leaders like MacArthur, it appears that a significant branch of biblical counseling believes precisely that. MacArthur has articulated this perspective again in "The Sufficiency of Scripture," *The Master's Seminary Journal* 15 (2004): 165–74. On 165 we read, "Scripture is comprehensive, containing everything necessary for one's spiritual life," and on 173, "I am convinced that many who submit to various kinds of extrabiblical therapy do so precisely because they are looking for a way of solving their problems without surrendering to what they know God's Word requires of them." To be consistent with this logic, even *biblical* counseling would not be needed, only preaching, since nothing in the Bible ever approximates any form of professional counseling. And certainly modern medicine would be excluded!

107. This all-too-common attitude provides the explicit rationale for the much more balanced book by Gerald R. McDermott, *Can Evangelicals Learn from World Religions? Jesus, Revelation and Religious Traditions* (Downers Grove, IL: InterVarsity, 2000).

108. For full details, see throughout Bruce A. Demarest, *General Revelation: Historical Views and Contemporary Issues* (Grand Rapids: Zondervan, 1982).

109. Arthur F. Holmes, *All Truth Is God's Truth* (Grand Rapids: Eerdmans, 1977; Downers Grove, IL: InterVarsity, 1983).

110. Paul D. Feinberg, "God, Man and Christ" (class lecture, Trinity Evangelical Divinity School, Deerfield, IL, Summer 1978). The quotation marks do not indicate that I recall his words exactly, merely the gist of what he said, but I use them to set his thoughts off from mine.

111. Christian Smith, *The Bible Made Impossible: Why Biblicism Is Not a Truly Evangelical Reading of Scripture* (Grand Rapids: Brazos, 2012), 4–5. He labels the nine "divine writing," "total representation," "complete coverage," "democratic perspicuity," "commonsense hermeneutics," "solo [*sic*] scriptura," "internal harmony," "universal applicability," and "inductive method."

112. Ibid., 5.

113. Ibid., 4.

114. Ibid., 8–10.

115. Ibid., 57.

116. Grand Rapids: Zondervan, 1994.

117. Grand Rapids: Zondervan, 2010.

118. On moving from the Bible to theology, see also Gary T. Meadors, ed., *Four Views on Moving beyond the Bible to Theology* (Grand Rapids: Zondervan, 2009).

119. See, e.g., Alister E. McGrath, *Christian Theology: An Introduction*, 5th ed. (Oxford and Malden, MA: Wiley-Blackwell, 2011).

120. See Craig L. Blomberg, *Christians in an Age of Wealth: A Biblical Theology of Stewardship* (Grand Rapids: Zondervan, 2013).

121. William W. Klein, Craig L. Blomberg, and Robert L. Hubbard Jr., *Introduction to Biblical Interpretation*, rev. ed. (Nashville: Nelson, 2004), 451–75.

Chapter 3: Can We Trust Any of Our Translations of the Bible?

1. See esp. C. John Collins, Wayne Grudem, Vern S. Poythress, Leland Ryken, and Bruce Winter, *Translating Truth: The Case for Essentially Literal Bible Translation* (Wheaton: Crossway, 2005).

2. See the classic study by John Beekman and John Callow, *Translating the Word of God* (Grand Rapids: Zondervan, 1974). This is the philosophy of most of the modern-language translations produced worldwide by the United Bible Societies, pioneered by Eugene A. Nida in *God's Word in Man's Language* (New York: Harper, 1952). See also Jan de Waard and Eugene A. Nida, *From One Language to Another: Functional Equivalence in Bible Translating* (Nashville: Nelson, 1986).

3. See, e.g., opinions discussed by Matt Slick, "Hasn't the Bible Been Rewritten so Many Times That We Can't Trust It Anymore?" (http://carm.org/hasnt-bible-been-rewritten-so-many-times-we-cant-trust-it-anymore). He also gives some good replies to those misconceptions.

4. The most exaggerated and misinformed statement I have ever come across to this effect appears in Kevin Davidson, "Which Bible Translation?" (http://www.davnet.org/kevin/articles/bibletrans.html): "The Christian religion described in the New International Version is not the same religion described in the New American Standard Bible."

5. A bright, middle-aged professional Jewish woman and regular attender at one of my students' neighborhood Bible studies shared precisely this misconception with us when I guest-led one week in the spring of 2009.

6. For a succinct history of Bible translations, see Paul D. Wegner, *The Journey from Texts to Translations: The Origin and Development of the Bible* (Grand Rapids: Baker, 1999), 241–399.

7. All the quotations below are from the Bible Works 9.0 computer software program or from www.biblegateway.com.

8. Other translations, for example, speak of "earrings of gold, studded with silver" (NIV) or simply "gold jewelry, . . . accented with silver" (HCSB). See further Richard S. Hess, *Song of Songs*, BCOTWP (Grand Rapids: Baker Academic, 2005), 66.

9. How the last two Hebrew clauses in this verse are related is the main question here, because they are juxtaposed without a connective word. Some translations have also proposed emendations in the verse. For full details, see Bruce Waltke, *A Commentary on Micah* (Grand Rapids: Eerdmans, 2007), 73–77. Interestingly, Moisés Silva uses the KJV of this very verse (Mic. 1:11, "Pass ye away, thou inhabitant of Saphir, having thy shame naked: the inhabitant of Zaanan came not forth in the mourning of Beth-ezel; he shall receive of you his standing") as an example of a word-for-word translation that we could not call accurate or faithful because of its unintelligibility ("Are Translators Traitors? Some Personal Reflections," in *The Challenge of Bible Translation: Communicating God's Word to the World*, ed. Glen G. Scorgie, Mark L. Strauss, and Steven M. Voth [Grand Rapids: Zondervan, 2003], 59).

10. This does occur once in a great while elsewhere. E.g., the NJB of Matthew 1:25 states that Joseph "had not had intercourse with [Mary] when she gave birth to a son; and he named him Jesus." What the Greek actually says is that he did not know her (i.e., have sexual intercourse) "until she gave birth to a son" (*ouk eginōsken autēn heōs hou eteken huion*). But this suggests that she subsequently did have normal marital relations with her husband, which denies the Roman Catholic doctrine of the perpetual virginity of Mary. But such examples are few and far between.

11. Both verses are unchanged from the original editions of these two Bible versions.

12. Walter Bauer, Frederick W. Danker, William F. Arndt, and F. Wilbur Gingrich, *A Greek-English Lexicon of the New Testament and Other Early Christian Literature*, 3rd ed. (Chicago: University of Chicago Press, 2000), 543.

13. For excellent resources to these ends, see Jack P. Lewis, *The English Bible from KJV to NIV: A History and Evaluation*, 2nd ed. (Grand Rapids: Baker, 1991); Bruce M. Metzger, *The Bible in Translation: Ancient and English Versions* (Grand Rapids: Baker Academic, 2001); and Gordon D. Fee and Mark L. Strauss, *How to Choose a Translation for All Its Worth: A Guide to Understanding and Using Bible Versions* (Grand Rapids: Zondervan, 2007).

14. Metzger, *Bible in Translation*, 29–35.

15. Ibid., 67–69.

16. For the history of English translations prior to the KJV, see Wegner, *Journey from Texts to Translations*, 271–304.

17. See, e.g., Alister McGrath, *In the Beginning: The Story of the King James Bible and How It Changed a Nation, a Language, and a Culture* (New York: Anchor Books, 2001).

18. Lewis, *English Bible from KJV to NIV*, 33–34.

19. Cf. Metzger, *Bible in Translation*, 164–67.

20. Ibid., 117–22.

21. A point widely acknowledged today by evangelical scholars. See, e.g., already in John N. Oswalt, *The Book of Isaiah: Chapters 1–39*, NICOT (Grand Rapids: Eerdmans, 1986), 207–8. Cf. Gary V. Smith, *Isaiah 1–39*, NAC (Nashville: B&H, 2007), 213–14.

22. Lewis, *English Bible from KJV to NIV*, 111–13.

23. Wegner, *Journey from Texts to Translations*, 370–73.

24. Kenneth L. Barker, ed., *The NIV: The Making of a Contemporary Translation* (Grand Rapids: Zondervan, 1986). Cf. idem, *The Accuracy of the NIV* (Grand Rapids: Baker, 1996); and idem, *The Balance of the NIV: What Makes a Good Translation* (Grand Rapids: Baker Books, 2000).

25. See further Bruce M. Metzger, Robert C. Dentan, and Walter Harrelson, *The Making of the New Revised Standard Version of the Bible* (Grand Rapids: Eerdmans, 1991).

26. Cf. Metzger, *Bible in Translation*, 127–31, 151–53.

27. Cf. Wegner, *Journey from Texts to Translations*, 363–68, 381–84.

28. Fee and Strauss, *How to Choose a Translation for All Its Worth*, 151.

29. E. Ray Clendenen, "The Holman Christian Standard Bible (HCSB)," in *Which Bible Translation Should I Use? A Comparison of Four Major Recent Versions*, ed. Andreas J. Köstenberger and David A. Croteau (Nashville: B&H, 2012), 117–56.

30. Information provided by Biblica (formerly International Bible Society) and Zondervan at annual meetings of the Committee on Bible Translation.

31. See esp. Leland Ryken, *Word of God in English: Criteria of Excellence in Bible Translation* (Wheaton: Crossway, 2002).

32. Wayne Grudem, "The English Standard Version (ESV)," in Köstenberger and Croteau, *Which Bible Translation Should I Use?*, 42.

33. Thomas P. Nass, "Some Thoughts on the ESV and Bible Translation," *Wisconsin Lutheran Quarterly* 108 (2011): 176–200, 267–88. Nass concludes, fairly it would seem, that the ESV "is not the silver bullet that does everything perfectly in regard to English Bible translation. It is not some sort of 'high road' for all conservative, Bible-believing, complementarian Lutherans. Simply put, *it is a doctrinally acceptable, somewhat unidiomatic and inconsistent evangelical revision of the RSV* [emphasis original]. Nothing more and nothing less. [*sic*] It is a translation that promises more than it actually produces."

34. Allan Chapple, "The English Standard Version: A Review Article," *Reformed Theological Review* 62 (2003): 61–96.

35. See esp. Leland Ryken, *The Legacy of the King James Bible: Celebrating 400 Years of the Most Influential English Translation* (Wheaton: Crossway, 2011).

36. See further Fee and Strauss, *How to Choose a Translation for All Its Worth*, 145–58.

37. The NASB is the most woodenly literal of the three, and the NRSV is the most fluent.

38. I have listed them in slightly descending order of reading levels required.

39. The NIV represents and targets the broadest international and theologically most heterogeneous audience. For an even more nuanced taxonomy of most of the major translations, see Fee and Strauss, *How to Choose a Translation for All Its Worth*, 147.

40. Clendenen, "Holman Christian Standard Bible," 117–21. "Optimal equivalence" is also used in a highly technical sense for a combination of formal and functional equivalence (going well beyond the processes these translations employ) by James D. Price, *A Theory for Bible Translation: An Optimal Equivalence Model* (Lewiston, NY: Edwin Mellen, 2007).

41. Cf. Beekman and Callow, *Translating the Word of God*, 23–24.

42. Grudem, "English Standard Version," 42–44.

43. On the details of this verse, see further Chris A. Vlachos, *James*, EGGNT (Nashville: B&H, 2013), 67–68, and the literature cited there.

44. See esp. throughout Dave Brunn, *One Bible, Many Versions: Are All Translations Created Equal?* (Downers Grove, IL: InterVarsity, 2013).

45. Eugene A. Nida and Charles R. Taber, *The Theory and Practice of Translation* (Leiden: Brill, 1969), 99–162.

46. But the GNB is the translation that most consistently follows the actual theory of creating a dynamically equivalent translation. The NLT translators were kept from following it completely because they were tasked with preserving Ken Taylor's original language of the LBP whenever it was acceptable as a bona fide translation.

47. Wayne Grudem ("English Standard Version," 61–62) misleads when he claims that such use of "brothers and sisters" is application, not interpretation. This is not the normal meaning of "application." Application typically asks who or what corresponds to the referents of biblical terms in a different context or culture. If a biblical writer was addressing only men, but today we employ that teaching with both men and women, then that is application. But if a biblical writer was addressing both men and women when using a word like "brothers," *then a generic meaning, including men and women alike, is part of the original meaning* and thus proper interpretation and translation. We might choose to subdivide this meaning into "sense" and "referent," so that the sense of *adelphoi* in this context is spiritual kin, and the referent is the men and women in the immediate Jewish or Christian community the writer is addressing, but in neither instance can the issue of gender inclusivity be limited to application. See further D. A. Carson, *The Inclusive-Language Debate: A Plea for Realism* (Grand Rapids: Baker, 1998), 75–76.

48. See throughout Mark L. Strauss, *Distorting Scripture? The Challenge of Bible Translation and Gender Accuracy* (Downers Grove, IL: InterVarsity, 1998), esp. 87.

49. Clendenen, "Holman Christian Standard Bible," 117–21.

50. The 2009 update of the HCSB (available, as of this writing, primarily just in electronic form) now reads, "My brothers, do not show favoritism as you hold on to the faith in our glorious Lord Jesus Christ."

51. Attempts to link these translations much more closely with purely formally equivalent translations seem to reflect less firsthand familiarity with both the goals and contents of the translations. See, e.g., Grudem ("English Standard Version," 43), who mistakenly includes the NET and the HCSB with essentially literal translations.

52. Overall the NJB falls in between a fully dynamically equivalent translation and an optimally equivalent translation.

53. Cf. Fee and Strauss, *How to Choose a Translation for All Its Worth*, 149.

54. Indeed, Stanley E. Porter argues that we need to pay more attention to even larger contexts of individual words (i.e., up to entire discourses) than we usually do ("Assessing Translation Theory: Beyond Literal and Dynamic Equivalence," in *Translating the New Testament: Text, Translation, Theology*, ed. Stanley E. Porter and Mark J. Boda [Grand Rapids: Eerdmans, 2009], 117–45).

55. When a genitive noun *y* modifies another noun *x*, if *x* functions as a verbal noun

(or "noun of action") in a given context, the two options for classifying the genitive noun *y* are subjective and objective (or possibly, in rare occasions, both). See Daniel B. Wallace, *Greek Grammar beyond the Basics* (Grand Rapids: Zondervan, 1996), 112–21.

56. Cf. Wegner, *Journey from Texts to Translations*, 372–73.

57. On James 2:1, see further Craig L. Blomberg and Mariam J. Kamell, *James*, ZECNT (Grand Rapids: Zondervan, 2008), 106–7, and the literature cited there.

58. Walter R. Martin, *The Kingdom of the Cults*, rev. ed. (Minneapolis: Bethany House, 1977), 64.

59. Robert H. Countess, *The Jehovah's Witnesses' New Testament* (Phillipsburg, NJ: P&R, 1982), 41–56.

60. Ron Rhodes, "Jehovah's Witnesses," in *A Guide to New Religious Movements*, ed. Ronald Enroth (Downers Grove, IL: InterVarsity, 2005), 31–36.

61. Countess, *Jehovah's Witnesses' New Testament*, 57–75.

62. For representative viewpoints on the JST, see esp. Robert L. Millet and Robert J. Matthews, eds., *Plain and Precious Truths Restored: The Doctrinal and Historical Significance of the Joseph Smith Translation* (Salt Lake City: Bookcraft, 1995).

63. For more on choosing a translation, see David Dewey, *A User's Guide to Bible Translations: Making the Most of Different Versions* (Downers Grove, IL: InterVarsity, 2004).

64. See further Carson, *Inclusive-Language Debate*, 27–38.

65. For a detailed timeline of events, see Vern S. Poythress and Wayne A. Grudem, *The Gender-Neutral Bible Controversy: Muting the Masculinity of God's Words* (Nashville: Broadman & Holman, 2000), 15–28.

66. "The one who acquits . . . the one who condemns . . ." is equally possible. See further Bruce K. Waltke, *The Book of Proverbs: Chapters 15–31*, NICOT (Grand Rapids: Eerdmans, 2005), 55. But even by the CSG, a gender-inclusive translation is permissible here. It should therefore be preferred.

67. Ibid., 111–280.

68. A claim repeated in Vern S. Poythress, "Gender in Bible Translation: Exploring a Connection with Male Representatives," *Westminster Theological Journal* 60 (1998): 225–53; and Poythress and Grudem, *Gender-Neutral Bible Controversy*, 246–50.

69. Cf. Mark L. Strauss, "Current Issues in the Gender-Language Debate: A Response to Vern Poythress and Wayne Grudem," in Scorgie, Strauss, and Voth, *Challenge of Bible Translation*, esp. 127–36.

70. Poythress and Grudem, *Gender-Neutral Bible Controversy*, 91–99.

71. See further Richard S. Hess, "Adam, Father, He: Gender Issues in Hebrew Translation," *Bible Translator* 56 (2005): 144–53, esp. 150–53.

72. Rightly Carson, *Inclusive-Language Debate*, 130–31; Strauss, *Distorting Scripture?*, 147–51.

73. The only approach allowed by Poythress and Grudem, *Gender-Neutral Controversy*, 223–32.

74. E.g., Grudem, "English Standard Version," 69–70.

75. Most of the CBT, however, was saddened by this decision because of the way it would inevitably pit the two editions of the NIV against each other. See Douglas J. Moo, "The New International Version (NIV)," in Köstenberger and Croteau, *Which Bible Translation Should I Use?*, 84.

76. Contrast Poythress and Grudem, *Gender-Neutral Bible Controversy*, 133, with Moo, "New International Version," 85.

77. I have had the privilege of being involved, to varying degrees, with four major Bible translations discussed here: the NLT, ESV, HCSB, and updated NIV. I was one of three translators commissioned to produce Matthew for the NLT. I was a second-tier consultant for the drafts of Matthew for both the ESV and the HCSB, and I have served on the CBT of the NIV since 2008.

78. Eric Reed, "Bible: Southern Baptist Convention Rejects TNIV Translation," *Christianity Today*, August 5, 2002, http://www.christianitytoday.com/ct/2002/august5/9.17.html.

79. The letter was read at the meetings of the CBT in Holland, Michigan, June 2008. Nothing in the formal doctrinal statements of the SBC excludes women deacons; this is just widespread practice. That makes Colson's observations all the more poignant.

80. In light of the close connection between the HCSB and the Southern Baptists, it is natural that a frequently asked question addressed on the translation's website is "Does the HCSB represent any particular tradition or denomination?" The answer provided is that the translation "is rooted, not in any one tradition or denomination, but in the original languages of the biblical authors" (http://hcsb.org/pages/hcsbpages/faq.aspx). Of course, identifying the textual base of the translation doesn't really answer the question about the ideology of those who sponsored it.

81. Most of the non-gender-related revisions to the NIV adopted in the TNIV were retained. For an overview of some of the best and most important of these, written before I ever imagined I would be invited to join the CBT, see Craig L. Blomberg, "*Today's New International Version*: The Untold Story of a Good Translation," in *Perspectives on the TNIV from Leading Scholars and Pastors* (Grand Rapids: Zondervan, 2004), 85–115; repr. in *Bible Translator* 56 (2005): 187–211. I included my thoughts at that time about the most important gender-related changes as well.

82. E.g., Poythress and Grudem, *Gender-Neutral Controversy*, 126.

83. Ibid., 120.

84. Ibid., 112.

85. Cf. Carson (*Inclusive-Language Debate*, 109) on the furor in some circles when "thee" and "thou" were first done away with in Bible translations.

86. Cf., e.g., Anthony Thiselton, *The First Epistle to the Corinthians: A Commentary on the Greek Text*, NIGTC (Grand Rapids: Eerdmans; Carlisle, UK: Paternoster, 2000), 316. For additional examples, see Dean Deppe, "You and You: John 1:50–51," in *Devotions on the Greek New Testament: 52 Reflections to Inspire and Instruct*, ed. J. Scott Duvall and Verlyn D. Verbrugge (Grand Rapids: Zondervan, 2012), 43–47.

87. Grudem ("English Standard Version," 72) is particularly candid about this. Despite a leading complementarian, Scott Baldwin, having argued for "assume authority" as an appropriate translation of *authentein* in 1 Timothy 2:12, despite John Calvin having supported this rendering as well, despite the KJV having used "usurp authority," Grudem's bottom line is that egalitarians could too easily use this translation to further their agenda, which he simply can't abide. Why does he not resort to the approach he insists on others using with gender-exclusive language—simply explaining the true meaning to those who might misunderstand it? The depth of Grudem's passion to fight evangelical egalitarianism is clear when he writes,

> I think the NIV committee failed to appreciate that evangelical feminists who want to become pastors are not going to take "assume authority" in a positive sense at all. They will uniformly take it to prohibit wrongful "self-assumed authority" and then say they are not "assuming authority" on their own but just accepting it from the church. Consequently, 1 Timothy 2:12 in the NIV has become useless in the debate over women's roles in the church. In any church that adopts the 2011 NIV, no one will be able to answer their argument using this English Bible. ("English Standard Version," 72)

This last sentence seems completely unfounded. For readers who don't understand gender-exclusive language intended to refer to both men and women, Grudem recommends adding a simple explanation of how "he" or "man" can refer to both men and women. The same thing could be done for 1 Timothy 2:12, with something like "Scholars are divided on the meaning of *authentein* in this passage. Some think it refers only to the exercise of some wrongful kind of authority; others, to a positive use of authority as well." The CBT chose this particularly happy translation because one can "assume authority" both in a wrong way and when it is not one's to assume at all. Neither complementarian nor egalitarian need feel excluded, and supporters of either view will need to take all the Bible's teaching into account anyway as they make their decisions. More important, to censure a certain translation because it doesn't, in one's opinion, make it easy to exclude a view one personally disagrees with, even though other equally gifted, godly, and academically qualified evangelicals hold the view, is to go far beyond the purview of any translator, *especially* someone who supports essentially literal translations!

88. See "An Evaluation of Gender Language in the 2011 Edition of the NIV Bible: A Report from the Council on Biblical Manhood and Womanhood," June 6, 2011, http://www.bible-researcher.com/cbmw.niv2011.2.pdf; Denny Burk et al., "The Translation of Gender Terminology in the NIV 2011," *Journal of Biblical Manhood and Womanhood* 16, no. 1 (2011): 17–33, http://cbmw.org/uncategorized/the-translation-of-gender-terminology-in-the-niv-2011/.

89. SBC Net, "SBC Resolutions: On the Gender-Neutral 2011 New International Version, June 2011," http://www.sbc.net/resolutions/amresolution.asp?id=1218.

90. Cf. Moo, "New International Version," 87.

91. Patricia T. O'Conner and Stuart Kellerman, "On Language: The All-Purpose Pronoun," *New York Times*, July 21, 2009, http://www.nytimes.com/2009/07/26/magazine/26FOB-onlanguage-t.html?_r=0. See also the usage note in *Merriam-Webster's Collegiate Dictionary*, 11th ed. (Springfield, MA: Merriam-Webster, 2003), s.v. "they."

92. See, e.g., "Wednesday Afternoon/Morning Running Blog," *Baptist Press*, June 15, 2011, http://www.bpnews.net/blog/article.asp?id=335.

93. Nass, "Some Thoughts on the ESV," 196.

94. The CBT compiled a series of "flashpoint" texts about which critics of the TNIV had most commonly complained, and almost all of them were revised.

95. This is all the more ironic, because while there is translation that involves "ideological gender sensitivity," neither the NIVI, nor the TNIV, nor the updated NIV has ever contained examples of it, but rather they use "translational gender sensitivity." The former fights patriarchalism; the latter seeks to translate each text accurately in accord with its entire context. See further Darrell L. Bock, "You Make the Call: Are Gender-Sensitive Translations Safe or Out?," *Bible Translator* 56 (2005): 170. Denny Burk is so misled about the actual nature of modern translations that he calls both the NIV and the NRSV dynamic equivalent renderings and claims there are three main approaches to Bible translation today: formal equivalence, dynamic equivalence, and paraphrase. See his "Why All the Translations?" in *Evidence for God: Fifty Arguments for Faith from the Bible, History, Philosophy, and Science*, ed. William A. Dembski and Michael R. Licona (Grand Rapids: Baker Books, 2010), 222. But paraphrase is not even an approach to *translation*, and it is hardly prominent today. Apparently Burk has not actually read any of the documents describing the translation philosophies of either the NIV or the NRSV, nor does he appear to be familiar with their contents in enough detail to describe them accurately, nor does he seem to be aware of the optimally equivalent option (under any name) that actually is more common now than either the dynamically or formally equivalent options. And why wouldn't CBMW or the SBC want to consult people who were actually involved in the translation processes they seek to evaluate and who, as a result, have the ability to report on what actually occurred?

96. Grudem, "English Standard Version," 48.

97. Ryken, *Word of God in English*, 157–72.

Chapter 4: Don't These Issues Rule Out Biblical Inerrancy?

1. Cf., e.g., A. T. B. McGowan, *The Divine Authenticity of Scripture: Retrieving*

an Evangelical Heritage (Nottingham, UK: Apollos; Downers Grove, IL: InterVarsity, 2007), 162 and throughout.

2. Jack B. Rogers and Donald K. McKim, *The Authority and Interpretation of the Bible: An Historical Approach* (San Francisco: Harper & Row, 1979; Eugene, OR: Wipf & Stock, 1999).

3. Carlos R. Bovell, *Inerrancy and the Spiritual Formation of Younger Evangelicals* (Eugene, OR: Wipf & Stock, 2007); Christian Smith, *The Bible Made Impossible: Why Biblicism Is Not a Truly Evangelical Reading of Scripture* (Grand Rapids: Brazos, 2011); Kenton L. Sparks, *God's Word in Human Words: An Evangelical Appropriation of Critical Biblical Scholarship* (Grand Rapids: Baker Academic, 2008). A work more difficult to categorize is Peter Enns, *Inspiration and Incarnation: Evangelicals and the Problem of the Old Testament* (Grand Rapids: Baker Academic, 2005). See the helpful summary comments of the two ways the book can be read in Ben Witherington III, *The Living Word of God: Rethinking the Theology of the Bible* (Waco: Baylor University Press, 2007), 48–49.

4. See esp. Craig L. Blomberg, *The Historical Reliability of the Gospels*, rev. ed. (Nottingham, UK: Inter-Varsity; Downers Grove, IL: InterVarsity, 2007); and idem, *The Historical Reliability of John's Gospel* (Leicester, UK: Inter-Varsity; Downers Grove, IL: InterVarsity, 2001). For a representative rejection, see, e.g., Enns (*Inspiration and Incarnation*, 65): "It is a distortion of the highest order to say Jesus must have cleansed the temple twice." If the emphasis is on the word "must," I agree. But as for the serious possibility, see E. Randolph Richards, "An Honor/Shame Argument for Two Temple Clearings," *Trinity Journal* 29 (2008): 19–43. For OT examples and for excellent inerrantist replies, see Richard Schultz, "Theological Diversity in the Old Testament as Burden or Divine Gift? Problems and Perspectives in the Current Debate," in *Interdisciplinary Perspectives on the Authority of Scripture: Historical, Biblical, and Theoretical Perspectives*, ed. Carlos R. Bovell (Eugene, OR: Pickwick, 2011), 133–63. Bovell is to be commended for assembling this anthology of pro- and anti-inerrantist perspectives, esp. given his frustration with the current state of inerrantism.

5. See esp. Norman L. Geisler and William C. Roach, *Defending Inerrancy: Affirming the Accuracy of Scripture for a New Generation* (Grand Rapids: Baker Books, 2011), 132–59, 180–85, 193–211; F. David Farnell, "Form Criticism and Tradition Criticism," in *The Jesus Crisis: The Inroads of Historical Criticism into Evangelical Scholarship*, ed. Robert L. Thomas and F. David Farnell (Grand Rapids: Kregel, 1998), 185–232; and Robert L. Thomas, "Redaction Criticism," in Thomas and Farnell, *Jesus Crisis*, 233–67. Cf. also idem, "The Rationality, Meaningfulness, and Precision of Scripture," *The Master's Seminary Journal* 15 (2004): 175–207; and idem, *Evangelical Hermeneutics: The New versus the Old* (Grand Rapids: Kregel, 2002), 271–322. Other important evangelical scholars blacklisted in these works include Robert Stein, Kevin Vanhoozer, William Klein, Robert Hubbard, James Edwards, William Lane, Stanley Grenz, Moisés Silva, Marianne Meye Thompson, Joel Green, R. T. France, Peter Cotterell, Max Turner, I. Howard Marshall, Michael Wilkins, James Brooks, Robert Mounce, and Scot McKnight.

6. For the diversity of perceptions and realities, see Mark A. Noll, *Between Faith and Criticism: Evangelicals, Scholarship, and the Bible in America*, 2nd ed. (Grand Rapids: Baker, 1991), esp. 142–61.

7. See, e.g., John Gribbin, *In Search of the Multiverse: Parallel Worlds, Hidden Dimensions, and the Ultimate Quest for the Frontiers of Reality* (Hoboken, NJ: John Wiley, 2009).

8. This inference has been criticized, but see G. K. Beale, "Can the Bible Be Completely Inspired by God and Yet Still Contain Errors? A Response to Some Recent 'Evangelical' Proposals," *Westminster Theological Journal* 73 (2011): 1–22.

9. Vern S. Poythress, *Inerrancy and Worldview: Answering Modern Challenges to the Bible* (Wheaton: Crossway, 2012), 248.

10. See esp. B. B. Warfield, *The Inspiration and Authority of the Bible* (Philadelphia: P&R, 1948), 167–226; John W. Wenham, *Christ and the Bible* (London: Tyndale, 1972; Downers Grove, IL: InterVarsity, 1973). For some helpful tweaking of the Warfield-Wenham line of thought, see Craig Allert, "Issues in Forming a Doctrine of Inspiration," in Bovell, *Interdisciplinary Perspectives*, 259–88; and J. P. Moreland, "How Evangelicals Became Overcommitted to the Bible and What Can Be Done about It," in Bovell, *Interdisciplinary Perspectives*, 289–302.

11. See esp. Alvin Plantinga, "Is Belief in God Properly Basic?," *Nous* 15 (1981): 41–51.

12. E.g., Michael J. Kruger, *Canon Revisited: Establishing the Origins and Authority of the New Testament Books* (Wheaton: Crossway, 2012), esp. 188–222.

13. Reprinted in Norman L. Geisler, ed., *Inerrancy* (Grand Rapids: Zondervan, 1979), 494–502.

14. Paul D. Feinberg, "The Meaning of Inerrancy," in Geisler, *Inerrancy*, 294. David S. Dockery tweaks this definition to produce the following: "When all the facts are known, the Bible (in its original writings) properly interpreted in light of which culture and communication means had developed by the time of its composition will be shown to be completely true (and therefore not false) in all that it affirms, to the degree of precision intended by the author, in all matters relating to God and his creation" (*Christian Scripture: An Evangelical Perspective on Inspiration, Authority, and Interpretation* [Nashville: Broadman & Holman, 1995], 64).

15. I. Howard Marshall, *Biblical Inspiration* (London: Hodder & Stoughton; Grand Rapids: Eerdmans, 1982), 59.

16. A select bibliography would include Walter C. Kaiser Jr., *The Old Testament Documents: Are They Reliable and Relevant?* (Downers Grove, IL: InterVarsity, 2001); Kenneth A. Kitchen, *On the Reliability of the Old Testament* (Grand Rapids: Eerdmans, 2003); Iain W. Provan, V. Philips Long, and Tremper Longman III, *A Biblical History of Israel* (Louisville: Westminster John Knox, 2003); Alan R. Millard, James W. Hoffmeier, and David W. Baker, eds., *Faith, Tradition, and History: Old Testament Historiography in Its Near Eastern Context* (Winona Lake, IN: Eisenbrauns, 1994); Jens B. Kofoed, *Text History: Historiography and the Study of the Biblical Text* (Winona Lake, IN: Eisenbrauns, 2005); Craig L. Blomberg, *Historical Reliability of the Gospels*; idem, *Historical Reliability of John's Gospel*; Paul R. Eddy and Gregory A. Boyd, *The Jesus Legend: A Case for the Historical Reliability of the Synoptic Jesus Tradition* (Grand Rapids: Baker Academic, 2007); and Colin J. Hemer, *The Book of Acts in the Setting of Hellenistic History*, ed. Conrad W. Gempf (Tübingen: Mohr Siebeck, 1989). But for all possible questions, the most detailed evangelical commentaries on individual books of the Bible are necessary. See esp. the New International Greek Testament Commentary, New International Commentary, Baker Exegetical Commentary, Zondervan Exegetical Commentary, New American Commentary, Word Biblical Commentary, Expositor's Biblical Commentary Revised, Apollos Old Testament Commentary, and Pillar New Testament Commentary series.

17. See esp. Greg L. Bahnsen, "The Inerrancy of the Autographa," in Geisler, *Inerrancy*, 151–93. This dispenses with the largely straw-man argument of John J. Brogan ("Can I Have Your Autograph? Uses and Abuses of Textual Criticism in Formulating an Evangelical Doctrine of Scripture," in *Evangelicals and Scripture: Tradition, Authority and Hermeneutics*, ed. Vincent Bacote, Laura C. Miguélez, and Dennis L. Okholm [Downers Grove, IL: InterVarsity, 2004], 108–9) that limiting inerrancy to the autographs gives no pastoral guidance to people dealing with modern translations based on existing manuscripts.

18. E.g., Albert C. Mohler Jr., citing a personal conversation with Carl F. H. Henry, in Molly Worthen, "The Reformer," *Christianity Today*, October 1, 2010, http://www.christianitytoday.com/ct/2010/october/3.18.html.

19. See, e.g., all four participants in James R. Beck, ed., *Two Views of Women*

in Ministry, rev. ed. (Grand Rapids: Zondervan, 2005).

20. See esp. Klyne R. Snodgrass, *Stories with Intent: A Comprehensive Guide to the Parables of Jesus* (Grand Rapids: Eerdmans, 2008), 9.

21. Feinberg, "Meaning of Inerrancy," 300. Cf. further Poythress, *Inerrancy and Worldview*, 34–42.

22. John M. Frame, *The Doctrine of the Word of God* (Phillipsburg, NJ: P&R, 2010), 177–78.

23. For this freedom of interpretation, see Timothy Ward, *Words of Life: Scripture as the Living and Active Word of God* (Downers Grove, IL: InterVarsity, 2009), 133–34. For specific interpretations of Genesis 1, see Ronald F. Youngblood, ed., *The Genesis Debate: Persistent Questions about Creation and the Flood* (Grand Rapids: Baker, 1990); Richard F. Carlson and Tremper Longman III, *Science, Creation and the Bible: Reconciling Rival Theories of Origins* (Downers Grove, IL: InterVarsity, 2010); and John H. Walton, *The Lost World of Genesis One: Ancient Cosmology and the Origins Debate* (Downers Grove, IL: InterVarsity, 2009).

24. Marshall, *Biblical Inspiration*, 72; Smith, *Bible Made Impossible*, 197n19; Sparks, *God's Word in Human Words*, 251.

25. Feinberg, "Meaning of Inerrancy," 299.

26. See esp. Craig S. Keener, *Acts: An Exegetical Commentary* (Grand Rapids: Baker Academic, 2012), 1:258–319. Cf. also Hemer, *Book of Acts*, 415–27; Conrad W. Gempf, "Public Speaking and Published Accounts," in *The Book of Acts in Its Ancient Literary Setting*, ed. Bruce W. Winter and Andrew D. Clarke (Grand Rapids: Eerdmans; Carlisle, UK: Paternoster, 1993), 259–303.

27. Victor P. Hamilton refers to Yahweh's "interpretative quotation" of Sarah, adding, "This is what Sarah had in mind, but that is not exactly how she said it" (*The Book of Genesis: Chapters 18–50*, NICOT [Grand Rapids: Eerdmans, 1995], 13). If God can do this, let no human ever criticize the biblical authors for doing so or insist that we adopt a different standard in interpreting what they are doing!

28. Gary Knoppers, "The Synoptic Problem: An Old Testament Perspective," *Bulletin for Biblical Research* 19 (2009): 11–34.

29. James Callahan, *The Clarity of Scripture: History, Theology and Contemporary Literary Studies* (Downers Grove, IL: InterVarsity, 2001), 105–26.

30. A remarkable consensus has coalesced around the technical definition of John J. Collins, "Introduction: Toward the Morphology of a Genre," *Semeia* 14 (1979): 9: "'Apocalypse' is a genre of revelatory literature with a narrative framework, in which a revelation is mediated by an otherworldly being to a human recipient, disclosing a transcendent reality which is both temporal, insofar as it envisages eschatological salvation, and spatial insofar as it involves another, supernatural world."

31. Cf. esp. Robert H. Mounce, *The Book of Revelation*, NICNT (Grand Rapids: Eerdmans, 1977), 302–3. I have cited the unrevised edition because this viewpoint is expressed more clearly in it than in the revised edition of 1998.

32. But, from a broader evangelical perspective, see the very helpful suggestions throughout John Goldingay, *Models for Scripture* (Grand Rapids: Eerdmans; Carlisle, UK: Paternoster, 1994).

33. Frame (*Doctrine of the Word of God*, 174) improves on matters by suggesting that "*inerrant language makes good on its claims*" (emphasis original). But this still leaves unanswered the question of what is claimed in texts like those used as examples here.

34. A point often missed by those who pit propositional versus performative or personal revelation—as does Mark Hargreaves, "Telling Stories: The Concept of Narrative and Biblical Authority," *Anvil* 13 (1996): 127–39. There is no literary form or personal relationship that communicates meaning and does not presuppose or build on certain propositions. Cf. Craig L. Blomberg, *Interpreting the Parables*, rev. ed. (Nottingham, UK: Apollos; Downers Grove, IL: IVP Academic, 2012), 158–59.

35. Cf. Tremper Longman III, *How to Read the Psalms* (Downers Grove, IL: InterVarsity; Leicester, UK: Inter-Varsity, 1988), 71.

36. Cf. Richard S. Hess, *Song of Songs*, BCOTWP (Grand Rapids: Baker Academic, 2005), 27–29.

37. Douglas J. Moo, *The Letter of James*, PNTC (Grand Rapids: Eerdmans; Leicester, UK: Apollos, 2000), 123–24.

38. William W. Klein, Craig L. Blomberg, and Robert L. Hubbard Jr., *Introduction to Biblical Interpretation*, rev. ed. (Nashville: Nelson, 2004), 344–50.

39. See the excellent suggestions for Christian application throughout Richard S. Hess, "Leviticus," in *The Expositor's Bible Commentary*, ed. Tremper Longman III and David E. Garland, rev. ed. (Grand Rapids: Zondervan, 2008), 1:563–826.

40. Craig S. Keener, "Kissing," in *Dictionary of New Testament Background*, ed. Craig A. Evans and Stanley E. Porter (Downers Grove, IL: InterVarsity; Leicester, UK: Inter-Varsity, 2000), 628–29.

41. Luke T. Johnson, *The First and Second Letters to Timothy: A New Translation with Introduction and Commentary*, AB (New York: Doubleday, 2001), 208–9.

42. E.g., Craig S. Keener, *Paul, Women and Wives: Marriage and Women's Ministry in the Letters of Paul* (Peabody, MA: Hendrickson, 1992), 107–13.

43. Often this difference has corresponded to the British (Commonwealth) versus American origin of the writer, respectively. For the larger context of the differing emphases, see Stephen R. Holmes, "Evangelical Doctrines of Scripture in Transatlantic Perspective," *Evangelical Quarterly* 81 (2009): 38–63.

44. Cf. Frame, *Doctrine of the Word of God*, 143.

45. For the debate, see Gregory A. Boyd and Paul R. Eddy, *Across the Spectrum: Understanding Issues in Evangelical Theology*, 2nd ed. (Grand Rapids: Baker Academic, 2009), 15–31.

46. Thomas Buchan, "Inerrancy as Inheritance? Competing Genealogies of Biblical Authority," in Bacote, Miguélez, and Okholm, *Evangelicals and Scripture*, 42–54.

47. See esp. throughout John D. Woodbridge, *Biblical Authority: A Critique of the Rogers/McKim Proposal* (Grand Rapids: Zondervan, 1982).

48. David W. Bebbington, *Evangelicalism in Modern Britain: A History from the 1730s to the 1980s* (London: Unwin Hyman, 1989), 3. He calls this "biblicism" (in a broader sense than Christian Smith uses the term; see "Avoiding the Opposite Extreme" in chap. 2 above). The other three tenets are conversionism, crucicentrism, and activism.

49. Sparks, *God's Word in Human Words*, 229–59.

50. Stanley J. Grenz and Roger E. Olson, *20th-Century Theology: God and the World in a Transitional Age* (Downers Grove, IL: InterVarsity, 1992), 71. John D. Morrison ("Barth, Barthians, and Evangelicals: Reassessing the Question of the Relation of Holy Scripture and the Word of God," *Trinity Journal* 25 [2004]: 187–213), however, argues that Barth did not separate Scripture from the Word of God to the extent that most have perceived him doing.

51. Enns, *Inspiration and Incarnation*, 17–21.

52. On Jesus and the Bible both as the Word of God, see further Ward, *Words of Life*, 67–78.

53. Smith, *Bible Made Impossible*, 3–54, with the list on 22–23.

54. Ibid., 25.

55. Of course, not all pedobaptists frame things in this way, but after studying the passages they typically cite in defense of their case, I have found their arguments singularly unpersuasive. See the magisterial study by Everett F. Ferguson, *Baptism in the Early Church: History, Theology, and Liturgy in the First Five Centuries* (Grand Rapids: Eerdmans, 2009). Cf. also Thomas R. Schreiner, *Believer's Baptism: Sign of the New Covenant in Christ* (Nashville: B&H, 2006).

56. See esp. Robert G. Clouse, ed., *The Meaning of the Millennium: Four Views* (Downers Grove, IL: InterVarsity, 1977); Darrell L. Bock, ed., *Three Views on the Millennium and Beyond* (Grand Rapids: Zondervan, 1999).

57. Joel B. Green, "Kaleidoscopic View," in *The Nature of the Atonement: Four Views*,

ed. James Beilby and Paul R. Eddy (Downers Grove, IL: InterVarsity, 2006), 157–85. In other words, the four views in this volume are actually the three discrete ones mentioned here, followed by Green, who affirms elements of all three simultaneously.

58. See Pat E. Harrell, *Divorce and Remarriage in the Early Church* (Austin: Sweet, 1967); and David Atkinson, *To Have and to Hold: The Marriage Covenant and the Discipline of Divorce* (Grand Rapids: Eerdmans, 1981).

59. See further Craig L. Blomberg, "Marriage, Divorce, Remarriage, and Celibacy: An Exegesis of Matthew 19:3–12," *Trinity Journal* 11 (1990): 161–96.

60. The same phenomenon results if one compares the contents of the major evangelical systematic theologies, even when they represent quite different denominational or theological traditions. Cf., e.g., Donald Bloesch, *Essentials of Evangelical Theology*, 2 vols. (New York: Harper & Row, 1982); Alister McGrath, *Christian Theology: An Introduction*, 5th ed. (Oxford: Blackwell, 2011); J. Rodman Williams, *Systematic Theology from a Charismatic Perspective* (Grand Rapids: Zondervan, 1996); Charles C. Ryrie, *Basic Theology: A Popular Systematic Guide to Understanding Christian Truth*, rev. ed. (Chicago: Moody, 1999); Thomas C. Oden, *Classic Christianity: Systematic Theology* (New York: HarperCollins, 1992); Millard C. Erickson, *Christian Theology*, 3rd ed. (Grand Rapids: Baker Academic, 2013); Michael S. Horton, *The Christian Faith: A Systematic Theology for Pilgrims on the Way* (Grand Rapids: Zondervan, 2011).

61. After making the relevant comparisons among works like those cited in the previous note, contrast any of them with their nonevangelical counterparts. See, e.g., Paul Tillich, *Systematic Theology*, 3 vols. (Chicago: University of Chicago Press, 1973); Wolfhart Pannenberg, *Systematic Theology*, 3 vols. (Grand Rapids: Eerdmans; Edinburgh: T&T Clark, 1998); Francis S. Fiorenza and John P. Galvin, *Systematic Theology: Roman Catholic Perspectives*, 2nd ed. (Minneapolis: Fortress, 2010); William Placher, *Essentials of Christian Theology* (Louisville: Westminster John Knox, 2003); and Marcus J. Borg, *Speaking Christian: Why Christian Words Have Lost Their Meaning and Power—And How They Can Be Restored* (New York: HarperOne, 2011).

62. Compare, e.g., the contents of each of the works in the previous note with each other; the disagreements outweigh the agreements.

63. On how thoroughgoing relativism paves the way for Nietzsche's godless "will to power" to fill the vacuum left by the denial of all transcendent absolutes, see Douglas Groothuis, *Truth Decay: Defending Christianity against the Challenges of Postmodernism* (Downers Grove, IL: InterVarsity, 2000), 198–202.

64. Carlos Bovell, *Rehabilitating Inerrancy in a Culture of Fear* (Eugene, OR: Wipf & Stock, 2012), 55–58. See esp. throughout Kevin Vanhoozer, *Is There a Meaning in This Text? The Bible, the Reader and the Morality of Literary Knowledge* (Grand Rapids: Zondervan, 1998).

65. On speech acts more generally, see esp. J. L. Austin, *How to Do Things with Words*, 2nd ed. (Oxford: Oxford University Press, 1975); and John R. Searle, *Speech Acts: An Essay in the Philosophy of Language* (Cambridge: Cambridge University Press, 1969).

66. Many of the signers of the Chicago Statement on Biblical Inerrancy presupposed a correspondence view of truth, even though the expression does not appear in the document per se. See, e.g., Feinberg, "Meaning of Inerrancy," 295.

67. Even fellow evangelicals sometimes resort to inflated condemnation. See, e.g., Gerald L. Borchert's (*John 1–11*, NAC [Nashville: Broadman & Holman, 1996], 160) calling the theory of two temple cleansings (based on the differences between John and the Synoptics on context and details) "a historiographical monstrosity."

68. For details, see Craig L. Blomberg, "The Legitimacy and Limits of Harmonization," in *Hermeneutics, Authority, and Canon*, ed. D. A. Carson and John D. Woodbridge (Grand Rapids: Zondervan, 1986;

Grand Rapids: Baker, 1994; Eugene, OR: Wipf & Stock, 2005), 169–73.

69. Paul Merkley, "The Gospels as Historical Testimony," *Evangelical Quarterly* 58 (1986): 328–36.

70. Blomberg, "Legitimacy and Limits of Harmonization," 166–68.

71. Harold Lindsell, *The Battle for the Bible* (Grand Rapids: Zondervan, 1976), 174–76.

72. Cited in Robert H. Stein, *Difficult Passages in the Gospels* (Grand Rapids: Baker, 1984), 12.

73. Ironically, the parallelism between the correct and incorrect uses of the two disciplines is missed *both* by those like Thomas ("Redaction Criticism"), who altogether reject redaction criticism, *and* by those like Sparks (*God's Word in Human Words*), who altogether reject harmonization.

74. For representative uses, see Vern S. Poythress, *Inerrancy and the Gospels: A God-Centered Approach to the Challenges of Harmonization* (Wheaton: Crossway, 2012).

75. See esp. Richard Bauckham, *Jesus and the Eyewitnesses* (Grand Rapids: Eerdmans, 2006), 319–57.

76. See, e.g., Bart D. Ehrman, *Jesus: Apocalyptic Prophet of the New Millennium* (Oxford: Oxford University Press, 1999), 51–52.

77. James D. G. Dunn, "Altering the Default Setting: Re-envisaging the Early Transmission of the Jesus Tradition," *New Testament Studies* 49 (2003): 139–75.

78. A classic example from the twentieth century is the Jewish chronicling of Nazi atrocities in Germany in hopes of preventing another Holocaust. See Richard Bauckham, *Jesus and the Eyewitnesses*, 399–405.

79. Cf. Michael F. Bird, "The Formation of the Gospels in the Setting of Early Christianity: The Jesus Tradition as Corporate Memory," *Westminster Theological Journal* 67 (2005): 133, and the literature cited there.

80. See esp. Blomberg, *Historical Reliability of the Gospels*, 221–25; idem, *Historical Reliability of John's Gospel*, 187–88, 237–39, 246–47.

81. Craig L. Blomberg, "A Constructive Traditional Response to New Testament Criticism," in *Do Historical Matters Matter to Faith? A Critical Appraisal of Modern and Postmodern Approaches to Scripture*, ed. James K. Hoffmeier and Dennis R. Magary (Wheaton: Crossway, 2012), 346. Sparks (*God's Word in Human Words*, 164n68) cites the page number of E. J. Young's work (*Thy Word Is Truth* [Grand Rapids: Eerdmans, 1957]) as 174, but the quotation actually appears on 124.

82. I cannot imagine Young applying it to my argument either, given his even more frequent use of additive harmonization in resolving problems among Gospel parallels than I am comfortable with. See Young, *Thy Word Is Truth*, 128–36. Sparks is apparently either unaware of or has chosen to ignore what Young thought was and was not a strained or forced harmonization. That he also misidentified the page on which the Young quote appeared (see the previous note) does not inspire confidence in the care with which he undertook his research at this point.

83. See further Blomberg, "Constructive Traditional Response," 357–60.

84. See now also Kenton L. Sparks, *Sacred Word, Broken Word: Biblical Authority and the Dark Side of Scripture* (Grand Rapids: Eerdmans, 2012).

85. See Thomas and Farnell, *Jesus Crisis*.

86. Thomas, "Redaction Criticism," 380. Given that the unforgivable sin, also known as blasphemy against the Holy Spirit (Mark 3:29), appears in its biblical context as ascribing to Satan what is actually the power of the Spirit (vv. 22–30), I have no idea how a self-confessed evangelical Christian author dares to use such language in speaking of fellow evangelical Christians!

87. E.g., Robert L. Thomas, "The Hermeneutics of Evangelical Redaction Criticism," *Journal of the Evangelical Theological Society* 29 (1989): 447–59; idem, "A Critique of Progressive Dispensational Hermeneutics," in *When the Trumpet Sounds*, ed. Thomas Ice and Timothy Demy (Eugene, OR: Harvest House, 1995), 413–26; idem, "Current Hermeneutical Trends: Toward Explanation or Obfuscation," *Journal of the Evangelical Theological Society* 39 (1996): 242–56.

88. Geisler and Roach, *Defending Inerrancy*, 43–211.

89. Ehrman, *Misquoting Jesus*, 9–14.

90. See esp. William P. Brown, ed., *Engaging Biblical Authority: Perspectives on the Bible as Scripture* (Louisville: Westminster John Knox, 2007).

91. See further Michael Bauman, "Why the Noninerrantists Are Not Listening: Six Tactical Errors Evangelicals Commit," *Journal of the Evangelical Theological Society* 29 (1986): 318–19, 322–23.

92. Jeff Robinson, "Theological Society Retains Open Theists Pinnock, Sanders," *Baptist Press*, November 20, 2003, http://www.bpnews.net/bpnews.asp?id=17132. Contra Geisler and Roach (*Defending Inerrancy*, 38–39, 342–43), who have mistakenly referred to the percentage of the vote against Sanders as the percentage of the vote against Pinnock.

93. The original work that Geisler attacked was Murray J. Harris, *Raised Immortal: Resurrection and Immortality in the New Testament* (Grand Rapids: Eerdmans, 1995). The published version of the attack came in the form of Norman L. Geisler, *The Battle for the Resurrection* (Nashville: Nelson, 1989). In response, Harris clarified his views and cataloged the plethora of factual errors and misrepresentations of his views that permeated Geisler's work, in Murray J. Harris, *From Grave to Glory: The Resurrection in the New Testament, Including a Response to Norman L. Geisler* (Grand Rapids: Zondervan, 1990).

94. Wayne Grudem, *Systematic Theology: An Introduction to Biblical Doctrine* (Grand Rapids: Zondervan, 1995), 611.

95. E.g., Geisler and Roach, *Defending Inerrancy*, 39–40, 227–32, 302, 342–43.

96. Norman L. Geisler and F. David Farnell decide "the time has come to expose people like Blomberg who enjoy wide acceptance in certain evangelical circles but who denies [*sic*] the historic evangelical doctrine of inerrancy" ("The Erosion of Inerrancy among New Testament Scholars: A Primary Case in Point—Craig Blomberg," [2012], http://www.normangeisler.net/articles/Bible/Inspiration-Inerrancy/Blomberg/DenialOfMiracleStory.htm). This is just one of an extraordinary number of factual inaccuracies that characterize this blogpost. For twelve of the most substantive, directly involving me, see chap. 5, n. 113, below.

97. As reported to me in each instance by former colleagues who for obvious reasons would prefer not to be named and incur his further wrath.

98. See esp. the three-volume series edited by James H. Charlesworth and Petr Pokorný, based on the two Princeton-Prague Symposia on Jesus Research, titled, *Jesus Research: An International Perspective* (Grand Rapids: Eerdmans, 2009–). Cf. also a majority of the chapters in the magisterial four-volume set edited by Tom Holmén and Stanley E. Porter, *Handbook for the Study of the Historical Jesus* (Leiden: Brill, 2011).

99. A classic example is John W. Loftus, *Why I Became an Atheist: A Former Preacher Rejects Christianity*, rev. ed. (Amherst, NY: Prometheus, 2012). See further James S. Spiegel, *The Making of an Atheist: How Immorality Leads to Unbelief* (Chicago: Moody, 2010); cf. Thomas Nagel, *The Last Word* (Oxford: Oxford University Press, 1998), 10–11.

100. Biblical authority "is *not* the power to control people and crush them and keep them in little boxes. The church often tries to do that—to tidy people up. Nor is the Bible as the vehicle of God's authority meant to be information for the legalist. . . . Rather, God's authority vested in Scripture is designed, as all God's authority is designed, to liberate human beings, to judge and condemn evil and sin in the world in order to set people free to be fully human. That's what God is in the business of doing. That is what his authority is there *for*. And when we use a shorthand phrase like 'authority of Scripture,' that is what we ought to be meaning" (N. T. Wright, "How Can the Bible be Authoritative?" *Vox evangelica* 21 [1991]: 16).

101. Cf. esp. Robert W. Yarbrough, "Inerrancy's Complexities: Grounds for Grace in the Debate," *Presbyterion* 37 (2011): 85–100. This essay is reprinted as chap. 4 in *Did God*

Really Say? Affirming the Truthfulness and Trustworthiness of Scripture, ed. David B. Garner (Phillipsburg, NJ: P&R, 2012).

Chapter 5: Aren't Several Narrative Genres of the Bible Unhistorical?

1. E.g., John Loftus, *Why I Became an Atheist: A Former Preacher Rejects Christianity* (Amherst, NY: Prometheus, 2008), 141–46. Of many mistakes Loftus makes, his first is to consider the book of Jonah a "typical" prophetic book (141). In fact, it is regularly recognized to be unlike any of the others in the OT, so that whatever one concludes about its historicity need not affect one's opinion on any of the other prophetic books.

2. See, e.g., Roland E. Murphy, "Job," in *The International Bible Commentary: A Catholic and Ecumenical Commentary for the Twenty-First Century*, ed. William R. Farmer (Collegeville, MN: Liturgical Press, 1998), 759.

3. So even Brevard S. Childs (*Introduction to the Old Testament as Scripture* [Philadelphia: Fortress; London: SCM, 1979], 316–25, 611–13), who otherwise emphasizes the final, literary unity and canonical shape of OT texts as much as anyone.

4. E.g., John J. Collins, *Introduction to the Hebrew Bible* (Minneapolis: Fortress, 2004), 67–77; Marvin A. Sweeney, *Tanak: A Theological and Critical Introduction to the Jewish Bible* (Minneapolis: Fortress, 2011), 55–61.

5. E.g., see throughout Carl R. Holladay, *A Critical Introduction to the New Testament* (Nashville: Abingdon, 2005); and Delbert Burkett, *An Introduction to the New Testament and the Origins of Christianity* (Cambridge: Cambridge University Press, 2002), both ad loc.

6. As in the voluminous writings of such popular authors as Hal Lindsey, Tim LaHaye, Jerry Jenkins, and Joel Rosenberg.

7. For details, see esp. William W. Klein, Craig L. Blomberg, and Robert L. Hubbard Jr., *Introduction to Biblical Interpretation*, rev. ed. (Nashville: Nelson, 2004), 323–448.

8. See esp. Harvey K. McArthur and Robert M. Johnston, *They Also Taught in Parables: Rabbinic Parables from the First Centuries of the Christian Era* (Grand Rapids: Zondervan, 1990).

9. For the major approaches to biblical interpretation current today, see Stanley E. Porter and Beth M. Stovell, eds., *Biblical Hermeneutics: Five Views* (Downers Grove, IL: InterVarsity, 2012).

10. "The Chicago Statement on Biblical Inerrancy," in *Inerrancy*, ed. Norman L. Geisler (Grand Rapids: Zondervan, 1979), 495.

11. Ibid., 496.

12. Craig L. Blomberg, *Interpreting the Parables*, 2nd ed. (Nottingham, UK: InterVarsity; Downers Grove, IL: InterVarsity, 2012), 295–303.

13. Ibid., 299–302.

14. E.g., Randy Alcorn, *Heaven* (Carol Stream, IL: Tyndale House, 2004), 62.

15. Blomberg, *Interpreting the Parables*, 257–59.

16. Classically in Henry M. Morris, *The Genesis Record* (Grand Rapids: Baker, 1976), 29.

17. See esp. John C. Whitcomb and Henry M. Morris, *The Genesis Flood* (1961), repr. as 50th anniversary ed. (Phillipsburg, NJ: P&R, 2011), 474–89.

18. Scientific creationists frequently allege that they alone adopt the plain meaning of Genesis 1 and that it is wrong ever to reinterpret the biblical text in light of apparently scientific findings, rather than vice versa. But whenever they propose a date for creation significantly earlier than what the biblical genealogies add up to (4004 BC), they are reinterpreting the "plain meaning" of the text to accommodate *their* scientific theories. So it is disingenuous of them to object to other people doing the same thing in other places.

19. For an excellent, recent evangelical introduction to the scientific question, see Davis A. Young and Ralph F. Stearley, *The Bible, Rocks and Time: Geological Evidence for the Age of the Earth* (Downers Grove, IL: InterVarsity, 2008).

20. There can, of course, be hybrid theories. Bruce Waltke with Charles Yu, for example,

argue for theistic evolution throughout the first five creative "days" but then insist on the direct creation of humanity on the sixth (*An Old Testament Theology: An Exegetical, Canonical, and Thematic Approach* [Grand Rapids: Zondervan, 2007], 202–3).

21. For good overviews of varying perspectives, see throughout Ronald F. Youngblood, ed., *The Genesis Debate: Persistent Questions about Creation and the Flood* (Nashville: Nelson, 1986); and Richard F. Carlson and Tremper Longman III, *Science, Creation and the Bible: Reconciling Rival Theories of Origins* (Downers Grove, IL: InterVarsity, 2010).

22. John H. Walton, *The Lost World of Genesis 1: Ancient Cosmology and the Origins Debate* (Downers Grove, IL: InterVarsity, 2009).

23. See esp. Samuel D. Giere, *A New Glimpse of Day One: Intertextuality, History of Interpretation, and Genesis 1.1–5* (Berlin: de Gruyter, 2009); cf. Mark A. Noll, *The Scandal of the Evangelical Mind* (Grand Rapids: Eerdmans; Leicester, UK: Inter-Varsity, 1994), 177–208.

24. See now esp. Peter Enns (*The Evolution of Adam: What the Bible Does and Doesn't Say about Human Origins* [Grand Rapids: Brazos, 2012]), who makes the most sophisticated case to date for accepting this interpretation within the context of a high view of Scripture.

25. E.g., Kenneth A. Mathews, *Genesis 1–11:26*, NAC (Nashville: Broadman & Holman, 1996), 109–11.

26. The problem of the "talking snake/serpent" need not be nearly as difficult as many make it. This is Satan (cf. Rev. 12:9; 20:2) speaking through the animal, and not an indication that all snakes once talked! Nor is this an inappropriate reading of the OT in light of the New; cf. Bruce K. Waltke with Cathi J. Fredricks, *Genesis: A Commentary* (Grand Rapids: Zondervan, 2001), 90.

27. For a similar critique, see esp. Stewart Goetz and Charles Taliaferro, *Naturalism* (Grand Rapids: Eerdmans, 2008).

28. Derek Kidner, *Genesis: An Introduction and Commentary*, TOTC (Leicester, UK: Inter-Varsity; Downers Grove, IL: InterVarsity, 1967), 28–29.

29. Ibid., 29, for both of the last two quotations.

30. Ibid., 30.

31. Quoted in C. John Collins, *Did Adam and Eve Really Exist? Who They Were and Why You Should Care* (Wheaton: Crossway, 2011), 129.

32. Ibid., 130.

33. On the distinct literary form of Genesis 1–11, see esp. Richard S. Hess and David T. Tsumura, eds., *I Studied Inscriptions from Before the Flood: Ancient Near Eastern, Literary, and Linguistic Approaches to Genesis 1–11* (Winona Lake, IN: Eisenbrauns, 1994).

34. John Goldingay, *Genesis for Everyone* (Louisville: Westminster John Knox, 2010), 1:29.

35. George W. Coats, *Genesis with an Introduction to Narrative Literature* (Grand Rapids: Eerdmans, 1984), 38.

36. Kenneth A. Mathews, *Genesis 1–11:26*, NAC (Nashville: Broadman & Holman, 1996), 109.

37. John E. Hartley, *Genesis*, NIBC (Peabody, MA: Hendrickson; Carlisle, UK: Paternoster, 2000), repr. in UBC series (Grand Rapids: Baker Books, 2012), 56.

38. See esp. throughout James K. Hoffmeier and Dennis R. Magary, eds., *Do Historical Matters Matter to Faith? A Critical Appraisal of Modern and Postmodern Approaches to Scripture* (Wheaton: Crossway, 2012).

39. Brief references to Sabeans (Job 1:15) and Chaldeans (1:17) teach us little.

40. E.g., Robert L. Alden, *Job*, NAC (Nashville: Broadman & Holman, 1993), 25–28.

41. E.g., John E. Hartley, *The Book of Job*, NICOT (Grand Rapids: Eerdmans, 1988), 38; Francis I. Andersen, *Job: An Introduction and Commentary*, TOTC (Leicester, UK: Inter-Varsity; Downers Grove, IL: InterVarsity, 1976), 32. Even David J. A. Clines calls it "a fresh and independent creation" (*Job 1–20*, WBC [Dallas: Word, 1989], lx).

42. Cf. John H. Walton, *Job*, NIVAC (Grand Rapids: Zondervan, 2012), 26.

43. On which see esp. Millard J. Erickson, *Christian Theology*, 3rd ed. (Grand Rapids: Baker Academic, 2013), 210–29.

44. On the theology of Job, see esp. Robert S. Fyall, *Now My Eyes Have Seen You: Images of Creation and Evil in the Book of Job* (Leicester, UK: Inter-Varsity; Downers Grove, IL: InterVarsity, 2002). See also many of the articles in *Sitting with Job: Selected Studies on the Book of Job*, ed. Roy B. Zuck (Grand Rapids: Baker, 1992; repr., Eugene, OR: Wipf & Stock, 2003).

45. Moshe Greenberg, "Did Job Really Exist? An Issue of Medieval Exegesis," in *Sha'arei Talmon: Studies in the Bible, Qumran, and the Ancient Near East*, ed. Michael Fishbane and Emanuel Tov with Weston W. Fields (Winona Lake, IN: Eisenbrauns, 1992), 3–11.

46. Walton, *Job*, 25. Cf. H. H. Rowley, *Job*, rev. ed., NCB (London: Marshall, Morgan & Scott; Grand Rapids: Eerdmans, 1976), 5.

47. Tremper Longman III, *Job*, BCOTWP (Grand Rapids: Baker Academic, 2012), 32–34.

48. Cf. Leslie C. Allen, *The Books of Joel, Obadiah, Jonah and Micah*, NICOT (London: Hodder & Stoughton; Grand Rapids: Eerdmans, 1976), 180. Allen makes the same point with the examples of Lady Macbeth and Oliver Twist.

49. R. Reed Lessing, *Jonah*, ConcC (St. Louis: Concordia, 2007), 13.

50. Richard D. Patterson, "Jonah," in *Minor Prophets: Hosea–Malachi*, by Richard D. Patterson and Andrew E. Hill, Cornerstone Biblical Commentary (Carol Stream, IL: Tyndale House, 2008), 244–45.

51. For many years, the theory was popular that Jonah 2:2–9 was not part of the original text, but this is not widely held today. For the reasons for both trends, see T. Desmond Alexander, "Jonah," in *Obadiah, Jonah, Micah: An Introduction and Commentary*, by David W. Baker, T. Desmond Alexander, and Bruce K. Waltke, TOTC (Nottingham, UK: Inter-Varsity; Downers Grove, IL: Inter-Varsity, 2009), 63–69.

52. See throughout the detailed survey of proposals by Kenneth M. Craig Jr., "Jonah in Recent Research," *Currents in Research: Biblical Studies* 7 (1999): 97–118.

53. Esp. Roger Syrén, "The Book of Jonah—A Reversed Diaspora-Novella?" *Svensk exegetisk årsbok* 58 (1993): 7–14.

54. Esp. Alastair G. Hunter, "Creating Waves: Why the Fictionality of Job Matters," in *Sense and Sensitivity: Essays on Reading the Bible in Memory of Robert Carroll*, ed. Alastair G. Hunter and Phillip R. Davies (Sheffield: Sheffield Academic Press, 2002), 101–16. For the use of Jonah as a primer to illustrate a wide range of methods in hermeneutics, see E. M. Conradie, L. C. Jonker, D. G. Lawrie, and R. A. Arendse, *Fishing for Jonah: Various Approaches to Biblical Interpretation* (Bellville, South Africa: University of the Western Cape, 1998).

55. Alexander, "Jonah," 111–12.

56. Lessing, *Jonah*, 187.

57. Allen, *Books of Joel, Obadiah, Jonah and Micah*, 176n5.

58. Tracy Kimball, "Shark Swallows Fisherman—Then Spits Him out Alive!" *Weekly World News*, January 21, 1992, 6, http://books.google.com/books?id=we0DAAAAMBAJ&printsec=frontcover&source=gbs_ge_summary_r&cad=0#v=onepage&q&f=false. Lessing (*Jonah*, 187) cites the date of the article as June 16, 1987.

59. "Great White Shark Attacks: Defanging the Myths," *National Geographic News*, October 28, 2010, http://news.nationalgeographic.com/news/2004/01/0123_040123_tvgreatwhiteshark_2.html.

60. "The fact that the vehicle [the fish for getting Jonah to Nineveh] is a wholly fantastic one is something which the interpreter must not try to rationalize away. With humor as his instrument, the narrator confronts Jonah's miscalculated flight (1:3) with the incalculable potentialities of his God" (Hans W. Wolff, *Obadiah and Jonah: A Commentary*, CC [Minneapolis: Augsburg; London: SPCK, 1986], 133).

61. Ernst R. Wendland, "Text Analysis and the Genre of Jonah," *Journal of the Evangelical Theological Society* 39 (1976): 373–95.

62. James Bruckner, *Jonah, Nahum, Habakkuk, Zephaniah*, NIVAC (Grand Rapids: Zondervan, 2004), 21–22.

63. See esp. Murray J. Harris, *The Second Epistle to the Corinthians*, NIGTC (Grand Rapids: Eerdmans; Milton Keynes, UK: Paternoster, 2005), 8–51.

64. Frank J. Matera, *II Corinthians: A Commentary*, NTL (Louisville: Westminster John Knox, 2003), 29–32.

65. Craig L. Blomberg, *Jesus and the Gospels: An Introduction and Survey*, 2nd ed. (Nashville: B&H; Nottingham, UK: Inter-Varsity, 2009), 197–201.

66. For a clear, concise introduction by an evangelical, who has outlined the "four human voices" in Isaiah (the prophet himself as "ambassador," a subsequent "disciple" who edits chaps. 1–39, a "poet" who pens chaps. 40–55, and a "preacher" who produces chaps. 56–66), see John Goldingay, *Isaiah*, NIBC (Peabody, MA: Hendrickson; Carlisle, UK: Paternoster, 2001), repr. in UBC series (Grand Rapids: Baker Books, 2012), 2–5.

67. For a good overview of the historical and religious background to Isaiah 1–39 during the reign of kings Uzziah, Jotham, Ahaz, and Hezekiah, along with an overview of the life of Isaiah himself, see Gary V. Smith, *Isaiah 1–39*, NAC (Nashville: B&H, 2007), 25–40. We do not know the dates of Isaiah's birth or death, but his prophecies are correlated with events of the second half of the eighth century BC (roughly 750 [or 740]–700 BC).

68. For a complete list of texts with full quotations, see G. K. Beale, *The Erosion of Inerrancy in Evangelicalism: Responding to New Challenges to Biblical Authority* (Wheaton: Crossway, 2008), 126–28.

69. Bryan E. Beyer (*Encountering the Book of Isaiah: A Historical and Theological Survey* [Grand Rapids: Baker Academic, 2007], 159), however, highlights a handful of these references, including the four used as illustrations here, that are more naturally taken to refer to the man Isaiah as the person who first uttered prophecies now found in chaps. 40–66.

70. Simon J. DeVries (*1 Kings*, WBC [Waco: Word, 1985], 170) goes so far as to call 1 Kings 13:2 an after-the-fact misreading of 2 Kings 23:19–20 by the final redactor of 1 Kings!

71. For the view that the main reason for understanding Isaiah as composite is "always" the conviction that prophecy could or would not predict such specific events this far in advance, see J. Ridderbos, *Isaiah*, BSC (Grand Rapids: Zondervan, 1985), 8. But now see Jacob Stromberg (*An Introduction to the Study of Isaiah* [London: T&T Clark, 2011], 2–3), who uses Isaiah 63:7–64:12 as an example of a passage that he believes *presupposes* the Babylonian exile. Stromberg adds, "The argument here is not that prediction of different sorts is impossible and that therefore all of these references in [Isa.] 40–66 must have been written after the fact. That would be a misunderstanding of what has been said. Rather, the argument is that 40–66 *presumes* rather than *predicts* the Babylonian exile, setting its authorship in a time far later than Isaiah the prophet" (3).

72. Richard L. Schultz, "Isaiah, Isaiahs, and Current Scholarship," in Hoffmeier and Magary, *Do Historical Matters Matter to Faith?*, 249–50.

73. For a survey of the growing trend to identify a redactional unity throughout Isaiah, even while presupposing the critical consensus on its tradition history, see Roy F. Melugin, "Isaiah 40–66 in Recent Research: The 'Unity' Movement," in *Recent Research on the Major Prophets*, ed. Alan J. Hauser (Sheffield: Sheffield Phoenix, 2008), 142–94.

74. Kenneth A. Kitchen, *On the Reliability of the Old Testament* (Grand Rapids: Eerdmans, 2003), 380. See already Joseph A. Alexander, *Commentaries on the Prophecies of Isaiah*, vol. 2 (Princeton: Princeton Theological Seminary, 1847), ed. and repr. with vol. 1 by Merrill F. Unger, ZCCS (Grand Rapids: Zondervan, 1953), 176 (and not mentioned by Kitchen).

75. J. Alec Motyer, *The Prophecy of Isaiah* (Leicester, UK: Inter-Varsity; Downers Grove, IL: InterVarsity, 1993), 28–29.

76. Sixteen times in the Hebrew of chaps. 1, 2, 7, 13, 20, 37, 38, 39. For clarity, many English translations (including the NIV) add

Isaiah's name at 7:13, where the Hebrew lacks it.

77. Even if Beale (*Erosion of Inerrancy in Evangelicalism*, 158–59) is correct that the NT references prove direct Isaianic authorship, he still overstates himself in concluding that "the prophet Isaiah authored the complete book." This may be a *likely* corollary, but logically all that the NT references prove, on Beale's interpretation, is that the prophet Isaiah authored the specific passages that the NT writers cite. And Beale, Schultz, Motyer, and other contemporary evangelicals who defend the unity of Isaiah regularly allow for Isaiah's followers to have put the text in its final form across all main sections of the book anyway, sometimes citing the ancient rabbinic tradition that the editing was done by Hezekiah and his associates. See, e.g., Richard L. Schultz, "How Many Isaiahs Were There and What Does it Matter? Prophetic Inspiration in Recent Evangelical Scholarship," in *Evangelicals and Scripture: Tradition, Authority and Hermeneutics*, ed. Vincent Bacote, Laura C. Miguélez and Dennis L. Okholm (Downers Grove, IL: InterVarsity, 2004), 166–67. Waltke with Yu (*An Old Testament Theology*, 67) declare, "The authorship of these chapters ought not be a test of orthodoxy."

78. These equations are agreed on even by those who see this chapter as genuine prophecy from four centuries earlier. E.g., Stephen R. Miller, *Daniel*, NAC (Nashville: Broadman & Holman, 1994), 291–304.

79. This is recognized even by those who see the text as the composition of the second century BC and Daniel 11:36–45 as still referring to Antiochus. E.g., John Goldingay, *Daniel*, WBC (Dallas: Word, 1989), 304–5.

80. See esp. throughout John J. Collins, *Daniel*, Hermeneia (Minneapolis: Fortress, 1993).

81. It starts with Adam and Eve and selectively narrates highlights of Israelite history up through the time of the Maccabean Revolt. All the main characters of the biblical narrative appear as animals of various kinds, including sheep and goats as in Daniel. In both documents, more opaquely depicted events then follow, culminating in the day of final judgment and reward (cf. Dan. 12).

82. Cf. Desmond Ford, *Daniel*, Anvil Biblical Studies (Nashville: Southern Publishing Association, 1977), 30–31.

83. Robert I. Vasholz, "Qumran and the Dating of Daniel," *Journal of the Evangelical Theological Society* 21 (1978): 315–21; William S. LaSor, David A. Hubbard, and Frederic W. Bush, *Old Testament Survey: The Message, Form, and Background of the Old Testament*, 2nd ed. (Grand Rapids: Eerdmans, 1996), 574–76.

84. Ronald K. Harrison, *Introduction to the Old Testament* (Grand Rapids: Eerdmans, 1969), 1110.

85. For a concise overview of the problems and the *statis questionis*, see Alan R. Millard, "Daniel in Babylon: An Accurate Record?" in Hoffmeier and Magary, *Do Historical Matters Matter for Faith?*, 263–80.

86. A view classically associated with James A. Montgomery, *A Critical and Exegetical Commentary on the Book of Daniel*, ICC (Edinburgh: T&T Clark, 1927), 96–99. That the Aramaic sections of Daniel span 2:4b–7:28 militates against this.

87. Tremper Longman III, *Daniel*, NIVAC (Grand Rapids: Zondervan, 1999), 280–83. Cf. Joyce G. Baldwin, *Daniel: An Introduction and Commentary*, TOTC (Leicester, UK: Inter-Varsity; Downers Grove, IL: InterVarsity, 1978), 197–203.

88. Ernest C. Lucas, *Daniel*, AOTC (Leicester, UK: Apollos; Downers Grove, IL: InterVarsity, 2002), 308–9. The references are to Collins, *Daniel*; and to John E. Goldingay, "The Book of Daniel: Three Issues," *Themelios* 2 (1977): 45–49. See also Goldingay, *Daniel*, xxxix–xl. Contra Andrew E. Steinmann, *Daniel*, ConcC (St. Louis: Concordia, 2008), 18–19.

89. Robert H. Gundry, *Matthew: A Commentary on His Literary and Theological Art* (Grand Rapids: Eerdmans, 1982); 2nd ed. as *Matthew: A Commentary on His Handbook for a Mixed Church under Persecution* (1994).

90. Gundry, *Matthew*, 623–40 (in both editions). The second edition (xi–xxx) also

contains a completely new preface, responding to scholarly critique of the first edition.

91. See esp. D. A. Carson, "Gundry on Matthew: A Critical Review," *Trinity Journal* 3 (1982): 71–91; Douglas J. Moo, "Matthew and Midrash: An Evaluation of R. H. Gundry's Approach," *Journal of the Evangelical Theological Society* 26 (1983): 31–39; and Scott Cunningham and Darrell L. Bock, "Is Matthew Midrash?," *Bibliotheca Sacra* 144 (1987): 157–80.

92. Which is precisely what has resulted. Indeed, Gundry's subsequent work on Mark (*Mark: A Commentary on His Apology for the Cross* [Grand Rapids: Eerdmans, 1993]) resoundingly defended its historicity; and a recent anthology of twenty of Gundry's essays from throughout his career is titled *The Old Is Better: New Testament Essays in Support of Traditional Interpretations* (Tübingen: Mohr Siebeck, 2005).

93. One that was repeatedly mentioned, though not at all representative of Gundry's overall approach, was the suggestion that Matthew had turned Luke's shepherds into magi in his infancy narrative. I record these comments as one who was present throughout these proceedings at the ETS national conference in Dallas, December 15–17, 1983. For a published summary of the key events, and their larger context, see David L. Turner, "Evangelicals, Redaction Criticism, and Inerrancy: The Debate Continues," *Grace Theological Journal* 5 (1984): 37–45.

94. Carson, "Gundry on Matthew," 77.

95. The recent critique by Norman L. Geisler and William C. Roach (*Defending Inerrancy: Affirming the Accuracy of Scripture for a New Generation* [Grand Rapids: Baker Books, 2011], 296–97) certainly does not address any of these issues and mistakenly equates midrash with allegory.

96. Carson, "Gundry on Matthew," 91.

97. Geisler and Roach, *Defending Inerrancy*, 297. The reference is to "Appendix A: The Chicago Statement on Biblical Hermeneutics," in *Hermeneutics, Inerrancy, and the Bible*, ed. Earl D. Radmacher and Robert D. Preus (Grand Rapids: Zondervan, 1984), 884. Geisler and Roach errantly ascribe the quotation to article 14 of the document. It actually appears in article 13. In a parenthetical reference within the text, they also wrongly ascribe it to "EH," an abbreviation for Geisler's "Appendix B: Explaining Hermeneutics: A Commentary on The Chicago Statement on Biblical Hermeneutics Articles of Affirmation and Denial" (as they specify on 284), which spans 889–904 of *Hermeneutics, Inerrancy, and the Bible*, even though they have just acknowledged it as part of the original Statement itself.

98. The Chicago Statement on Biblical Hermeneutics has not had nearly the lasting effect that the Chicago Statement on Biblical Inerrancy did, which is a shame, because in many ways it is the superior of the two documents.

99. For the argumentation behind each verdict, see the NT introductions listed in note 5 of chapter 5 (above) or just about any major nonevangelical NT introduction of somewhat recent vintage. See now esp. M. Eugene Boring, *An Introduction to the New Testament: History, Literature, Theology* (Louisville: Westminster John Knox, 2012).

100. See esp. Andreas J. Köstenberger, L. Scott Kellum, and Charles L. Quarles, *The Cradle, the Cross, and the Crown: An Introduction to the New Testament* (Nashville: B&H, 2009); D. A. Carson and Douglas J. Moo, *An Introduction to the New Testament*, 2nd ed. (Grand Rapids: Zondervan, 2005). Unique in presenting very balanced cases for each side, without taking sides himself, is Mark A. Powell, *Introducing the New Testament: A Historical, Literary, and Theological Survey* (Grand Rapids: Baker Academic, 2009).

101. In evangelical circles, no one argued more strenuously for this than David G. Meade, *Pseudonymity and Canon: An Investigation into the Relationship of Authorship and Authority in Jewish and Early Christian Tradition* (Grand Rapids: Eerdmans, 1987). See now also Donald A. Hagner, *The New Testament: A Historical and Theological Introduction* (Grand Rapids: Baker Academic, 2012), 426–35.

102. Particularly frequently cited are Tertullian, *Against Marcion* 4.5 ("that which Mark published may be affirmed to be Peter's, whose interpreter Mark was. For even Luke's form of the Gospel, men usually ascribe to Paul") and Mishnah, *Berakot* 5.5 ("a man's representative is like himself").

103. For a study of Greco-Roman pseudepigraphical epistles in their own right, see Charles D. N. Costa, *Greek Fictional Letters* (Oxford: Oxford University Press, 2001).

104. When the established scholar has done more of the work, the assistant's role is acknowledged by "with," as in Craig L. Blomberg with Jennifer Foutz Markley, *A Handbook of New Testament Exegesis* (Grand Rapids: Baker Academic, 2010). But I have yet to see an established scholar's name appear second, after the preposition "with," even when it is well known that the scholar did far less work!

105. See esp. Terry Wilder, *Pseudonymity, the New Testament, and Deception* (Lanham, MD: University Press of America, 2004). Cf. also Eckhard J. Schnabel, "Paul, Timothy, and Titus: The Assumption of a Pseudonymous Author and of Pseudonymous Recipients in the Light of Literary, Theological, and Historical Evidence," in Hoffmeier and Magary, *Do Historical Matters Matter to Faith?*, 383–403.

106. For an outstanding study of the role of Jewish Christianity in the formation of the Jesus movement, esp. as it became a decided minority, see Oskar Skarsaune and Reidar Hvalvik, eds., *Jewish Believers in Jesus: The Early Centuries* (Peabody, MA: Hendrickson, 2007).

107. "Chicago Statement on Biblical Inerrancy," 497.

108. Ibid.

109. See esp. I. Howard Marshall with Philip H. Towner (*A Critical and Exegetical Commentary on the Pastoral Epistles*, ICC [Edinburgh: T&T Clark, 1999], 57–92) with respect to what they dub "allonymity." Cf. Hagner, *New Testament*, 637.

110. R. C. Sproul wrote a commentary on the Chicago Statement on Biblical Inerrancy to clarify what its various articles mean. Geisler and Roach (*Defending Inerrancy*, 31) highlight, among other parts, his explanation of article 18: "'By biblical standards of truth and error' is meant the view used both in the Bible and in everyday life, viz., a correspondence view of truth." Sproul does not indicate whether or not he means modern everyday life in Western cultures or ancient everyday life in biblical cultures. In either instance, it would be hard to imagine how a correspondence view could be applied to all everyday utterances. Children of all cultures have loved to have their parents read or recite to them the kind of narrative fiction that presents itself entirely as if the events actually happened. But by a fairly young age, those same children know the events did not actually occur.

111. This has been Geisler's standard ploy throughout his career. When he is trying to get someone removed from an organization that upholds inerrancy, he contacts all the living members of the original committee that drafted a given document on inerrancy to see if they had intended to allow the position currently in dispute. Of course, the answer is always "no." No one had thought about the issue in question at all at that earlier date, because the controversy is always about some creative new idea. So it is unhelpful even to frame the question as "Did you have this in mind when you first drafted the document?" The question is rather a logical one of whether or not the new idea is consistent with the text of the statement as it stands. Besides, what happens when all the framers die? The meaning of documents, in and outside the Bible, must be tied to the meaning of texts as well as authorial intention, because when authorial intention becomes inaccessible, texts are all that are left.

112. New York: HarperOne, 2011.

113. This is precisely what Norman L. Geisler and F. David Farnell claim about me in "The Erosion of Inerrancy among New Testament Scholars: A Primary Case in Point—Craig Blomberg," (2012), http://www.normangeisler.net/articles/Bible/Inspiration-Inerrancy/Blomberg/DenialOfMiracleStory.htm. I am stunned by the

number of factual errors in this piece. The following is a list of the most obviously false statements made about my writings: (1) that I "aggressively attacked" scholars like Geisler and Mohler (I called for an apology for *their* attacks on Michael Licona and pled for them to stop ruining people's lives); (2) that I have made a "significant, substantive shift in hermeneutics" (the most objectionable work cited was among the first few I ever published—in 1986); (3) that I hold to a "blend of historical-critical ideologies with the grammatico-historical hermeneutic" (the other views, elements of which I adopted, were explicitly distinct from historical-critical ideologies); (4) that I chose to ignore the 1998 book *The Jesus Crisis* (I responded to it directly, as they later acknowledge); (5) that I denied the historicity of the miracle of the coin in the fish's mouth (my whole point is that the text—Matthew 17:27—is a command rather than a narrative, so that there is no story or account either to affirm or deny); (6) that I advocate pseudonymity in the NT (I do not; I merely argue that certain forms of it are not incompatible with inerrancy); (7) that I advocate Ehrman's specific view of pseudonymity as forgery (I most emphatically do not, and I argue that Ehrman's form is *not* compatible with inerrancy); (8) that I demonize my opponents (I do not; rather, it is in the *Jesus Crisis* and in Geisler and Farnell's online article that terms like "satanic" and "demonize" appear); (9) that I claim that anyone who advocates inerrancy as expressed by the ETS and the Chicago Statement is responsible for causing some people to leave the faith (no, I specifically mention that I am speaking of *the way* in which one advocates these views—in heavy-handed, authoritarian, political fashion that censures those who disagree); (10) that my approach in some of my writings in arguing for as much historical reliability of the Bible as possible without presupposing inerrancy means that I never *presuppose* inerrancy in other situations (simply false); (11) that no one has ever moved from a more skeptical to a less skeptical position on the basis of the kind of historical evidence I marshal (I know of many who have done so); and (12) that I do not hold to the historic, orthodox view of biblical inerrancy (utterly ludicrous). When two writers so distort and misrepresent someone with whom they disagree, one wonders about their ability to discern what does or does not constitute an error in *any* document, to say nothing of Scripture!

114. Leo G. Perdue, "Pseudonymity and Graeco-Roman Rhetoric: Mimesis and the Wisdom of Solomon," in *Pseudepigraphie und Verfasserfiktion in frühchristlichen Briefen / Pseudepigraphy and Author Fiction in Early Christian Letters*, ed. Jörg Frey, Jens Herzer, Martina Jannsen, and Clare K. Rothschild with Michaela Engelmann (Tübingen: Mohr Siebeck, 2009), 59.

115. Eibert Tigchelaar, "Forms of Pseudepigraphy in the Dead Sea Scrolls," in Frey et al., *Pseudepigraphie und Verfasserfiktion*, 85–101.

116. David E. Aune, "Reconceptualizing the Phenomenon of Ancient Pseudepigraphy: An Epilogue," in Frey et al., *Pseudepigraphie und Verfasserfiktion*, 794, citing Marco Frenschkowski, Wolfgang Speyer, and Joseph A. Sint.

117. Gordon D. Fee and Douglas S. Stuart, *How to Read the Bible for All Its Worth*, 3rd ed. (Grand Rapids: Zondervan, 2003), 249–64.

118. See esp. the commentaries by the following authors: David E. Aune, *Revelation*, 3 vols., WBC (Nashville: Nelson, 1997–98); Grant R. Osborne, *Revelation*, BECNT (Grand Rapids: Baker Academic, 2002); Stephen S. Smalley, *The Revelation to John: A Commentary on the Greek Text of the Apocalypse* (Downers Grove, IL: InterVarsity, 2005); Robert H. Mounce, *The Book of Revelation*, NICNT (Grand Rapids: Eerdmans, 1977); Ben Witherington III, *Revelation*, NCBC (Cambridge: Cambridge University Press, 2003); Craig S. Keener, *Revelation*, NIVAC (Grand Rapids: Zondervan, 2000); Gordon Fee, *Revelation: A New Covenant Commentary*, NCCS (Eugene, OR: Cascade Books, 2011); Michael J. Gorman, *Reading Revelation Responsibly: Uncivil Worship and Witness; Following the*

Lamb into the New Creation (Eugene, OR: Cascade Books, 2011); and Eugene H. Peterson, *Reversed Thunder: The Revelation of John and the Praying Imagination* (San Francisco: Harper & Row, 1988).

119. The phenomenon is hardly limited to our day. See esp. the thorough history in Bernard McGinn, *Antichrist: Two Thousand Years of the Human Fascination with Evil* (San Francisco: Harper SanFrancisco, 1994).

120. For a responsible approach, see Craig L. Blomberg and Sung Wook Chung, eds., *A Case for Historic Premillennialism* (Grand Rapids: Baker Academic, 2009).

121. See, however, the case made by Daniel M. Gurtner ("Interpreting Apocalyptic Symbolism in the Gospel of Matthew," *Bulletin for Biblical Research* 22 [2012]: 525–46, esp. 535–40) for treating this as an apocalyptic symbol.

122. Recent scholarship on the passage is unusually sparse, but see also Kenneth L. Waters, "Matthew 27:52–53 as Apocalyptic Apostrophe: Temporal-Spatial Collapse in the Gospel of Matthew," *Journal of Biblical Literature* 122 (2003): 489–515; and Ronald L. Troxel, "Matt 27.51–54 Reconsidered: Its Role in the Passion Narrative, Meaning and Origin," *New Testament Studies* 48 (2002): 30–47.

123. E.g., David L. Turner, *Matthew*, BECNT (Grand Rapids: Baker Academic, 2008), 670–71; John Nolland, *The Gospel of Matthew: A Commentary on the Greek Text*, NIGTC (Bletchley, UK: Paternoster; Grand Rapids: Eerdmans, 2005), 1216; and R. T. France, *The Gospel of Matthew*, NICNT (Grand Rapids: Eerdmans, 2007), 1082.

124. Michael R. Licona, *The Resurrection of Jesus: A New Historiographical Approach* (Downers Grove, IL: InterVarsity; Nottingham, UK: Apollos, 2010), 548–53.

125. Danny Akin, Craig Blomberg, Paul Copan, Michael Kruger, Michael Licona, and Charles Quarles, "A Roundtable Discussion with Michael Licona on *The Resurrection of Jesus: A New Historiographical Approach*," *Southeastern Theological Review* 3 (2012): 74.

126. For details, see Bobby Ross Jr., "Interpretation Sparks a Grave Theology Debate," *Christianity Today*, November 7, 2011, 14 (http://www.christianitytoday.com/ct/2011/november/interpretation-sparks-theology-debate.html).

127. R. Albert Mohler Jr., "The Devil Is in the Details: Biblical Inerrancy and the Licona Controversy," September 14, 2011, http://www.albertmohler.com/2011/09/14/the-devil-is-in-the-details-biblical-inerrancy-and-the-licona-controversy/.

128. Akin et al., "Roundtable Discussion," 97.

129. See esp. Edward T. Babinski, *Leaving the Fold: Testimonies of Former Fundamentalists* (Amherst, NY: Prometheus, 2003).

130. See also Scot McKnight and Hauna Ondrey, *Finding Faith, Losing Faith: Stories of Conversion and Apostasy* (Waco: Baylor University Press, 2008).

131. See the candid autobiographical remarks by Bart D. Ehrman, *Misquoting Jesus: The Story behind Who Changed the Bible and Why* (San Francisco: HarperSanFrancisco, 2005), 1–14.

132. This was the mantra I heard more times than I care to recall in my undergraduate studies in religion. Former students of Ehrman at the University of North Carolina or of Hector Avalos at Iowa State University have repeatedly told me of comments these professors make in their classes regarding their desire to disabuse their students of anything like historic Christian faith. Many other students have reported similarly stated goals by "lesser lights" in universities around the country as well. On Sparks's rhetoric, see "Debates about Harmonization" in chap. 4 above.

133. The problem with scientific creationists is that they tend to be very exclusivist in allowing only their own interpretations of Scripture (and science!) as legitimate. When non-Christians come to believe that all true Christians must hold to this position and yet recognize the almost insuperable scientific obstacles to the view, they then too often reject all of Christianity out of hand. But they do so needlessly, given the other

evangelical options. Scientific creationists need to join the proponents of the other perspectives in acknowledging the diversity of legitimate thought on the topic. Cf. further Conrad Hyers, *The Meaning of Creation: Genesis and Modern Science* (Atlanta: John Knox, 1984), 26.

134. See Craig L. Blomberg, *From Pentecost to Patmos: An Introduction to Acts through Revelation* (Nashville: B&H, 2006), 473–76. Cf. also Ben Witherington, *Letters and Homilies for Hellenized Christians* (Downers Grove, IL: InterVarsity, 2008), 2:260–72.

135. Hal Lindsey, *The Late Great Planet Earth* (Grand Rapids: Zondervan, 1970). For a fascinating survey of the entire history of failed prophecy surrounding the end of the world, most of it heavily based on a similar approach to the book of Revelation, see Francis X. Gumerlock, *The Day and the Hour: A Chronicle of Christianity's Perennial Fascination with Predicting the End of the World* (Atlanta: American Vision, 2000).

136. Useful here, too, are Tom Greggs, "Reading Scripture in a Pluralist World: A Path to Discovering the Hermeneutics of *Agape*," in *Horizons in Hermeneutics*, ed. Stanley E. Porter and Matthew R. Malcolm (Grand Rapids: Eerdmans, 2013), 201–16; and idem, "Biblical Hermeneutics and Relational Responsibility," in *The Future of Biblical Interpretation: Responsible Plurality in Biblical Hermeneutics*, ed. Stanley E. Porter and Matthew R. Malcolm (Downers Grove, IL: InterVarsity, forthcoming).

Chapter 6: Don't All the Miracles Make the Bible Mythical?

1. E.g., Gerd Lüdemann, "Opening Statements," in *Jesus' Resurrection: Fact or Figment? A Debate between William Lane Craig and Gerd Lüdemann*, ed. Paul Copan and Ronald K. Tacelli (Downers Grove, IL: InterVarsity, 2000), 45: "If you say that Jesus rose from the dead biologically, you would have to presuppose that a decaying corpse—which is already cold and without blood in its brain—could be made alive again. I think that is nonsense." At the annual meeting of the Society for New Testament Studies in Birmingham, UK, August 1997, Lüdemann phrased it almost exactly as I have put it above. See also throughout his *The Resurrection of Christ: A Historical Inquiry* (Amherst, NY: Prometheus, 2004).

2. E.g., Robert C. Koons, "Science and Theism: Concord, Not Conflict," in *The Rationality of Theism*, ed. Paul Copan and Paul K. Moser (London: Routledge, 2003), 72–90; R. J. Berry, "Divine Action: Expected and Unexpected," *Zygon* 37 (2002): 717–27.

3. See, classically, Peter Medawar, *The Limits of Science* (San Francisco: HarperSanFrancisco, 1984; Oxford: Oxford University Press, 1985). Cf. also Stephen M. Barr, *Modern Physics and Ancient Faith* (Notre Dame, IN: University of Notre Dame Press, 2003); and Francis S. Collins, *The Language of God: A Scientist Presents Evidence for Belief* (New York: Free Press, 2006).

4. See esp. Craig S. Keener, *Miracles: The Credibility of the New Testament Accounts* (Grand Rapids: Baker Academic, 2011), 1:107–208, and the literature cited there.

5. Ibid., 1:211–599.

6. Ibid., 2:788–856.

7. An extraordinarily wide-ranging set of studies, *Miracles: God, Science, and Psychology in the Paranormal* (ed. J. Harold Ellens, 3 vols. [Westport, CT: Praeger, 2008]), analyzes biblical, historical, and contemporary "miracles" from just about every perspective on a spectrum from purely natural to purely supernatural, but with a definite emphasis on the possible psychological forces involved. Yet a few chapters resemble Keener's work in miniature by documenting modern-day miracles remarkably similar to NT ones.

8. Keener, *Miracles*, 1:197. In fact, Hinduism is the only other major world religion in which miracles have been *widely* claimed. Cf. David K. Clark, "Miracles in the World Religions," in *In Defense of Miracles: A Comprehensive Case for God's Action in History*, ed. R. Douglas Geivett and Gary R. Habermas (Downers Grove, IL: InterVarsity, 1997), 200–213. Yet in many religions, folklore tends

to add claims of the miraculous to ancient traditions the further away from the founding events one proceeds. See also Kenneth L. Woodward, *The Book of Miracles: The Meaning of the Miracle Stories in Christianity, Judaism, Buddhism, Hinduism, Islam* (New York: Simon & Schuster, 2000).

9. Edwin Yamauchi, *Jesus, Zoroaster, Buddha, Socrates, Muhammad*, rev. ed. (Downers Grove, IL: InterVarsity, 1972), 40.

10. A point Richard J. Mouw intriguingly explores as one possible explanation of Joseph Smith's ministry. See his *Talking with Mormons: An Invitation to Evangelicals* (Grand Rapids: Eerdmans, 2012), 72–89.

11. The televangelist was the well-known Oral Roberts. My aunt's name was Luella Edwards, living in Chicago.

12. The church was Mission Hills Baptist Church, Greenwood Village, Colorado. I served as elder in 1998–2001 and again in 2003–5.

13. Similar events, usually interpreted as angelic appearances, are too numerous to catalog. See Keener, *Miracles*, 1:585–87, and the literature cited there. Cf. also Joan Wester Anderson, *In the Arms of Angels: True Stories of Heavenly Guardians* (Chicago: Loyola, 2004). For theological interpretations, see esp. Anthony N. S. Lane, ed., *The Unseen World: Christian Reflections on Angels, Demons and the Heavenly Realm* (Carlisle, UK: Paternoster; Grand Rapids: Baker, 1996).

14. For earlier exorcisms in our church, see Mike Sares, *Pure Scum: The Left-Out, the Right-Brained and the Grace of God* (Downers Grove, IL: InterVarsity, 2010), 84.

15. My mother is Eleanor M. Blomberg. The home was in Rock Island, IL.

16. The students were Jennifer Louise (Gigi) Townsend (now Mooi) and Tom Hall, respectively.

17. See, classically, Raymond A. Moody Jr., *Life after Life: The Investigation of a Phenomenon—Survival of Bodily Death*, 25th anniversary ed. (New York: HarperOne, 2001). From an evangelical Christian perspective, cf. Gary R. Habermas and J. P. Moreland, *Beyond Death: Exploring the Evidence for Immortality* (Wheaton: Crossway, 1998), 155–218.

18. Jeffrey Long with Paul Perry (*The Science of Near-Death Experiences* [New York: HarperOne, 2010]) have analyzed over 3,000 near-death experiences and focus on those in which patients with absolutely no brain waves over a period of time are resuscitated and able to accurately describe events that occurred precisely during the time they had no scientifically known reason for being able to do so.

19. Eben Alexander, *Proof of Heaven: A Neurosurgeon's Journey into the Afterlife* (New York: Simon & Schuster, 2012).

20. Perhaps a close second to Alexander's experience is that of Colton Burpo. See Todd Burpo with Lynn Vincent, *Heaven Is for Real: A Little Boy's Astounding Story of His Trip to Heaven and Back* (Nashville: Nelson, 2010).

21. One thinks esp. of the so-called health-wealth gospel, with its "name it and claim it" theology. For a good recent survey and critique of developments, see David W. Jones and Russell S. Woodbridge, *Health, Wealth and Happiness: Has the Prosperity Gospel Overshadowed the Gospel of Christ?* (Grand Rapids: Kregel, 2011).

22. Keener, *Miracles*, 1:236–38. The survey was titled "Spirit and Power: A 10-Country Survey of Pentecostals."

23. See esp. D. A. Carson, *How Long O Lord? Reflections on Suffering and Evil*, 2nd ed. (Grand Rapids: Baker Academic, 2006). Cf. Aída B. Spencer and William D. Spencer, *Joy through the Night: Biblical Resources for Suffering People* (Downers Grove, IL: InterVarsity, 1994); Daniel J. Harrington, *Why Do We Suffer? A Scriptural Approach to the Human Condition* (London and Franklin, WI: Sheed & Ward, 2000); Jeffrey R. Wisdom, *Through the Valley: Biblical-Theological Reflections on Suffering* (Eugene, OR: Wipf & Stock, 2011).

24. Skeptics sometimes complain that Christians fill in "God" wherever they have no scientific explanation, calling this a "God-of-the-gaps" approach. But they are at least as guilty of a "naturalism-of-the-gaps"

approach when they have no scientific explanation for apparently miraculous phenomena. Cf. Keener, *Miracles*, 2:697–704.

25. See, e.g., Gerd Theissen and Annette Merz, *The Historical Jesus: A Comprehensive Guide* (Minneapolis: Fortress, 1996), 281–325; John Dominic Crossan, *The Historical Jesus: The Life of a Mediterranean Jewish Peasant* (San Francisco: HarperSanFrancisco, 1991), 303–53.

26. See the overview of perspectives in Craig L. Blomberg, *The Historical Reliability of the Gospels*, 2nd ed. (Nottingham, UK: Inter-Varsity; Downers Grove, IL: InterVarsity, 2007), 112–27.

27. For a good survey, see Jack Finegan, *Myth and Mystery: An Introduction to the Pagan Religions of the Biblical World* (Grand Rapids: Baker, 1989).

28. See throughout Everett Ferguson, *Backgrounds of Early Christianity*, 3rd ed. (Grand Rapids: Eerdmans, 2003), 148–318.

29. Hans-Josef Klauck, *The Religious Context of Early Christianity: A Guide to Graeco-Roman Religions* (Minneapolis: Fortress, 2003), 250–330.

30. Still very useful in this respect is J. Gresham Machen, *The Virgin Birth of Christ* (New York: Harper & Row, 1930; repr., London: James Clarke, 1987), 317–79. Much more briefly, cf. the catalog of supposed parallels in W. D. Davies and Dale C. Allison Jr., *A Critical and Exegetical Commentary on the Gospel according to Saint Matthew*, ICC (Edinburgh: T&T Clark, 1988), 1:214–16.

31. A point that remains clear in Paul M. Fullmer (*Resurrection in Mark's Literary-Historical Perspective* [London: T&T Clark, 2007], 58–170), despite his focus on partial parallels that have often been underscrutinized.

32. For the English translations of the most important miracle stories in Philostratus's biography of Apollonius, see Craig A. Evans, *Jesus and His Contemporaries* (Leiden: Brill, 1995), 245–50.

33. B. F. Harris, "Apollonius of Tyana," *Journal of Religious History* 5 (1969): 189–99.

34. See Robin L. Fox, *The Search for Alexander* (Boston: Little, Brown; London: Allen Lane, 1980).

35. Gerd Lüdemann with Alf Özen, *What Really Happened to Jesus: A Historical Approach to the Resurrection* (Louisville: Westminster John Knox, 1995), 15.

36. Cf. Gary R. Habermas, "The Resurrection of Jesus Time Line," in *Contending with Christianity's Critics: Answering New Atheists and Other Objectors*, ed. Paul Copan and William L. Craig (Nashville: B&H, 2009), 113–25.

37. For detailed demonstration of this from all branches of early Christianity, see Larry W. Hurtado, *Lord Jesus Christ: Devotion to Jesus in Earliest Christianity* (Grand Rapids: Eerdmans, 2003).

38. N. T. Wright, *The Resurrection of the Son of God* (Minneapolis: Fortress, 2003), 129–206.

39. Lüdemann with Özen, *What Really Happened to Jesus*, 82–129, esp. 99.

40. Nor have they elsewhere occurred over a forty-day period (Acts 1:3), in different places, to more than five hundred people (1 Cor. 15:6), who are known to be defeated in outlook and not expecting anything miraculous to happen (John 20:19). See John J. Johnson, "Were the Resurrection Appearances Hallucinations? Some Psychiatric and Psychological Considerations," *Churchman* 115 (2001): 227–38.

41. For a recent example in the Western world, see Andrew Moran, "Smiling, Weeping Virgin Mary Statue Attracts Hundreds to Ontario," *Digital Journal*, November 3, 2010, http://digitaljournal.com/article/299743.

42. See further Finegan, *Myth and Mystery*, 203–12; Antonia Tripolitis, *Religions of the Hellenistic-Roman Age* (Grand Rapids: Eerdmans, 2002), 47–57; and Ronald H. Nash, *The Gospel and the Greeks: Did the New Testament Borrow from Pagan Thought?*, rev. ed. (Phillipsburg, NJ: P&R, 2003), 133–38.

43. Blomberg, *Historical Reliability of the Gospels*, 138.

44. See further Mary Jo Sharp, "Is the Story of Jesus Borrowed from Pagan Myths?," in

In Defense of the Bible: A Comprehensive Apologetic for the Authority of Scripture, ed. Steven B. Cowan and Terry L. Wilder (Nashville: B&H Academic, 2013), 183–200. Sharp also debunks even more remote so-called parallels. Recent television documentaries and popular books and blogs have proved highly misleading in talking about a common pattern in ancient mythology of virgin births, sacrificial deaths, and bodily resurrections, which in fact is nonexistent.

45. See further G. W. Bowersock, *Fiction as History: Nero to Julian* (Berkeley: University of California Press, 1994), 121–43.

46. See throughout Erkki Koskenniemi, *The Old Testament Miracle-Workers in Early Judaism* (Tübingen: Mohr Siebeck, 2005). The quotation is from page v.

47. Leah Bronner, *The Stories of Elijah and Elisha as Polemics against Baal Worship* (Leiden: Brill, 1968), 50–134.

48. One rabbinic way of counting the number of miracles of Elijah and Elisha finds the former doing eight and the latter sixteen. This approach highlights the conceptual parallels between many of them, as a way of confirming that God gave Elisha a double portion of the S/spirit he had given Elijah (2 Kings 2:9). See Nachman Levine, "Twice as Much of Your Spirit: Pattern, Parallel and Paronomasia in the Miracles of Elijah and Elisha," *Journal for the Study of the Old Testament* 85 (1999): 25. Whether or not it works out this neatly, there is no doubt that the similarities between the two sets of miracles are clear. For our purposes, explaining the nature and rationale of one set will almost certainly clarify the other set also. Less widely noted but also significant are parallels between Elijah and Moses, not just with respect to miracle stories but also more generally. See esp. Havilah Dharamraj, *A Prophet Like Moses: A Narrative-Theological Reading of the Elijah Stories* (Milton Keynes, UK: Paternoster; Eugene, OR: Wipf & Stock, 2011). On Elisha as a second Joshua, see Andrew D. Carr, "Elisha's Prophetic Authority and Initial Miracles (2 Kings 2:12–25)," *Evangelical Journal* 29 (2011): 33–44. On the *differences* between the miracles of Elijah and Elisha, see Yael Shemesh, "Elisha and the Miraculous Jug of Oil (2 Kings 4:1–7)," *Journal of Hebrew Scriptures* 8, no. 4 (2008): 1–18. On the parallels between Elijah's and Elisha's miracles on the one hand and Jesus's miracles on the other, see Philippe Guillaume, "Miracles Miraculously Repeated: Gospel Miracles as Duplication of Elijah-Elisha's," *Biblische Nötizen* 98 (1999): 21–23.

49. Conrad Hyers, *The Meaning of Creation: Genesis and Modern Science* (Atlanta: John Knox, 1984), 53.

50. Douglas S. Stuart, *Exodus*, NAC (Nashville: Broadman & Holman, 2006), 131–32.

51. Ibid., 278–81.

52. Gordon J. Wenham, *Genesis 1–15*, WBC (Waco: Word, 1987), 128.

53. We cited the section on Greco-Roman religions above: Machen, *Virgin Birth*, 317–79; on alleged Jewish parallels, see 280–316. For a thorough, up-to-date study of Jewish backgrounds, see Eric Eve, *The Jewish Context of Jesus' Miracles* (London: Sheffield Academic Press, 2002).

54. Machen, *Virgin Birth*, 284.

55. Cf. Craig L. Blomberg, "Matthew," in *Commentary on the New Testament Use of the Old Testament*, ed. G. K. Beale and D. A. Carson (Grand Rapids: Baker Academic, 2007), 4.

56. The word carries no sexual connotations, and "the mysterious action is hidden from the gaze of curious humans" (David E. Garland, *Luke*, ZECNT [Grand Rapids: Zondervan, 2011], 82).

57. Particularly helpful on this and other rationales for the commands to war against the Canaanites is Andrew Sloane, *At Home in a Strange Land: Using the Old Testament in Christian Ethics* (Peabody, MA: Hendrickson, 2008), 128–41. See now also Heath A. Thomas, Jeremy Evans, and Paul Copan, eds., *Holy War in the Bible: Christian Morality and an Old Testament Problem* (Downers Grove, IL: IVP Academic, 2013).

58. Tremper Longman III, *How to Read Exodus* (Downers Grove, IL: InterVarsity, 2009), 102.

59. Carol Meyers, *Exodus*, NCBC (Cambridge: Cambridge University Press, 2005), 111–12.

60. Peter Enns, *Exodus*, NIVAC (Grand Rapids: Zondervan, 2000), 274.

61. See esp. Colin Humphreys, *The Miracles of Exodus: A Scientist's Discovery of the Extraordinary Natural Causes of the Biblical Stories* (San Francisco: HarperSanFrancisco, 2003), esp. 111–49. Humphreys appears to overstate his case considerably, but commentators have regularly observed that there is a logical, natural progression to the various plagues.

62. See further James K. Hoffmeier, *Israel in Egypt: The Evidence for the Authenticity of the Exodus Tradition* (Oxford: Oxford University Press, 1996); idem, *Ancient Israel in Sinai: The Evidence for the Authenticity of the Wilderness Tradition* (Oxford: Oxford University Press, 2005). More briefly, cf. Kenneth A. Kitchen, *On the Reliability of the Old Testament* (Grand Rapids: Eerdmans, 2003), 241–312.

63. R. Dennis Cole, *Numbers*, NAC (Nashville: Broadman & Holman, 2000), 274–75.

64. Gordon J. Wenham, *Numbers: An Introduction and Commentary*, TOTC (Leicester, UK: Inter-Varsity; Downers Grove, IL: InterVarsity, 1981), 170–71.

65. Timothy R. Ashley, *The Book of Numbers*, NICOT (Grand Rapids: Eerdmans, 1993), 458.

66. David M. Howard Jr., *Joshua*, NAC (Nashville: Broadman & Holman, 1998), 125.

67. J. Michael Thigpen, "Lord of All the Earth: Yahweh and Baal in Joshua 3," *Trinity Journal* 27 (2006): 245–54.

68. Daniel E. Fleming, "The Seven-Day Siege of Jericho in Holy War," in *Ki Baruch Hu: Ancient Near Eastern, Biblical, and Judaic Studies in Honor of Baruch A. Levine*, ed. Robert Chazan, William W. Hallo, and Lawrence H. Schiffman (Winona Lake, IN: Eisenbrauns, 1999), 211–28.

69. Richard S. Hess, *Joshua: An Introduction and Commentary*, TOTC (Leicester, UK: Inter-Varsity; Downers Grove, IL: InterVarsity, 1996), 129.

70. Robert L. Hubbard Jr., *Joshua*, NIVAC (Grand Rapids: Zondervan, 2009), 297: "The interpretation of verses 12–14 is difficult, but an important starting point is to take seriously its poetic nature—that its thought world is phenomenological and metaphorical rather than historical or scientific."

71. John H. Walton, Victor H. Matthews, and Mark W. Chavalas, *The IVP Bible Background Commentary: Old Testament* (Downers Grove, IL: InterVarsity, 2000), 226.

72. Cf. Howard, *Joshua*, 249. A recurring urban legend, particularly over the last three-quarters of a century, has claimed that NASA was once trying to determine why certain calculations extrapolating backward over the millennia were not working until someone added an extra day to the chronology based on Joshua 10. There is no shred of truth to this story! Unfortunately, this has not kept the legend from being published in some otherwise respectable publications. For its impossibility, see, e.g., Tommy Mitchell, "NASA Found Joshua's Missing Day: Arguments Christians Shouldn't Use," Answers in Genesis.Org, August 24, 2010, http://www.answersingenesis.org/articles/2010/08/24/joshua-missing-day.

73. Richard D. Patterson and Hermann J. Austel, "1, 2 Kings," in *Expositor's Bible Commentary*, ed. Tremper Longman III and David E. Garland, rev. ed. (Grand Rapids: Zondervan, 2009), 924: "Certainly there is no need to postulate any reversal of the earth's rotation or receding of the sun. The fact that the miracle was felt only 'in the land' (i.e., Judah; cf. 2 Chr 32:31) makes such solutions most dubious. . . . A simple localized refraction of the sun's rays would be sufficient to account for the phenomenon. Keil, 465, reports that such a case was noted in AD 1703."

74. Daniel I. Block, *Judges, Ruth*, NAC (Nashville: Broadman & Holman, 1999), 273. Cf. also K. Lawson Younger, *Judges, Ruth*, NIVAC (Grand Rapids: Zondervan, 2002), 187–88.

75. Robert D. Bergen, *1, 2 Samuel*, NAC (Nashville: Broadman & Holman, 1996), 267.

76. Sharon Beekmann and Peter G. Bolt, *Silencing Satan: Handbook of Biblical Demonology* (Eugene, OR: Wipf & Stock, 2012), 79–83.

77. Joyce G. Baldwin, *1 and 2 Samuel*, TOTC (Leicester, UK: Inter-Varsity; Downers Grove, IL: InterVarsity, 1988), 207.

78. Cf. Herbert Lockyer, *All the Miracles of the Bible* (Grand Rapids: Zondervan, 1961), 25–26.

79. See esp. Graham Twelftree, *Jesus, the Miracle Worker: A Historical and Theological Study* (Downers Grove, IL: InterVarsity, 1999); René Latourelle, *The Miracles of Jesus and the Theology of Miracles* (New York: Paulist, 1988); Leopold Sabourin, *The Divine Miracles Discussed and Defended* (Rome: Catholic Book Agency, 1977); Hendrik van der Loos, *The Miracles of Jesus* (Leiden: Brill, 1965).

80. Cf. Jack Deere, *Surprised by the Power of the Spirit* (Grand Rapids: Zondervan, 1993), 117–43.

81. Most interpreters understand Jesus's comment in John 9:3b (lit., "in order that the works of God might be displayed in him") to be an explanation of why the man was born blind (vv. 1–3a). But this clause could also modify the next one, giving the reason for why Jesus must do the work of the one who sent him (v. 4). See Gary M. Burge, *John*, NIVAC (Grand Rapids: Zondervan, 2000), 272–73. In this case the text simply would not supply the reason for the man's congenital condition.

82. See esp. Michael H. Burer, *Divine Sabbath Work* (Winona Lake, IN: Eisenbrauns, 2012), 103–35. The Mishnah (*Yoma* 8.6) forbade healing of non-life-threatening injuries or illnesses on the Sabbath.

83. See further Darrell L. Bock, *Luke*, BECNT (Grand Rapids: Baker Academic, 1996), 2:1079–82.

84. See throughout David Seccombe, *The King of God's Kingdom: A Solution to the Puzzle of Jesus* (Carlisle, UK, and Waynesboro, GA: Paternoster, 2005).

85. The issue was not merely that God alone could forgive sins, because priests regularly announced God's forgiveness of sin, but that Jesus was doing so apart from the temple cult. See Nicholas Perrin, *Jesus the Temple* (London: SPCK; Grand Rapids: Baker Academic, 2010), 140.

86. See further Craig L. Blomberg, "The Miracles as Parables," in *The Miracles of Jesus*, ed. David Wenham and Craig Blomberg, vol. 6 of *Gospel Perspectives* (Sheffield: JSOT, 1986; Eugene, OR: Wipf & Stock, 2003), 327–59.

87. Robert H. Stein, *Mark*, BECNT (Grand Rapids: Baker Academic, 2008), 245–46.

88. Cf. Caitrin H. Williams, "'I Am' or 'I Am He'? Self-Declaratory Pronouncements in the Fourth Gospel and Rabbinic Tradition," in *Jesus in Johannine Tradition*, ed. Robert T. Fortna and Tom Thatcher (Louisville: Westminster John Knox, 2001), 343–52.

89. Cf. esp. John P. Heil, *The Transfiguration of Jesus: Narrative Meaning and Function of Mark 9:2–8, Matt 17:1–8 and Luke 9:28–36* (Rome: Biblical Institute Press, 2000).

90. Eric K. Wefald, "The Separate Gentile Mission in Mark," *Journal for the Study of the New Testament* 60 (1995): 3–26.

91. Timothy Wiarda, "John 21.1–23: Narrative Unity and Its Implications," *Journal for the Study of the New Testament* 46 (1992): 71.

92. Cf. Colin G. Kruse, *The Gospel according to John: An Introduction and Commentary*, TNTC (Leicester: Inter-Varsity; Grand Rapids: Eerdmans, 2003), 91–96.

93. Cf. esp. William R. Telford, *The Barren Temple and the Withered Tree* (Sheffield: JSOT, 1980).

94. Jesus sends Peter, along with the rest of the Twelve, to do this already during Jesus's lifetime (Matt. 10 pars.). Paul's miracles in Acts strikingly parallel Peter's in Acts. See Andrew C. Clark, *Parallel Lives: The Relation of Paul to the Apostles in the Lucan Perspective* (Carlisle, UK: Paternoster, 2001), 209–29.

95. See esp. Graham H. Twelftree, *In the Name of Jesus: Exorcism among Early Christians* (Grand Rapids: Baker Academic, 2007).

96. Cf. David G. Peterson, *The Acts of the Apostles*, PNTC (Nottingham, UK: Apollos; Grand Rapids: Eerdmans, 2009), 209–11.

97. "There is important symbolism here. The false prophet sits in darkness as Paul works. The temporary nature of the judgment is like that which fell on Zechariah in Luke 1, a judgment from which Zechariah learned to believe God. Paul accuses the magician of being full of deceit and villainy as well as being opposed to righteousness" (Darrell L. Bock, *Acts*, BECNT [Grand Rapids: Baker Academic, 2007], 445–46).

98. Graham H. Twelftree, *Jesus the Exorcist: A Contribution to the Study of the Historical Jesus* (Tübingen: Mohr; Peabody, MA: Hendrickson, 1993), 63–64.

99. It is not a coincidence that this occurs in Ephesus, home to so much ancient "magic"—i.e., occult practices. Luke was particularly "concerned to claim that Paul could beat the Ephesian magicians at their own game" (C. K. Barrett, *A Critical and Exegetical Commentary on the Acts of the Apostles*, ICC [Edinburgh: T&T Clark, 1998], 2:907).

100. The fullest recent anthology of studies of the resurrection, demonstrating this from numerous perspectives, is Geert van Oyen and Tom Shepherd, eds., *Resurrection of the Dead: Biblical Traditions in Dialogue* (Leuven: Peeters, 2012).

101. Michael R. Licona, *The Resurrection of Jesus: A New Historiographical Approach* (Downers Grove, IL: InterVarsity, 2010), 133–98.

102. For these and similar arguments, see throughout William L. Craig, *Assessing the New Testament Evidence for the Historicity of the Resurrection of Jesus* (Lewiston, NY: Edwin Mellen, 1989).

103. See, e.g., Joseph Smith, History 1.21, in *The Pearl of Great Price* (Salt Lake City: Church of Jesus Christ of Latter-day Saints, 1981 [orig. 1851]), 50.

104. Paul Alexander, *Why Pentecostalism Is the World's Fastest Growing Faith* (San Francisco: Jossey-Bass, 2009).

105. See further William K. Kay, *Pentecostalism: A Very Short Introduction* (Oxford: Oxford University Press, 2011); Allan Anderson, *An Introduction to Pentecostalism: Global Charismatic Christianity* (Cambridge: Cambridge University Press, 2004); and Walter J. Hollenweger, *Pentecostalism: Origins and Developments Worldwide* (Peabody, MA: Hendrickson, 1997).

106. For a representative exposition, see Richard B. Gaffin Jr., "A Cessationist View," in *Are Miraculous Gifts for Today?*, ed. Wayne A. Grudem (Grand Rapids: Zondervan, 1996), 25–64. Cf. John F. MacArthur Jr., *Charismatic Chaos* (Grand Rapids: Zondervan, 1992); Samuel E. Waldron, *To Be Continued? Are the Miraculous Gifts for Today?* (Merrick, NY: Calvary Press, 2005).

107. Demonstrating the weaknesses in the cessationists' treatment of key passages, while modeling exemplary exegesis himself, is D. A. Carson, *Showing the Spirit: A Theological Exposition of 1 Corinthians 12–14* (Grand Rapids: Baker, 1987).

108. E.g., Sinclair B. Ferguson, *The Holy Spirit* (Leicester, UK: Inter-Varsity; Downers Grove, IL: InterVarsity, 1996), 223–37.

109. Roy E. Ciampa and Brian S. Rosner, *The First Letter to the Corinthians*, PNTC (Grand Rapids: Eerdmans; Nottingham, UK: Apollos, 2010), 614.

110. In fact, considerable steps in both directions have been taken over the past generation, but there remain holdouts in both the charismatic and noncharismatic camps.

111. One thinks esp. of churches and other Christian organizations that require members or employees to sign a doctrinal statement that includes belief in cessationism or to refrain from any exercise of the more supernatural charismata. Particularly egregious is interference with someone's personal devotional life when the person is completely theologically orthodox. Yet the Southern Baptist Convention in 2005 disallowed its foreign missionaries from even using tongues as a private prayer language and had those who could not comply in good conscience resign! In 2007, it changed its ban from a "policy" to a "guideline," apparently allowing room for some dissent, but to what degree and in what ways is by no means clear. See Audrey Barrick, "Southern Baptist Trustees Approve Leeway for Speaking in Tongues," *The Christian Post*, May 10,

2007, http://www.christianpost.com/news/southern-baptist-trustees-approve-leeway-for-speaking-in-tongues-27339/.

Conclusion

1. For the first and fourth of these tasks, see "A Working Definition" and "Debates about Harmonization" and their related notes in chap. 4 above. For theological coherence, see esp. Charles H. H. Scobie, *The Ways of Our God: An Approach to Biblical Theology* (Grand Rapids: Eerdmans, 2003); Bruce K. Waltke with Charles Yu, *Old Testament Theology: An Exegetical, Canonical, and Thematic Approach* (Grand Rapids: Zondervan, 2007); I. Howard Marshall, *New Testament Theology: Many Witnesses, One Gospel* (Downers Grove, IL: InterVarsity; Leicester, UK: Inter-Varsity, 2004). For biblical ethics, esp. after sifting the prescriptive from the merely descriptive, see esp. Christopher J. H. Wright, *Old Testament Ethics for the People of God* (Leicester, UK: Inter-Varsity; Downers Grove, IL: InterVarsity, 2004); Walter C. Kaiser Jr., *What Does the Lord Require? A Guide for Preaching and Teaching Biblical Ethics* (Grand Rapids: Baker Academic, 2009); R. E. O. White, *Biblical Ethics* (Exeter, UK: Paternoster; Atlanta: John Knox, 1979); Glen H. Stassen and David P. Gushee, *Kingdom Ethics: Following Jesus in Contemporary Context* (Downers Grove, IL: InterVarsity, 2003). Ranging widely over several of these areas with a distinctive focus on the OT is John Goldingay, *Key Questions about Christian Faith: Old Testament Answers* (Grand Rapids: Baker Academic, 2010).

2. In a bizarre example of redefining individuals out of existence, many liberal biblical scholars do not even include evangelicals when they write about what a majority or minority of scholars believes. I include scholars of all ideological stripes worldwide when I speak about majority or minority positions.

3. See the profound reflections on this in Mark A. Noll, *The Scandal of the Evangelical Mind* (Grand Rapids: Eerdmans, 1994), 241–54.

4. See further Arland J. Hultgren, *The Earliest Christian Heretics: Readings from Their Opponents* (Minneapolis: Fortress, 1996).

5. "The style marks a serious act of divine judgment. But this judgment is brought upon the self. It is almost as if Paul says, 'If someone destroys, . . . such a one is *thereby* destroyed.' Without publicly naming and shaming a culprit, Paul refers to those who feed the splits. Here is perhaps their last warning that the effects (for the church *and* for them) are entirely beyond what they imagined when they began a little, 'innocent' power play. They are playing with forces that threaten the holiness of God's own temple, in effect pitting themselves against the Holy Spirit. By their attitude they also despise the humility of the cross and the love of Jesus" (Anthony C. Thiselton, *1 Corinthians: A Shorter Exegetical and Pastoral Commentary* [Grand Rapids: Eerdmans, 2006], 68).

6. Norman L. Geisler and David Farnell write, "While Blomberg is irenic and embracing with Mormons, he has great hostility toward those who uphold the 'fundamentals' of Scripture" ("The Erosion of Inerrancy among New Testament Scholars: A Primary Case in Point—Craig Blomberg" (2012), 6, http://www.veritasseminary.com/THE%20EROSION%20OF%20INERRANCY%20AMONG%20NEW%20TESTAMENT%20SCHOLARS.pdf). Neither of these claims is true. I am irenic but *not* embracing with Mormons, at least not in general. But I embrace anyone of any background whom I discover has enough doctrinal and experiential common ground with my faith to lead me to believe that we are true Christian brothers or sisters, and I have found *some* within Mormonism of whom I believe this to be true. I hold no hostility toward those who uphold the fundamentals of the faith *because they uphold those fundamentals*; rather, I applaud them. But when fundamentalists add nonessential items to the fundamentals, or uphold the fundamentals with unnecessary judgmentalism against those with whom they disagree, they inevitably and unnecessarily scare many people away from the faith. Then biblical ethics demands that we sternly

rebuke them (e.g., Matt. 23; Gal. 1:6–9; Phil. 3:2–11).

7. Craig L. Blomberg, "The New Testament Definition of Heresy (or When Do Jesus and the Apostles Really Get Mad?)," *Journal of the Evangelical Theological Society* 45 (2002): 59–72.

8. Essential reading for anyone who finds this assessment surprising is Philip Yancey, *What's So Amazing about Grace?* (Grand Rapids: Zondervan, 2002). Also very helpful are Tom Hovestol, *Extreme Righteousness: Seeing Ourselves in the Pharisees* (Chicago: Moody, 1997); and idem, *Spiritual Profiling: How Jesus Interacted with Eight Types of People and Why It Matters for You* (Chicago: Moody, 2010).

9. In addition to works already cited above in the introduction, see Craig S. Titus, *Christianity and the West: Interaction and Impact in Art and Culture* (Washington, DC: Catholic University of America Press, 2009); Rodney Stark, *The Victory of Reason: How Christianity Led to Freedom, Capitalism, and Western Success* (New York: Random House, 2005); and Peter Harrison, *The Fall of Man and the Foundations of Science* (Cambridge: Cambridge University Press, 2009).

10. August H. Konkel, *1 and 2 Kings*, NIVAC (Grand Rapids: Zondervan, 2006), 463–66.

11. See esp. Philip Yancey, *What Good Is God? In Search of a Faith That Matters* (New York: Faith Words, 2010).

12. On which, see esp. David W. Jones and Russell S. Woodbridge, *Health, Wealth, and Happiness: Has the Prosperity Gospel Overshadowed the Gospel of Christ?* (Grand Rapids: Kregel, 2011).

13. Of many excellent sources, one important recent one is Neil Martin, *Keep Going: Overcoming Doubts about Your Faith* (Phillipsburg, NJ: P&R, 2008).

14. For an excellent primer that discusses the range of historic Christian views on some of the most debated doctrines, see Gregory A. Boyd and Paul R. Eddy, *Across the Spectrum: Understanding Issues in Evangelical Theology*, 2nd ed. (Grand Rapids: Baker Academic, 2009).

15. To help counter this, see Paul Copan, *"True for You but Not for Me": Overcoming Objections to Christian Faith*, rev. ed. (Minneapolis: Bethany House, 2009).

16. See esp. James S. Spiegel, *The Making of an Atheist: How Immorality Leads to Unbelief* (Chicago: Moody, 2010). Agreeing from an atheist perspective, cf. Thomas Nagel, *The Last Word* (Oxford: Oxford University Press, 1997); idem, *Mind and Cosmos: Why the Materialist Neo-Darwinian Conception of Nature Is Almost Certainly False* (New York: Oxford University Press, 2012).

17. This is the view of Peter Enns, *Inspiration and Incarnation: Evangelicals and the Problem of the Old Testament* (Grand Rapids: Baker Academic, 2005); and Kenton L. Sparks, *God's Word in Human Words: An Evangelical Appropriation of Critical Biblical Scholarship* (Grand Rapids: Baker Academic, 2008).

18. E.g., Marcus J. Borg, *Reading the Bible Again for the First Time: Taking the Bible Seriously but Not Literally* (San Francisco: HarperSanFrancisco, 2001).

19. See the anthology of approaches in William P. Brown, ed., *Engaging Biblical Authority: Perspectives on the Bible as Scripture* (Louisville: Westminster John Knox, 2007).

20. The one affirmation in the Chicago Statement with which I would disagree is not part of its description of the meaning of inerrancy but a closing reflection (the last sentence of the last article, article 19) on its significance: "We further deny that inerrancy can be rejected without grave consequences, both to the individual and to the Church" ("The Chicago Statement on Biblical Inerrancy," in *Inerrancy*, ed. Norman L. Geisler [Grand Rapids: Zondervan, 1979], 497). I agree that the consequences can be detrimental and that sometimes they can be grave, but to imply that they are *always* grave is too strong a statement, not borne out by actual experience.

21. See throughout David Basinger and Randall Basinger, eds., *Predestination and Free Will: Four Views of Divine Sovereignty and Human Freedom* (Downers Grove, IL: InterVarsity, 1986).

22. I. Howard Marshall, *1 and 2 Thessalonians*, NCB (London: Marshall, Morgan & Scott; Grand Rapids: Eerdmans, 1983), 180: "To be separated from God and his blessings—and to be for ever in this situation—is for Paul the worst of prospects. This is the reality for which the other pictures used are merely symbols."

23. "It would seem that Our Lord finds our desires not too strong, but too weak. We are half-hearted creatures, fooling about with drink and sex and ambition when infinite joy is offered us, like an ignorant child who wants to go on making mud pies in a slum because he cannot imagine what is meant by the offer of a holiday at the sea. We are far too easily pleased" (C. S. Lewis, *The Weight of Glory, and Other Addresses* [New York: HarperCollins, 2000 (orig. 1949)], 26).

24. For some other debunkings of key misunderstandings about the end times and the life to come, see Craig L. Blomberg, "Eschatology and the Church: Some New Testament Perspectives," *Themelios* 23, no. 3 (1998): 3–26; repr. in *Solid Ground: 25 Years of Evangelical Theology*, ed. Carl P. Trueman, Tony J. Gray, and Craig L. Blomberg (Leicester, UK: Inter-Varsity, 2000), 84–107.

25. The problem with this analogy, of course, is that no one has yet come up with absolute conclusive proof that the building is burning. Smoke keeps appearing here and there, some items show signs of charring, burnt smells come and go, the alarms periodically go off, but the building for now still stands. So those who keep on warning us about the fire eventually become unwelcome. Still, if it is clear that the person keeps speaking about the danger out of genuine concern and care for those in the building, and out of the sincere belief that the fuse to a huge explosion is becoming very short, most of us would at least tolerate the person's periodic warnings even if we disagreed with their assessments.

26. At the same time, our desires are considerably reshaped. As Eugene H. Peterson puts it, "This is not a paradise for consumers. St. John's heaven is not an extension of human cupidity upwards but an invasion of God's rule and presence downwards. Heaven in the vision, remember, *descends*. The consequence is that 'the dwelling of God is with men.' If we don't want God or don't want him very near, we can hardly be expected to be very interested in heaven" (*Reversed Thunder: The Revelation of John and the Praying Imagination* [San Francisco: HarperSanFrancisco, 1988], 185, emphasis original).

27. For the antidote, see esp. Randy Alcorn, *Heaven: Biblical Answers to Common Questions* (Wheaton: Tyndale, 2006).

Scripture Index

Old Testament

Genesis

Exodus

Leviticus

Numbers

Deuteronomy

Joshua

Subject Index